Someone Gay

Someone Gay

Memoirs

Don Clark

www.lethepressbooks.com
lethepress@aol.com

Printed in the United States of America

Book design by Toby Johnson
Cover credits:
  photo: Steve Savage (bottom row far left)
  photograph by Rink Foto (bottom row third from left)
  Portrait by Robert Morgan, 1987

Published as a trade paperback original
by Lethe Press, 118 Heritage Avenue, Maple Shade, NJ 08052.

First U.S. edition, 2007

ISBN 1-59021-067-0

Library of Congress Cataloging-in-Publication Data

Clark, Donald H., 1930-
  Someone gay : memoirs / Don Clark. -- 1st U.S. ed.
    p. cm.
  ISBN 1-59021-067-0
  1. Clark, Donald H., 1930- 2. Gay men--United States--Biography. 3. Gay
psychologists--United States--Biography. 4. Psychologists--United
States--Biography. I. Title.
  HQ75.8.C59A3 2007
  306.76'62092--dc22
  [B]
                    2007015436

CHAPTERS

Portrait by Robert Morgan

DEDICATION

For my husband, Michael,
Our loving family

And
Those individuals everywhere in this world
Who are finding their way gay.

Chapter 1

Unwanted

Each of us begins life with the seeds of a unique genetic inheritance. Then, even before memory begins, circumstances and events plant additional seeds that will have long lasting influence. In my life seeds of guilt, shame and fear were put in place with the pretense that my mother was not pregnant. My family pretended and the two student doctors at the nursing school nearby also pretended that she was not pregnant because abortions were illegal in New Jersey in 1930.

"They gave me all kinds of awful poisons to drink to kill the tumor that was growin'," she told me as an often repeated childhood story masking her own shame and guilt as well as her need to confess. "Then they operated to cut the tumor out of me and found you in there. We wasn't ready. No baby clothes. Not even a name, so you was named for the two doctors who found you." Shame, failure and guilt were abundant in our world, the usual ghosts that haunt the poor and oppressed.

I am a man who has spent most of my life experiencing, then investigating, then understanding and finally learning how to overcome feelings of shame, failure, guilt and fear. Fortunately, my early attraction to writing pointed to a safe haven in which I could store and sort my observations and feelings.

To everyone's surprise, including my own, I found my way to formal education; undergraduate experiences that fed a latent zeal for social justice and the Ph.D. and clinical training in psychology that propelled me across the great chasm that separates lower class from middle class. It took only one more giant step for me to clarify my gay identity, announce it, and defy medical, psychological, legal and religious establishments with the writing of *Loving Someone Gay* in the mid-1970s.

The publicity surrounding the publication of the first edition of that book put me in touch with like-minded professionals and students eager to learn and help to refine the gay-oriented psychotherapy that I practiced. Contrary to the *homosexuality-is-a-sickness* orientation inherent in *respectable* psychotherapies at the time, this therapy called into question all negative thoughts, feelings and teachings about homosexuality. It celebrated homosexual feelings and experiences as natural and worthy. It offered genuine, heart-felt support to the client as he or she threw off damaging, oppressive past learning and became reoriented. A surprising amount of the damage done is hidden in the seemingly ordinary moments of childhood, homophobic remarks or experiences ingested and accepted without question. An ongoing questioning review of one's life in search of one's own truth is the inevitable outcome of gay-oriented psychotherapy.

It is necessary, as Socrates pointedly told his students, to examine one's life. Only by so doing may you free yourself of the prejudices that harm yourself and others. I was fortunate to be set on that path long before I had ever seen or heard the name Socrates and long before anyone had heard of a gay-oriented psychotherapy.

This book is the story of me, someone gay. It is a true story, though I have altered some names when I thought the person would prefer privacy. It is based on my memories and the journals I have kept since childhood. It is the story of my own reorientation as I searched for my own truth. Homosexual desire and behavior exist in many animal species but for humans, *claimed gay identity* and *gay pride* must be earned.

The last child born to poor parents at the start of the Great Depression, I was an unwelcome addition to their overwhelming problems. Like many parents, then and now, they knew how babies were made but not how to protect and care for them.

My forty-year-old father's last remaining teeth showed only when he laughed, three of them, stained a dark yellow from chewing tobacco. He could neither read nor write. He had a job as a laborer for the town's public works department but with the Depression just under way, lay-offs were about to begin. My overweight mother, thirty-six years old, had a fourth grade education, full dentures, a driver's license, years of experience in factory work, hidden fears, strong opinions and an amiable but frightened and helpless husband.

With four children already, they had six mouths to feed and the bank to pay. They had built a small cabin, with the help of relatives, a few of my father's co-workers and a loan from the bank. It was a simple four-room place. A second loan from the bank made indoor plumbing possible. But those loans were more complicated and dangerous than they seemed.

I managed to survive the early surgical intervention. Born alive, I was sent home to the care of my oldest sister, fourteen, who was instructed to boil beets and other vegetables and then feed the water to the new anemic baby. My mother was "kept for another operation," a sterilizing hysterectomy probably.

Families tell stories to one another. Those stories that are repeated again and again are coded family oral history, the part that fills gaps and explains the mysteries in the more open family history. Some of the stories told repeatedly in my family had to do with accidents that threatened my survival in the first years of my life. There was, for instance, "the time you was crawling around the kitchen and drank the kerosene under the stove." Years later, finally able to decode the meaning of these tales, I faced the fact that the family simply could not afford me but neither my *sickly nature* nor the various accidents freed them of me. The persistent survival of the quiet frail baby provoked more shame, guilt and remorse in them, as well as some love and pity.

In my earliest memories I believed that there was something about me that was wrong. I felt guilty but did not know why. My crime, of course, had been arriving as the intruder, unwanted and unwelcome, a last-straw burden. Additionally, my apparent innocence confronted family members with their wishes and actions to rid themselves of me. I was the face of their shame and I absorbed that shame. It became my identity, soon reinforced by the experiences of poverty.

Shame and poverty easily crush a child by destroying self-esteem. Yet it may have been my ill-defined guilt that helped to keep me going. Ever anxious and fearful of impending punishment, I became not only wary but intensely curious, alert to any evidence that might solve the mystery of my guilt by revealing the nature of my wrongness.

There are countless thousands of children in our world, overlooked, forgotten or abused, now as then, some starved, murdered, beaten, raped, tortured or sold into slavery. I was lucky, and I know it. I had a bath once a week usually. Clothes were too big or too small, frayed, mended or darned, but I had clothes. Shoes were tight, stuffed with cardboard in winter to keep out the cold if not the rain and slush, but I had shoes. Absence of food never lasted more than a few days and there was always clean water to drink. Fear and loneliness were constant companions but I had a place to sleep at night. Though much of my childhood was a matter of getting through the hour or the day, it helped me to learn to endure.

I learned to read early and in later years I learned to hear music, to laugh and to feel both appreciation and deep gratitude for the variety that can be found in the world. I am fortunate also to have grown up relatively free of inner anger. There was plenty of anger around me every day but it looked dangerous and futile to me. It still does.

My mother wanted that indoor plumbing. She was a risk taker. Something would come along, she thought, and somehow they could pay the money back to the bank quickly. But my father lost his job working for the Borough. They were unable to make payments, the bank started foreclosure proceedings and finally took the house. It was 1934 by then. There were rumors of work in Miami. Another risky decision was made. We would go to Florida.

The seven of us packed into an old faded blue Buick and drove there from New Jersey, sleeping and eating in the car. Going had been my mother's decision. She was a person who was not content with her life and who was incapable of taking the safe, small steps that might build a more secure life. She had dreams and hopes and she was ready to take any chance to win and step into a life she wanted.

She was the ultimate authority in the family, the one who made all of the final decisions. She was the one with the driver's license. Yet, tellingly, in another of those repeated family tales, this one about that migration to Florida, the decision she had made to pull off into a side road for a night's sleep was always good for a laugh. At dawn we seven sleepers were awakened by someone rapping on the car's window. We were parked not on a quiet side road but on a working railroad track and the morning train was due.

We arrived in Miami Beach after the art deco building boom had faded but we stayed a year, scraping together the wherewithal to return to New Jersey. We lived at first in a shack there, surrounded by the south's poor of all colors, a shaming for my prejudice-afflicted family.

I liked it. I was nearing my fourth birthday and gaining in awareness every day. It was warm and sunny. I could see the world outside by looking through the spaces between the boards.

There were sunburns with blisters, bug bites and terrors such as a near drowning after being thrown into the surf by two of my siblings, but coconuts grew on palm trees and they could be cracked open to yield sweet milk and chewy white meat. I liked the clean smell of soap and bluing that came with the rhythms and warm tones of southern women's voices over the scrubbing sounds on washboards at the communal washhouse. I felt safe at that washhouse.

Four clear memories have stayed with me from that year in my life, each a step in awakening. The first happened soon after we had found that first place to live. The sun was high overhead in a pale blue sky with no clouds. I sat in the sandy yard with a pail and shovel, digging. Someone had told me that if I dug deep enough I would see China.

Suddenly I felt pain. The top of my head hurt. I put the shovel down and felt through the blond curls. My hair was hot, too hot. I looked around and saw no one. I was alone, really alone. No one was home. No one was watching me. I would have to take care of myself. I already knew enough to come in from the rain, now I would know enough to come in from the burning sun, to watch out for myself.

The second happened on the day before my fourth birthday. We had moved to a small ramshackle house a few days earlier. This one had a dark kitchen and four steps from it down to a small back yard. I was making my way down the steps carefully, intent on exploring the new yard when a woman in the house next to ours said a cheery "hello" in a voice with a European accent. She called to her daughter in the house, "Trudy, come play with the nice little girl who just moved in next door." Her mistake was due to my shoulder length curls in the style popularly sported by both girls and boys at the turn of the century when my parents had been children.

I turned, marched into the kitchen and demanded a haircut. The demand was denied but I persisted. A new awareness was dimly seen but strongly felt. I was neither a toy nor a doll. I was a person who happened to be a boy and that meant I needed a boy's haircut. The curls required too much combing and pulling every morning anyway. They were in my way. I could insist, make a fuss. I got the haircut for my birthday.

The third happened some weeks later. I saw a smiling, athletic young man go into an outdoor wooden shower stall at the beach. The louvered door hid his mid-section from sight but I could see muscular shoulders, arms and chest. I saw white soapsuds in his dark hair and on his handsome face. I saw his wet swimsuit drop to the wooden floor slats as water and suds cascaded down the hair on tanned legs and onto his feet. I felt desire for the first time in my young life. I wanted to get into that shower with him and hug myself close to him. I *needed* to be with him, yet something stopped me. I knew that it was forbidden. I must not do it. How do we teach children such taboos so early in life without ever using the words? I was awakened then and there to my desire and to my loneliness, hiding my loss for fear of shame.

The fourth happened like a sudden Miami thunder and lightning storm. My sister had been working as a live-in baby-sitter somewhere in Miami. A man who had a nice smile, maybe her employer, maybe connected with the citrus industry, brought crates of oranges and grapefruits as gifts each time he came to pick her up.

At supper one evening, for no reason that I knew anything about, my father's rage exploded. It had something to do with this man, though he was not there at the time. My father shouted, paced and threw things. His words did not make sense to me but there was danger in the tone and volume. "I'll kill the son-of-a-bitch." *Those* words were clear. The next day we were packing. We were going to leave Miami.

I was alert to the danger that lurked within this family. Danger was not only in the world outside. There was lethal anger in the family, simmering usually, but it could be ignited at any time and then there might be *hell to pay*, in my father's words. I was careful and quiet, wary and watchful. Safety was not to be found within the shifting alliances of these people.

There it was. Another sweet, good-natured, gay boy child was coming awake at the age of four in a mean world. Even at that tender age I wanted to make things nicer. I tried, first and foremost, not to add to trouble. I was looking for ways to quell or lessen the endless quarrels and unhappiness that I saw the people around me causing one another needlessly. The empathy, tolerance, compassion and altruism that are personality traits researchers have found in abundance in populations of gay males were peeking out, setting the foundations for a characterological need to nurture, make peace and build bridges of understanding. And there was that erotic attraction to the handsome young man in the shower.

We returned to New Jersey, to a cold winter in an uninsulated garage behind the house where my mother's youngest sister lived with her husband and children. There I learned that sleeping too close to the garage wall could lead to something painful called frostbite on my ear, but that was less a problem than the scarcity of food. We were hungry.

We were Republicans, a family tradition or habit since the time of Lincoln and my father's father's Civil War service as a fifteen year old in the Union Army. Such unquestioned politics and false pride kept us away from Welfare help or *relief* as it was called then. But my father did get a W.P.A. job for a few days that winter and it led to bags of groceries from a food distribution center. That meant shame for the family, of course, but I felt only gladness and wonder seeing those big paper bags filled with food.

My father tried to teach me how to tell time on the clock that spring, sitting in the thin sunlight in front of open garage doors. I was impressed that he knew how and that he wanted to pass the skill on to me. But I could not follow his teaching. He abandoned it finally, another failure for him, another something wrong with me, another frustration for both of us.

Later that Spring my mother took me along in the car with her one morning to a huge, echo-filled, chilly, damp warehouse across the street from a pier in a nearby town. The newspaper wrapped bundle we took back to the car was filled with little shrimp. Back in the garage she rinsed the shrimp, coated them with flour and fried them. With biscuits it made a delicious evening meal. Many times I asked if we could go and get more but was shushed each time. No reasons were given but we never went there again. Years later, during a dinner party, the difference in size of shrimp used for shrimp cocktails in New York and California came up in the conversation. Someone pointed out that on the East Coast the very small shrimp are used for bait.

The house we moved into the following summer seemed big. Inland from the ocean and on the wrong side of the main street, it must have failed to rent for the season. It had an upstairs, a downstairs, three bedrooms, a bathroom and a cellar.

One morning I passed the open door of my parents' bedroom where my mother was dressing after a bath. She was putting Cashmere Bouquet talcum powder on her breasts. Nakedness did not happen in our family. I stopped and stared. She was wearing a pink slip, the straps down. I was startled by the sight.

"These was your dinners," she said, explaining her breasts. "And these are the nickels," I thought she said. Stunned, I filed away the exotic information, informing other equally ignorant children for years after of the correct anatomic names for *dinners* and *nickels*. It did not make sense but there was so much of our world that did not make sense.

I slept in a borrowed crib at the new house but sometimes I was allowed to squeeze into a bed with siblings. If a thunder and lightning storm was coming, for instance, we had to pull all the window shades down, wrap knives, forks and spoons in dish towels quickly so as not to attract the lightning and then crawl under a bed or get into the bed together and pull the covers over our heads. Waiting for the storm to pass there might be sex play between my youngest siblings. I was allowed to know about it but knew not to speak about it ever.

Waiting my turn to use the bathroom one morning, a small red rubber ball dropped from my hands, rolled into my parents' bedroom and into the closet there. Retrieving it, I saw an unfamiliar blue box on the floor in the farthest corner, a hidden supply of sanitary napkins for menstruation. When my mother came out of the bathroom I asked her what was in the box. She brusquely told me it was none of my business, to stay away from it and "stop poking around in other people's business."

Later that same morning I was intrigued by the way the forced air from the floor register that was between the living room and dining room flared out the dresses of my mother and sisters when they walked over it. I promptly lay on my back next to it so that I could look up their skirts. My mother yelled, "Get up off that floor. You know too damn much for your own good, Mister. Don't play dumb." Unclear to me, but more evidence of my wrongness.

A few days after my fifth birthday, I was alone in that house with my oldest brother who was sixteen. I wanted to get a pad of colored paper and a pencil that had been birthday presents. They were in the bedroom in which he was taking a nap. His bed was behind the door which was open just a crack. I could see the pad and pencil on a table under the window. Carefully, I pushed the door open just wide enough to squeeze through and then tiptoed to the table. When I turned to retreat I was startled to find him awake and holding an enormous erection, the first I had seen. He told me that I could touch it if I wanted. I was in awe of both it and of his generous, gentle invitation. It was exciting. I offered him an equal invitation but he declined. I felt honored and excited by his offering, but I also felt rejected, not desirable.

I started kindergarten that September. The younger of my two brothers, seven years older than I, and the younger of my two sisters, nine years older, walked the two miles each way with me. My sister had been labeled *slow* and had been put into the *Opportunity Class* to serve out her sentence weaving baskets until she reached the legal age to leave school and get a factory job. Good natured and accepting, she made the best of it, though bullied and made miserable by other children every school day. Our brother toughed it out, keeping a distance from us except at lunchtime.

We were forced together at lunchtime, scrambling to get to a small green-topped table in the corner at the far end of the school lunchroom. Our lunch was sandwiches of homemade bread with sugar covered bananas sliced lengthwise or homemade biscuits spread with homemade jelly. They were wrapped in a clean but thin dishtowel and carried in a brown paper bag that was to be saved to be used again.

At other tables children pointed at us, laughed and sometimes made ugly threats. There was a disinterested teacher on duty who kept a loose semblance of order. On the playground at the dreaded morning and afternoon recesses there was a teacher on duty also but she intervened only if a full-fledged fist fight was underway. Classroom time was tense and boring, the playground was scary. School was part prison and part jungle, from nine in the morning until three in the afternoon.

I quickly started learning to read. A school nurse came to the house to talk to my mother. I was sent upstairs. It may be that the kindergarten teacher had noticed signs of malnutrition, bad teeth, poor vision, bad hygiene, the constant running nose, the lazy eye or my timid, wary shyness. I was never told why she had come but I knew that my mother was not pleased and that it was my fault.

Danger could erupt in our house at any time. The brother and sister closest to my age were at home with me one rainy afternoon. They started to play a board game which quickly led to accusations of cheating, then to my brother getting angry and chasing my sister around the house. Scared, I begged them to stop. She made the mistake of trying to escape by running down the steps into the darkness of the cellar. He grabbed the axe that was beside the steps and threw it down the stairs in her direction as she fled. Thrown hastily, it missed its mark but I had seen that axe split tree trunks with its sharp blade. I knew what might have happened.

I wanted people to read to me. Words in books attracted me. My teacher was amused that I liked the big word *picturesque* and learned to recognize it. A few times she sent a picture book home. Otherwise we had only an old family bible and a half dozen inherited adult books that were never opened. We had a few pictures that went from house to house with us also and someone once had cut out the top of a candy box and wedged it into a frame that hung above that crib I slept in until I was six. A colorful wreath of flowers on the white cardboard surrounded a small poem. I liked to have the rhyming lines read to me until I could read them myself:

> *Silver and gold*
> *May tarnish away*
> *But a good education*
> *Will never decay.*

The summer following kindergarten we were still in the same house and I met my first friend. He had moved into the house across the street facing ours. We were the same age and even had the same first name. We liked one another, both of us shy and content to be together. But the friendship was ended quickly by our mothers. Something was very wrong. Years later I realized it must have been the difference of our skin colors. Maybe it also made them uneasy that we were not playing like real boys, no dares, no rough stuff, just enjoying our peaceful companionship.

Our family was rich in prejudices and the crude language used to express them. The town was full of *niggers, wops, kikes, mackerel snappers, krauts, summer people, polocks* and other *foreigners.* Lowest on the social pecking order were the local-born poor whites who fished and dug clams. Our family had come from the big city, Newark. The local poor were the untouchable caste, the *clam diggers.* Every poor white person in town feared that label. No matter how hungry we were, digging clams and fishing were not options. Such was the family's strange false pride.

Chapter 2

Depression Years

The weekend after Labor Day, just after the start of the first grade, we moved to a summer house on a street near the ocean where my father could sheetrock walls during the winter. Norma Mercy, who had been in my kindergarten class, lived there. She greeted me on the corner the day that we moved, blond hair and blue eyes sparkling in the sun, agenda front and center. "I'll show you mine if you'll show me yours," she said by way of greeting.

During the year that we lived there Norma recruited most of the neighborhood kids for one or another of her show-and-touch anatomy classes, held more frequently in the off-season months when most of the homes in the area were deserted. Built on pilings, many had ample space under them since their backyards sloped down towards the sea. Various theories about variety in anatomy were proposed and considered but even with willing attempts to simulate what some kids swore to have seen, we were unable to verify the *tab A in slot B* theory of baby production. Amazingly, the only angry shaming that came from it all was on the day my mother arrived home and discovered Norma and me in the bathroom together. We feigned innocence to no avail.

Thirteen years later I was summoned home from college for an emergency visit because my mother had been taken to the hospital for gall bladder surgery described as very risky. While she was in surgery I took a walk in the hospital hall and found myself suddenly facing Norma Mercy, now straight backed with ample bosom, wearing a starched white nurse's uniform and cap, still blond and bright blue eyed. We were both surprised, having not seen one another since elementary school because we had gone to different high schools. I was shocked to find her looking so grown up, official and professional. She was shocked to learn that I was a college student in far away Ohio. We had not grown up with people who went to college. Becoming a nurse had been a real achievement. She was married and had three children she told me.

Hitch hiking back to school a few days later I smiled often thinking of Norma. Her spunk, curiosity and attraction to anatomy had taken her a long way. Meeting one another's eyes in that hospital corridor, I knew that we both were amused by the unspoken recollection of the same memories. There she was, professional, responsible and respectably able to continue her hobby of comparative anatomy study.

Winter in that summer house near the ocean was very damp and cold. My sleeping place, a wicker couch on the sun porch was moved into the small, cramped living room on the coldest nights, Christmas Eve among them. Work of any kind was still scarce. Christmas gifts were unlikely, I was told, but my father and oldest brother cut down a pine tree and hauled it from the edge of town on a sled.

We set to work decorating it. Our trees never had lights but there were a few wonderful old ornaments that came from before my time when the family had lived in an apartment in Newark. At school we had learned how to make paper chains. Scraps of construction paper from school were best but any kind of paper could be used, the more colorful the better, though even newspaper strips other than the comics would do. All we needed was scissors, some flour and water to make library paste to form the paper loops and maybe some glitter from school.

The tinsel we called *rain* or *icicles* were taken off the tree each year at holidays' end, one by one, and carefully laid flat on tissue paper, then folded away, ready to add light, sparkle and magic to the next year's tree. Putting on and taking off that tinsel, one piece at a time, was a painstaking job that I enjoyed. It was orderly and required my expert patience, each piece a silver prize. I was the keeper of its magic.

My father had temper tantrums. They came suddenly, like a fissure appearing in volcanic soil before lava erupts. He was a man just barely resisting a forced admission of defeat. The world had not made a place for him and did not offer him respect. His attempts at amiable good humor and hard work had earned him no rewards.

One of his temper outbursts could be predicted each Christmas at tree decorating time. From the moment the first ornament was hung it was just a matter of time. A dropped ornament or the discovery that the tree was a bit crooked would do it. He would roar and shout his loud curses. To my child eyes it seemed like rays of dangerous fury shot from his body as the pent up, impotent rage and general unfocused hatred poured out. It destroyed whatever fragile joy might have been building, each and every time.

My mother would tersely tell him to shut up. One brother or sister would bump into another prompting another lesser shouting match. I would tearfully plead for peace and ask why we could not just be nice to one another. Ignored, I realized again each time that I did not fit in this family. I was the odd one, alone.

The scene would burn out, leaving an odor of burned joy in the acrid air. No physical harm was done. My mother, probably as a result of having been knocked around by her own hot-tempered father, absolutely forbade any hitting except for ritual punishment spankings administered only by her.

Words were another matter. Either parent might try to have the final word by telling the other parent or one of the children to "go shit in your hat and pull it down over your ears" or "go outside and blow the stink off yourself." An additional stray, gruff, and meaningless, "So's your Aunt Tillie" could indicate that the battle was finished. From somewhere in the puritan family history, it was understood that such sins as alcohol and makeup were forbidden, fortunately. I can only imagine how it might have been if there had been heavy drinking.

The tree and its decorations were particularly important that Christmas that I was six years old because there was no money for gifts. Yet at bedtime I was instructed to hang a stocking for Santa Claus. Might there be a Santa Claus after all? A stocking most years would be stuffed with an orange, an apple and some hard candy.

I do not know how it was done but what happened seemed a miracle. Maybe my mother's parents who lived only half a dozen blocks inland and always seemed to have enough food for themselves made a last minute contribution.

Whatever the source of the miracle, I awoke that freezing cold Christmas morning to find the stockings full! Added to the usual allotment were a few dates and one unwrapped chocolate in each stocking. And there were gifts! Family members gave up things they already had. One brother gave me a box of shiny colored paper that could be made into shapes. My oldest sister gave me the violin she had once bought from her factory wages and struggled to learn to play. Now it was mine. Santa still seemed unlikely but a miracle had happened.

My first grade teacher that year, Miss Miller, had a habit of holding the skin of her neck between thumb and forefinger when she spoke in a warbling voice like a young Eleanor Roosevelt. She was a stickler for order, routine and classroom cleanliness. I liked that. However, living in her world meant getting to school on time and that meant getting my brother and sister up and out of the house early enough. There was no incentive for either of them to get to their respective torture on time so I was often late and shamed for it.

I wanted, more than anything, to fit in and go unnoticed. But late arrivals were noticed. The first morning that I did manage to get the three of us to school on time, Miss Miller wrote "Donald is here on time today" all the way across the blackboard. Everyone looked at me and laughed. I was humiliated.

Miss Miller was bothered by my frequent absences due to sickness. These absences interfered with her schedule and her sense of order. I understood that. It made it difficult for me to keep up with the reading lessons and spelling tests. But I tried. I spelled the word *chance* as c–h–a–n–c–h and *attitude* as a–d–d–i–t–u–d–e, incorrect spelling but the way words were pronounced in our local dialect. The first report card read,

"Donald is very slow but very thorough." In the space for parents' remarks and signature my mother wrote, "He comes by it natural."

My mother was a peculiar mixture of defensiveness, desires, needs and chaotic determination. She had worked in a chocolate factory as a child, a female first child disappointment to her petty tyrant, Victorian father with his pretensions to aristocracy. He saw no reason for a girl to go beyond fourth grade in school. That first factory job addicted her to chocolate for life. Poor as we were, through the years, tiny stashes of chocolate were to be found hidden in a corner of a top shelf in the kitchen, a coat pocket in a closet or the glove compartment of the car. During the scarcity and rationing of the war years, one of my assignments was to try to score a chocolate bar for her whenever and wherever possible.

She dreamed of living in Florida or California someday. There was a golden framed picture always hung on the living room wall in each house showing a snow capped mountain as background for a sunny green meadow full of colorful wildflowers. Under the picture was one word: *California*. She was determined to get there.

Old photographs showed her to have been a spunky beauty as a girl. In one, at nineteen she sat on a motorcycle wearing boy's clothes. She was a dancer, too. Sometimes, if we were alone in the house and she was in a good mood, she would dance around the dining room table in the arms of an imaginary partner as she whistled and hummed tunes of years gone by. She encouraged me to follow her. "Watch my feet. It's easy."

She fell down stairs often and sprained an ankle or a wrist now and then, caught colds, got headaches and complained of stomach pains and bloating "from those adhesions after the operations." She had had mastoiditis as a child, aggravated by her father "boxing my ears". The damaged ear hurt, sometimes releasing a discharge with a distinct sour smell. A puckered scar on her neck "where the goiter was cut out" hurt too, especially during rainstorms. Even as a young child I could see that she needed someone to take care of her and give her attention.

It was while we were living in that same summer house that I first heard the family story of my mother's arrest or detention by the local police when I was a baby. She had been carrying me, wrapped in a blanket, on her way to the grocery store when a policeman stopped her. He looked at me and at a picture he was carrying and took us to the police station where "they took you away from me until some city Jew cops came and undressed you and then later gave you back."

The Lindbergh baby had been kidnapped and the resemblance was close enough. When I once met Anne Morrow Lindbergh at a cocktail party while I was in graduate school I temporarily had forgotten the family tale fortunately. I knew of her then only as the woman who had written *A Gift from the Sea*. I was, however, struck by the quick, warm, easy conversational connection we made, both of us admittedly shy and unsure of our appearance in a big cocktail party. Later of course, remembering, I wondered at how different my life might have been had she been my mother.

A few months before we left that summer house I devised a way of teaching myself to tell time. We had a wind-up clock someone had left behind that had a rotating metal ring of numbers representing the twelve hours. I would check the time on it and then run to the clock in my parents' bedroom and check the big hand and the little hand until the connection finally was clear to me.

When the numbing chill of a second winter in that house began, we moved to my mother's parents' house, taking over the upstairs while they moved to a smaller downstairs apartment that they rented to summer people in season. Nervous and scared, the teasing at school got worse for me and included daily threats of being beaten by one or more of the school toughs.

But my mother had gotten piecework at the women's underwear factory that was beside the railroad track near school. That was good for several reasons. We had some money for food, money to pay my grandparents rent and I could escape the bullies by making a quick run along the tracks after school to the car parked outside the factory just one long block away. I could lock the car from the inside, slump down to hide and be safe waiting there until she finished work when it got dark.

The factory was a sweatshop. The women tore part of a ticket from each garment sewed. At the end of the week the tickets had to be sorted and assembled on a white sheet of paper made sticky by wetting it. They were paid only for submitted tickets. It was important to make sure that each ticket stuck firmly to the white paper. I took on that job.

A week before Thanksgiving that year some children, including me, were given a green slip of paper to take home. It was an invitation to a *Thanksgiving dinner with all the trimmings* that would happen during vacation, the day before Thanksgiving. Each child must be accompanied by a mother, however.

We arrived at Lodge Hall at the appointed time. Two long tables created with boards and sawhorses, had been covered with tablecloths. I took very little notice of decorations. I saw ladies in fancy dresses and hats carrying steaming bowls and platters of food to the tables.

Each child was seated on a folding wooden chair; mothers were standing just behind the chairs. I had never seen such an abundance of food. My dish was filled with ample portions. A few of the ladies made little speeches and then we began to eat. It was delicious. The aromas and the warmth of the food filled me with gladness. Mothers leaned forward to help cut turkey on the dishes. But then I realized what was not happening. The mothers were not eating. I knew my mother was just as hungry as I was. The food lost its appeal, empathy and shame replacing it.

I realized that my mother, standing behind my chair, hungry, was shamed by these ladies feeding her child while she and the other mothers stood in presumed gratitude. I also understood that I dared not offer to share my food with her. I ate some and we left. There was no discussion of that Thanksgiving meal then or ever.

There was lots of snow that winter. Several times I woke early on a Sunday morning, quietly got out of my blanket on the living room sofa, dressed and let myself out of the front door into a world covered by a white purity that quieted all sound, big snowflakes continuing to float to earth like messages from the sky above. I could walk through the nearly knee deep snow all the way to the beach. I was alone, cold but safe from the school bullies and safe from the harsh world of home. There was nothing to do but admire the beauty of the snow and the majesty of the ocean with its awesome, changing, never-ending waves. The ocean was hypnotic, a magnet for me in those years as it has continued to be throughout my life.

My mother started baking more that winter. Maybe she was inspired by being in her own mother's kitchen or maybe it was because the factory job brought in enough money to afford such luxury. She always had baked bread and biscuits. Those and boiled potatoes were the mainstays of our food supply. But now she baked cakes and pies. She said that she learned it all from her *Dutch* grandmother, perhaps a friend of the family when she was a child in the city.

As winter neared its end I began to earn money by finding metal scraps, newspapers and old soda bottles to take to the junk yard. I was eight years old. Money earned by anyone in the family was turned over for *room and board* with some given back for spending. I had my own money then.

Nickels paid my way into the Rivoli Theater for Saturday matinees. I went alone. First came the newsreel, then *Abbott & Costello, Three Stooges,* or *Marx Brothers* shorts, and then I would sink into the feature, whether a Tarzan tale or a drama. On the walk home, I hoped that I would find my mother in the kitchen starting to get supper ready so that I could tell the entire story of the movie. Telling it, I could see it all again in my mind's eye.

In one of those black and white films, seen on a Saturday afternoon, a man and a woman were in their bedroom talking. There was tension between them, some sort of argument. But they were being nice to one another despite the disagreement. In fact, everyone in the movie seemed considerate of one another.

To me it seemed proof that there really were people like that somewhere. I had suspected that it was not necessary for people to be mean, angry, sarcastic and suspicious with one another. Somewhere in the world there were people like these people. I needed to find them. I was with the wrong people in the wrong place.

In the movie the man took a fresh shirt from a drawer that held several and said something like, "Well, if I can't be good looking, I can at least dress nicely." It was an important clue. I would remember that. Going to sleep that night my mind was racing, full of the movie images. There were people like that somewhere. I would find them. Maybe they would let me live with them if I could find them.

We moved again in the spring, leaving my grandparents' house so that they could rent to summer people. We went from Belmar to the less developed, cheaper West Belmar, farther inland, away from the desirable beaches. Starting third grade I had to change to the smaller West Belmar school with its front entrance for adults, one side entrance for girls and the other for boys. Girls played girls' games on the girls' side playground. Boys played baseball on their side. Boys like me, scrawny, timid, possibly cursed with poor eyesight and coordination, were doomed to cling to the building's shadows and the shame of being sissies.

Factory work had dropped off and the money my father and brothers were able to make caddying at the Spring Lake Golf & Country Club in the summer was not enough to carry us very far into winter. There was a stepped up effort to find junk, soda bottles and newspapers. My oldest brother went off to a Civilian Conservation Corps camp. There were cold days with no food.

As the least likely to be refused, it fell to me to go to the corner store two blocks away now and then with a request for a pound of ground meat, some suet, a quarter of a pound of butter, some potatoes, a can of tomatoes, a carrot and maybe some soup bones. Then at the end I was to ask the man to "put it on the cuff" and "I'll bring the money Friday," which meant maybe Saturday or the following week. A few times he turned me down, putting the food away again saying "you haven't paid for last week and the week before yet." With burning ears I would feel other people in the store looking at me and trying not to look at me as I left.

But there were always a few kids at school who had to face worse misery. There was the boy with the clubfoot whom everyone called "Gimp." The more he smiled, the more they taunted him. Or the girl whose family car had been hit on the railroad track crossing. Her parents had been killed and she had been left with a face full of scars. Naturally, she was called "Scarface." Her tears had no effect on tormenters. I was nicknamed "Mortimer Snerd" after Edgar Bergen's wooden dummy that was stupid and spoke in a dead, flat voice, a reflection of my depression no doubt.

The fourth grade teacher, Mrs. Titus, had large breasts. On the first day she stood at the front of the class, hands palm out in from of her breasts, and boomed, "I stand here like the blinkers at the railroad crossing, telling you that if you do not memorize the multiplication tables from one to twelve you will never leave this fourth grade. *Never.*"

It was another worry. I felt unable to do it. But she had activated more than my fear and anxiety. I decided that I would have to develop a strategy so as not to get found out. I began devising methods for quick additions or subtractions and visualized multiplication tricks that made memorization unnecessary and later served me well in algebra. I left fourth grade without learning the *times tables*, as they were called, having learned instead that I was able to break the rules.

For more than three years at that school I had waves of cramping and diarrhea that came on as soon as I got to school. I had to ask to be excused to go to the boys' toilet in the basement whenever it seemed like I dared wait no longer. The teachers were suspicious and it provided more ammunition for teasing on the schoolyard.

Chapter 3

War Begins

But into that time of endurance a dog appeared, an all black mongrel. She followed me home from school at the end of the third week of the fourth grade. I noticed her as I was walking on the path that cut through a corner vacant lot just a block from our house. She was trailing me at a distance, keeping her eye on me. When I went into the house, she cautiously settled herself on the bottom step.

When I looked out of the window later she was sleeping there. As usual, there was no food to spare but I took a small bowl of water out to her, approaching slowly. She watched my face but made no move. She drank the water quickly so I filled the bowl for her again and then sat on the top step. She drank more and then settled back into her place, head down but looking at me. Finally she stood and climbed up to the top step, licked my hand and sat beside me.

She had no collar or tags but that was not unusual. It seemed clear that she was either lost or abandoned. My guess was that summer people had left her behind when they packed up to return home. After our supper I took her scraps from my share of the meal and filled the water bowl again. She was there in the morning, on the bottom step, waiting. She had decided to stay and had claimed her place. Best of all, no one had raised any objections to her.

I named her Peggy. She belonged to all of us, I suppose, but more to me. She started as an outside dog but when the winter storms began she gained house rights bit by bit. I gave her baths and begged scraps for her at the small butcher shop nearby. In fact, she added to our food supply. The scraps and bones I begged for her went into a big soup pot with backyard vegetables canned in summer. We could get two meals from that plus a sandwich of marrow scraped out from the center of the larger bones. Peggy got the bones after they had been boiled clean. She also got the first rinse of the soup pot, any scraps of bread and any nourishment that could be found licking the soup bowls.

Peggy and I scouted backyards of summer houses, vacant lots, the main highway and other roads together, looking for soda bottles that could be returned for deposit money or newspapers and scrap metal that could be put into a rusty wagon and pulled to the junk yard where the man who was missing one finger weighed first the newspapers and then metal in a big hanging scale. He would silently dole out coins that became grocery money.

In summer, always the youngest, skinniest, saddest looking and most shy, I went door to door selling homemade fudge squares neatly wrapped in waxed paper. Summer people could afford the luxury. I was glad to have Peggy with me. We heard "no" more often then we saw the kind smile that would yield a nickel for one square or a dime for three squares.

We also hunted back behind town in summer for wild blueberries, blackberries and the cherries that could be reached on low hanging branches. We got to the beach when we could. Peggy never tired of barking at the big waves that came crashing in, chasing the water as it retreated and then running from it again as the next wave chased us. She listened to my feelings and my confusion. She listened to it all. She taught me how to listen and how to love.

Before we were able to afford a radio or pay the electric bill our lighting came from kerosene lamps and evening entertainment could be me creating a costume for patient Peggy with scraps of cloth pinned into dresses and improvised hats. Catching sight of a cat or a squirrel in the woods across the road on a summer evening and taking off after it in a flurry of flying rags provided a reliable source of laughter for the family.

We were an isolated family, isolated from others and isolated from one another. But like strangers on a long cross-country bus ride, sometimes there was a rallying of spirits, something that pulled us together for more than a meal. About the time that my oldest brother left for the C.C.C. camp, my sister in the Opportunity Class became old enough to leave school and my oldest sister quit high school. Both joined my mother at the factory when work picked up there. That meant some spare money. Alice, my oldest sister, bought copies of the current issues of ten-cent song books. They had the words to popular songs. After supper, once or twice a week we would sit in the living room and sing the songs together, hostilities relaxed. It was fun.

Next to our house was a vacant lot with wild grass that grew to four feet in summer, turning golden and dying off each fall. Across the street was a stretch of woods. Neither was as good a place to be alone as the ocean but I could hide in either location.

Early in the summer between Fourth and Fifth grades new people moved into the house on the other side of the vacant lot, a family named Himmelman. The mother and father had German accents. Their two girls and one boy were all close to my age. Of course I was told to steer clear of them since they were foreigners but, anxious to make some connection before the school year started, they sought me out for *club mee*tings in the high weeds between our houses. They brought beer to our first meeting. I tasted the forbidden substance but it was bitter. They also took me to meet Ray, the seventeen-year-old boy who lived with his mother in the attic apartment of their house.

Ray's mother worked with their parents somewhere so we had the house to ourselves. Ray baked chocolate cake for us. We ate it warm. The second visit, he baked another chocolate cake and dared everyone to take their clothes off. He said he would do it too. It was exciting. We were half undressed when we heard someone come into the house downstairs and had to make a fast retreat to our club space in the weeds, leaving Ray to wash his dishes.

Two weeks later we heard that Ray's mother had sent him out of the apartment on Sunday and told him not to come back until supper time. Then she put her head in that same oven that had baked our cakes and turned on the gas. She was dead when he came home.

That winter, about a year and a half after she adopted me, Peggy disappeared. She was missing for three days. I looked for her everywhere. My father spotted her finally, late in the afternoon of that third day, lying in a vacant lot not far from the house, partly covered with the snow that had begun to fall, too weak to stand. He carried her home. I was allowed to make a bed of rags for her on the floor in the kitchen, out of the way but near the warmth of the stove.

I gave her water from a spoon because she could not lift her head. By the next day she was able to move around the house, stiff and slow, unsure in balance but better. Before long we saw that she was going to have puppies. When the big day came, late in April, she had eight. There were three sets of identical twins, each set looking like a different breed plus two odd individual pups. She cleaned and nursed them. But after the births she was tired and sick.

I was told I could keep one of the puppies. But homes would have to be found for the others. I claimed one of the two odd individuals, a fluffy black and white ball of energy I named Teddy. The summer people had begun to return in May. I did not want to beg, but it was that or they would go into the ocean in a burlap sack. With a lot of begging I found homes for them

In September the unwelcome prospect of another school year loomed. I would be back in school, as would my next youngest brother. It was 1941. The war was coming but we did not know it. My oldest brother had gone from the Civilian Conservation Corps to the National Guard. There were some jobs available. No one would be home on the days my father found work.

Poor Peggy got sicker and sicker. She vomited often and stairs were a problem for her. She had too little strength to go more than a few feet from the house when I carried her outside. As I feared, I was told that Peggy was too sick and that we would have to call the SPCA and get rid of her. I begged for time, prayed often and talked to Peggy, urging her to get well.

But on the Wednesday before Labor Day, the SPCA truck came for her. I was the only person home that day waiting with her and Teddy. The SPCA man's footfall was heavy on the steps to the porch.

He carried a big net on a long pole. Peggy barked more fiercely than I thought she could and scuttled under the rusting sofa glider on the porch while Teddy jumped up and down adding his higher pitched bark.

The man started to drag the glider and poked his pole under it toward Peggy. I told him to stop and said I would bring her out to the truck. I put Teddy inside the house, closed the door and reached under the glider for Peggy.

Frail and weak, she did not resist. I lifted her into my arms and carried her off the porch, down the steps and out the driveway to the cage with the open door on the back of the pickup truck. One last lick of my face, then the man shut the cage door. Peggy did not struggle. She yielded, helpless. But she managed to sit up in the cage, facing me, looking at me questioningly. Her eyes looked into mine, mine into hers. I could not say goodbye. The man bolted the cage door, lit a cigarette, got into the truck, started the engine and began the slow drive down the dirt road, Peggy's eyes on me, still managing to sit. We looked at one another until we could no longer see one another.

There was no crying. I had just turned eleven. I had given up useless crying, trading it for grim feelings of emptiness. I remember that after the truck had gone, I felt hopeless emptiness inside of me and outside. My prayers had done no good.

The first weeks of the sixth grade went by in a blur. On a sunny Monday morning of the second month a handsome New Jersey State Trooper appeared in his blue uniform on stage at a special assembly for sixth, seventh and eighth graders. He told us that he needed some help. Safety patrol monitors were needed to get kids across the streets near the school safely. Each monitor would wear a large polished brass arm badge and was to be strictly obeyed by children and motorists. It would mean reporting for duty at the school forty-five minutes early and staying at your assigned post for thirty minutes both before and after school. It was a job to be taken seriously. An oath would be administered and there was to be an inspection meeting after duty on Friday afternoons.

Shy as I was, I volunteered. I was chosen. Being tall probably helped. I polished my brass badge every Thursday evening. At the end of the year I would get a big official recognition certificate from the State of New Jersey with the State seal embossed in gold. My stomach problems ended on my first day of duty.

Teddy and I managed. I talked with him less than I had confided in Peggy. I did not talk about missing her. We got through the school year together, punctuated as it was in December by the Japanese attack on Pearl Harbor, far away in a place called Hawaii. They were *the enemy*, quickly joined by Germans and Italians. *Japs*, *Krauts* and *Wops* they were called in our town. It was confirmation that foreigners were not to be trusted, except maybe the English and French. The word *war* was attached to everything said or done. Everything was about the war and *the war effort*. But there was work now and more food for us, even though there were shortages and rationing. Wonder Bread replaced homemade bread because we could afford it.

The following summer I turned twelve. I carried golf bags at the Spring Lake Golf and Country Club for overweight men more than twice my size who smoked cigars and did not see me. Money earned entitled me to go down the narrow back stairs of the club house to the caddies' cellar kitchen and buy a hot dog with mustard for lunch. I remember still that very tempting smell of mustard and hot dogs wafting up that stairway. Teddy and I played in the back yard in late afternoons or took walks in the woods across the road.

One month into seventh grade, in October, we moved back to Belmar, into one side of a double house. It was closer to the ocean and to transportation. Gas was rationed. I was to change schools again. There were air raid drills, blackouts, army truck convoys to and from the new nearby army camp, food rationing, blackened headlights, a Victory Garden in the back yard, and always rumors about the war.

The people on the other side of the house had a dog who looked enough like Teddy that people in the neighborhood could not tell them apart. The two dogs hated one another and we had to try to be careful not to let them out of the house at the same time or there would be a guaranteed dogfight. Like tribal people around the world, then and now, the two dogs could not or would not overcome their useless primitive instincts, settle their claims to territory and agree to live together in peace.

Soon after the start of the school year I developed stomach pains again, but worse than any I had ever had. I was treated at home with a sweet tasting opiate to relieve the pain if not the fever. It was appendicitis. It ruptured finally on the way to the hospital and was followed by pneumonia. For me it was the beginning of life getting better, however. There was ample food in the hospital. Nurses seemed glad to bring me fruit juices and Jell-O between meals. During the long recuperation at home I was moved from the living room sofa to a bed of my own.

Teddy kept me sweet company and comforted me as I wandered into and out of fevers. The old patterned wallpaper had water stains. I used the paper's patterns and the stains to create people and animals, Rorschach style. I gave the people identities and names that changed to suit the stories I made up about them. Teddy was a good audience.

The war was changing everything. My father found occasional odd jobs, my second brother skipped his senior year of high school to join the Marines and my mother went to Washington, D.C. to get work and to be with my sisters who were working and living there.

My father's brother who walked with a squeaking wooden leg lived nearby. His wife had been laid off from the women's underwear factory while they converted it to war work so she came in once each day to check on me and give me a meal while I recuperated from the pneumonia. My oldest sister signed me up for a junior book club and the first book was a biography of Abe Lincoln. Life was good.

I stalled my recovery as long as possible. When I returned to school in March I was genuinely weak and confused about the seventh grade school work. I began to have bad headaches. I was allowed to stay home many days and it led to having my vision checked and to getting glasses.

I was allowed to take the train to Washington to visit my mother and sisters. My mother quit her job as a uniformed counter waitress at a downtown Washington five & ten cent store while I was there. They ordered her around too much she said and the tips were not big enough. She did not say it but I could see that she also was embarrassed to be in that yellow uniform with its checkered brown and white trim on the cap and apron. I cringed when I visited the counter and heard them yell criticisms and call her by her first name. She was the only *girl* with gray hair.

I definitely did not want to go back to school. There were more sick headaches, sometimes exaggerated. My oldest sister offered to take me back to Washington to share her room there for a month before she left for the army. She was lonely.

It was wonderful. She had breakfast and dinner with me each day at the government employee's cafeteria and bought me a public transit pass that gave me the whole city to explore. I was twelve years old. I found every public building that would permit free entrance, thereby accidentally beginning a real education.

Since the appendectomy I had been on a holiday of sorts. No one, including me, noticed that I was getting an education. But State law demanded a return to school. I was to go back for the last few weeks of the seventh grade.

The Friday before my return to class I woke to a bright, sunny, very cold morning that followed on the heels of a late two-day winter storm. I bundled myself up and walked to the ocean, troubled by the impending return to school. The ocean was my place to go with troubles. It could both distract and comfort me.

Icy wind whipped spray foam, blowing it over powerful waves. It was early morning and I was alone. Suddenly I was stunned by what I saw. The beach was littered with packing crates, some still whole though most had split open in the surf, spilling unlabeled food cans onto the sand. There was black oil tar on the beach everywhere, a residue of war. Somewhere out there, not too far from shore, a ship had gone down in battle or in the storm. Down the beach I saw something that seemed to be shooting sharp rays of light, reflecting sunshine. When I got to it I found a brass bowl half buried in the sand. It was horizontally ornamented with rings of some strange foreign script.

I found a spot partially sheltered from the wind by two waterlogged crates and sat studying the bowl, wondering. I imagined that it might have been the last prized possession of a Japanese sailor in a life raft after his ship had been torpedoed. Or it might have been an American or German sailor with a war prize. But how had it made it to shore? It must have managed to stay afloat riding piggyback on one of the crates, maybe put there by a dying sailor. I took it home, showing it to my parents later that day. My father said, "Some damn Jap thing." I took it to my bedroom and hid it.

The first week back in school the local chamber of commerce gave both the seventh and eighth grades a lunch with speeches. I remember the pumpkin pie. After everyone had been served dessert we were given permission to begin eating it. On my third or fourth bite I realized that some of my classmates were pointing at me, trying not to laugh out loud. Everyone else was eating with a fork, the pie still on a dish. I had mine in my hand. A teacher told everyone to stop laughing. "There's nothing funny here."

She was right. There was not much that was funny in any of our lives. The Depression and the war had seen to that. People only laughed when they made fun of one another. The few truly funny people on radio and in films were prized. Jack Benny was the best. He knew how to laugh at the human predicament, using himself as a lightning rod for laughter. His most ingenious joke was the one about being held up by a robber saying, "Your money or your life." That was followed by his long calculated moment of silence before the robber repeated his demand, Jack finally answering, "I'm thinking." It struck a deep chord in a world of people who had learned to value money too much during the Depression and the war.

The Belmar kids were not much better than my classmates had been in West Belmar. The only Black, Clara, made a puddle under her seat several times because she was afraid to ask to be excused and the two Jewish kids paid for their special holidays with a shower of ethnic taunts when they returned to school. The star glamour boy was Pete Positella who had spent a year and a half at the Rahway State Reform School. A good looking, wiry boy with dark hair, flashing eyes and a pug nose, he smoked and had pubic hair that he showed off in the boys' room to anyone who risked looking as he had to "rearrange my stuff" because underwear apparently got twisted as it carried its extra large burden.

He had a smart mouth and could be counted on to say things in line when the teacher could not hear him. To a tall skinny girl with acne he would say, "Hey, Bea, you want my pole up your hairy hole." To a boy almost tough enough to challenge him he might say "My pals are going to work your ass under the boardwalk if we catch you near Bernice and her big tits. Those are mine." I tried to stay out of his path and out of his line of vision.

Our seventh grade got a new student soon after my return. He had just moved into town. Like me, Mike was lost in the new class work. We were vulnerable outcasts, both strangers among established alliances. I tried to leave school quickly each day, before trouble started, but one Friday Mike asked me if I wanted to come to his place to play. The word *play* was not one that any of the other boys would have dared to use but he was not embarrassed to use it. He was not a sissy either. He was a good looking, well built boy though he did wear thick plastic rimmed glasses.

Mike and his mother lived in an apartment near the school, upstairs over a store on the main street. That was unusual too. Our side of town was dilapidated but everyone lived in a house. I stayed an hour and he asked me to come over the next day. His friendly mother invited me to stay for lunch. I had never eaten a meal at a friend's home. In his room Mike showed me his toy soldiers and other prized possessions. I told him about the bowl I had found on the beach, told him how I had found it and promised to show it to him. He was impressed. He did not seem to have a father. I wondered if his father had died or was away in the army.

I did not know how to have a friend. My family did not have friends, only tedious duty visits with relatives. There having been a rift sometime before I was born, my father's family in Newark were never seen. Only his brother with the wooden leg and the wife with hyperthyroid eyes who lived alone in a tiny house in Belmar were visited. My mother's brothers and sisters who also lived in the city would call on us periodically. All were friendly, each odd in his or her own way, and all very ready to conclude a brief visit after recounting again the virtues and oddities of other relatives I had never met.

But all of a sudden I had a friend, my first real friend. Love blossomed in me, simply and easily. His mother invited me to stay for dinner too on that Saturday but I did not dare to wear out my welcome and *dinner* sounded different. At our house it was supper that came at the end of the day.

After a couple of weeks, my mother asked where I had been going so often on my bicycle. I told her I had a friend from school. My father asked what his last name was.

"Paternoster," I said.

"Catholics," was my mother's instant verdict. Incompetent as parents, they were acute, strong and sure in their prejudices. I was not to go there again and that was definite. I worried about how I would tell him or get around the edict.

But there was no need. The following Monday he was gone again. The teacher told us that he had moved. Gone. No goodbye. No knowing why. I ached for him, looking at his empty place in the classroom. My friend gone and no one cared but me.

When school let out in June I got a job at Lil's Luncheonette, across the street from the beach and boardwalk. I was an illegal worker. Another boy and I, both tall enough to pass but a year too young to be legal, were paid one dollar for each nine hour day, seven days a week. We were kept mostly in the small kitchen, out of sight, making thin hamburgers and washing dishes. We had a half hour for a lunch break, out of the kitchen with one greasy hamburger and a coke each day.

I studied the city teenagers who wandered in for food, cigarettes, sun tan oil, camera film and postcards or to drink coke and play the jukebox on cloudy and rainy days. They were summer people, most of them bored and surly. They were another breed, not the people I had seen in the movies and hoped to find someday.

In those summer evenings Teddy and I would go into the Victory Garden in the back yard to pick the tomatoes, corn, lima beans and string beans my father had planted. I watered the plants, checked for eggs and cleaned the chicken coop. Teddy liked to chase the chickens when they dared to get close enough. They would spread their wings, squawk and lift a few inches off the ground. Sometimes we sat on the back steps in quiet while I petted him and he looked up at me, tongue out, panting in the summer heat. I would look west towards where the sun was setting somewhere, sending rose red rays into our sky. I wondered if we would be bombed, when the war would ever end and why my friend, Mike, had left.

I discovered a set of books someone had stored in an upstairs bedroom. There were a dozen books, all bound in matching red, black and gold covers that appeared never to have been opened, the complete works of Shakespeare, whoever he was.

The endless rumors, talk of torpedoed ships, German submarines sighted just offshore, and secret codes had permeated my pubescent mind. A few looks into the books and I recognized the words as mostly English, but peculiar. Some sort of code.

Each day I hurried home from school, trying to avoid the thugs, bullies, and patriotic future war killers who were my classmates. I let Teddy out to do his business after making sure the dog next-door, Butch, was nowhere to be seen. Then I got two or three slices of Wonder Bread, spread them with mayonnaise, cut the crusts off carefully, rolled each piece and cut it into slices to make my invention of pinwheel snacks, went into the living room, turned on the radio and sat beside Teddy on the floor, listening to *Stella Dallas* and *Mary Nobel, Backstage Wife* as Teddy and I slowly snacked on our treat, he getting the cut off crusts in one dish and I getting most of the fancy hors d'oeuvres that I did not yet know might have been called that.

When the radio announcers from New York City spoke at the start, intermission and finish of each program, I would listen attentively and imitate them, word for word, trying to speak exactly the way they did. It sounded better than the local flat *clam-digger* Jersey dialect that surrounded me.

That done, I put potatoes in a pot of water, turned the gas burner on low so they would boil for dinner and went upstairs with Teddy to the bookcase and the code. He would inspect the book of the day and the bookcase, sniffing, perhaps checking for tampering, bombs or booby-traps, I imagined. I would choose a section of this code by Shakespeare at random and made my best try at cracking the code, translating it aloud into normal English spoken in my radio-announcer's clear speech while Teddy listened, sometimes wagging his tail and sometimes barking. I took both as his enthusiastic war-effort support for my code breaking efforts. But some days it was more tedious and Teddy would doze off.

I asked two girls out on dates because that was what was starting to happen in eighth grade. They were among the more attractive girls in the class. The challenge was to call them from the telephone at the corner store, ask while not sounding scared, wait a day or two for the answer, pick them up at their home, walk to the early evening movie on Saturday, manage to casually get an arm over their seat back and then over their shoulders during the show, leave it there to be seen by others when the lights came on, then take her for a lemon or cherry coke at the drugstore, walk her home, and kiss her on the lips just before she went in the door. It was a job that required skill.

The most amazing thing that school year was that the teacher, Bessie Pierce, noticed me. I had made it my business not to be noticed in school but she noticed me. I do not know what she saw in that nearly six-foot tall, stoop-shouldered, skinny, shy, scared kid with bad skin, bad teeth and glasses, but she noticed me and moved me into a front row seat.

Her passion was English grammar, especially diagramming sentences. I paid attention. She asked me questions. I knew the answers. I became the star, a whiz at diagramming sentences. I dared to say some words the way the New York City announcers said them. She smiled. She appointed me chairman of the graduating eighth grade yearbook committee that met in the library for an hour each day and I, in turn, began to produce a yearbook in raw but rhyming poetry form for her, writing most of it with no help from the committee.

I did not tell all of this to Teddy because I did not know how to say what these changes were that were happening. I did not understand them or have words that explained them. I did tell him about my new sexual thoughts and feelings. I also gave him a thorough sexual examination and encouraged him to do likewise with me but a few sniffs here and there were enough to satisfy his modest curiosity.

Half way into that school year, a new boy arrived in class. His name was Neal. He was not as handsome as Mike had been but Neal was easy going, amiable and smart. He seemed almost like someone from that as yet unfound place where nice people lived. The teacher asked me to help him with class work so that he could catch up.

We drifted into friendship. Neal liked to read and introduced me to the town library. It was near his house in the better part of the town. Since he was not colored and his last name was clearly English he was not suspected by my parents of being Jewish, Catholic or from any of the other forbidden ethnic groups. He did not invite me inside his home but that seemed normal since no friends were ever invited into ours either.

I admired Neal's parents. His father was an engineer, Neal told me. He wore a necktie to work. Both parents smoked cigarettes and loved to read. Through their living room windows, I saw them sometimes sitting in comfortable chairs, an ashtray and bright light between them, immersed in their books.

Neal and I talked, walked, rode our bikes, tried to get forbidden sex books from the top shelves at the library and told what we knew and did not know of the facts of life. Eventually we confided some of our fears and hopes.

In April the rains were awful. It was 1944. The war ground on, seeming endless. I began to wonder if I, too, was destined for the Army, Navy, Air Force or Marines. On one rainy, dark Friday afternoon I got home from school, let Teddy outside and stood by the side of the street with him in the downpour watching to make sure Butch would not be let out at the same time. Cars were rare, especially at that time of day, partly because of the gas rationing. But suddenly a car appeared from nowhere it seemed, going fast, screeching tires as it turned the corner and headed our way. Teddy was startled and lunged towards it. I heard the thud, then his yelps, dog screams of pain as the car sped on down the street, disappearing as fast as it had appeared.

He lay in the wet road, twitching, but could not move normally and the awful yelps of pain continued. My vision blurred by tears and rain, I knelt by him in the road, repeating his name again and again. He was alive but could not stand. I got my arms under him and carried him into the house.

When my parents got home Teddy and I were on the worn linoleum of the kitchen floor. Bleeding had stopped and I had cleaned him and the floor as best I could. I explained what had happened. My parents let me have a couple of old sheets destined for rags and permitted me to make a bed for him in a protected place, under the buffet sideboard in the dining room. They also let me stay with him after they had gone to bed for the night.

Teddy had grown steadily more quiet in the hours since the accident. I hoped that was a good sign. I brought food and water but he would not eat. He would take small amounts of water from my cupped hand. It seemed to comfort him that I was there with him. I lay down beside him, being careful not to touch any places that hurt.

He was my fallen, wounded comrade of the war, my buddy, my loved friend. Sometime in the early morning hours of the night both of us dozed off, him first with heavy but steady breathing.

When the Saturday dawn woke me he was quiet. He was gone. I lay there beside him and talked to him for the last time and cried. He was gone. I knew that he was gone but I talked to him anyway. I buried him in the back yard later that Saturday, near the fence, a safe distance from the chicken pen and the garden and I said a prayer for him.

I had been exploring the churches in our town on Sundays for months. There was no real place in any of them for a kid like me. I could feel it. Each and every one of them seemed too cold and smug. People looked at me like an interloper and I guess I was. To me, they seemed foolish, dumb in their prayers too, asking God to help our side kill more people than the other side in this war, busy with the same old prejudices and segregation they took for granted as right. More than anything the long-winded sermons were boring. But I still hoped there was a God and I prayed each night at bedtime. I prayed my heart out that cloudy Saturday for Teddy, sitting by his grave on the damp dirt. I wanted God to hold him, to keep him safe, love him and to take care of him.

May was a very lonely month without him. Neal did not know what to say. He had never had a dog. As graduation neared I wanted him to go with me to look for work but he was certain his parents would not let him work until he was of legal age.

In June Bessie Pierce wrote the usual "Best Wishes" on the chosen colored page in each of her students' graduation autograph books. But on mine she wrote a poem:

> *Dare to do right,*
> *Dare to be true,*
> *You have a job*
> *No other can do*
> *Do it so nobly,*
> *So full and so well,*
> *Angels will hasten*
> *Your story to tell.*

The mysterious wonder of Bessie Pierce treating me as someone different *and* worth her special attention. I read it again and again. A third angel, this one in human form. Peggy and Teddy were gone. My childhood had ended and everything was changing. But a teacher had noticed me, someone special to her. Before that I had been a throwaway kid. It was my first look at that fact. I did not know what to do with it.

After eighth grade graduation I took a job that I hated, Saturdays and then all week for a dime an hour, helping a disorganized, slightly crazy and verbally abusive man harvest spare parts and make repairs on broken pinball machines in his backyard workshop near the boardwalk.

I turned fourteen a month later, got the working papers I had applied for from the State, a Social Security card from the Federal government and a minimum wage legal job as a stock boy in J. J. Newberry's Five and Dime in Asbury Park, four miles away. Neal joined me there a couple of weeks later. There was nothing glamorous about the dust-laden stockroom work and half my pay went for room and board but that left a few dollars for spending money. I was able to buy some clothes for high school and Neal and I had the summer together.

Evenings in late summer we rode home from work on the open top of the double-decker bus that traveled along the oceanfront between the two towns. We walked on the boardwalk breathing in the warm summer salt-water air, ate double dip ice cream cones and watched the frantic jitterbug dancing of wartime sailors, soldiers and their girls at the open air pavilion. Neal's attention was on the girls whose skirts flew above their waists in frantic dance gyrations, mine was mostly on handsome servicemen in snug fitting uniforms.

We dreaded the end of summer. Our town was located between two high schools so we had a choice. Perversely, his book loving parents chose the one that was known for athletics. I had chosen the more college-preparatory school that my drop-out brother had attended. I assumed that there would be less trouble in the more study-oriented school. It was also located in the larger town where more jobs could be found.

Chapter 4

High School

It was 1944. I knew that the war was a very big war and that we were in it. At the beginning it was movies like *Casablanca* that showed the war to me. People far away in places that were exotic and dangerous, trapped in intrigues of romance, fear, hope and betrayal. It was all foreign. But *Mrs. Miniver*, a Hollywood film set in a suburban village outside of London, shook me awake fully and brought it all closer. It showed a family of the sort of people I still hoped to find someday as they were pulled from a life of polite mutual consideration and advantage into one that involved real German bombs shattering parts of their home as well as killing family and friends in their village.

Government ordered black-outs, air raid drills, the top half of headlights painted black and rationing stamps had quickly become normal parts of our everyday wartime lives, just as they had for the people in the film. All of those changes were taken in patriotic stride, hardly noticed yet there always, lurking like the invisible enemy who was out there somewhere trying to harm us.

The stars and stripes flew from the small, leaning front porch on our half of the double house on Sixteenth Avenue every day that it did not rain or snow and the small gold tasseled, red bordered flag in the living room window showed three blue stars against a white background. The stars represented one soldier brother in Europe, a soldier sister in Oklahoma and a marine brother in the South Pacific. In addition to pride, it enlisted community hope that no blue stars would be replaced by the gold stars representing patriotic, military deaths in the family.

My other sister, working as a filing clerk at the War Department in Washington, did not show up on the starred flag in the window. She was the one the local school had deemed *slow* and kept in the *Opportunity Class* weaving baskets until she was old enough to make a legal escape. Maybe she did not try to enlist in the military for fear that she would find herself the object of ridicule again, or maybe because she had learned by then that she was no more capable of harming another person than Mrs. Miniver who, in the film, impulsively slapped a wounded German flier she had found hiding in her garden after he made a terrible and unlikely Nazi propaganda speech. But she also fed him and gave him milk in her kitchen, choosing to hide his gun rather than use it to harm him. I feared that I too, like Mrs. Miniver, was far more capable of offering nurture and healing to a wounded young man in any uniform than I would be of pointing a gun at him and firing it. Did that make me unpatriotic and a coward? What would I do if I had to go into the service? No one knew how long the war might last.

I understood *Casablanca*, sharing Ingrid Bergman's tears in that final scene, being sent away from love in a crazy world of intrigues and fear. But *Watch on the Rhine* confused me. Bette Davis took it in stride when her anti-fascist German husband shot a collaborator bully to death while in evening clothes after a dinner. He then received the blessing of her affluent family, nice people living just outside of Washington, DC. The message seemed to be that we were the good guys and that alone justified doing bad things, or maybe it was just supposed to be every man for himself in a mixed up world. Yet Humphrey Bogart had made a choice that was hard, turning his back on Ingrid Bergman's love because the good of the world demanded that sacrifice. I was sorting life's questions.

Neal and I went to a Sunday matinee just about every weekend, not only during that summer between elementary school and high school but during the first year of high school as well. Movies were our windows on the world as well as our magic mirror, showing us ourselves and our neighbors as we were and as we might become.

We got an eye-opening look at how dirty, bloody and mean the war could be as we watched Claudette Colbert and her group of nurses tend the wounded on Bataan and Corregidor in *So Proudly We Hail*. They and the troops had been left by their generals as a means of delaying the advancing Japs, heroic people sacrificed. I could imagine myself in the shoes of most of the nurses, tending the wounded but I could not imagine myself as one of the fighting soldiers or marine killers, definitely not as Veronica Lake wanting to kill all Japs including wounded prisoners and finally walking with her long blonde hair flowing, hands raised in false surrender into a group of them so that the grenade she put into her shirt would explode and kill them as well as herself. The repetitive message seemed to be that what was right, wrong, good, bad, virtuous or treacherous depended on which uniform was worn and which language was spoken.

Both Neal and I agreed that *To Have and To Hold* was a dumb story but we liked Lauren Bacall's sultry character. We did not know how to think about it or put it into words exactly but that particular film and many others were changing the seemingly unchangeable belief system that had formed us. A new morality had arrived. Good and bad were no longer clear. The end justified the means. Even sex without marriage could be okay. What counted was having your heart in the right place, not letting your friends down, being willing to take risks, being patriotic and being on our side in the war.

Hitchcock's *Lifeboat* had everything we needed in a movie. Not only was there the loathsome, untrustworthy, ungrateful, dangerous Nazi they had saved but the sweet, dumb, innocent William Bendix who got his leg amputated only to be murdered after his endurance, and the totally fabulous Tallulah Bankhead whose raw courage and goodness surged through her shockingly casual amorality.

The summer job as stock boys at J. J. Newberry's Five & Ten Cent Store ended on the Saturday of Labor Day weekend. The girls at the soda fountain treated us to ice cream sodas while Frank Sinatra, the

Andrews Sisters and Bing Crosby serenaded us with war songs. We were not really sorry to leave. The work was dirty and boring, hauling heavy boxes from the truck dock up to the roof with a crane, unpacking them in an airless attic stockroom layered with years of greasy dust and then carting items down the stairs to the store so that the counter girls could have the fun of cleaning them up, making them pretty and arranging displays. The job ended on Saturday. We had a full long weekend to get nervous about going to our high schools.

We got some distracting chuckles and belly laughs from *Arsenic and Old Lace*, a dose of patriotic morale fluff from *Stagedoor Canteen* and instruction in eternal goodness from Bing Crosby in *Going My Way*. But after seeing *The White Cliffs of Dover* we needed to change the subject. We did not know how to speak about the fear, hope and choked back tears of sadness that came up in that particular kind of war movie. England was just far enough away as a setting to let our feelings bypass defenses and get into our gut. We were really scared and that definitely was not a feeling that fourteen-year-old boys, soon old enough to volunteer with parental consent, dared to show in our patriotic world.

Neal came up with the idea of stopping in at a used record store that had opened on the main street near our old elementary school. It was small and disorderly with piles of old records at discount prices. I spotted one that looked new in its crisp paper jacket. No nicks or scratches, it was fifteen cents, labeled *The Last Spring* by Grieg. It was a bargain and my accidental introduction to classical music. Neal's parents had moved to a larger house earlier that summer. It had a back stairway that allowed us to go to his room without going through the rest of the house. We played our bargain records on the portable phonograph he had inherited when his parents bought a new one. We both thought the Bing Crosby record he bought was okay but he thought my *Last Spring* was a dud. I liked it and I played it on my brother's record player when no one was home. If my parents were there they would have the radio on and tell me to "turn off that damned racket."

A new Acme Supermarket had been built that summer across from the old A & P on the main street in Belmar. I persuaded Neal to go with me to find out about jobs. Signs in the window said they were hiring and the Grand Opening was to be in two weeks. I applied for a stock boy job and got it, two weekday afternoons after school plus full days on school holidays and full time in the summer. Neal's parents would not let him work during the school year but I promised to try to help him get taken on when summer came.

The first thing that was different about high school was taking a school bus to get there. It was important to get to the bus stop at least ten minutes early. Both the old yellow bus and the old driver with poor eyesight and slow reflexes were unreliable and unpredictable. The bus might arrive early or late. But, mysteriously, they delivered us to the school in time for the homeroom bell each morning without fail.

The first day in homeroom we were issued not only basic textbooks but soft yellow paper composition pads with blue lines and a blue cover displaying the school's logo and name printed in black ink. School rules were laid out in homeroom which we were told was the place where we would have attendance taken and receive grades and punishment such as study hall detention.

We were also given two weeks to choose an academic track that would branch the second semester. The choices were *Classical* for the college bound, *Technical* for those who might go for further training after high school, *Commercial* for those going straight into jobs and *Domestic Science* for the left-overs and brides-to-be. I chose *Technical* knowing that I wanted to leave the area and get something better than a factory job. Optional courses were allowed and I chose the typing course, a skill that I thought could be used to earn money.

It was clear to me the first week that I had chosen the right high school. It was larger than Neal's, so I could stay hidden in the crowd. Even the school bus people were quieter, tired early in the morning and those of us who caught the first bus in the afternoons were either heading off to too much homework or to jobs. The jocks and club kids took the late bus. The bullies had gone off to Neal's school. He did not say anything about it but I could see that he was not enthusiastic about the school his parents had chosen for him.

School wasn't great for me but it was good. There were rules and the teachers were strict but if you paid attention and did all of the assigned homework there was no trouble. Elementary algebra made sense because it worked, there were clear answers. General Science introduced me to a new way of looking at what was true. I did not like turning a helpless frog into a paraplegic in Biology so that it could be cut open without protest but I was intrigued by the ways both plants and animals were constructed and functioned.

Best of all was Freshman English. My teacher, Miss Vickers, was young, fresh out of teacher training. I liked her enthusiasm and her assignments. When she told us to write a story poem, I went home and dug out the long one I had written secretly the year before, touched it up and handed it in. It was the story of an old tramp who "at four o'clock does not ask for tea, but only the shade of a friendly tree." He had a sad death at the end.

She read the entire poem aloud to the class, mercifully not telling who wrote it. Then she asked me to stay a moment as we were leaving at the end of the period and asked my permission to show it to a few of the other teachers. I was embarrassed, impressed and pleased. A teacher asking my permission!

Homeroom study tips included concentrating on homework during the monitored study hall period each day and also doing homework at the same time and place at home each day, allotting a definite minimum time for each subject and not putting off work on a particular subject. I heeded the advice, going directly to my homework immediately after getting home from the school bus on the three weekday afternoons I did not go to the Acme, giving equal time to each subject.

I liked my job at the Acme. I felt useful and needed and I definitely liked being around all of that food. We had to punch in and out on a time clock. There were two or three stock boys on duty at all times. We roamed the aisles looking for depleted supplies, got a box from the stockroom and made the shelf displays neat and attractive.

There were *damaged* packages of cookies or crackers in the stock room always, a favored brand that had to be eaten so that mice would not be attracted. I liked the orderliness and the smells of the new, clean cardboard boxes in the stockroom and the store's mingled aromas of food. The manager had his cubicle office in a front corner of the store, where he kept an eye on everyone and everything. His plump daughter, the head cashier, worked her own check-out register and kept her eye on the girls working the other registers. Girls worked the cash registers, boys did the stock and when it got busy went to the front to bag.

On Saturdays we had forty-five minutes for lunch. I went across the street, brown pay envelope in my pocket, first stepping into the quiet bank on the corner to make a weekly deposit of seventy-five cents into my Christmas Club Account and getting my book stamped. If I managed to make all of the payments since joining at the start of the summer, it would pay fifteen dollars for Christmas presents in the first week of December. Half of my take-home pay went for room and board and I needed lunch money for the school cafeteria but that still left enough to go to the Drug Store Luncheonette two doors down from the bank for lunch.

After the first few weeks, Miss Salli recognized me as a Saturday regular. A thin middle-aged woman who more often than not had a cigarette in her mouth, she would say, "The usual, Hon?" My *usual* was a liverwurst sandwich on toasted white bread with iceberg lettuce and plenty of mayonnaise plus a coke. I was a regular working guy sitting on a stool at the counter, having my lunch, paying with my earned money.

The war carried us all along with a dull hum of anxiety. Movies were a medicine, the distraction a relief. One summer evening I went alone to the Rivoli Theater. The movie was *Cover Girl*, starring Gene Kelly and Rita Hayworth. I got lost in it. Sitting closer to the screen than usual, suddenly Gene Kelly enveloped me. He was singing directly to me. "Lone ago and far away, I dreamed a dream one day, and now that dream is here beside me…"

I was stunned. He was so beautiful, one of them, the people I wanted to know and live with someday. It should be Rita Hayworth I wanted but it was him. It was on my mind often for a long time after that. I had a secret.

Patriotic duties included saving tin foil, rolling it into a heavy ball, saving all left over cooking grease in a Crisco can to be turned in at the butcher shop, locating hard to find chocolate for my mother and mixing the capsule of coloring into the white margarine to make it look like butter. Until the war made butter disappear my mother had not permitted margarine or lard in the house, butter and Crisco only. She had definite rules that were not questioned.

I also wrote at least one V-Mail letter each week to my uniformed sister and brothers. I followed the suggested form for morale building, a positive everyday family or town news tidbit, something about my school work, a joke of some kind and a statement about how proud all of us were.

In November I heard an advertisement on the radio that gave me an idea. My mother did not own a wristwatch, none of us did. But for a special price of thirty-four dollars and ninety-five cents it was possible to buy a lady's watch with two genuine diamond chips on each side. I went to the store, put a dollar down to hold it and wrote to my brothers and sisters asking each for a seven dollar contribution to the collective gift. It worked. Each of them sent the money to me and no one spoiled the surprise.

During the second semester my father got a steady job at the new nearby army camp as a janitor. What had been the ladies' undergarment factory was now making army uniforms as fast as they could so my mother had a job too. Groceries were rationed and shortages were frequent but there was money. Short cold winter days meant getting out to the bus stop while it was still dark but Chiquita Banana sang me out of the front door with her radio commercial at the same time each morning, my stomach full of warm oatmeal. I had decent looking clothes and there were no holes in my polished shoes.

In our homeroom briefing in September we had been warned that we were no longer children and were expected to comport ourselves as decent young men and women. That included *decent* dresses and skirts for the girls. Boys were expected to wear neckties and slacks as well as sweaters or jackets. I had one shirt, a sweater and one pair of slacks so I had to buy another shirt. During the winter I managed to buy a second tie, another pair of slacks and a new sweater.

In that second semester I relaxed enough to look around at the other students. Some were still little kids, some fully grown women with breasts and men who had to shave every morning. Some were really students, some stars in their private fantasies. The shortage of teachers caused the physical education requirement to be relaxed. Anyone with an after-school job was excused. Physical education had been torture in elementary school so I was relieved. But the school had an active football and basketball program. Muscular team members in team sweaters strutted the halls between classes. Sex was in the air.

In Freshman English II, Miss Vickers took us step by step through *Ivanhoe, The Rime of the Ancient Mariner* and Edgar Allan Poe. She put me in a front row seat by the windows and smiled at me often. Once, when bowed heads groaned as she announced an assignment of a report on the meaning of a poem by Alfred Lord Tennyson, she gave me a conspiratorial wink. I got a steady supply of A's from her both semesters.

Spring seemed just around the corner on April 12. That afternoon the radio announced that President Roosevelt had died in a place called Warm Springs, Georgia. My parents said, "Good riddance" since he was a Democrat. The next day everyone at school was stunned. Roosevelt was the only President of the United States most of us had known of during our entire lifetimes. Now suddenly there was a new president named Harry Truman. It sounded funny. His name did not fit after the word *president*. And how would it affect the war?

Battle reports were more frequent. There was a touch of hope in them. The trees did leaf green again, flowers bloomed, people replanted their backyard Victory Gardens and beach businesses geared up for the season. Suddenly, on May 8, the war in Europe ended. It was over! There was an explosion of relief and hope. People celebrated any way they could invent. Cars honked horns, flags waved, sirens sounded, people cried, people laughed and some danced invented jigs on the boardwalk

Movie newsreels showed pictures of ruined, bombed out German and Italian cities; Mussolini's body was hung, and then dragged through the streets by angry Italians. Concentration camps were opened, the horrors of their contents spilling out the unimaginable pain and suffering insanely planned and inflicted. We had to open ourselves to the reality of it, groaning and gasping as we sat in those darkened movie theaters. Here was the ultimate proof for me of where prejudice takes people. It was hard for me to believe that people could do such things to other people and yet I did know it. It was confirmation of what I knew to be true but had tried hard to disbelieve. There was something dark inside people, all people, not just *the enemy*. It had to be curbed somehow.

But war in the Pacific was still happening. Might the Japanese win the war? I remembered the soldiers, sailors, marines and nurses in *So Proudly We Hail*. How many more of them were being tortured and slaughtered in sacrificial delaying actions? What was happening to the old people, children and women, the civilians in all of those places?

Feelings were churning in me. I could not find the words to say it or anyone who might want to hear it, not Neal and certainly not my parents. But I did give my parents some of it. I argued against their habitual, careless prejudice. I tried to show them how it was as bad as Hitler when they spoke that way. From their angry, startled reactions I could see that they were seeing me more than ever as the stranger hatched in their nest and hiding in their midst.

Neal and I continued our friendship. Neither of us had made any friends at school yet. When that first year of high school ended Neal got the job at the Acme. We each worked a scattered forty-hour week Monday through Saturday but always were done by five o'clock.

We compared our rival high schools, went to the movies more than once a week, shared the scare rumors that were so much a part of the war years, went to the library, rode our bikes, talked, confided a bit and even wrestled playfully sometimes. But if body contact led to any hint of arousal we backed off quickly. The natural erotic pull that had been there with Mike Paternoster in seventh grade was not there with Neal. We were just pals.

August was hot. We walked the boardwalk and got ice cream cones in the evening. There was news of an atomic bomb dropping on Japan and then a second one. What were they? We saw pictures of them in the newsreels. Then August 14, suddenly, dancing in the streets and on the boardwalk again. Car horns, sirens, screams; the war was over, really over. Japan had surrendered unconditionally. The whole war was done!

As hard as the war had been to understand, that there now was no war seemed almost harder to grasp. It had started when we were eleven years old and now at fifteen it was ended. Everything would change again, but how?

Chapter 5

A Wider World

I did not like my sophomore year geometry course. I saw no way that I might ever make use of it. The other courses were okay. The war years had siphoned off more and more males from the job market and they did not return immediately. The third week of school I overheard an older student tell his buddy that he was quitting school and also his job as an usher at the biggest, most expensive theater in town to move to a cousin's in Jersey City and take a job in a factory that would pay more. The theater was not far from school. The next afternoon I went to apply for the job.

It was a huge, ornate palace near the beach, an imaginative architectural rendering of a castle, built originally as a vaudeville theater with concrete tiered dressing rooms connecting its backstage to another large theater done in art deco style. Wide cement sidewalks outside sparkled with glitter in the cement. The two theaters occupied the entire block.

All of the doors from the street to the outer and inner lobbies were elaborate heavy wrought iron shielding thick glass. The floor of the outer lobby was made of large stone tiles. The floor of the inside lobby was thickly padded red carpet that continued up the wide curved stairway to the lobby located outside the loge and balcony. There were heavy velvet curtains everywhere and huge fake stone columns reaching three stories to the blue ceiling painted with stars between the wide fake wood beams.

The cashier in the outer lobby buzzed for Mr. Brown, the manager. He emerged from the inner lobby, a thin man in his early thirties who was wearing a suit and necktie. He led me past the uniformed ticket taker and through the doors to the darkened interior of the orchestra where a hidden release button on the back wall opened the door to his office. He snapped on a light after closing the door behind us and began to ask questions without looking at me. He said it was good that I was tall but that since I was only fifteen years old I could not work nights until my birthday the following summer. He could schedule me for some afternoons after school and the full matinee shift on Saturdays and Sundays. The pay would be five cents an hour more than I was making at the Acme.

As I was leaving he mentioned that whenever I wanted a pass to any of the other four theaters in town, either he or the assistant manager could write one. I could hardly believe it but I asked no questions.

I was sent to their tailor two blocks away where I was fitted for the uniform, double breasted dark blue jacket, brass buttons, light blue shoulder braid, pale blue trousers with darker blue stripes down the sides and a midnight blue bow tie. Back at the theater the head usher, Bruce, issued me two stiff white cardboard shirt front dickeys, two white cardboard collar bands and a brass collar stud that attached the collar to the dickey. I was to appear neat and clean at all times, purchasing clean collars and dickeys as needed. I would share a padlocked dressing room back stage with another usher and appear for uniformed inspection ten minutes before each shift time.

The first movie I saw in uniform was *Rhapsody in Blue*. The theater was never full in weekday matinees on school days. I had to stand straight at all times, nonetheless, show people to their seats with my flashlight and hush any disturbances. If anyone failed to heed my directions I was to let the head usher, assistant manager or manager know about it. If a situation persisted one of them would call the retired policeman, Pete, who had a badge and worked all of the theaters.

Seeing a movie from start to finish while sitting down is a very different experience than seeing it in pieces. Seeing it in pieces is even more different when the pieces are seen repeatedly. I soon learned to see each movie off duty, start to finish sitting down, as early in its week long run as possible. I also learned to patrol my assigned section of the theater every fifteen minutes when there were no patrons coming from the outer lobby since walking was easier than standing.

Rhapsody in Blue was a mess when viewed repeatedly. Except for Gershwin's agent and the mysterious rich divorcée in Paris the characters were too simple and sweet to be believed, acting was unconvincing and the music was served up in slices that, heard repeatedly, became annoying. Even the popular tunes lost value. The serious music, long and incomplete, was a bad combination.

The movies that followed showed me that even in the world of well dressed, well fed people not everyone was good and wholesome. That was certainly clear in *Mildred Pierce* and *Leave Her to Heaven*. Even a movie as innocent as *The Dolly Sisters* revealed darker human motivations.

But then came *A Song to Remember*, the story of the life and death of Chopin. I already had a crush on Cornel Wilde as the handsome, noble and mistreated writer husband of Gene Tierney in *Leave Her to Heaven* but I fell deeply and solidly in love with both Wilde and Chopin when *A Song to Remember* portrayed the life and death of Chopin with poor Wilde once again misunderstood, more sweet and handsome than ever and in the grip of another bossy, crazy woman.

Georges Sand as portrayed by Merle Oberon was icy and scary. She was a vampire. I wanted to protect him, comfort him and be comforted by him. I wanted to sit at his feet and touch him, listening to his amazing piano playing forever. I wanted to climb into his sick bed with him, feel his tears on my chest, hold him, heal him, and love him back to a life that included me. I loved the music, all of it, every note, every phrase. He made a big mistake being seduced by power, wealth and glamour but I forgave him and made note to be wary of ever making that mistake myself.

In the three years that I worked as an usher I saw more than three hundred films, half of them repeatedly. In high school I was going through the paces of passing courses so that I could get a high school diploma and get a better job in a better place but the five theaters in town were the campus where my education really was taking place. It may not have been a reading of the world's one hundred best books but it was the best and the worst of life as shown in the awesome variety of stories that Hollywood had to offer in the final months of the war and the first years immediately following the war, as the world reconstructed itself and looked with increasing daring at social values and previously unquestioned taboos.

As winter was easing into spring, Rita Hayworth filled the weekend shows from the first matinee until closing, sizzling as *Gilda*. It was held over for a second week. I was able to get Neal hired to work weekend matinees. He just missed *Gilda* but was in time for *Spellbound*.

That movie got my full attention. I was attracted to both Ingrid Bergman and Gregory Peck. I wanted to be like her and save someone like him. I did not say it that way to Neal but I wanted to talk about the picture with him. I said I thought it must be great to know how people's minds really worked and be able to do what she did as the brave psychologist in the story.

Neal was not very interested in discussing the film or the story. His feet hurt. He had learned, as had I, that standing military straight for a full shift with movement allowed only to show someone to a seat, quiet a disturbance or check on the general condition of an assigned portion of the theater looked glamorous and lent surprising authority but was mostly tedious and tiring. He made it through what was left of the school year but then quit to take a summer desk job offered at his father's office. Our friendship was ending.

Maybe that was what inspired us to arrange a June trip to New York City the weekend after he quit. He had to tell his parents that he was going away for an overnight trip with the parents of a school friend. We had the head usher, Bruce, older and with a deeper voice, lined up and ready to play the phone voice of the father if needed. I arranged to get the weekend off. We made a hotel reservation at the Dixie Hotel near Times Square and took a Saturday train to Pennsylvania Station.

The war had ended just nine months earlier, the cumulative tension of the war years was easing. We walked around Times Square, and got subway directions to Coney Island. Arriving there at dusk, it was big, busy and fun. Barkers called out to us, "Step right up Gentlemen, happy hour drinks, three for the price of two." We were tempted. Neither of us ever had a real drink. His parents drank sometimes but, like smoking and makeup for women, it was something strictly forbidden in my family. Both of us had started secret smoking during that school year. We bought a pack of Lucky Strikes and considered it.

After hot dogs, we decided to go ahead and try the drinks. The popular drink during the war was rum and Coca Cola. Confronted with two shot glasses and two larger glasses we tried to appear casual during a whispered conference about which glass held what. I deduced that the large glasses must hold the rum and Coke while the smaller glasses must contain what I had heard called *chasers*, something to rinse it all down at the end.

We stood at the bar, trying to be two relaxed guys having our drinks, not in a hurry but watching for effects. The drinks did seem to relax us and make things funnier which fitted with what we had heard. Having finished the big glasses we tasted from the little glasses. I did not like mine, so Neal drank his and the second half of mine. The bartender asked if we wanted our free third drink as part of a second round. We feigned indifference and strolled away casually.

By the time we got back to the hotel we were both drunk. Neal was happy. I was coping with the circular swimming of the ceiling when I flopped into bed. We slept soundly, waking with dry mouths. I reminded Neal of the scary lesson of Ray Milland in *Lost Weekend*. We found a place on 42nd Street for breakfast, then packed up and caught a return train, feeling satisfyingly worldly. Mission accomplished, we had given ourselves a graduation present, commemorating our moving away from childhood, the war and from one another.

Anna and the King of Siam occupied me the first week after school let out. I worked all seven days that it was showing. It was another reminder of how different life could be in other parts of the world and the rewards awaiting those with the courage to leave familiar home territory.

The day of my sixteenth birthday, *Night and Day* started. I was old enough to work nights and they needed me. The story of Cole

Porter's life brought in the summer crowds. Working nights with a popular picture was more a matter of crowd control than showing people the way to their seats with a flashlight. Since there were four shows a day with intermissions only long enough to empty the half of the seats taken at the start of each show, people had to be herded into holding pens at the back of the orchestra or the entrance to the loge and balcony and then released and led in quietly as seats were vacated during the show.

Working evenings after sixteen changed my world again. I was earning more money and I began to pay attention to myself. I improved my posture, bought clothes and decided to get my teeth fixed. I found a dentist a few blocks from the theater who offered general anesthesia and a weekly payment plan. He fitted me for partial upper and lower dentures and pulled half of my teeth, the bad ones and the crooked front ones. I wanted to be able to smile.

Now a regular staff member, I became better acquainted with the others. The men were managers, assistant managers, ticket takers, projectionists and ushers. Women were cashiers and waited on the candy counter customers. Bill was the old guy who worked the backstage ropes that opened and closed curtains for our theater and the adjoining one. Gilli, the colored porter, emptied ashtrays, swept candy wrappers into his long handled brass dust pan and kept the men's rooms of both theaters clean while his wife, Ottie, did the same for the ladies' rooms.

Jay, an older usher who said he was twenty-two but I thought was probably seven or eight years older, had thinning dark blond hair and manicured fingernails. He was tall, good looking and had eyes that seemed to enjoy a private joke. He took an interest in me and told me the gossip about other employees and people in the New York City management.

He and a few women who worked in the theaters went to a bar called *Anchors Away* after closing. They invited me along. I was five years underage but tall and they knew the bartender. The women liked to dance and wanted male company on evenings when too few soldiers and sailors showed up. They bought me rum and coke and taught me how to drink it. They also taught me how to dance. Some of the women who congregated there earned extra money leaving the bar with lonely servicemen who knew it was a quick and easy pick-up place if they had the money.

Pamela, a thirty-year-old floater, worked in several of the theaters as a relief cashier and sometimes at one of the candy counters. I liked her. She felt good in my arms when we danced, a real woman. She wore dark red lipstick and the aroma of perfume. She looked directly into my face when we talked and never seemed phony. I saw worry and sadness behind her eyes too, even when she smiled or laughed. She was divorced, had two children and lived with her mother. Thanks to her I always got away in time to catch the last bus home. She had to face an argument with her mother if she stayed out too late. Me too. My mother told me I had better not be drinking booze, *or else*. But I was paying my room and board regularly.

The Postman Always Rings Twice closed out the summer season and then I had to change to working full shift only on Fridays, Saturdays and Sundays. In my second period Spanish class, Alan Warshawski took the seat beside me. A bit overweight, braces on his teeth, glasses with dark plastic frames, he was a friendly, likable and serious student. He asked me which colleges I was hoping to get into. I avoided the question. It was a foreign idea. But I began to consider what it might be like to go to college, at least for a semester or one year, just to see that world. It was a possible way out, I thought.

In October I confessed that I did not know how to pick a college or apply. Alan said that I should talk to the vocational guidance teacher. She had college catalogues in her office. I could also write to colleges and ask them to send me information He suggested a few, including the state college. "It's really tough to get in anywhere," he said, "because of all the veterans with the G.I. Bill." He advised me to start thinking about two teachers and a professional person from the community to recommend me, to get involved in some school clubs and to get my grades up as high as possible. I told him that I did not know a professional person in the community. He said he would ask his dentist father and that generous man sent word back to me that he would be happy to recommend me.

Mrs. V., the vocational guidance counselor, was not enthusiastic. She advised me to think about training for a trade. But I said I wanted to find out about college anyway and sat silent. Finally, she said

I could look at her catalogues during study hall if I was really that interested.

I began to save money and do what I could in school to fit a profile that might get me accepted into a college. I did improve my grades and got onto the honor roll, joined two school clubs and, shy as I was, appeared in both a school play, and the following year, a musical. I was warned repeatedly by Mrs. V. that competition for college entrance was really tough. But I decided that I could try. There was nothing to be lost by trying.

The school year was moving fast. Autumn turned quickly into winter. I had to limit my visits to *Anchors Away* to Saturday nights, skipping those during bad weather when there were few customers and bus service was less reliable. I discovered a new secret attraction when Alan Ladd appeared bare-chested in *Two Years Before the Mast*. *It's a Wonderful Life* and *Razor's Edge* were the hits of the Christmas and New Year's holidays. I worked as many shifts as I could so as to save some money just in case I got into a college.

The winter storms were fierce. I was one of the two late shift people left to close our theater on a Sunday evening. Several people had not shown up for work and there had been few customers. It had been snowing since the previous night, harder since early afternoon with a veil of huge wet snowflakes blowing into drifts.

The assistant manager, Sonny Royce, lived only a few blocks from the theater and had come to work with boots. Coat collar up, scarf around his ears, he trudged off in the direction of his home after the last key was turned in the locks of the outer lobby. The wide sidewalk leading to the adjoining theater was free of really deep snow since Gilli had shoveled it clean only an hour before we closed. I walked out to the main street, standing in front of the other theater, sheltered in its outer lobby where I would be able to see the bus coming.

The theater's lights were being turned off. The manager and the late shift usher appeared, bundled up, ready to lock the outer lobby doors. The manager lived within walking distance but the usher was worried. He said he had not seen a bus in either direction for nearly an hour. He and I stood outside and waited together.

When, at last, we saw the headlights of a bus approaching slowly, we stepped out to the curb. But when it stopped the driver told us that he was taking the bus in and there would be no more service that night because drifts in some areas had gotten too big. We were stuck. The town had shut down. The luncheonette at the end of the block was closed. The theaters were locked up and we were cold.

The only hope seemed to be a small blue neon sign across the street announcing *rooms*. It was on the second floor of a house set back behind the street shops. Many houses in the beach area rented inexpensive rooms in season. Neither of us had ever noticed this one before and it seemed unlikely that they were open for business at this hour on a winter night but the sign was lit. We checked our money. I had two and a half dollars. He had about four dollars.

His name was Billy. I had noticed him only twice before, once on a summer evening when he was high on a ladder, changing the letters of the brightly lit marquee. I remembered his blond curls blowing in the summer breeze, highlighted by the marquee lights. I had met him the second time just the previous evening, Saturday, when the snow started falling. We were both closing that night but their show was to let out later than ours. I had exited from the backstage dressing rooms by way of their theater as an eye catching, full bosomed and very beautiful Kathryn Grayson appeared on screen in sparkling Technicolor singing *You Are Love*, the tune from *Showboat*. I had stopped to talk to him and ask if the picture was worth seeing.

He was my age, old enough to work nights but not yet old enough to drive a car. I had noticed his thick curly hair and the hair on his wrists, sparkling gold in the bright lobby lights. Like me, he seemed shy. We had commiserated on the slow late night bus service. He lived in the next town, but did not go to my high school. I guessed that he went to St. Mary's High.

We leaped and stepped across the road, through snow that varied from ankle deep to knee deep, climbed the stairs and pushed the doorbell under the blue neon sign, stamping cold, wet feet on the top step, shaking off snow. A light came on finally and a woman came to the door tugging at her bathrobe. She had been asleep and was not pleased to see us. We explained our situation, told her we worked in the theaters across the street and also told her that we did not have much money. After a minute of consideration she told us there was one room made up and we could have it for five dollars, "bathroom down the hall." Billy asked if he could use the telephone to call his folks and let them know where he was. "A dime for the call. Telephone's on the table in the room across the way." There was no telephone at my house.

Our room was small and unheated but it had a double bed with sheets, a blanket and a quilt. There was an old bureau with a crooked mirror against one wall and hooks on the back of the door. The linoleum in the room and in the hall leading to the bathroom was ice cold on bare feet.

We stripped down to underwear and quickly got into a bed with squeaking springs. Lying very still, awake in the darkness, a far streetlight dimmed by the falling snow cast a surreal glow on the window. We were waiting to get warm, not daring to move lest warmth be lost to the cold sheets. I listened to his breathing and was aware that he also must be listening to mine as we lay there unmoving. Warmth came slowly. And then it happened. I moved a hand slightly in his direction and met his moving to me. We held hands in silence. I held my breath. My heart was racing.

Then, slowly, gently, our hands were everywhere. We did not remove underwear at first but found our careful way inside tee-shirts and jockey shorts. Arms, legs, chests, stomachs, muscles and hair were discovered and explored. An awful hunger was being satisfied. The bed lost its chill but the room and its floor were as cold as ever I discovered when I got out of the warm bed to get a handkerchief that was in the back pocket of my pants.

Sometime before dawn we fell asleep, warm in one another's arms, a peaceful sleep. I was deeply happy. A missing part of me had been found, a chasm of yearning filled. I was safe now, my flesh touching his. We were together.

Morning came too soon, glaring sunlight reflecting from snow to the mirror. Billy showered quickly, using the one thin towel in the room. I said that I would wash up later, just washing face and hands for now. Snowplows had been out already and the bus would be running soon.

The luncheonette down the street was open. Without discussion we headed for it, hungry. On the street, between the theater and the luncheonette I wanted to say something to him, to celebrate this happiness, but I did not know what to say. Just for the pleasure of saying it, a name now mine to say, I said "Billy."

He looked at me quickly, in a hurry, moving through the cold air. In the luncheonette the waitress behind the counter let us each have French toast and coffee while saving enough change for bus fare. I promised to bring the rest of the money to her the next day.

Watching butter melting into steaming hot syrup I said something to Billy about being hungry and how good the food tasted but he did not answer or look at me. I said his name again, "Billy?" Sitting there beside me at the counter, he did not answer or look at me.

My stomach muscles tightened. I understood. He was lost, deep in feelings of shame. My happiness died.

He never spoke to me again. The next day, I brought him the money that I owed him. He took it without comment and without looking at me. He quit his job a week later. I never saw him again.

I was in agony, afloat in grief and hurt, all of it a secret, unspoken and unspeakable. The pain was a feeling of being in pieces, alone. I went to school, did my homework, worked my shifts and wondered about him every day for days that became weeks, weeks that became months. I wonder about him still today and hope that he has survived and found his own measure of happiness. He *was* love for me, found and lost, all in a matter of hours. I turned my attention to dating girls, determined to become a good person.

Winter yielded to spring. I saw *Duel in the Sun* in the theater next door, Billy's theater, where he was no more. It was a tale of passion and sexual attraction that leaped boundaries, killing the lovers who broke the rules but not killing their love.

When school let out I started working full time again. I asked for extra overtime shifts and was promoted to doorman or ticket taker. *The Best Years of Our Lives* was packing the theater. The film was portraying the shocks everyone was facing in a world that had changed its rules while changing many of the people too.

Before my dinner break, while things were slow, Sonny, the assistant manager suggested that I try palming a few whole tickets once in a while instead of ripping them in half. He showed me how to keep old stubs in one hand and give them to any customer who bothered to keep a hand out for stubs. When there was only one cashier and she needed a ladies' room break, he said he would re-sell the tickets and we would split the money. It was wrong. I was surprised but easily inducted. At the end of the day he slipped a twenty dollar bill into my uniform pocket.

A week later, deciding I could be trusted, he told me that both of the cashiers were involved also in the ticket resale arrangement and that the more tickets I could palm in crisp condition the better. Money would be split four ways. They called it *skimming*. It had been going on for years, he said. In fact, the elderly and very straight-laced seeming head cashier had been taught the art by the theater's owner in the early days when the place had first opened its doors. He, himself, had palmed the tickets and she resold them, thereby keeping some of the income free of taxes and the split with distributors.

There was no way to know whether each of us received the same amount of cash since the cashiers said that they could not always resell all of the tickets. It had to be an undetectable fraction of the gross they said, and sometimes there was a checker from the film distributor standing in the lobby, hand in a pocket clicking a counter button, counting people entering. I was a temporary, but trusted by the others.

I was scared because we were doing something wrong and illegal. But I was also excited by doing something that broke rules, having more spending money and a much better chance to save for college.

Sonny asked me what I was doing with the money and I told him I was saving most of it in case I was able to get into a college. He said, "Just don't start throwing it around in a way that people might notice, especially Bruce. He's such a Boy Scout he'd have to tell his Mommy and everybody else."

With my pay and the skimming, by the end of the summer I had saved one hundred and ten dollars altogether, enough to buy an old 1932 Chevrolet, not stylish but it had four wheels and it ran. I also had lent nearly a hundred dollars to my parents and I had a hundred dollars saved towards college.

With a car it was easier to date girls. I dated two girls. Reenie was Jewish, had big breasts and lived in a big house. We dated several times. She like to have her breasts handled but did not want to go all the way. Theresa was very pretty but gave clear hints that she would do nothing unseemly unless we became engaged. I was given the honor of being an usher at her brother's elaborate Italian Roman Catholic wedding where she was the bride's maid of honor. The next year I took her to the senior prom.

I was breaking all the rules I had grown up with except one. I was keeping my strongest desires a secret still, but I was going along with the tide like some of the characters in the movies, getting tainted money skimming. And I was sailing way out beyond family and community prejudices. I was beginning to make friends at school and, as one of them pointed out to me, all of them were Jewish. I was incorporating Yiddish words in my vocabulary. I liked these people and they liked me. A few of us played hooky several times and drove to Union City in my dilapidated car to see the strip teasers in the smelly burlesque theater there. Being a member of a formal wedding party in a rented tuxedo in a Catholic church was one more thing I did not explain clearly to my parents because I did not want to be bothered arguing with them.

One afternoon, Gilli took his resting position, leaning against a pillar and a door to the outer lobby, partly hidden in the shadows there behind my ticket-taking stand and repeated a conversation he had heard between the manager and the assistant manager. "They talkin' about 'them Jews' this and 'them Jews' that and I'm thinking un-huh 'cause you know if they talkin' that way about the Jews when I'm there you *know* what they sayin' about my kind behind my back. You get my meanin'?"

I told him that I did. I really did. I had grown up with it all around me every day and I was not taking it anymore. Gilli must have overheard me one or more times tell someone that "I don't like that kind of talk" or "you're talking about people like my friends." I was finding my way.

The theater crowd were amused that I was considering college as if it were a real possibility. I joined them at Anchors Away some Saturday nights after work and they introduced me to the high life on a couple of jaunts to New York City, going to the Latin Quarter Nightclub, but none of it looked like real fun or adventure to me. They were trying to help me find my place in my own social class but it was too late. I had stepped out of my old life, already looking for my new path.

Jay, the older usher continued to show an obvious interest in me. Pamela teased him about it sometimes, "Stop picking on teenagers, Jay. He's *my* dance partner." She said that he was twenty-seven, ten years older than me. He had hinted a couple of times that guys could pick up extra money the same way the women did at *Anchors Away*.

Early one Saturday afternoon just after Labor Day he said he wanted me to meet an old friend, Miss Eva. "Some of the girls from Anchors Away call her Mama. She lives just a few blocks from the theater. We have time before the theater opens. You're not due on until three o'clock today anyway. Come on. She's a character. It'll be fun."

Miss Eva was sitting on a pillow-laden glider on her front porch, an extremely ample pale figure more or less covered by a sleeveless thin cotton print dress. She languidly waved a cardboard fan that pictured Jesus with halo on one side and advertising for a funeral home on the other.

"I want you to meet a friend of mine, Miss Eva," Jay said as we climbed the few steps to her shaded perch.

"Why good afternoon, Sir," she said in an alcohol and tobacco worn baritone voice. "You must stay for tea." She smiled. "Do you take it with whisky," she asked lifting one huge breast with one hand, "or with buttermilk?" she asked, switching her fan deftly and lifting the other breast with the other hand. "I am always delighted to meet a charming young man." Both she and Jay burst into raucous laughter that left her flushed and coughing. "May June Louise, bring us out a pitcher of lemonade," she called into the house. "We got company out here."

I had no idea how I was supposed to behave. I smiled. We did have a glass of lemonade from the large pitcher brought out by a dark skinned girl who winked at me as we spoke of the hot weather. Finally, I said I had to go to work. "Come see me anytime," Miss Eva said as we were leaving. "I mean that," she called after us. "You're a nice, clean, quiet type. I might have some interesting work for you."

I suspected that Jay must have guessed my secret. He managed to get me drunk a half dozen times during my senior year. Once we were in New York City and he took me to the Everhard Baths "for a swim to sober up". I swam alone in the pool and later went upstairs where I saw men having sex together in shadowed places.

It was another world discovered. It intrigued me and scared me. I wanted to stay and I wanted to run. It looked wicked. I needed to get away from it. Finally Jay appeared, smiling broadly and asked if I had had a good time. "Meet anyone interesting?"

He also took me to a bar on West 72nd Street once after a few drinks in Greenwich Village. I froze when he said it was a queer bar as we entered. Everyone there seemed to know him. He sat me down next to Johnny, an extremely handsome professional ice skater who was nineteen years old. Johnny put his hand on my leg and placed mine on his, setting off a wave of trembling in my whole body that I could not control. It was noticed. "Johnny won't bite you," Jay laughed, highly amused, but he agreed to leave after fifteen minutes.

His own attempts to seduce me also did not work. Everything this man showed me scared me. It all seemed shameful, bad, wrong, evil and tempting. I knew that if Johnny and I had been alone somewhere I would have yielded even though I was afraid that giving in to my desire for other males would trap me. I would become one of them; caught, held in shadows like them. I wanted the life of a respectable person, not an outcast.

There was one evening late that spring that was different. After a couple of drinks in the Village, Jay said he was taking me to a "place on the east side. You'll like it." A woman named Mabel Mercer sat at a piano, playing and singing haunting songs in an unusual voice. Men at small tables sipped drinks, smoked cigarettes, applauded and smiled at one another. A few smiled at me. It was strange and scary but he was right. I did like it. It was better than the other gay places. It seemed safer, more respectable. But we did not go there again.

My discovery of classical music was well underway by then. After my discovery of the bargain record of Grieg's *The Last Spring*, I had been pushed into Gershwin with *Rhapsody in Blue*, fallen in love with Chopin and Cornell Wilde during the run of *Song to Remember*, had teasing glimpses of Franz Liszt and his music along the way, heard plenty of unidentified classical music as background themes in action and mystery films, got a dose of Rimsky-Korsakov's music in *Song of*

Scheherazade in my junior year and then Schumann and Brahms in *A Song of Love* in my senior year.

I was managing to do well with school grades and clubs even though the only course that interested me was my senior English class. My teacher, Mrs. Phelps, had a kind of chaotic glamour. She dressed casually in expensive clothes. On her a simple silk blouse, wool skirt, silver necklace and bracelet reeked of sophistication in some way I did not yet understand. A student who lived near her said that she drank and played classical music on a grand piano, sometimes into the early morning hours. It was an intensely romantic vision.

She came to school with a black eye and her hair disheveled one day, scrapped the lesson planned and said she wanted to introduce us to Medea. She spent that period reading Euripides aloud to us. She *was* Medea, playing to a silenced audience. She introduced us not only to Medea but to real theater that day. She ended the reading putting down the book, looking at us and saying, "Each of us makes mistakes, some more terrible than others. The most terrible are those from which we do not learn."

Her clever device at the beginning of the year had been to have each of us pick a poem and to learn what we could about the poet before reading it aloud to the class and into a brand new reel-to-reel tape recorder. We also told what we knew about the poet and then our reading was played back to us so that we could hear ourselves as others heard us.

Her assigned term project was to pick any author of novels, read *every* novel that author had written and then write about the person as well as his or her books. I chose Steinbeck simply because his books up to that time were small. Her plan worked. I was hooked forever, of course, later reading every book by or about Steinbeck.

I graduated from high school with no great honors except being on the scholastic honor roll. I wore a cap and gown and marched down the aisle and up across the stage to receive my diploma from the Principal and the Superintendent of Schools. I had done it, the first person in my family to graduate from high school. My parents surprised me with a graduation gift, a wristwatch. They were proud of me.

I continued to work through to the end of the third week of August. I was paying more careful attention than ever to particular films. A sleeper playing in one of the smaller theaters that spring was *The Search*, a tender, heartbreaking film about a child and a mother finally reunited after the concentration camp. It introduced me to a new star who stirred my romantic interest, Montgomery Clift. I was making a strange peace with my secret desires, letting them remain secret as I sought a respectable future life.

A Foreign Affair with Marlene Dietrich was billed as a comedy but I went with her into the life of her character in bombed out Berlin. It was no joke. I understood when she sang "Want to buy some illusions?" and the "You take art, I take Spam," line from the *Black Market* song. *Snake Pit* reawakened the interest in psychology, first started by Ingrid Bergman and Gregory Peck in *Spellbound*.

Gentlemen's Agreement sparked a final shouting argument with my parents. One of them said something that contained one of their ordinary insults to Jews during the week the picture was showing. I exploded and said I had had enough of their ignorant prejudices. They retaliated. "So's your Aunt Tillie." "You're getting too big for your britches, Mister." "You're not as smart as you think you are." "You keep up with this shit and you can forget about college." "You're not going anywhere, Mr. Smart Stuff, you're staying right here where you belong."

Something broke. It felt as if they might actually be able to carry through on the threat and keep me there. It was an empty threat, of course, since they had lost control of me long before but I stumbled up the stairs to my bedroom and shut the door, sobbing gut wrenching sobs as if my hopes and dreams really were shattering. Maybe I was crying for the loss of my own illusions, scared by my true aloneness, confronted with my own vulnerability, embarking on a journey into an unknown world beyond boundaries.

Although the vocational guidance counselor had told me I would be better off looking into training for a trade, I had applied to three colleges and was accepted by two of them. One was the state college and one was in Ohio. The cost was about the same at both, approximately five hundred dollars per semester for room, board, tuition and fees. But the Ohio school had a work-study program that would mean guaranteed jobs for half of the year.

I had five hundred and eighty dollars saved by the end of that last summer working as many extra shifts as possible. I calculated it would get me through one semester. Then, if I could get a part time job while on campus and another part time job while off campus in addition to the work-study job, I might be able to get through a full year of college and be that far ahead in looking for a job and my new life.

It was going to happen. I was going to get out of Belmar. I was going to see what college was like and what the people who go to college were like. At least it might lead to a different kind of job in New York City or even some far away place like Florida or even California. I would get married to someone nice and find respectable work where I would wear a suit, a clean shirt, shined shoes and necktie, something better than factory work.

The last week of August, wearing a freshly dry cleaned suit, clean shirt, necktie and shined shoes, carrying a checkbook that showed a balance of five hundred and fifty-six dollars, I boarded the old dirty steam engine powered train headed for New York City where I would transfer at Pennsylvania Station to the clean streamlined electric powered train called the Jeffersonian that would head west at sunset, making a stop the next day in Ohio. I was going to Antioch College in Yellow Springs. I was excited.

My parents solemnly accompanied me to the train station, as they had with my brothers and sisters going off to war. My mother kissed me and my father shook my hand. "Take care of yourself," they said. They stood on the platform looking bewildered and stoic, a small town post-war American Gothic picture. I did not own a camera but the picture is as clear in memory today as it was to my eye when the lurching train, wheels screeching metal on tracks, slowly pulled me away.

It really was the beginning of a new life. I did meet the kind of people I had hoped were out there in the world somewhere. I did find my way, thanks in no small part to having picked the right college for the wrong reasons.

Chapter 6

A Try at College

When I arrived at Penn Station in New York City I had an hour still before boarding time for the Jeffersonian. I carried my suitcase to a lunch counter and ordered the least expensive meal, a grilled cheese sandwich and a cup of coffee. Following the school's suggestion I had bought a footlocker, filled it with most of my belongings and had it shipped to Ohio two weeks earlier by Railway Express.

The Jeffersonian really was streamlined, lots of chrome inside and out. Boarding it was exciting. There were people searching for Pullman sleeper cars, some were going as far as Chicago, some all the way to California. I had my own reserved sleeper seat that was upholstered and reclined.

When we emerged from the darkness of the tunnel under the Hudson River a large August sun was setting, flooding New Jersey with hues of orange, crimson and dark blue. I had hoped I might see Sandy on the train. He was one of the three boys I had done the musical skit with in high school; *Three Sharps and a Flat* we called ourselves. We were not really friends but he was one of the honor roll guys who had skipped school and crowded into my old Chevrolet to go to the Burlesque Theater in Union City. He had told me that he too was going to Antioch and would be on the Jeffersonian but I had not seen him in the station. Two hours after we left Penn Station it was dark. A young man and a young woman, or a guy and a girl as they were called in 1948, were working their way through the train asking people of the right age if they were heading to Antioch. I told them I was and they said that we were gathering in the Club Car at the rear of the train.

I walked through the swaying cars and found that there was, indeed, a club car with a bar, just like ones I had seen in movies. There was one empty seat. When the waiter asked for my drink order I thought about ordering a rum and Coke but I was not sure of the age requirement or the price so I ordered just Coke.

More people came in, the girls were given seats, the boys stood or sat on the carpeted floor. Everyone seemed friendly. Several started conversations with me as people moved around. I responded to questions but did not know how to keep a conversation going. It did not seem polite to ask more than where a person was from. Many were from New York and most of the New Yorkers were Jewish, like Sandy, who I saw when I arrived, already in a lively conversation with a group at the far end of the car.

The few people in my high school that I knew and liked were Jewish but since I was not, I did not have that easy connection that I saw others using with a well placed Yiddish word or the imitated inflections of the worried mother or grandparent who had seen them off at Penn Station. The two girls seated opposite me seemed to be a magnet for cheer, laughter and conversation. One had a perfect figure and a large nose. She raised her arms over her head often, accentuating a shapely bosom. The other had not yet lost her baby fat but was eagerly interested in everything anyone had to say and managed an appreciative laugh for any attempt at humor. They were Bobbie and Joanie.

Our stop came early the next morning. It was not a usual stop for the Jeffersonian but it had been arranged to accommodate this flotilla of young people traveling unaccompanied into strange territory. It was a small town with a tiny station just a few miles from Yellow Springs. On the road beside the track stood Jeff, a lanky older physics major who had been sent to collect us in an old school bus. Fitting everyone and their suitcases into the bus was a problem. Fortunately there was also a pick-up truck for luggage and a few of the boys rode on top of the pile of suitcases. This was not how I imagined it would be.

In July, Pamela had given me the early August issue of a men's magazine featuring *Men at College*. It was a token. She wanted to show me that she was on my side. While the others snickered about my crazy college ideas, she thought it was probably a good idea. I read every word and studied every picture in the articles having to do with college.

The pictures showed young men wearing suits and neckties gathered around a fireplace or a bar in their rooms, driving convertibles and showing off on tennis courts and in swimming pools. I did not know that all of the pictures were of models and had been taken at Ivy League schools, but then I also did not know there was such a thing as the Ivy League.

On the basis of what I had seen and read I had shopped and filled my new footlocker accordingly. I had a crème colored sport jacket with blue sleeves, a pair of winter tweed suits that each came with an additional contrasting pair of slacks and a vest bought at a two-for-one winter close-out sale, four dress shirts, ten neckties, one pair of brown shoes and one black, two swim suits, one red flannel sport shirt, one pair of blue jeans, a black belt, a brown belt, a calf length tweed overcoat and a new pair of glasses with clear Lucite frames.

As suggested, we had arrived the day before Freshman Orientation Week was to begin. Classes would not begin until the following Monday. Everyone I saw there, male or female, had changed into old jeans, work pants or hiking shorts with equally old looking sport shirts or sweat shirts.

The campus was an instant disappointment. There was a cluster of red brick buildings, two of them dormitories, with a library in one. The building with the small tower, called the *Main Building*, had offices, classrooms, a bookstore and a mailroom. Scattered out from this center were a big military Quonset hut that housed the cafeteria and a bungalow that was the *Tea Room* where students, faculty and town people could eat at a higher price, served at tables by student waiters and waitresses. Farther from the center was a new upper class women's dorm, a low slung name-architect designed place called Birch Hall, a smaller red brick dorm in the other direction for upper class males, a converted two-story house for women students, the fairly new and bland-modern Science Building, a gym with no swimming pool and, out by the athletic field, a cluster of military barracks that housed second-year male students. On the edge of the campus was the large new Fels Research Center building, not officially a part of the college. The entire tour took an hour.

All first-year male students were housed in one of the central red brick buildings, South Hall. First-year women were in North Hall. The buildings had two dorm units on each floor, twenty-two students, two to a room, with one room in each unit reserved for two upper class *hall advisors*. One of them, Dick, was on hand to greet arrivals. He was the son of the head of the Psychology Department.

I was in *Anchors* on the ground floor, in an end across from the advisors' room. That meant two windows rather than one. The room contained an old double-deck, metal framed bunk bed, probably Army surplus; two nicked and scraped desks; two equally well-used small bureaus; one closet and a small sink and mirror in the corner by the door. The door itself hung casually on one hinge, leaning out into the hall.

"Not sure how that happened," Dick said, walking toward me with hand extended in welcome and name at the ready. "We'll have to see if we can't get someone to fix it." He was a tall, skinny twenty year old wearing, of course, old jeans, work shoes, and a plaid shirt with a hole in one sleeve. It was clear that I had picked the wrong college. It was a dump.

I had picked Antioch because of its co-op work-study program; four quarters each year, twenty weeks on campus in classes and twenty-six on a job related to your major and six free summer weeks. The jobs were in locations all over the country. It was a five-year program rather than four but I expected to be there only one year at most anyway. I was not too keen on the idea of classroom study but I liked the idea of working in far away places. Also, my financial plan involved not only a job on or near campus but also a good-paying job during the work periods.

Dick told me that during Freshman Orientation Week I would need to set up an account in the Bookstore, check in at the mail room, look over courses offered to first- year students, meet my Academic Advisor and my Co-op Job Advisor, take the Placement Exams given to incoming first-year and transfer students to determine which, if any, of the basic required courses could be skipped and then actually register for my first semester courses with a probable major field indicated.

"Don't worry too much about the major," he said. "Almost everyone changes their major a couple of times once they get out on their co-op jobs." He laughed. "It's sort of expected."

I liked Dick. He was a peculiar mix of ill-at-ease and assured, grown-up but not entirely sure how his lanky frame should move, sit or stand, and whether he was telling the full and exact facts. "You can get unpacked today, sort of get settled in. The Bookstore and Mail Room open tomorrow. Tea Room won't open until next week but the Cafeteria's open. You'll have to use money there today but tomorrow you can buy food coupons. There'll be a charge for them on your bill. Coffee Shop's in the Cafeteria when it's not meal hours, no cashier, you pay on the Honor System. Oh, yeah, and the Bookstore sells both new and used textbooks. They buy books back at the end of the semester if they're usable."

My roommate arrived, apple-cheeked Dan from a small town in Washington state, eyes bloodshot from his long train trip but bubbling with enthusiasm and excitement. Like the people I had met on the train, Dick and Dan were impressively friendly. And as others arrived during the day, they too were friendly. It seemed odd.

Dan was dressed up when he arrived but soon dug an old pair of jeans and a rumpled sport shirt out of his suitcase. Walking across campus, everyone I passed looked me directly in the eyes, smiled and said "hi." I was surprised, amazed. These people really were friendly! During my growing up years, any male who looked directly into the face and eyes of an unknown male was asking for something, trouble usually.

Many of the incoming male students were veterans. Military fatigues and dress pants broke the monotony of jeans. We had four vets in Anchors. They were easy to spot not only because of the scraps of GI clothing but because they were older.

We had a Hall Meeting that first evening with Dick and Chad, for purposes of introductions and general orientation questions. We told our names, where we were from and how we had gotten to Yellow Springs. Only one other person in our Hall, a vet named Don Brown, had come on the Jeffersonian. He was from Long Island and had been a Second Lieutenant in the Signal Corps until his discharge in June. He smoked Marlboros, one right after another, was soft-spoken and had the sullen, shy good looks of an off-screen Montgomery Clift.

Chad, the other Hall Advisor, seemed less interested in us than Dick was. He did, however, tell us that we would be asked to put on a Hall skit at a Freshman Follies show on Thursday evening and we might want to get a jump start by getting together some ideas that evening.

Dick explained how extensive the Honor System was and how it worked in everything from paying for a morning donut and coffee in the Bookstore to exams that could be taken in your room or under a shady tree on the lawn.

Chad explained, "It's the real democratic experiment that is Antioch, lots of responsibility." There were rules, he told us, such as when women could be in a men's dorm and vice versa and the hours and use of common rooms for dating "and it's all under the Honor System. Almost any rule can be changed if enough people want it changed and if we agree to change it."

He explained that the school was governed by an elected Community Council, students with faculty and administration representatives and the Administrative Council, with student representatives. "We've got a new president this year, Doug McGregor from M.I.T., who's really hot on group dynamics so get ready to be in a lot of groups deciding everything from whether we should keep the total enrollment at a thousand with a little more than half of us on campus at any time, to whether bikes on campus should be registered."

Another vet, Wayne Higley, with a dark blond crew cut and neutral toned plastic framed GI issue glasses, made sure he was noticed by asking lots of questions. His throaty theatrical laugh was an exhalation usually accompanied by a plume of cigarette smoke.

His brand was Pall Mall. It was he who, as the meeting was winding down, suggested we get some ideas together for our skit right away. It was also he who suggested we might want to do something similar to a traveling GI show he had seen that ended with the guys wearing improvised skirts and string mops on their heads while singing in a prancing, high-kicking chorus line. He volunteered to play the piano. A silly story line slowly emerged from throw-away suggestions.

I was surprised at the staid and shy types that seemed to back the idea, Don Brown included. The sticking points were that no one knew how to do a high-kicking chorus line or could come up with a silly ditty to sing. I said that from watching many movies as an usher I knew that the chorus line was easy, "just a matter of getting everyone in synch, like a drill, and holding on to one another for balance." I even knew a tune and some silly lyrics. They especially liked the closing lines. "We use sandpaper on our kneezies. All of this we have to do to get the one we woo."

It was set. Dick told us where we could find a practice room with a piano. We agreed on a quick first run through right after the meeting. Wayne rounded up a smaller group after our rehearsal to go to the tavern in town for beers. I declined, saying I had some things to do. I knew I needed to be careful with my money. Wayne pushed, "Oh, come on," but backed off after my second refusal, given firmly and without any explanation that might be argued or ridiculed out of the way. He had enlisted Don and four others and settled for that. A social group was taking shape.

There was a general welcoming of new students the next afternoon followed by a campfire meeting that evening in Glen Helen. Doug McGregor spoke to us there, saying that as the incoming President he considered himself a new Antioch student also and he hoped that we could help one another to learn how to continue to make this community an excellent example of democracy with social conscience. He cited the school's history of breaking taboos, taking Negro students in Civil War times and pioneering co-ed and co-op education. He quoted the inscription on the monument statue of Horace Mann that stood near the Main Building saying that both the person and the inscription could be a daily reminder: "Be ashamed to die until you have won some victory for humanity."

We then were asked to break into small *buzz groups* of six to eight people and share what had caused us to choose this school as well as what we hoped to do with the education gained in five years here. Immediately six other students gathered in a tight circle with me. Strangers to one another, they began to speak seriously and intimately. One's father had been killed in the war. He wanted to work at the U.N. for world peace. Another was from a family who had fled from the Nazis in Europe. She wanted to work with emotionally disturbed children. Another vaguely hoped there was some way he could help to put an end to racial discrimination in our country. I turned to the boy sitting on my left who, like me, seemed uncomfortable.

"Hey, what's going on?" I whispered. "I don't get it. There are no teachers." There were no supervisors or monitors listening in on us to see to it that we followed instructions and said good things. It was just us. He did not answer, just looked puzzled. When it was my turn I said I wanted to see what college was like and I liked the fact that we would be going out on jobs to different places in the country. There was a discreet silence during which I realized that my answer had not been on a par with the others, then the intimate, hushed, sincere sharing of dreams, hopes and ambitions continued. I was amazed. The quiet student on my left was from Central America. He confessed he was having some trouble keeping up in English. As puzzled by them as they probably were by me, I was nonetheless thoroughly impressed.

After the buzz group the professor who was head of the Music Department was introduced. He was a Negro! I had never seen a colored teacher nor had I even thought about not having seen one, and this one was a college professor! He invited us to end the evening with some singing.

Everyone sang. "You are my sunshine...," rounds of "Row, row, row your boat...," "She'll be comin' round the mountain when she comes...," "Oh Danny boy..." Voices began to call out suggestions and immediately the singing would begin, "Roll out the barrel...," and then songs unknown to me: "There once was a union maid who never was afraid...," "Go tell Aunt Rodie...," "I dreamed I saw Joe Hill last night...," "This land is your land...," "Go down Moses...," ending the evening with "Tell me why the stars do shine...."

There had been many songs. The mood was mellow but alive with a camaraderie I had never before witnessed. But how did they all know the words to all of those songs? I liked these people and they gave me every reason to believe that they were welcoming me in as one of them but I was missing something. What was the key to the club?

In our room the next day Dan, my rosy-cheeked roommate, was as cheerful as ever. "Did you know all of those songs last night," I asked, daring to betray my ignorance. "Some of them I just faked and mumbled along," he answered, giggling with lack of concern as he combed his blond hair and stuck out his tongue at the mirror.

At lunch in the cafeteria a girl who sat down at my table seemed to know the answers to everything. "Hi, I'm Peggy but you can call me Pigeon. You must be you." She wore a low-cut Mexican peasant blouse, exuded a worldly, bored sexiness but yet was curiously friendly, asking where I was from and did I think we would survive five years on the kind of food being dished up in the cafeteria.

I tried to sound equally casual when I said it seemed like everyone had been singing all of the words to all of the songs the night before. "Oh, Honey, they've got lots of songs to learn yet," said Peggy / Pigeon. "What do you expect? Every one of those tired old things was a camp song."

"Camp?"

"Summer camp," she said breaking into a mirthful trill. "You do speak *summer camp*, senor?"

"Yo no hablo *summer camp*, senorita. Muchas gracias." I was saved by fragments of high school Spanish and some silliness. She liked the humor. But *summer camp*? I had never heard of it.

Freshman week ended with the Freshman Follies. From the laughter and the applause, Anchors seemed to be the favorite. Even one guy losing his string mop wig, another his skirt, and another falling down during the high-kicking chorus line finale seemed planned and fired the calls of "Encore, encore!"

Saturday night there was a dance at the gym. Most of the older students had returned by then. Everyone changed for the dance. Jeans were discarded. People were dressing up! Girls showed up in make-up, satin dresses and ballerina skirts over puffy crinoline petticoats and tight girdles. Boys were in jackets, most with neckties. This cast of characters in the new world had many faces. I was still unsure of my place in this crowd but dancing was one thing I knew that I knew how to do and I did it, clearing the floor with a girl named Rita Cohen who moved with me as if we were truly joined at the navel and had been dancing together all of our lives.

At the impromptu dorm party that followed the dance, I intended to go to bed as soon as possible. I had been declining invitations to go out for beer all week, usually seated at my desk where I was studiously trying to make sure that I would be fully prepared for the first week of classes.

Wayne called me into his room which seemed to be Party Central. He and Don had stocked it with beer, ice, pretzels and a wide variety of liquor. "You're one hell of a dancer but you don't drink, is that right?" Wayne asked. "Well, how about a ginger ale or a Coke?" His speech was a bit slurred. He was playing to the crowd that had packed into the room.

"Now whatever you do, watch out for this stuff," he said, holding a bottle of vodka aloft. "Looks like water but it's not for lightweights. Want to try it?"

"Sure," I answered.

He handed me the bottle and a small glass with two ice cubes. "Just take a little," he cautioned. I filled the glass to the top, let it stand a minute as the room hushed, looked at it, fished out the ice cubes and threw them into the sink and then drained the glass, finishing with an exhale of satisfaction. "Not bad!" I said, turning to leave the room. I had not watched all of those male initiation challenges in all of those movies for nothing.

"Hey, watch out, you'll fall down," Wayne called as I reached the doorway. There was less taunt now and some real concern in his voice.

"I doubt it," I said, giving him a farewell wave. "That wasn't my first drink." The movies had also taught me the value of exit punch lines.

I knew that he now did not know what to make of the studious boy in Lucite-framed glasses. I had cut out a role for myself in the emerging group. I was a mystery and I was in. I counted. Now to find out how that role might play out.

Cheerful Dan and I both snored in deep sleep through the night, with him looking less rosy-cheeked in the morning. It had been his first drinking experience, "except once when one of my cousins gave me a beer behind the barn when we were helping with the harvest last year," he said. I took an aspirin and gave him one.

My Academic Advisor was a History professor. He wore thick glasses and rumpled clothing, seemed distracted and was ill at ease advising. I declared a major of Business Administration and signed up for required introductory courses. The two-semester Life Sciences sequence contained psychology. I looked forward to that but was ultimately disappointed in it and my grades reflected it. The head of the two-person Psychology Department was a dedicated Behaviorist who loved lab rat studies and anything having to do with conditioned response including increasing the efficiency of factory workers. It was a far cry from *Spellbound*. He thought "Freud, Jung and company" were "frauds and charlatans."

One course required a *Life Aims Paper* that would be followed in the fifth year by a corresponding *Senior Paper*. The idea of the first was to look at who we were as individuals, where we had been before and where and how we might go during college and after college. We were to examine the influences of our life experiences, as well as the ethics, morality and responsibilities involved and see how all of it fit into a changing personal philosophy of life. "Question your basic assumptions," we were told. We also had to do a personal money budget.

The Placement Exams had unexpectedly excused me from the physics and chemistry sequence. I was not excused from geology, however, which was tedious, boring and time-consuming. Bound by the Honor System, we each had to dig out a collection of rock samples from Glenn Helen with no help, then label and explain them for a final project. But then there was the Humanities sequence that contained American literature and creative writing. There was no possible way for a slow reader like me to read all of the books and stories, but the teacher's oblique reference to Joseph Conrad and *Lord Jim* one day made me curious.

The book swept me away. I made time budget deals with myself to read five or ten more pages. Partly it was the adventure in the story and exotic setting but, more, it poked at those questions I was asking myself for the *Life Aims Paper*. Was there really such a thing as a second chance? Can a person change, run away or overcome mistakes made? Was there any real difference between a coward and a hero? And the concept of destiny was new to me. Did each of us have a destiny that included accountability and would mine, like Lord Jim's, hunt me down finally?

In the creative writing segment the teacher asked us to write something drawn from our personal experiences that was unresolved or unclear to us and to write it in the form of blank verse. The assignment agitated and excited me. He explained free association also, letting it all come on its own from some deep inner place.

When I knew that Dan was going to be out of our room for several hours one afternoon I locked our door, got a pad and pencil, pulled down our shades and lay on my bed with eyes closed, waiting. Two hours later I had a quartet of small blank verse poems, each about some experience that the four and five-year-old voice speaking inside of me did not understand. They included finding myself alone digging in the sand under hot sun in Miami and being lifted to kiss the cold wax face of dead Aunt Dot as her husband cried quietly nearby. The professor put a long note on my paper, saying that he was moved by the poems, that he thought I had genuine writing talent and that he hoped I would continue to write!

There were only eight fast weeks of classes in the first quarter and then we would be out on jobs. There was no work to be found on campus or nearby. Yellow Springs, population two thousand, did not need an usher or any other college student employee. The only paying jobs on campus were working in the bookstore, the mail room or waiting tables in the Tea Room and these were all filled by upper class students. Careful as I was, my money was going too fast.

I read through all of the files of co-op jobs open to first year students, met with my Job Advisor and requested as first choice the filing clerk's job in the mail order department of Charles Scribner's Sons Publishers on Fifth Avenue in New York City. Second choice was a live-in job in an institution for mentally retarded children somewhere in New York State.

There had been two letters from my mother, both in pencil with easily read handwriting saying they hoped I was okay in Ohio and asking what people ate there. The second one contained a ten dollar bill "to help out" and asked how was the weather. I wrote and tried to tell how wonderful this new world was. I tried to communicate it in words that they would understand but knew it would not work. There was also a short letter from Jay, the older usher. He was moving to New York City and hoped to see me there.

The Scribner's job came through. I wrote Jay and told him that I would be working and living in New York in November and December and asking if he knew of any cheap places where I might rent a room. He wrote back immediately saying he would be sharing an apartment and there was a chance they could rent me space there. He gave me the telephone number of the apartment and said that I should call when I get into the city.

The semester ended with a *Div Dance*, short for the *"Division A" Dance*. Division B. was the students out on jobs with whom we would be exchanging the next week. The core party group of Anchors had made an alliance with several girls from Dodd Hall. Bobbie and Joanie from the Jeffersonian were in that group. So was Peggy. It relieved us of worries about having a date for dances and permitted us to avoid the complications of one to one dating. We went to the dance on a group date, happy to have completed the first academic segment of our first year of college, excited to be going out on our first work-study jobs soon and glad to have found one another as friends. At the party that followed we drank too much. We commiserated in the morning at the cafeteria, then packed and began to head out.

I had been told by a few older students that to hitchhike to New York was a matter of about twenty-four hours usually. Mostly it was big rig truck drivers wanting someone to talk to them so that they could stay awake. The hardest part was getting from Yellow Springs to the Pennsylvania Turnpike. I could not afford the train or the Greyhound Bus, so at ten-thirty on Saturday morning, large suitcase in hand, I walked out to the main street of Yellow Springs, followed it to the edge of town and put my thumb in the air.

Chapter 7

Wanting More

During the daylight hours there were short lifts with long waits. But as the darkness approached a semi-rig pulled off to the side of the road and I had my first lesson in the difficulty of getting myself and a suitcase up and into the high cab where the driver waited. He was not going onto the Pennsylvania Turnpike he told me but would be passing an entrance to it and would drop me there. I was grateful. "Them cars won't stop for you at night," he said. "Folks get scared of their shadows at night but truckers like company to help us stay awake."

There were lights at the entrance to the Turnpike and after a twenty minute wait a trucker did stop for me. "I'm fixin' to get some food in about thirty miles and gettin' off at the next exit after then but you're welcome to come along. You'd have a better shot at a ride at the rest stop there. More people going through, more traffic, and they can see you in the lights. Chance to get some food too if you want." I sat at the counter with him, had a hamburger and coffee, thanked him and moved on while he took his time with his full dinner.

The next truck was good for a hundred miles. The driver was about my age, said he wished he had gone to college but now he had a wife and two kids to support. He dropped me at his exit where I waited an hour as traffic sped by. I looked at the stars and lifted my collar against the cold wind. It was not an easy spot for someone driving fast to see me and decide to pull over.

But it did happen finally, a double rig that came to a full stop some distance away, lights flashing. I ran to it with my suitcase and climbed aboard. "Goin' all the way," the driver said. He also told me it was the end of a long haul and he was sleepy, "so keep talkin' to me, if you don't mind."

Indeed his eyelids did try to close fairly often. I watched his eyes, the steering wheel and the line on the road. I told him stories about where I grew up, the people I knew, college life, courses at school and scary things that I had seen in movies. Whenever his lids began to lower or the steering wheel threatened to take us off course, I asked him a sudden question about himself or his opinion relating to the current tale. Dawn came as we rolled through the fields of oil storage tanks in New Jersey. I could see him then, a man of forty or so who needed a shave and who in a different life might have been handsome. He popped one last *No Doz* pill and washed it down with water from a jug. "Looks like we made it," he said as we entered the Lincoln Tunnel.

He asked me where in the city I was going and I told him I was not sure. Jay had given me the phone number and said to call when I got into the city. "There's a Y.M.C.A. on Thirty-Fourth Street if you get stuck," he said as he pulled over to let me out on the corner of Seventh Avenue. "Subway downtown right there will take you to Thirty-fourth." He shook my hand. "Thanks for keeping me awake. You did a good job. Good luck in college."

I found a public telephone booth in the street, wedged my suitcase into it with me and dialed the number. Busy signal. I went into a luncheonette and ordered coffee and toast. Back to the telephone booth, no answer. I dialed it again and let it ring a long time. No answer. I took the subway to Thirty-Fourth Street, found the Y.M.C.A. and tried again, using a telephone in the lobby. No answer. Maybe Jay had not gotten to New York yet. I did not know his roommate's name or if he knew about me. I asked the price of a room for one night and if I could leave my suitcase there the next day. I was tired and worried about the fact that I was to report for work the next morning at Scribner's at nine o'clock sharp. I wanted to be rested and make a good impression.

The man at the desk said "no personal checks, cash in advance only." I needed to sleep. I emptied my pockets on the bed and counted my money, three dollars and sixty-four cents. I showered and tried to sleep but could not quiet myself. I was hungry. I decided to try the telephone in the lobby again, find something to eat and look around. No answer on the telephone. I walked to the Automat on Forty-Second Street that I remembered from my visit to Times Square with Neal. I looked in the small Automat windows for the cheapest things and the largest quantity for the fewest coins, and then went for a walk to think about it.

I noticed that the stand-up sidewalk counter of Nedick's offered a morning orange drink, a donut and a cup of coffee for fifteen cents. That would be breakfast the next morning before work. I bought a cheese sandwich at the Automat, ate half of it and saved half for dinner. I decided to walk to Scribner's, study the entrance and then time how long it would take me to walk between there and the Y.M.C.A. by way of Nedick's, no need to spend a nickel on the subway.

There was no answer at the telephone number up to nine o'clock that evening. I hung out my suit, shirt and tie for the next morning and went to sleep, setting an alarm for six-thirty to give myself plenty of time to shower, shave, dress, pack up, store the suitcase downstairs, try to reach Jay again, get my breakfast at Nedick's and report for work a few minutes before nine o'clock. I had been told to ask for Mrs. MacMillan in the Mail Order Department on the mezzanine level. She would be my supervisor.

The bookstore was not open when I arrived at fifteen minutes before nine. It was a bright sunny morning and I was excited. The Scribner's building looked elegant, elaborate black framing and spotless windows. Fifth Avenue was crowded with people hurrying to work. Some were going in a doorway beside the bookstore that was a part of the building so I tried that, asking a man who entered just behind me if the elevator went to the Mail Order Department on the mezzanine level. "Sure," he answered, "but the stairway there is faster." He pointed to the stairs beside and just beyond the old elevator. I took a deep breath and put my foot on the first stone step.

This was it, my first day on the job in New York City. A new life was beginning.

Mrs. MacMillan, a pleasant looking, plump woman with bifocal glasses was standing beside the first desk waiting. "Are you our new Antioch student?" she asked, peering over the tops of the metal-framed glasses and smiling. "We got here early so that we could welcome you properly. We've always had girls before; you're our first man. This is going to be fun. And this is your desk right here and mine is the next one squeezed in just in front of yours."

Front meant in the direction away from the street and toward the windowless rear of the store which could be seen below through small glass panels that were tilted slightly open for ventilation, parts of the large rounded frosted glass windows that were the architectural décor of the store. Front was in the direction of Mr. Horn's desk in the dark far end of the narrow mezzanine. She worked her way up the ladder of importance introducing me.

Next in the line was an empty desk and then the only one turned to face away from the store. "This is Miss Connely." The deeply lined, impatient face of slim Miss Connely managed a hint of a smile, exhaled a cloud of cigarette smoke from a scarlet slash of mouth as she placed her cigarette in an overflowing ashtray and said "How do you do?" in a rusty voice. She placed her hand briefly in mine before retrieving her cigarette and coughing.

Next came Mr. Simpson, painfully thin and stoop shouldered in a worn black suit now too large for him, an unstylish dark necktie, white shirt with a collar too large, a shy welcoming smile and a voice uncertain of its tones as he said "It's a pleasure to meet you," putting his nervous, bony hand in mine for several shakes.

Then, "This is Hennie, Miss Henrietta Strunk, actually, our ray of sunshine and Mr. Horn's secretary." Hennie was an attractive, plump woman probably about ten years older than I, blond permanent waved hair, two silver bracelets, modest makeup and an air of cheerful confidence. "I'm the girl from Queens." she said, "Glad to meet you."

"And finally this is Mr. Horn," Mrs. MacMillan said with deferential flourish, stepping back a bit so that he and I could make contact. Mr. Horn, almost as tall as I, a decade older than Hennie, had a gruff yet soft voice, a suit that fit and a neutral face as he shook my hand firmly, asked if this was my first year at college and wished me luck. "Mr. Horn somehow manages to make all of this work," Mrs. MacMillan said with a flutter of girlish laugh. "Some days I think it is the most amazing thing!"

Just then a rustle of activity back near the empty desk announced the nearly late arrival of Miss Polly. "This is our lovely helper who is here some days and some days not but will one day be gracing the stages of Broadway and beyond. Miss Polly is an actress."

She was not much older than I, perhaps twenty-one or twenty-two, dressed in a smart maroon jacket and skirt, simple white blouse, high heels and necklace of tiny ceramic beads. Long dark hair swept neatly into a soft roll at the nape of her neck. Perfect makeup included the framing of her sparkling dark eyes. "Hi, I'm Polly," she said, fishing her cigarettes out of a dark leather sack. "I'm the temp."

My work was explained in ten minutes. I was to go through the mailing list kept on cards in file boxes that lined the shelf that ran almost the entire length of the office, make new cards on my typewriter for any changes of address that came in, hunt down missing cards or replace them if necessary and be on the look-out constantly for cards "that have the funniest way of wandering off on their own," Mrs. MacMillan said. It was easy. Too easy. It was boring. But soon the office staff had become a friendly family soap opera in close quarters with new developments each day.

Mrs. MacMillan could be counted on to find an amusing aspect of any event, "It was so funny, being jostled aside like that and not getting that taxi and then to have the rain stop the very next instant!" That would be Miss Connely's cue in her throaty chain-smoker's voice to say, "There is very little civility left in this city these days." Hennie would look for a change of topic as needed, Mr. Simpson would quietly murmur a possibly related literary quote and Mr. Horn would telephone someone, dictate a letter to Hennie or hurry off to see someone in the Shipping Department. "They lost an order of fifty books that was supposed to go to the Canary Islands," Polly might mouth in a half whisper to me with one arched brow as she rolled new sheets of stationery with carbon paper into the typewriter.

There was a birthday cake on birthdays and, to celebrate the occasion, Mr. Simpson could be persuaded to recite *The Face on the Barroom Floor, Mighty Casey* or a favorite poem by Poe. He delivered his recitations near his desk, standing with one hand on a file cabinet like a Roman orator. These were brave and memorable performances by a shy man, always followed by our sincere applause as well as his deep embarrassment and covert pleasure.

At lunch time that first day I asked if it was permissible to use the telephone to make a personal call. The others had left the office and Mrs. MacMillan was putting on her hat. "We're actually not supposed to make personal calls but it *is* lunch time so if it's not long distance and not too long I don't see the harm."

There was no answer. I took a walk around the area and bought a pretzel with mustard from a street vendor for my lunch. In the afternoon Mrs. MacMillan asked if I had found pleasant housing. "Honestly, some of the students have gotten into the funniest situations renting rooms." I told her about trying to find my friend and the problem of the cash policy at the Y.M.C.A.

"Honestly! What a funny rule to have. Maybe the cashier in the store will cash a check for you since you work here. Why don't you run downstairs and ask."

The answer was no. I assured Mrs. MacMillan that there was no need to worry. "That's true I'm sure," she said, "Honestly, people are so funny about money. I'm sure the manager at the Y.M.C.A. will make it all work if you speak to him. I mean you *are* a college student and you *are* employed at Scribner's. Honestly!"

The manager of the Y, after careful consideration of my story and my credentials said that he would accept a check from me each day for that day's rent only. "But no cash. Sorry, that's the best I can do. And you'll have to pack up and check out each morning and then see if we have a room open at the end of the day."

The next morning Mrs. MacMillan told me that Mr. Horn had arranged with the Payroll Department to give me my pay in cash on Friday afternoons. I was earning twenty-seven dollars and fifty cents a week. "Also," she said, looking uncomfortable, "Miss Connely and I, funnily enough, found we have fifteen dollars in our purses that we will not be needing before Friday afternoon, but please, no checks," she said laughing, "cash only, like your Y.M.C.A. man. You can pay us back on Friday."

"Absolute nonsense the way young men are treated in that supposedly Christian hotel," Miss Connely added gruffly. She then went into a fit of coughing. "Pardon me."

Jay was there when I telephoned at lunchtime. "A friend invited me to Fire Island for a few days and I couldn't refuse. We got involved and stayed until today. Sorry. And Albert's been working odd shifts at the hospital. He's a nurse's aide. Write down the address. It's on Seventy-Fourth Street between Central Park West and Columbus. Get your suitcase at the Y and take the Seventh Avenue Express uptown to Seventy-Second Street."

It was seven o'clock that evening when I located the brownstone and carried my suitcase up to the second floor front apartment. "I hope the spaghetti sauce isn't burned," Albert said. He was a busy, breathless, aproned, rounded man with thinning hair. I guessed him to be close to thirty.

"Chef Albert's been slaving over a hot stove," Jay giggled. "Canned tomatoes in canned sauce but the spaghetti goes into the boiling water now. The really hard part was the salad."

"That'll be enough out of you Mr. Smart Pants," Albert said, hurrying over to the wall of the living room that had a stove, sink, small refrigerator, small table and a cabinet with two drawers. "We'll be seeing if you can't get a job as a dishwasher someplace north of Hundred and Twenty-Fifth Street."

Albert switched on the radio. Perry Como crooned "I'd like to get you on a slow boat to China." Albert served large portions of the pasta and I ate it all. "I see someone here appreciates my cooking," he said with pursed lips and raised eyebrows.

What had once been one large living room facing the street was now divided into a kitchen and living area plus a small bedroom. There was a shared bath down the hall. "Jay says you're just here for seven or eight weeks. You can stay here if you want to. You can have that little closet under the windows. There's a fold-up army cot in there with a full sheet, a pillow and a blanket. Everything has to be put away in the morning. I can't stand a messy house. Rent would be five dollars a week plus a dollar in the kitty any night I cook and you eat here. You can have one half of one shelf in the refrigerator if you want."

During my senior year of high school it seemed clear that *Jay worked both sides of the street*, as Pamela had discreetly put it once after a couple of drinks but now I had stepped into Albert and Jay's world. I supposed they might represent the *free thinkers* or *bohemians* my friends at college had described admiringly when talking about Greenwich Village. Homosexuality was in the air—definitely. It was foreign. It scared me and titillated me. And where else could I get rent that cheap?

I learned that a fold-up canvas and wood frame army cot can be quickly assembled and disassembled, creaks and groans if you attempt to change position during the night, and is uncomfortable but offers a night's sleep once you are tired enough to yield. *Miss Albert*, as Jay called him, was talkative, bossy and always busy. Jay was unemployed "but always looking" and muscular Mel, the warehouseman who had a room one flight up was often there for dinner. It was a dollar and a half in the kitty for him. "He makes good money and only pays rent on that dinky little room," Albert said. "If it wasn't for all those muscles and him stripping down to his undershirt on hot evenings I'd let him starve."

To Jay's ill-concealed annoyance, Mel took a liking to me. He was twenty-seven years old and close to handsome when he was shaved and showered, a requirement for Albert's dinner. He had thick dark hair that was unruly, hairy arms and chest, had broken up with his girlfriend at the end of the summer and was every bit as muscular as Albert had described him. With the four of us sitting around in the living room area that had one sofa and one old chair with worn upholstery, Mel did seem to maneuver so that his muscles and I were often in close contact.

"He's an animal," Jay said, rolling his eyes. "I think he likes you. That's how he shows it. He likes to get those big paws on you."

"He'd better be minding his manners in my living room or he'll be eating White Castle fatburgers. Throwing all that meat around here like that. I'm beginning to wonder about that boy," Albert added.

In the evenings when Albert was working and Jay was out, Mel would stop by after he'd had a sandwich somewhere and ask if I wanted to go get a beer at the corner bar. If I declined, thinking about money, he'd say "Oh, come on, my treat."

On his birthday he insisted. He definitely was treating, he said. "We're having boiler makers, one shot of whiskey for each beer." There was lots of touching at the bar. He wanted me to help him figure out why the muscles of his right thigh were bigger than those on the left. "I'm right handed. Could that mean something?" I was the college boy with all the answers.

He repeatedly took my hand and pressed it hard on one thigh or the other, sometimes brushing across a full crotch on the way. I got drunk in an hour and threw up into the gutter on the way home while Mel steadied me with his left hand and pressed his big right hand comfortingly against my lower belly. "Next time we celebrate we'll get some girls," he said.

We did. It was a Friday night but I had tucked most of my pay away after picking up my two clean shirts at the Chinese laundry on Amsterdam Avenue, buying a box of cereal and a quart of milk and leaving five dollars for Albert in the usual cup in the kitchen cabinet. It began with my agreeing to go out for one beer. But Mel wanted to celebrate getting a raise. He bought us a pitcher of beer and then said he needed a woman and was going to treat me to one. "Come on, we both need it."

He found a willing cab driver on Columbus Avenue who took us to a corner in Harlem where two girls ran over and hopped in when the driver flashed the headlights twice. They took us to a room with a double bed, a naked light bulb and a sink. One of them called upstairs to report to "Mama." They examined us, handed each of us a condom, quickly threw off skirts and heavy sweaters revealing dark skin and no underwear, switched off the light and said "Hurry up now, we ain't got all night."

It was not working for me, "Come on, Sugar, let's get going." From Mel's side of the creaking double bed there was moaning. "Hey, you wanna' switch?" he asked. "I got this baby all warmed up."

"No thanks." I wanted it to be over. With some faked groaning on my part when Mel groaned his loudest, we all declared it over, Mel paid, the girls were satisfied and we went out to catch a cab heading downtown. Days later the itch began. It was fierce.

Jay recommended a free public health clinic. The doctor called it *scabies* and by then it was clear how it got its name. He gave me a salve, said it would go away eventually, told me to wear clean underwear every day, iron my pants inside out with a very hot iron every morning and wear gloves to bed at night to stop the scratching.

It did not go away. It got worse. It was hard not to scratch during the day at the office. Finally Jay got "some poison medicine in a jelly jar from a witch in the Village." "It's turpentine and a couple of other things. You have to stand naked in the tub down the hall," he said giggling, "while I put it on you with a paint brush and then you can wash after fifteen minutes. Three days in a row." Jay had fun doing it. It hurt. But it worked.

I had been looking for a second job in the evenings. Jay had gotten a job as an usher at a large movie theater on Broadway, near Times Square, and said he would keep an eye out for something for me. At the end of my third week in New York City Jay told me that a friend of his told him there was a temporary job for an usher, last shift at a theater down at Union Square. "They said if you could work six to closing you could have it. Last show usually lets out around midnight. Oh, I also called home. There's some kind of big trouble. All the old crew at the theaters has been fired. Sonny wants you to call him right away. He said the bosses are trying to find out what college you're at."

Sonny told me that they had been caught in the act reselling tickets and the theater owners were trying to track me down since I had been one of the ticket takers the previous summer and they guessed it had been going on then, too. In fact, he reminded me that it had been going on for years. "Say nothing."

There was some hope it would blow over, he told me, because Bernice, the head cashier, had been involved in doing the same thing, with the owner, when the theater first opened. She was willing to say so in court if they pressed charges. "But you'd better call Junior at the New York office and say you heard they were looking for you before they find your college. Just don't give them any information they don't already have."

That was too close. My old life was threatening my new life. I telephoned the New York office and was told to be there the next morning at ten. I called in to work sick the next morning and went, terrified.

The owner's son and son-in-law had taken over the business. They kept me waiting in an outer office for half an hour and then called me in to Junior's large office. Switching a lever on a box on the desk, they warned me that everything I said would be recorded and that I had better answer all questions truthfully because my answers would be compared with what others had told them.

Most of what I said was "I don't know," "I don't remember," and "Maybe."

They were seated. I was standing. They smirked, threatened and laughed at me. "You must be proud of yourself, *college boy*. Are you as dumb as you seem or playing dumb for some kind of honor amongst thieves?" They warned me that I should be expecting to hear from the FBI and was facing a trial and jail time. "Get out of our sight, college boy," the son-in-law said. "You're trash."

I did not sleep that night. I was afraid to go into the brownstone. There might be FBI agents waiting inside. I watched for people who might be following me on the street or standing in the shadows near the brownstone as I passed it on the other side of the street several times.

That long night I considered ways of suicide. Sleeping pills were a luxury. I had no idea where to get them or how to pay for them. There was the subway, a bridge or jumping over a railing and into the winter water of the East River. The subway seemed easiest and surest. It would be fast. I could not face the shame of being exposed before my new friends and going to jail, taken down to a place lower than where I had begun. The door to the world I had just found was closing. I was going to be exposed as an imposter.

The need for sleep won out the second night. I crept back into the building late that night and on the nights following, checking shadows and looking from the curtained living room windows again before leaving for work each morning, looking for anyone standing nearby who might have handcuffs or a summons. I was delaying the suicide, worried but not noticing that the real possibility of it was growing dimmer each day.

I went down to Union Square to see about the late shift job and it was open still, four nights a week, sixty-five cents an hour. *Children of Paradise* was playing. It let out at ten minutes past midnight. With luck I could leave Scribner's at five, catch a downtown express at Times Square, get a cream cheese sandwich on raisin bread and a cup of coffee at Choc Full o' Nuts for fifteen cents, change into my uniform jacket before six o'clock, then catch an uptown express at Fourteenth Street and be on my cot at about one in the morning.

The work at the Mail Order Department was very tedious. My affection for the little office family grew deeper but so did my sleepiness in the afternoons. Albert got cranky about "all this coming and going at all hours." Mel said I could share his room and bed if I wanted. Hearing that, Albert relented "since it's only two more weeks to Christmas."

"He wants that five bucks and can't stand the thought of anybody else getting into Mel's bed," Jay said.

The day after Christmas I was excused early with much handshaking and good wishes. I had admired an anthology of poetry published by Scribner's that fall but, of course, could not buy it. Mrs. MacMillan had told me that if a damaged copy turned up I might buy it at half price. "One fell off the shelf in the Shipping Department yesterday," Mr. Horn said, not looking at me. "Corner's bent so we had to write it off. Merry Christmas."

"We're all looking forward to seeing you again at the end of March," Mr. Simpson said with his shy, affectionate smile.

Hennie had tears in her eyes.

"Study well," Miss Connely said. "You need it in this world."

Polly lamented that I would miss her workshop performance in *A Doll's House*.

"It's a pleasure, I must say, having another man in the office," Mrs. MacMillan said. "It's so funny that the school's never sent us a man before. Heavens!"

I took the train home to New Jersey because I did not yet know how to hitchhike out of Manhattan. After shopping for inexpensive Christmas presents I found I had managed to save only fifty dollars in the two months in New York. It was something, but not enough.

In the year since the previous Christmas my oldest brother had married a girl from a coal mining town he had met before he was discharged from the army and they had their first baby. A sister had married a soldier she had met in a service club in Washington and they had moved in with his family in a small town in the pine woods. There were new houses being built in the woods back of Belmar, no down payment and easy terms for returning vets. Using my oldest sister's GI benefits, my parents and she had gotten two small houses, next door to one another, each with two bedrooms, kitchen, living room and bathroom, small houses with small rooms, but they were buying now instead of renting. My other brother, discharged from the Marines, had bought a brand new car, gotten his high school diploma and was enrolled in a couple of courses at a junior college nearby.

All of that change and yet there was nothing to talk about still. "You got a lot of Jews at that college?" my father asked.

I said that two of my new friends were Jewish, Joanie and Bobbie, but what difference did it make? I told them the music professor was colored.

"A nigger teacher? Don't that take the cake! That's a good one," he said with a chuckle. "Does he dance the jig too?"

"You should have stayed here and gone to the business college," my mother said.

"Don't go marrying any of them Jew girls," my father said.

There was no way to tell them about the wonderful new world I had found. They were not interested. But my brother was interested that the vets I knew were using the GI Bill and that it paid fully for their tuition, fees, room and board plus giving them an allowance for spending money. "They get to keep the money earned on the co-op jobs?" He was going to look into it and might think about applying for September as a transfer student.

My oldest sister was working as a telephone operator and they had gotten a telephone installed. Wayne called from his parents' home in northern Ohio. He had gotten my family's telephone number from the school. Joanie was having a New Year's party on Long Island. He was definitely going to be there. Don lived only a few miles away from her and would be there. Bobbie was coming from her home near Philadelphia. Several other people who had been working in and around New York were coming. "It'll be fun. We can sleep on the floor at either Joanie's or Don's place. Say you'll come."

I wanted to go. I could not go. I felt guilty. I had said I would be home for the week between Christmas and New Year's. My parents would not understand but I mentioned the party, just in case there was a way out. "Very hoity-toity, huh?" my mother said. "They must be rich. Are they the Jews?"

I stayed, wishing that I could leave. The day after New Year's Day I was on the road hitchhiking with a three-sandwich lunch. "Don't that school even give you bus fare to get there? That's some joint you picked."

I made payments on my bills and stretched my money through the three months of the second semester. I was a part of our group of friends and I knew it. I had a place. Wayne shaped the group, I saw, bestowing praise on admired traits and dismissing dullness. He had an appetite for rich, famous and foreign people. Don began dating a raven-haired beauty who knew painters in Greenwich Village, who had posed nude for them, and who might or might not be a lesbian. Wayne was delighted. "But she's marvelous, whatever she is." He briefly flattered and pulled in Ida, another girl, who appeared to be disoriented and had a heavy West Virginia accent but she faded and failed as an exotic source of amusement. He found and began dating a petite blonde beauty with Polish parents who was a third year student. Her outstanding physical beauty and willingness to bend to him was enough. He marveled at my ability to call up dialog and lyrics from a variety of old films that had been popular. My exotic status was certified as I slowly revealed my lower class background.

Wayne's father was in sales, his mother was a housewife. Don came from a family devoted to government service. His brother was an assistant ambassador. His father had committed suicide. Joanie's father made gold jewelry in New York City. Bobbie's father was a lawyer. My father was a janitor and my mother a factory worker. I grew up in a family that said "ain't'" and "shit" and I had been taught to dance by women, some of whom were of questionable repute. I was the most exotic.

We bought bottles of cheap red Chianti, put in candles that dripped onto the empty bottles and talked in the candlelight about Baudelaire's poems, the songs of Charles Trenet and Billie Holliday's life. Don and Wayne were reading Thomas Wolfe's *You Can't Go Home Again* and *Look Homeward Angel*. Bobbie had discovered Thomas Mann's *Magic Mountain* and Rilke's *Letters to a Young Poet*. Joanie pushed us for awareness of the workers' struggle and the coming purge of left-leaning politicians, socialists and former communists. Both Joanie and Don quoted *The New Yorker*. I seemed to be the only one worried about how to pay for school, so I did not talk about it.

We joined the picketing of the only barbershop in town whose proprietor said he could not and would not cut a Negro's hair because he did not know how. We boys went without haircuts. The girls taught us how to knit. We knitted socks and long scarves, seated conspicuously in the front row for large lectures in the Humanities and Life Sciences series.

I was wet when I arrived back in New York. It had rained hard during my hitchhiking trip and I had no raincoat. Jay and Albert had had a falling out but Jay had found another place one block away, on Seventy-Fifth Street. "Don't ask. Mel moved out of the building too. He's living somewhere in Brooklyn. We have to give the place up the first of June but Yours Truly has a job about then on Fire Island keeping house sort of for a rich old man. By the way, I hear that blow-up at the theater seems to be going away."

I did not take the bait and ask about the Fire Island job. I did not want to appear curious or to hear salacious details that he probably wanted to tell. Sharing this place on Seventy-Fifth Street would cost an additional two dollars a week but I would have my own bed. It was a second floor rear that probably had been a dining room and butler's pantry, nicked and scarred wood paneling, bricked up fireplace, crumbling decorative plaster ceiling with the chandelier missing and a large window. The shared bathroom was the next door in the hall. There was no refrigerator but we had a hot plate and two pans.

Jay was now open about being gay and often out on dates, a few times bringing one home for the night. "This is Juan. He doesn't speak English and that's probably good. Isn't he cute? Look at that smile. We'll try to be quiet until after you leave for work."

Jay seemed to be enjoying his life of *free love* as well as provoking my discomfort. I wanted to appear sophisticated and worldly like my new college friends. I did not want to reveal my own attraction to men. Jay was not attractive to me but Juan *was* cute and sexy. I would have liked to touch him. They were quiet, a few whispers, kisses and giggles in the darkness. I was interested but feigned sleep. I told myself I was learning what it was like to live like them. I could use it in my writing.

I could not find an evening job so I spent my evenings writing short stories and sending them off to *The New Yorker* with return postage on the enclosed envelope. Once I got a handwritten "nice!" on the rejection slip. Dinner was half a can of tamales in tomato sauce, the opened can heated in a pan of boiling water. One tin of sardines in mustard sauce could be made into two sandwiches, covering both lunch and dinner, and a heated can of spaghetti and meatballs could last for two dinners.

Wayne wrote to me at Scribner's, his full name on the return address, *L. Wayne Higley.* His school assistant job was ending at the end of May and he was coming to New York and wondered if we could share a room somewhere. My job at Scribner's ran until the alternating student came at the end of July.

We settled on what Wayne's petite blonde girlfriend said students called "the Hell of last resort," the Viking-Forsberg Apartments on the corner of One Hundred and Thirteenth Street and Broadway. The tall building had a multi-story sign painted on its brick back side that could be read from a distance as one walked uptown along Broadway. *The wages of sin are death but the gift of God is eternal life through Jesus Christ, our Lord. Amen. Luke.*

Large apartments had long ago been separated into single rooms onto the doors of which people had put hasps and padlocks. Each apartment had one dark kitchen alive with colonies of cockroaches and one none too clean bathroom to share. Our room had two small beds, each with creaking springs, sagging mattress and stained pillows plus an orange crate table and two damaged wooden chairs by the one window facing a brick wall five feet away. Wayne's girlfriend had a job as a live-in nanny a few blocks uptown in an apartment on West End Avenue and was able to borrow sheets and pillowcases for us.

Fortunately our window opened. It was a very hot summer with some days well over a hundred degrees. Air conditioning was available only in large and expensive movie theaters. Some nights we walked Riverside Drive until two o'clock in the morning. There was no movement of the hot air in our room. I learned that the initial L in Wayne's name was for Lawrence. He thought L. Wayne Higley had a better ring.

At the end of July, Mrs. MacMillan enlisted the help of a friend in the Billing Department and got me a job there typing invoices on a billing machine. There was a large fan there. Men were expected to wear suits and neckties to the office but the jacket could be hung on the back of the chair, the necktie loosened and shirt cuffs turned up once at work. I had bought a lightweight summer suit at the start of the summer, a bargain and a necessary expense, twenty-seven dollars at Robert Hall. Wayne and I took the subway out to the end of the line for a few of the weekends, meeting up with Don and staying at Joanie's home. Don borrowed his mother's car and we went to Jones Beach.

Their parents amazed me. Don's mother worked in a government office. When she got home from work she made Manhattans and lit a cigarette to celebrate the end of the workday and was ready to talk about world events.

Joanie's mother always seemed delighted to see us. She put out heaping platters of food which I learned to eat heartily since she did not seem to mind at all. "No, darling, really, eat *please*. It gives me such pleasure to see someone with an appetite." Her kindness, generosity and enthusiasm were then and are still an inspiration to me.

We listened to a few of the amazing new long-playing records, *The Pines of Rome* and Tchaikovsky's *Romeo and Juliet*, no need to change records. We sat in the sweltering top row of the top balcony for *Streetcar Named Desire* with young Marlon Brando.

On an impulse on my way to Scribner's one morning I stopped in the box office at Rockefeller Center where the Monte Carlo Opera was performing and squandered five dollars on a ticket for my first opera, *Madame Butterfly*. I loved it and returned three days later for *La Traviata*.

I was eager to return to campus at the end of the summer but I had been unable to save money. I had applied for tuition-reduction before I left but had been warned that there was very little of it and too many students applying for it. There were no scholarships and no loan programs. I had less than one hundred dollars left. It was not enough to pay for even one more semester. I would hitchhike back to school and hope for the best. I already had done one year of college.

But I wanted more.

Chapter 8

Antioch

Hitchhiking through that early September night, waiting for rides, there was plenty of time for worries about money and to anticipate seeing my new friends again. My brother was there on campus already, I knew. I hoped that he was enjoying the Orientation Week for new students. I had prepared him for it. "Be honest. Say what you think and feel. They're good people."

Lucky him, I thought, the war behind him and now no worries about money. The G.I. Bill would pay all of his expenses and even give him spending money. He could study and play, have time to enjoy new friends and new ideas.

Back on campus finally, the next evening, tired, I found the posted housing assignments and headed for the barracks out on the edge of the athletic field. Don Brown and I were going to be roommates in one named *Valhalla*.

My first stop after breakfast the next morning was the desk of the man in charge of Student Aid. My request for tuition-reduction had been denied, he told me. Even if I could find a job quickly and got permission for delayed payment I would not be able to pay for the semester. I was scared.

My friends were outraged. "If you don't qualify for full tuition reduction who the hell does?" Don Brown said. He, Wayne and Joanie took up my cause and paid a visit to the office later that morning. They reported back to me in the afternoon that it was hopeless. All of the funds had been allocated already. They were indignant and angry but had vague hope that we would think of something.

I did not go to dinner with them that evening but went with them into town for beer and free pretzels. I left them after one beer and returned to my room. What to do? Pack up and leave seemed to be the only option.

I walked out into the dark untended expanse of the athletic field. There was a definite chill in the air but it mixed with the earth's remaining end-of-summer warmth. Stars were gem bright in a black, cloudless sky. I spread my jacket on the ground and lay on it, looking up at the stars, wishing as I had in third grade that somehow I could go there to that elsewhere. I had hit a wall. I wanted to stay but I was being told to leave. I was being sent away from my new world.

I sat up and looked back across the field to the lights of the barracks windows. My friends were there. Tears came. Surprised and blinded by them, I fell back on the ground and gave up, sobbing. No one could hear or see me. I was alone. Holding myself, hugging myself as if I was coming apart, I cried until the tears were spent, then cried again, quieted again, on and on until all of the barracks windows had gone dark. I was lost. I had no questions and there were no answers. I might as well sleep. I crept back across the field and into my room where Don was snoring lightly. I put my jeans, shirt and jacket on my upper bunk and slid quietly between the sheets. Done, all of it. Antioch, my new life, it was done. Tomorrow would take me wherever it took me.

But it was not done. Don, Wayne, Joanie, and Pigeon were at a breakfast table in the cafeteria and called to me to join them. They insisted that I not give up. The Tea Room, the waiter-served campus restaurant, would be opening in two days. "Go see if they have a job, Honey," Pigeon said. "Insist," Wayne said. "Go to the Student Aid Office again," Don said. "Be a squeaky wheel," Joanie said.

I got lucky. Though all of the jobs at the Tea Room were spoken for already by the returning experienced waiters, I could be on call to come in if someone got sick or quit. "Stop by to check before lunch and dinner each day. You can bus tables if we're busy. It's the way to start," said Kenny, the manager.

Ben, Director of Student Aid, handed me the official brief note telling me that my application had been denied. "The reason, I think, is that the committee didn't see you as much of an asset to the community, not as much as other applicants were. You're not contributing by being on any of the community committees, for instance. You could get more involved and try for next semester."

"I can't pay the bill for this semester," I confessed.

"See Millie in the Finance Office and see if you can do delayed payment."

As I was leaving he said, "Oh, and there's a kind of obscure loan program you might qualify for next semester. It's the Devella Mills Foundation in New Jersey and only for people from New Jersey in out-of-state private colleges and it's competitive. You'd have to take an exam this semester, see how your score competes and how much they would lend but it's a low interest rate loan."

"Thanks," I said, "I'd like to try."

"You'll need to show them good grades and good community involvement too. Any of the campus committees interest you?"

"The Race Relations Committee," I answered.

"They're having an organizing meeting tomorrow afternoon."

I got permission for delayed payment and did get some of the money I needed on the competitive loan from the foundation in New Jersey for the second semester. I joined the Race Relations Committee and became its chairman, gradually increased the hours I worked at the Tea Room and managed four A's in the second year, compared with only one the first year. The pay as a waiter was low, sixty-five cents an hour, and community mores of equality strongly discouraged tipping, but I aimed for better paying jobs when off campus. My nose was above water. I held on, one semester at a time. I was not being sent away, not yet.

The first job period that second year was in the Circulation Department of Women's Day Magazine in Manhattan. Wayne and I found a room with shared bathroom, One Hundred and Tenth Street and Riverside Drive. Three of the girls from school had an apartment four blocks away on Broadway. We formed a meal co-op, chipping in money and taking turns with shopping and cooking dinners. The job was dull but I liked my co-workers and my boss. I could not find an after work job, though. That was bad news but it made it possible to enjoy our co-op dinners and the fun of astonishing the girls' local dates when Wayne or I emerged from the bedroom after helping one of them with dress and make-up.

The second job period assignment was a four month gift from the gods, part of a team of thirteen anthropometrists traveling the country by sleeper trains as far as New Orleans, Texas, California and Washington State to measure thousands of the most physically fit U. S. Air Force flight personnel, naked. It was a forerunner of the Space Program, furnishing the data needed in designing Space Suits and other equipment. Insurance for us as civilian contractors did not permit us to be flown on Air Force planes but at the bases we were housed in Officers' Quarters which meant cheap food and drinks as well as easy bus transportation to nearby towns and cities. The job painfully inflamed my secret desires, of course, but it also showed me parts of the country I had seen only in movies and helped my savings program considerably. Both jobs paid a third more than I had earned the first year and there were few expenses on the Air Force job.

The only grades below A that second year were two C's, one in Budget and one in Administrative Accounting. I started thinking about changing my major to Psychology, even giving some brazen thought to changing to Fine Arts with a focus on writing.

I had won the right to borrow a limited amount from the New Jersey foundation for one year. That gave me hope that I might continue to borrow, taking the competitive exam each year. Since I also had been granted some tuition reduction I hoped that it too might continue or be increased if I increased my visible community involvement and kept my grades up. My job as a waiter in the Tea Room was secure as a returning third year student and I could concentrate on finding future job assignments that paid better and permitted me to keep expenses down.

I was reading, books that were not required, books recommended by other students, odd books, interesting books. It started during second year when the professor teaching a required course on American Civilization spoke enthusiastically about the amazing journey of a cultured young French aristocrat, visiting the New World of America in 1831. I decided to take a peek at Alexis de Tocqueville's *Democracy in America* in the library and it quickly became a secret pleasure, squeezing a half an hour or fifteen minutes out of my schedule to read more and more of his amazing experiences, watching myself do this non-required reading, pleased and proud of it as a sign of real change in me.

The summer following that second year at Antioch, while I was touring the western United States courtesy of the nation's fledgling space program, Don Brown took a student ship to France. While there he visited a family his older brother had gotten to know while stationed in Paris. Don fell in love with the family's youngest daughter and they posted marriage banns according to local custom before he returned home. The plan was for him to return to France at Christmas for the wedding.

Don found a small apartment off-campus in a professor's home. It did not have much of a kitchen but he was sure that his French wife would make magic in it. Wayne and I also got permission to live off-campus in the two small upstairs rooms with a shared bathroom in the house of the Director of the Alumni Association. It was quieter and more private than dorm life, cheaper, and we were automatically invited to her literate Sunday brunch gatherings of chosen faculty, staff and students, a prestige prize for Wayne and another social class learning laboratory for me.

I was able to land a job in the campus bookstore for the two job periods that third year but had to vacate our private, quiet rooms for those periods since they were promised to returning students. It was not a problem for Wayne since he had work assignments elsewhere anyway. The best that I could find was a dilapidated apartment on the edge of town that I shared during the first job period with an amiable, habitually barefoot, guitar playing radical who I would see years later pictured in Time Magazine in a suit and necktie as a newly chaired professor and department head at Harvard.

He drifted off to some other place during the second job period and I shared the apartment with a soft spoken poet-aesthete who drank exotic teas, had a blond crew cut and sometimes let a very wicked sense of humor and talent for mimicry peek through his very refined façade. The Antioch community was small but had variety.

It was fun being on campus for a full ten months but I did hitchhike back east for the winter holiday break between semesters since the bookstore was closed and our whole gang had decided that we needed to be on the dock in New York to welcome Don and his new bride, Micheline, when they disembarked. Guilt required that since I was so close I should spend Christmas and a few days with my family in their little house in the pinewoods west of Belmar.

I counted the hours while there until I was free to go to my friends in New York. My mother and father, disgruntled as always, filled the air with sarcasm and dissatisfaction. They were uneasy, not knowing how to behave with me. I had changed. I was someone different, awake and eager for life. I never really had been one of them and was even less so now. From their vantage point I was on the way to being their social superior. They tested me with unfunny jokes and remarks about *kikes, wops* and *niggers*. I corrected their language to *Jewish people, Italians* and *Negroes,* explaining why the jokes were not funny.

My brother was there also, not much changed, out drinking with his hometown buddies, not much to tell about college. "It's okay." For me it was an amazing door that had opened, for him it seemed to be just the next thing he was doing.

The last day there it was clear that they thought I should stay longer. It was not so much their wanting my company but my short stay was one more item added to the list of the ways life cheated them. Remarks from my mother were designed to make me feel guilty. "If you wasn't so busy with those fancy friends you could stay here where you belong." My father softened a bit into his own peculiar joshing friendliness. "Don't go havin' to marry one of those Jew girls," he said with a twinkle in his eye. My mother, in a last dangerous try to engage me, followed that by saying, "Your brother says he thinks you like the boys better than the girls."

The bomb sat there ticking, between us in an unusual quiet in that tiny living room, the vivid floral wallpaper waiting, listening. "I like girls," I said finally. "I like Jews, too." I got up and left the room. End of discussion, end of visit.

I was able to pick up some evening shifts in the Tea Room during my bookstore job periods. The bookstore also offered the fringe benefits of being able to order odd books to look through before putting them on display, discounts to cost on all books and first pick of second-hand texts that were to be re-sold.

By the start of the second quarter I had been pretty sure that I would change my major to psychology by the end of the year. I volunteered for a research study at the Fels Institute adjoining campus. It meant taking a full battery of psychological tests, including the Wechsler Adult Intelligence Test, a Rorschach inkblot test, telling stories about pictures in the Thematic Apperception Test, and a few other projective personality tests. There was a life history interview before the testing and a follow-up feedback interview a month after taking the tests. A benefit offered, if desired, was ten free psychotherapy sessions following the feedback interview and they could be extended with another ten low-fee sessions if needed.

I was apprehensive about the results and surprised by them. I heard what sounded like compliments, phrases like "very high creativity", "unusual ability to use imaginative conceptualization in problem solving", "high compassion..." The intelligence test results, "quite mixed... low information but high ability..." added up to a score that told me I was really smart, if uneven.

It turned out that the psychotherapists were the psychologist researchers at Fels. They had little clinical experience but that was lucky for me. My kind, gentle therapist confessed immediately that he had little experience but promised to listen with care. A *presenting problem* was required so I said that mine was a fear of the current military draft that would send me to Korea. I hoped and feared that this therapist might find out my true secret and force me to deal with homosexual desires but I found myself first talking about the agonies of childhood poverty and social class differences. Only later did I blurt out my homosexual problem, halfway through the ten sessions.

Growing up I had not felt sorry for myself because we were poor. It was just the way we were. I wished we had more food when I was hungry or that my clothes were warm and that my shoes did not have holes. I wished that the bullies at school would not pick on me or that I might get sick more often so that I could stay home alone. But it did not occur to me to wish that we were not poor, just as it did not occur to me to wish that family members might hug me, kiss me or tell me that they loved me. We were as we were. Life was as it was.

It was only when my shocked college friends learned about my life and I met their families that I saw the differences and felt real envy. It was an envy that would lose its sting though, as I learned in the years to follow that life for most children in the world is at least as difficult as it was for me, too often more difficult.

My therapist seemed to like me and did not recoil in horror when my homosexual secret was revealed. We renewed for the second ten sessions at the rock bottom discounted rate and then went on for some additional sessions after that with me paying whatever I could come up with for payment. My breakthrough in therapy was a simple, wracking awareness of how extremely lonely and alone I felt and had felt all of my life. *Different.*

My good luck was his lack of doctrinaire training and his simple decent human kindness. I saw him search for truth in himself when he said that since I was attracted to some girls and could enjoyably function with them sexually, he thought I would do well to keep my secret, find a girl I could love, marry her, build a good life together and be happy. "And if you slip once in a while homosexually, try not to feel too guilty about it."

The uniform official professional stance among clinical psychologists and psychiatrists of that time was that homosexuality was either a *character disorder* or a serious degenerative psychopathology that required years of intensive treatment, possibly with hospitalization. It had a very bad prognosis. The *disease* was self-destructive and antisocial, the patient untrustworthy. New experimental treatments such as electric shock therapy, insulin shock therapy, aversion therapy that involved self-administered electric shock to the testicles, and in really bad cases, surgical lobotomy, severing neurons in the brain's frontal lobes might offer some hope of cure. Due to its illegality, jail rather than mental hospital treatment was always a possibility. I got off lucky with my therapist's advice, very lucky.

I was living in the Alumni Director's house during the third quarter study period when that advice was given. I began to review all of the girls I knew and my feelings for them. Other students my age were beginning to marry. I liked the idea of having a home. Don and Micheline were a glamorous couple. Ironically, Wayne was having a sexual affair with a very cute freshman boy and it was not at all well hidden. They were often in the room across the hall for an entire afternoon with the door firmly closed.

Our landlady pointedly told me and not Wayne that she was going out of town for a holiday weekend and that if I would like to entertain a guest for dinner I could use the downstairs. Even the good china, silver and the wood-burning fireplace were at my disposal. "Just clean up and be careful." It was a huge vote of confidence and trust.

I invited Bobbie, one of our gang. I liked her, was sexually attracted to her and especially enjoyed her sense of humor. I made a meat loaf, a big salad and bought a bottle of wine. She would not go all the way in front of the fire after dinner as I had hoped but we did get into heavy petting and had an intimate evening together talking about what we valued in life and what kind of life we wanted in future years. Our values, aspirations and temperaments matched. We might be a really good couple. I could imagine us in an envied marriage someday.

By the end of June when the campus bookstore was to close, I had decided to officially change my major to psychology. I needed work for the summer and I had learned that I could be placed in a new job the school was opening as a ward aide in a mental hospital in suburban Milwaukee. It paid better than any job up to then, and there was low-cost staff housing and meals. I could start the first week of July. It would last until early September when I would return to campus for classes and, as usual, an alternate student would take over the job.

The green grass lawns, giant shade trees, brightly colorful flower gardens and stately white buildings looked perfect, a gracious, calming private mental hospital or sanitarium for wealthy people recovering from mental illness. My room was in a cottage of four rooms and two bathrooms for male staff just a half block from the gated entrance to the sanitarium. My window looked out on the quiet, tree-lined suburban street.

I had arrived, hitchhiking as usual, on Sunday afternoon. Aldo, a burly ward attendant with a tattoo on each hairy, muscular arm had one of the other rooms in the cottage. He took me with him to the employees' dining room for dinner. "I do days on Men's Disturbed," he told me. "Pay's not bad."

Early Monday morning I reported to Administration and was sent to the Director's office. The well-dressed, soft-spoken secretary had me wait in the very comfortable lounge area surrounding her desk while she announced me. The director's office was large, as was his desk at the far end of the thickly carpeted room. The silver-haired doctor wore a dark blue suit, conservative necktie and rimless spectacles. He motioned me to one of the two leather chairs facing his desk.

"We are very pleased to begin this affiliation with your school for the purpose of training students," he told me. "This very day we are admitting a new patient, a young priest who is quite disturbed. While you will be a general aide on the ward, I want you to spend all time available with him, study his case and write a report for me as you near the end of this work period. I'll go over it with you before you return to your campus studies." He lifted the telephone and instructed his secretary to call the ward and have an aide sent to escort me to my assignment. The interview was finished.

Aldo appeared minutes later. "You'll need a couple of white shirts, white pants and a ring of keys," he told me as we left the Administration Building. "Our ward is in that building at the far end over there but I'll take you on the path behind the buildings. That's the one you use if you have to take one of our guys to another building for an x-ray or something. Our guys never get walked out front."

Inside the door we faced another door, locked, with a third locked door, just behind it. The third door had one small thick glass window panel. "You'll get to know your keys," Aldo said. "Don't ever unlock one of these doors until you've locked the other one behind you, especially leaving. You might get jumped."

The third door opened onto a wide linoleum floored hall with men pacing or sitting. It was loud. One man paced on crutches, spitting obscenities at anyone in his sight. "Watch out for Joe-boy's crutches. He's got good aim and could deck you," Aldo said. "Hey, watch out,

Joe-boy, we're coming through. Don't mess with us. Remember what happened yesterday," he called to him.

He delivered me to the nursing station, a slender room behind another locked door and a thick glass window where a plump middle-aged woman in white nurse's cap and uniform sat writing in charts.

"I'm Mrs. Tellis," she said. "So you're the college student." She looked at me with what seemed a tired or bored, appraising eye. "What are you taking up in college?"

I told her that I was majoring in psychology. "Well that's good," she said. "We got enough guys with muscles here; maybe you can use some psychology on these patients. Aldo will show you where to get your whites. Here's your keys. Keep them clipped to your belt. We do temperature, pulse and respiration at the start of each shift. Aldo can show you tomorrow morning. Temperatures are done rectally; face down on beds in their rooms, no exceptions. Write it all down before you leave the room and hand them in here when you're done. Write at least a one line note for the chart of each patient assigned to you before you end your shift. The rest Aldo can show you. He'll take you to the room they're putting the priest in as soon as you get into your whites." She picked up her pen, lit a cigarette and faced her charts again, then turned back to look at me. "Oh, yeah, and we need you to help in the Shock Room on Monday, Wednesday and Thursday mornings from ten to one."

The ward was a dangerous place in which I was to learn important basic lessons that would serve me well throughout the years of my professional career as a psychologist. I hated the place and dreaded approaching those locked doors every morning or afternoon of the two months I worked there.

The young priest was stripped naked, wild eyed with terror, shouting and crying as two tough aides yelled at him and wrestled him into the leather ankle and wrist restraints that would tie him to the bed. "Why are you doing this to me?" he screamed. "I am not Satan. I cannot stop the voices! It's their fault!"

His words were ignored. "Shut your mouth and quiet down," Stan yelled in his ear. "You're a fucking nut." I could see that he had gotten a few scrapes and one bleeding cut in the tussle. I asked if I could stay with him for a few minutes when they were satisfied that he was secured to the bed. "Suit yourself," Stan shrugged, walking to the door, "fucking nut don't know where he is anyway."

I was not able to calm or reassure him. I did not have any real calm of my own to offer. It was years before any tranquilizers. Available tools were sleep narcotics, restraints, shock treatments, lobotomies and simple human kindness. The latter was in short supply.

I remembered Olivia de Havilland in *The Snake Pit*. It was one of the last films I had seen as an usher. Now I had fallen into a nightmare male version of the film. Patients struck out at the men in white often. The men in white retaliated often. It was a battle zone. I did not really belong in either camp, a familiar theme of my life being played out again vividly each day.

It was necessary to go out for beers with Aldo and Stan at least two or three times a week. It was necessary to drink enough to show that I could do it. "For a college guy you're okay, not a pansy like fuckin' Percy who works Women's Discharge. What the fuck were they thinkin' anyway to call a fuckin' ward 'Women's Discharge'?" Stan gasped, expelling a cloud of cigarette smoke and punching Aldo in the arm as both staggered off their bar stools, hitting one another and themselves, roaring with laughter.

Aldo had been in combat in Germany, Stan in the Pacific. Percy had been a medic in San Francisco and Japan. We four lived together in the cottage. Though I shared a bathroom with Percy, I had no conversations with him. He showered after his shift and in the morning but spent his off-duty hours elsewhere.

Mr. Jamison was admitted on the Monday of my second week on the job. I was to escort him to various admission appointments for his physical and dental exams, x-rays and shots. He was a small, soft-spoken gentleman in an expensive suit, confused. His necktie, belt, suspenders, watch and wallet had been taken from him as part of the standard procedure within his first five minutes on the ward. His trousers were a bit loose which made it necessary for him to tug them up every now and then as we walked the dirt path behind the elegant buildings. He could not remember why his watch and belt were missing so he invented a nearly reasonable reason to explain the mystery to himself and me even though I chose at first to try to remind him of what had happened on the ward to reassure him that it was normal hospital procedure.

By the third day he had made an adjustment as best he could. He had collected some squares of toilet paper and put them into the inside pocket of his jacket, taking them out and sorting through them now and then, explaining to me and anyone else who would listen that he was trying to get his papers filed but seemed to have lost track of some of them.

His daughter came to visit during the allowed hours on Sunday and I was assigned to be their escort on the grounds. Visitors could see their patient in the guarded Visitors' Lounge in the outer lobby of our building or, with permission and an attendant, amid the flower gardens and lawns in front of the buildings briefly if the patient was well behaved.

I chose to be an unintrusive shadow, nearby but not so close as to overhear conversation. At the end of the allotted time as I was returning him to the ward, his daughter said she would like to speak to me if I could step out again after taking him inside.

She was only a few years older than I, not pretty but attractive and expensively dressed. She asked me how he was doing on the ward. I told her he was no trouble at all and, smiling to share the humor, how endearing it was "the way he shuffles those papers he carries in his pocket—treating them seriously like something very important."

I saw the tears begin to well up, then spill down her cheeks. She dabbed them away quickly with a handkerchief from her purse. Instead of creating a bond with her I had created distance. "Until three weeks ago my father was not only a sweet, very intelligent man but a highly successful and important attorney in Chicago," she said.

I mumbled an apology which I knew was inadequate. Lesson learned. Inadvertently, I had permitted myself to be contaminated with the staff attitude toward *those patients*. We were the sane ones and they were the caricatures of craziness we dealt with in the kennel. I felt well shamed as I endured her look of reproach. Her father was a person. Like every other patient on the ward, he deserved no less than my full respect. I knew little or nothing of who these people had been, who they might one day be, what their usual lives in the real world had looked like and what they might be experiencing currently.

"They think it's some sort of poisoning, a metal in his blood," she said. "He's very confused but he seems to trust you. Please do what you can to help."

"I will," I promised. I meant it.

I found some time to spend with him each day, listening, explaining confusing ward happenings, trying to help him remember who he was. I began to interact with every patient differently. My repeated calm explanations to the priest of the reasons they had put him in restraints helped to calm him enough that, one by one, the two wrist restraints and the two ankle restraints were removed. He was able to feed himself and move around inside his locked room.

I learned that the large man manacled by one arm to the heavy wooden chair in a room in the rear, more hidden, section of the ward had been on the ward for five years. He masturbated for hours each day, talking incoherently to his large erect penis as it if were another being. He had been an investment banker for thirty years and was a member of a prominent Milwaukee family. His roommate, Howard, laughed at him a lot and told him to "put that damn thing away and let's get some music going for dancing." Howard had been on the back ward for ten years, had forgotten his own name and sometimes spent weeks on his bed, staring at the ceiling, not speaking to anyone or simply calling out, "I'm dead. I'm not here."

The more I tried to engage each patient in respectful conversation, the more silly and "different" I seemed to the other attendants. They pegged me as "the college kid," not much help when it came to wrestling a restless, combative patient into restraints and too likely to disapprove when an extra punch was thrown after the patient was subdued. They were guys from the street, war veterans now fighting an *us* versus *them* battle with temporarily disadvantaged upper-class adversaries, proving that they were better because they were sane, somehow balancing the scales finally in small battles of retribution.

I found Dennis locked away in the most remote isolation room at the end of the back ward, the last room before the screened porch that overlooked the back path, tree tops and a deep ravine with a small creek at its bottom. He was just a year older than I, attractive on his good days, bright, educated, articulate and sometimes very crazy.

When I worked my turns on the evening and night shifts there was a smaller staff and less to do. I got permission to unlock his room and take him out to the screened porch for a cigarette when I had time if he had not been violent that day. We talked about everything, his life before hospitalization, music, books, even current world events relayed to him by me. His pattern was to be in and out of the hospital, a few months at a time, leading two lives. Smoking cigarettes on the porch at sunset one day, he asked "Aren't you afraid I might jump right through that screen and land at the bottom of the ravine and then run away if the fall didn't kill me?"

"I hope you won't do that," I answered.

He laughed. "I'm quick. I could do it," he said. "Aren't you afraid? Aren't you afraid of me sometimes?"

"I'd feel really awful if you hurt yourself or me," I said, searching for truth, "and I guess sometimes I am afraid of what you might do."

Work in the shock treatment room occupied most of three mornings each week. Patients had to be escorted, put into hospital gowns and settled onto narrow beds on wheels. The shock ward was a wing on the opposite end of our ward, matching in size the back ward wing. There were curtained partitions and one special room with a closed door where the doctor and the small shock machine were located.

Those who were to get insulin shock came in first, got set up with their I.V. and went into coma. Those there for electric shock were wheeled into the shock room when their turn came, each securely strapped to the table and then injected with curare which made it impossible to control their muscles.

The nurse would then put a wooden stick between the patient's teeth before applying Vaseline and electrodes to their temples. The doctor checked the positioning of the electrodes, set the dials on the machine behind the patient's head and pushed the button. The electricity coursed through the patient's brain. We held the body firmly as it convulsed violently to minimize the risk of broken bones and bruising. The convulsions finished, straps, electrodes and wooden stick were removed and the patient wheeled out to a curtained cubicle to await the regaining of consciousness and the slow remembering of where and who they were.

A few times, if a patient had been a troublesome management problem on the ward or assaulted staff, the doctor pressed the button twice inducing two series of convulsions. It was jokingly referred to as a *bloodless lobotomy*, usually leaving the patient disoriented and docile. It looked to me like punishment and revenge, part of the war. When the electric shock cases were done we monitored the insulin patients who by then were coming out of their comas, also confused and wondering who they were, where they were and why.

Blaise, a very large, very powerful and very combative man was the only patient sent away for a full frontal lobotomy while I was there. He returned from surgery a week later with two Frankenstein wounds healing on his forehead and an inability to control his bodily functions. After that he sat in a large chair in the hall wearing a large diaper, no longer combative.

The last two weeks that I was there I made time for Dennis every day. We sat on the screened porch and smoked cigarettes. He said he would miss me. We agreed that we might be friends someday, after his hospitalization.

Three days before I left I looked through the small window of his room and did not see him. The room appeared to be empty though he was supposed to be in it. I unlocked the door and tugged it open. Suddenly, there he was, his face inches away, totally naked except for a towel fashioned into a turban on his head. As I registered surprise his fist met my face.

Another attendant happened to be only steps away so we were able to get Dennis back into his room. "What's going on, Dennis?" I asked. He answered with a stream of gibberish that contained no recognizable words. "What's goin' on is he's nuts," the other attendant laughed.

The next day I was on the afternoon to midnight shift. The day shift said that Dennis had calmed down but was not talking. The day nurse left an order for him to have a sedative bath, "He could use a good cleaning anyway." I volunteered. It involved taking him into the tub room, filling one of the very large tubs with water, getting him out of whatever clothes he was in, putting the clothes in a locker and him in the tub, then fastening a rubber sheet over the tub and sitting there with him for an hour, possibly setting up a screen if another patient was put into another tub.

Dennis nodded his head when I told him a tub had been ordered and that I had volunteered to do it but he was not speaking. In the tub room, with the water running I told him that since the next day would be my final shift I thought this might give us some time to talk. I opened one of the lockers that lined one wall so that he could hang his clothes or give them to me to hang.

As I turned to face him, he was lunging at me. He threw me against the lockers, eye blazing, a fury of fists finding their targets on my body, making a terrible racket against the metal lockers echoing in the empty, tiled room. The two other attendants on duty heard the noise and came running. We got Dennis back to his room and I gave myself some minor first aid.

The next and last day I was on the day shift. I went to Dennis's room and looked through the window. When he saw me he put his hands over his eyes, then turned his back to me and put his hands over his ears. I knew that if there was another blow-up he would be put in restraints with plenty of unnecessary roughness.

Another lesson learned. I remembered the end of a brief summer friendship when I was ten years old. The other boy's family was due to return to the city in a few days and were planning to go elsewhere the next summer. Neither of us had any say in the matter, no power to alter our fate. A few days before he left we had our only argument. It escalated into name calling and shoving. We turned and walked away from one another in opposite directions on the dirt road where we had been standing, both with tears in our eyes.

This was worse. Dennis had no say in the matter, no power, and it was I who seemed to be choosing to leave him. Goodbyes are difficult at best when there is a bond of affection, easily bitter and hurtful when the bond has grown strong and the need is greatest in the person being left. I had not known enough to pay due attention to Dennis's feelings and the unfair reality of our situation.

I had submitted my report on the priest to the hospital's Director as instructed. In it I included my observations and negative opinions about how he was treated. The good doctor did not have time to review my report with me.

I had written my job report too and mailed it to the school a week earlier, as requested, since it was a new job and another student might or might not be sent to replace me. It was a long report describing the Snake Pit ward and the Shock Room duties. I recommended closing the job unless it was decided that there was justifiable educational value in witnessing and participating in what seemed to me to be bad treatment of patients in a beautiful looking, expensive mental hospital. The job was closed.

The evening of that last day I had been invited for dinner to the home of an Antioch student in Milwaukee, Judy. She also had changed her major to psychology and wanted to hear about my summer. I appeared in the hot evening in a short-sleeved shirt, bruises and Band-aids visible on my face and arms. I told my stories. We laughed about how some learning is more vivid than others. She was not deterred. We became good friends, taking our psychology classes together, graduating together and nearly going to the same graduate school where she would have been two years ahead of me because of the slice of my life to be taken by the United States Army.

Chapter 9

A College Graduate

Back on campus I signed up for the required psychology classes and a three credit elective course in ceramics. My new academic advisor was the chairman of the small Psychology Department. He raised an eyebrow at my choice of the ceramics course but said he guessed it was no more useless than the mental hospital jobs. In his opinion, he told me, a future psychologist's place was in the laboratory with rats. "This is a science," he said. He was known to be a strict Behaviorist, an admirer of Pavlov and Skinner. I did not tell him that the psychology students I knew were interested in Freud and Carl Rogers, planned to become clinicians and assumed there was at least as much art as science involved in the work.

The word among the students was that *the* best psychology job at that time was at Chestnut Lodge, just outside of Washington, D.C. in Rockville, Maryland. I put in an early request for the job. They took two students each semester to work in the Recreational Therapy department and there were always another one or two who had taken a full year out from school to work there as well.

It was as different from the previous mental hospital as it could possibly be. There were no staff uniforms. Psychoanalysis was the treatment and each patient had private sessions with their psychoanalyst each week. Most of the analysts' offices were on the first floor of the main building. They were the sacred places. Each time I walked by the double doors that sealed the sanctity of the offices I wondered what secrets might be being spoken inside the rooms and what the skillful healing techniques of the psychoanalysts might look and sound like if I could see and hear them. I had not forgotten Ingrid Bergman and Gregory Peck in *Spellbound*.

The Control Analyst was the famous Frieda Fromm-Reichman who had inherited the mantle from Harry Stack Sullivan. It was Sullivan's revolutionary Theory of Interpersonal Relations that set the tone for everything that happened in every staff-patient interaction. His books were required reading. Patients were to be listened to and treated with respect always. No exceptions.

I liked the sports activities assignments least since I felt inadequate in athletics. There was more than enough drama to be found on the wards, more drama still in escorting ladies from the fourth floor's *most disturbed* ward to the Friday Tea dances and sometimes far too much drama escorting patients into Washington for a ball game, an intimate dinner in a restaurant, a tourist outing, a bike ride or a movie.

I took two ladies to the opening baseball game of the season. We watched President Truman pitch the ball onto the field and then the fun began. Miss Zenia was hebephrenic and prone to long bouts of giggles stimulated by just about anything. Mrs. Ashley was an indecisive schizophrenic who, due to the unpredictable weather, had brought along a sweater and head scarf as well as her fur coat and fashionable hat. Since she had no interest in the game, she changed back and forth frequently to squeals of delight and peels of giggles from Miss Zenia while people behind us shouted "Down in front!" each time Mrs. Ashley stood to change her outfit again.

Thoroughly bored with the spectacle on the field finally, she decided she needed to "go to the Powder Room." Miss Zenia delightedly pointed out that it was at the very top of the stands, far from our seating area and she did not care to go along, realizing the dilemma that this presented for me. Sure enough, too much time went by without Mrs. Ashley returning. I had to insist that Miss Zenia come with me to check lest I lose both of them.

Mrs. Ashley was not to be found in the Ladies' Room. I headed for the main entrance and exit, holding Miss Zenia firmly by the hand. On the way we came to the place where the Presidential limousine was parked under the stands and there was Mrs. Ashley in her sweater and hat, carrying her fur coat and scarf, chatting with a Secret Service guard, trying her best to reassure him that "the President is a lovely man who certainly wouldn't mind at all if I just rested in the car for a few moments since the seats we've been sitting on are so terribly uncomfortable." He was looking unsure facing her absolute sureness and obvious aristocratic breeding. I excused us and we left him looking even more puzzled.

Another time I took Miss Zenia and Susan White to visit Mount Vernon. We were trapped in a pack of tourists on a narrow staircase between two floors when Miss White spoke out clearly in her Vassar accent. "Well I don't think it fair at all." She shot a look at me standing one step below her with Miss Zenia one step below me. Her delusion had taken this moment between floors to blossom. Addressing the crowd in a loud clear voice she asked "Do any of you find it fair that he rapes me night after night and then sends others to rape me also? I mean really, there must be a limit to it."

Miss Zenia was, of course, convulsed in giggles and the captive tourists were unsure how to respond in such an odd situation. "Susan," I said, hoping for a calm, firm voice, "this crowd will move in a moment. You and Miss Zenia and I can cancel this outing if it isn't working for you."

"Oh, no, of course I want to see the rest of it," she answered, looking at me with condescending patience. "I mean we've come all this way, it would be a shame to cancel, don't you think? Unless, of course, you're not willing to do your job. I'm certain Miss Zenia can get through it, can't you dear? Honestly! Where *can* good help be found these days?"

We students from Antioch and a few other staff members lived in a cottage on the grounds, two to a room. We had meals in the staff dining room in the main building. There was a bridge game almost every evening in our cottage living room, snacks and beer in the refrigerator and parties with dancing most weekends. Student nurses on a three-month assignment were housed in a separate building on the other side of the grounds but came to our cottage for the parties as did staff members who lived in apartments off the grounds. It was a compatible group, dedicated in our work and always needing to blow off steam on Saturday evenings. Often we would have Sunday morning recoveries in one of their apartments with the Sunday New York Times and its crossword puzzle as we listened to recordings of Bach, ate bagels, lox and cream cheese and drank many cups of coffee.

When I returned for the second job period there in January I knew the routines and the people. I felt as comfortable as I could feel in an environment that was so unpredictable. There were no tranquilizers, and pills would have violated the basic beliefs and guiding philosophy of the hospital anyway. Going up to the *most disturbed* women's fourth floor ward was a frequent assignment but rarely routine.

I might be met at the door by the young woman whose face would be only a few inches from mine and whose lips and voice echoed my words as soon as I had unlocked the door and stepped inside. A famous ballet dancer, now nearing forty, once grabbed the pen I had carelessly left in my shirt pocket, slipped it quickly into her vagina and laughingly said, "Come and get it, Big Boy!"

Another morning a young, talented, future novelist who had seemed inappropriately calm and sane during her first weeks at the Lodge found herself on the fourth floor after an explosive coming undone the day before. She was wandering about on the ward wrapped in a sheet. As I entered, she approached me, opened her arms wide to reveal her totally naked form, wrapped the sheet around both of us and said, "Let's dance." We danced a few steps as she hummed a Cole Porter tune. I thanked her for the dance and went on to the nursing station.

It was a crazy world in which anything that did no harm was accepted and, if possible, understood with words. I might pass Jamie on the grounds, the son of a very wealthy and socially prominent family, he had a penchant for drinking anything he could find that contained alcohol as one of its ingredients. Often he was in conversation with his voices.

"Hi, Jamie. You hearing those voices again today?"

"You hear them too, Honey. Aren't they a bitch?"

I hated most to be caught on the fourth floor when Gertrude exploded. A large, powerful, bright, well educated, articulate and very unhappy woman, you could see the storm clouds gathering for minutes or sometimes hours as her face darkened before she blew. Other women on the ward were well aware of her. If the ward grew suddenly quiet it was because all eyes were on her and very heavy furniture was about to start flying as she engaged in battle with a few patients, staff that rushed onto the ward to subdue her and anyone else caught up in the frenzy.

But, always, in all situations, in the moment or later when calm had been restored and the person released from a padded isolation room or unwrapped from a calming cold sheet pack that acted as a sedative—always there was one or more of the staff to discuss what had happened and try to make sense of it. Gained information and insight were written into the patient's chart to be of possible assistance to the psychoanalyst.

My biggest surprise came on a cool Friday afternoon when I arrived on the fourth floor to escort the ladies who would be going to the tea dance in another building. There were always three or four from that floor whose current behavior made it seem that they could handle a couple of hours in a social setting with men and women from the less disturbed wards. Staff spent the tea dance hours chatting with patients who were not being otherwise included or inviting them to dance. I was the smoothest, most relaxed and accomplished dancer and I made sure to have at least one dance with each willing lady present.

As I herded my few well dressed ladies to the fourth floor porch that particular Friday, I inserted my key to call the elevator and noticed Jeanne looking at me from her usual daytime spot, sitting on the porch floor, slumped against the wall facing the elevator, twenty feet away. She had been on the ward for years, silent or mumbling and grunting to herself, eating with clumsy use of her hands, slobbering, never responding to anything said to her.

It happened quickly yet seeming in slow motion. I was dressed for the dance in a suit and tie, hand on the key inserted in the call button for the elevator, talking to Mrs. Ashley. Jeanne rose from the floor, larger than I would have expected, took a few small lumbering steps in our direction and in an amazingly limber leap landed on me with her arms around my neck and her legs around my hips, her slobbering face close to mine.

I let go of the key to give her back support, looked into her eyes and, from some blessedly trained place in me, reassuringly said, "Jeanne, I think you're trying to tell me something. Is it that you would like to go to the tea dance?"

With the charge nurse's enthusiastic permission I returned to the ward after work that evening to see Jeanne. She was willing to sit on a bench on the porch with me. I told her that I was sorry that there had not been enough time for her to get dressed up and come to the dance that day and hoped that she might get ready and come along the next Friday.

Verbal response was not possible. She grunted and made agitated sounds but it was a one way conversation. She did grab hold of my arm when I started to leave though and I was able to say, "I think you're telling me that you don't want me to leave, Jeanne. Is that true?" It elicited only a more excited, louder series of grunts and the stamping of one foot.

I promised to visit her the next day. The nurse and aides recorded small but promising signs of improvement in the days that followed. I improvised a way to communicate during my visits with lots of easy questions from me and squares I drew on a small pad next to *yes, no, maybe, don't know* and *not sure*.

Within two weeks she was up to small walks on the grounds, leaning heavily against me, arm in arm, shuffling and stepping in an ungainly fashion, hunched, learning to walk again. In three weeks she was ready to go to the Friday tea dance, not the most beautifully dressed woman there, not graceful, not conversational, unable to produce words still, shuffling across the dance floor in my arms, needing help to drink from a tea cup, cookie crumbs and spills on her blouse, but she was there.

The staff sociologist, Morrie Schwartz, got word of the phenomenon from the nursing staff and her psychoanalyst. He arranged with the Recreation Director for me to have allotted hours with Jeanne regularly and to meet with him once each week in one of those first floor rooms with double doors to talk with him and his tape recorder, reporting, recording and answering questions about our interaction and Jeanne's strange progress.

Seven years later, during my internship year, I was a member of a car pool driving between San Francisco and the Palo Alto V.A. Hospital on the Peninsula with three staff social workers. One morning one of them mentioned an interesting course she had taken at Harvard from a sociologist. As she described the case study used by the sociologist who taught the course it began to sound more than familiar. "Was it Morrie Schwartz?" I asked. It was still years before his fame in *Tuesdays with Morrie*. "That was me at Chestnut Lodge when I was a fourth year Antioch student!"

By early summer everyone, including me, was amazed that I might try to take Jeanne by train to New York City for an overnight visit to her mother's apartment. We even managed a meal on the train in each direction. The train meals in our compartment and keeping Jeanne reasonably neat and clean through them, turned out to be the greatest challenge. But once in the city, I saw her take taxis in stride and become more the lady she had once been in her mother's apartment.

The end of July was changeover time when the new alternating Antioch students arrived. I had been able to earn extra money by working some night shifts as ward aide and also by taking Jeanne on extra outings. I asked if I could stay on through the remainder of the summer and permission was granted. I needed the money for my final year. I had borrowed to the limit from the foundation and had negotiated a small loan from my brother. Though I was fairly sure of tuition reduction since I had put in a year as a first-year dorm hall advisor and had been elected to the Community Council, money for the final year was going to be a problem.

There were three new Antioch students. Two were male and I was attracted to both of them but reminded myself to keep my distance. I was doing well at school and on the job and did not want any complications. Besides, a thirty year old woman on staff, who was divorced, had her own apartment in the next town, a convertible, classical music records, lots of books and a full bar had taken a liking to me, taken me into her bed and was teaching me how to enjoy frequent, uninhibited sex. Life was good.

At the end of the first week that the new students were on the job the Saturday evening cottage party fizzled. Too many staff people had vacations or other plans. We four Antioch students and one of the student nurses who had come hoping to find the usual music and dancing sat on the small porch of the cottage looking at the bright stars in the dark sky and listening to the quiet summer night sounds of nature.

The student nurse from West Virginia said it was like sitting in a poem. Then, one after another, we surprised each other by quoting favorite sections of poems. David, handsome and Jewish with a slight New York accent, seemed to have an endless supply ranging from e. e. cummings and Ogden Nash to Swinburne and Shakespeare. He and I drew closer in spirit in the darkness, as if singing verses to one another while supposedly offering them to everyone present.

A week later, on a rainy Saturday afternoon when we were both off duty, we decided after lunch to meet in his room overlooking the softball field and read poetry aloud. I had noticed that, like me, he limited his spending as much as possible.

Arriving in his room, looking out the window at the rain soaked ball field, I told him that I had noticed that he was an excellent softball player while I was inept at best. He said that where he grew up it was what he did because the people he lived with wanted him out of the house as much as possible. He also said he would help me to learn. "It's just about practice," he said.

He sat on the floor with his back against the bed and I lay on the bed, propping myself up with his pillows. He read Dylan Thomas to me. I read from the anthology I had gotten when I worked at Scribner's.

After an hour or so he said, "Rainy day nap time," and flopped down flat on his back, beside me on the small bed. It was close quarters. I turned on my side to make room and held the book in one hand, arm resting on his athletic chest. He closed his eyes, his chest moving with slow even breathing.

I closed my book and my eyes, placing my hand on the soft texture of the thin, pale blue sweater that had pulled up when he settled on the bed revealing the tan, tight skin at his slim waist. I could feel his heart beat. Like mine, it was too fast for people supposedly resting. We were two young men on a bed together, pretending to nap, touching. It was definitely forbidden territory. Neither of us moved until we heard his roommate coming in the front door.

Janet was an Antioch student, too. She had dropped out, taking a year or two to work full time to save money. It was something I had considered doing until I learned that if I tried it I would lose my student deferment and be drafted for military service in the Korean Police Action, the euphemistic name given to the current war. Janet recently had become sexually liberated. She and I went to bed once but it caused tension in her working relationship with the thirty-year-old divorcée so we were unsure if or when we might do it again.

She invited David and me for dinner one evening at the apartment she shared with a co-worker. The four of us had lively conversation and laughs during dinner and while washing and drying the dishes. There was a sexual tension in the air, too many sexual jokes told.

Her roommate finally announced that she was going to bed because she had to get up early the next morning. Janet said that before David and I left she wanted to play a record for us, her new discovery of Max Bruch's *Violin Concerto*.

She lit a candle and turned off the living room lamps, put the long-playing record on her portable phonograph and seated us on either side of her on the small sofa. "Just close your eyes and listen," she said. "It's amazingly beautiful music."

It was, beautiful and romantic. We sat close, Janet placing one hand on David's leg and the other on mine. David and I each put an arm behind her, along the low back of the sofa. Somewhere along the way, listening to the music, I realized that I could feel the warmth of David's hand close to the back of my neck. I could also feel the warmth of his shoulder next to my hand. An almost imperceptible shift and the skin of his hand was in contact with the skin of my neck. Forbidden territory for young men again.

I moved my hand slightly until I was in contact with his skin, above the collar of his shirt. His hand moved, a finger lightly stroking the hair at the nape of my neck. I reciprocated, slowly, carefully. As the sweet, romantic music rose in volume and through to its finish we quietly caressed the hair at the back of one another's neck and head. We made no mention of it on our walk back to the Lodge, simply saying goodnight, touching one another on the shoulder when we parted.

The next day I accompanied Mrs. B. on a bicycle tour of the nearby countryside. She was a bright, well-educated, athletic, bored, disappointed and sometimes heartbreakingly sad person in her late thirties. She was also paranoid. She was the former wife of a politically ambitious young man, cast off by him and his political family dynasty when she showed signs of questioning conformity.

"It is so glorious getting out for some exercise where sunshine, trees, flowers and birds abound," she said, pausing at the top of a hill to take in the view. "You know some of the wizards say that this craziness is a matter of not having gotten enough love, some say it's due to being smothered by it and others suspect it's due to a failure to open yourself to the kind you need."

She gave me what seemed to me to be a far too knowing glance. "Some days I think it's from failing to stop yourself from knowing too much, failing to control your knowing or your willingness to know. Some days I just take a next step carelessly and there I am in the world next door, the one where all that's swept under the rug comes to life and does a mad dance around you. Then another day, another step and there you are back in the world inhabited by only what's allowed and you're congratulated on your improvement. There's a good book by that title, you know, *The World Next Door*."

I told her that I had read it and learned a lot from it.

"You just had a birthday recently, I heard. Is that right? How old might you be?"

I told her that I had just turned twenty-two.

"Good boy," she said. "Don't know too much though. It opens up that world next door. Be careful, no careless steps." She climbed back onto her bicycle and started down the hill calling over her shoulder, "But get the love you need, the love you *need*, whatever it is, that's the main thing."

The summer was near its end. David would be staying and I would return to campus. Since we were on alternating work-study divisions we easily might not see one another again. But it was clear that we had become friends and a bit more. We promised to write.

In the next to last week before I was to leave, Morrie Schwartz had news for me. Frieda Fromm-Reichman had taken a great interest in the relationship Jeanne and I had established and Jeanne's improvement. It was understood that I had some financial difficulties. I was offered the opportunity to stay on for a full year or more working with Jeanne. In addition Frieda Fromm-Reichman would take me on for my own psychoanalysis for fifteen dollars per session, a huge discount.

For an aspiring psychologist it was an offer I could not afford to refuse. In addition, remembering the hurtful departure from Dennis on the back ward in Milwaukee, I had been worrying about the impending separation from Jeanne. Morrie was sure that, under the circumstances, the school would continue to certify my student status and thereby keep the draft threat at bay. I agreed.

Telegrams and telephone calls were exchanged between the Lodge and Antioch and between the school and my draft board in New Jersey. But the draft board said no. Unless I was on campus and enrolled in classes in September, I would be called for active duty immediately.

The final goodbye with Jeanne was terrible. I explained again why I had to leave. She would not speak but she cried, holding on to my arm with the grip of a strong and desperate child. The awful lesson again, do not invite trust and dependence if you cannot promise to be with the person when he or she needs you. I later heard that after I left Jeanne regressed, going back to sitting on the floor, grunting sounds, eating hand to mouth, the only intelligible word "damn!"

Back on campus for my fifth and final year I mapped out the courses I wanted and needed for upcoming semesters. After satisfying all requirements for my degree and the psychology major there was room for a few elective courses. I wanted too many but was able to fit in an art course called Basic Design, a Nineteenth Century Novel course and a course on weaving.

I was inspired to fit that last course in by the new young instructor who was very serious about the art, craft and philosophical implications of weaving. He appeared at the first class meeting outfitted in sport jacket, slacks, necktie and coat, announcing, "I wove everything that I am wearing as well as the tapestries, tablecloths, placemats and other garments I have at home."

It may have been that weaving course that sent my academic advisor, the chairman of the psychology department, over the edge. At our conference he told me bluntly that I would never be a psychologist. "You're a dilettante. You don't have the discipline required to be a psychologist or any other kind of scientist. What do you imagine you could possibly gain from a course about Nineteenth Century novels?"

I was frightened, hurt and angry. It was too close to the scene at home during my senior year of high school when my mother angrily told me I could "just forget about college." After the scene with my academic advisor I was comforted by friends, some of whom had taken psychology courses with me, but I was shaken. The other instructor in the department, more clinically oriented, told me not to pay too much attention to it. "You'll graduate, I'm sure. Your grade average is good."

I took the elective courses I had planned and have been grateful ever since for the learning in both the weaving course and the study of nineteenth century novels. I could not find time to read all of the novels fully, of course, and my final grade of C in the course reflected that but it did not reflect my educational gain. I kept the treasured reading list ready for the future.

Wayne and Don had graduated the previous June since both had job credit for their time in the military and had gained all of the necessary academic credits during four years. Don and his wife had moved into an apartment in Georgetown. He was settled in a job at the Department of State specializing in aid to countries in Africa. It was a career path he had begun on his work-study jobs.

Wayne also had settled in at the small, private, very progressive school where he had spent two job periods as an assistant teacher. It was his idea that I apply for a new opening as assistant kindergarten teacher for the first job period that year. I did. He reported that "they're all abuzz and thrilled with the idea of a man in the kindergarten for the first time." It was a good decision.

The School was in a woodsy, cloistered, rural suburban area miles out from Philadelphia. I had excellent luck hitchhiking, leaving campus an hour after my last class on a Thursday and arriving at the school early Friday morning. Wayne lived in a tiny one-room house on the grounds. He told me where to find a bathroom and left me to his bed while he went to work.

He popped in later with half a sandwich left over from lunch and a cup of coffee to rouse me as the children were dispersing. I freshened up at his makeshift sink and bathing area, dressed and stepped outside after the children were gone.

That was when Wayne introduced me to the Director. "This is Grace."

She had white hair, blue eyes and a smile that seemed easily to take in and accept all information. She was also wearing baggy old blue jeans and carrying a bucket of garbage.

"Oh, I'm so glad to meet you," she said. "Welcome."

"You're the director?" I asked, an incredulous tone escaping before I could stop it. I was staring at her baggy jeans and the bucket of garbage.

She saw what I was seeing. "Well I think I am," she said, laughing. "But, you know, somebody always has to take out the garbage. It's a good thing to remember in life. I'm just adding this to our compost heap. Come along and see. Everyone learns from the compost."

The kindergarten teacher, like Grace, had been one of the original founders of this radical little parent-run school twenty-three years earlier. She was an elderly widow now who wore dark cotton stockings and steel-rimmed glasses, her gray hair pinned securely in a knot. She lived with her even older sister in a little cottage just up the road from the school. She appreciated every attempt and achievement of every child, my own as well.

"That was a remarkable thing to do!" she said admiringly, after I chased a persistently anti-social five-year-old across the large, grassy playing field, caught him, put him on the ground and crouched astride him to keep him there "so that we could have a talk and sort things out."

She knew everything there is to know about young children yet went through the school day, as she did through life, with a sense of appreciative wonder, made happy by signs of learning and children's smiles, truly saddened only by tears that did not contribute in any way to learning.

Grace frightened me at first. She seemed so simple yet she knew so much. She was like a Buddha. It was my first close encounter with genuine wisdom in a generous, gentle, accepting person. Her teaching seemed effortless, as natural as her breathing.

She invited Wayne and me for meals. "Well, you've got to have food now and then, until you two find a room or an apartment or something." We often showed up at her house on Saturday mornings. She would make cinnamon and brown sugar rolls and start a pot of coffee while we settled ourselves at the red-topped table in her kitchen to talk about the school, children, books, movies, memories and, not infrequently, the tangled problems Wayne and I faced in our young lives.

I did not know that I was learning it, but Grace was teaching me the basics of psychotherapy. It was second nature for her. She was awed by the learned pronouncements of psychoanalysts, psychologists and psychiatrists, yet she was the enviable healing distillation of all of their best intentions.

"Well, what is wrong," she might say, or "What is it you're trying to figure out?" She then would listen intently as I took any amount of time to get it spelled out. Only then might she sigh deeply with genuine compassion, look worried and say "Well, what in the world can you do when you're in a spot like *that*?"

Partly in response to her worried concern I would scramble for some possible answers, finally picking out whatever seemed the best one available. At that her face reflected determined strength as well as relief. "Well if that's what you've got to do, then you must do that!"

Wayne and I laughed about how it always seemed to end with Grace saying, "Then that's what you have to do," sounding almost simple-minded yet we went back for more again and again and somehow it always helped. She was witness and companion, thereby becoming a quiet guide.

Sometimes we went to Grace's for dinner and then sat by her big fireplace and read poems to one another. Her favorite was Walt Whitman's *There Was a Child Went Forth*. She had been a radical in her youth, quitting college at one time to work in a knitting factory to help organize a union there. She had kept this strange and wonderful school going against all odds and kept its amazing integrity intact. She believed in life's possibilities. Above all she believed that the world's hope resided in listening to its children.

Wayne had a good eye for furniture arranging and bargains. Drawn to rich or powerful people, he also had a strong drive to make things happen. So it did not surprise me greatly when he showed me the stone barn just over the hill from the school. It was on an estate and the owners clearly had no use for it. It was slowly turning into a ruin. "We could tear down that old pigpen over there and use that beautifully weathered wood..." The estate owners were amused at the prospect of his imagined renovation. "There's even a flushing toilet in an outhouse down the path and there's running water near the barn!" Wayne enthused.

We did it. We built a beautiful, rustic Bohemian home with the bedroom in what had been horse stalls, a kitchenette with sink, hot plate, and an improvised oven on a shelf in front of the small window. Candlelit, tablecloth-covered planks over sawhorses made a dining table on a raised floor platform that compensated for the old cement trough run-off. A wood cabinet was constructed for the portable phonograph by the glass-paned door we nailed into an opening that caught the late afternoon sun. And there was a piano. Someone did not need their old piano. Wayne needed it.

We had dinner guests often for creative and inexpensive casseroles, garlic bread and wine. My bolts of hand-woven fabric were artfully draped over gaping holes. Wayne played pieces by Ravel and Chopin that he practiced before dinner each day. People were amazed.

I drove the small school bus in the early mornings and afternoons keeping the otherwise noisy children entertained with to-be-continued stories that included them as characters. It lengthened my workday but gave me a few more dollars toward tuition bills. It also gave me a view of how story telling works in writing.

Wayne and I were very compatible as roommates in our little home. There were problems, of course. The water in the hose leading from an outdoor spigot to our improvised kitchen froze and broke the hose twice. The large, heavy-footed rats who were our neighbors in the old hayloft above our ceiling began to intrude and had to be poisoned. Only years later did I learn that most people assumed that Wayne and I were lovers at the time. I would have been shocked and embarrassed by the thought then. I only knew that I had a compatible roommate with whom I was learning how to make the kind of home I wanted.

When school let out for the Christmas and New Year's holiday I found a job at Wanamaker's, the large department store in Philadelphia. I hated it. I stood behind a table in the noisy toy department demonstrating a toy war machine called the F-84 Thunderjet. It was my job to entice children who might in turn nag parents to buy the thing. To rescue myself from the insanity of the situation I brought neatly typed copies of *The Love Song of J. Alfred Prufrock* and other favorite poems to work, taping one at a time to the back of the table where I could see it in glances until I had memorized the entire poem.

A week before Christmas the post office advertised for extra mail carriers. It meant getting up in the dark each morning and carrying a heavy leather sack as I slipped, slid, and often fell in freezing rain and snow in the suburbs, but the job lasted through New Year's Eve, the pay was good and it got me out of the frenzy of the toy department.

Back on campus for the final academic semester I spent all of my spare time on two projects, the *Senior Paper* and my *Field Thesis*. Both were required, the former being the companion end piece relating back to the first year's *Life Aims Paper* and the latter demonstrating a grasp of one's major field of study.

My problem with the first, aside from my usual bad spelling, was finding the words to illustrate how complete the change in my life had been in five years and to sort out for myself the directions in which I hoped to continue to learn and develop. In the Senior Thesis I gave myself the problem of comparing psychoanalytic ideas and theories with the ideas and theories put forward by the chairman of the Psychology Department's beloved Behaviorists. I did neither paper to my satisfaction but they more than met the requirements. To the credit of the formerly discouraging Department Chairman, he wrote me a letter a month after I completed the paper congratulating me on my effort and its quality.

I had finished all requirements, including job credits, before the start of the final job period so I was free to take any work. The barn was waiting but the school had reluctantly cut the job of assistant kindergarten teacher due to a lack of funds and was depending on parents to fill in as teacher's helpers.

Wayne pointed out that I ought to find a real job with good pay so that I could make a dent in my debts. It would make sense to look there in the Philadelphia area. I could commute to the barn. There would be no rent to pay and food costs would be minimal. It sounded right but turned out to be wrong.

There were no jobs open to me. I read the want ads every day and tried applying for anything and everything, even an assembly line floor job in a helicopter factory. The problem was my draft status. I was a college student due to be drafted immediately after graduation in June. The school did find some money to hire me as the school bus driver again. I cut the grass at Grace's house and did any other odd job I could find but ended the semester with no money, hitchhiking back to Ohio for the graduation.

Antioch College had been founded one hundred years earlier. I did not know it at that time but some of my own ancestors, including people from the indigenous Wyandot tribe had lived in the area and might have been buried in the *Indian mounds*, one just a stone's throw from where one hundred and forty-two of us graduating seniors now sat on chairs facing the steps of Antioch's Main Building.

In the five years since I had arrived there on that August morning at age eighteen, to that star-filled warm, late June evening twenty days before my twenty-third birthday, my self had changed, my life had changed completely. The naïve, raw, unsure boy had changed into a responsible young man with more than average awareness of himself and the world around him. I was ready, eager and wanting to learn more and contribute to the world.

I sat there remembering the first time I had danced with a Black girl, a fabulous dancer named Coretta Scott and the conversation with her and questioning friends in the doorway to the Tea Room about the Deep South Black Baptist minister, Martin, whom she had been dating and said was *really different*; the conversations with Rod Serling, in his fatigues and combat boots, in front of the mail boxes when he told me that he wanted to be a writer for the new field of television where you could do a lot of social good; Gus, who I'd always thought was poor, telling me one morning that he had to go back to South America to manage the family's huge plantation because his father had died; the evenings sitting with my friends by candlelight as we listened to soulful Billie Holiday, Marlene Dietrich or Dylan Thomas's *Under Milk Wood*; the girl from Arkansas, scared and outclassed like me, who had dropped out in our first year and disappeared; Joe, who was killed on an icy road hitchhiking between school and job; hundreds of visions of the world opened for me by people here in this little spot in Ohio. I had a real life to live. I knew that for sure. I was keenly aware that much of what now was possible never would have been possible had I not made it to this moment in this place.

My heart was full. I was about to be granted a college degree. I had earned it. It was an achievement that had not been easy. I had accomplished something that very few people would understand. I had changed social class membership. I had moved from being a lower-class American to being a college educated, middle-class American.

Listening to the ceremony's speakers that evening I also felt my burdens. I had only a few dollars, was deep in debt and in two or three weeks I would be forced to become a soldier, a serial number who might by chance be shipped to a killing ground in Korea to actually kill or be killed myself as a pawn in the giant chess game played by the world's rulers, a game in which I had no say.

In one of life's sour jokes I had been forced to become a *voluntary draftee*. After graduation I would be drafted into the army but the date was uncertain, perhaps as late as October or November. I had no money and, because of my draft status, could not get a job. But I could request permission to apply to be drafted immediately, thereby becoming a *voluntary* draftee. I could then be inducted early the next month, the first week of July.

I had managed to establish an identity that included a sense of my own individual worth and a sense of my responsibility to promote social justice. The only control, however, that I had over the next two years was to volunteer to be drafted or go to jail. The ceremony finished. It had happened. I held the degree in my hands. For one long moment the future and the army did not exist.

I had become someone I had not known I could ever become. I was a young man who was a college graduate.

Chapter 10

Drafted

I shipped my footlocker, left one box of clothing and books in a dormitory attic and took one suitcase. That would be enough.

My plan was to hitchhike to the other end of the state to visit Wayne and his parents for a few days and thank them for their willingness to store my footlocker for the two years. Then I would hitch rides to Washington, D.C. where Don and Micheline Brown, now a year out of Antioch, had invited me to stay with them for a week. A three day stay with Grace in Rose Valley after that and finally a three day visit with my family would take me up to the day of induction. I had to make my thirty-six dollars last until I was guaranteed food, clothing and housing in the army.

Wayne borrowed the family car and picked me up at the Texaco station, where the last ride had dropped me just five miles from their house. It was close to nine o'clock at night but his mother had saved some dinner for me in the warming oven.

Wayne's mother and father really liked me and I really liked them. His mother had learned to play Canasta two weeks earlier and wanted to teach me. We spent one long rainy afternoon at her kitchen table enjoying the game and one another. Falling asleep on the couch on their screened porch that night, I heard Wayne's father say he admired my ability to be as big or as small as any situation required. "He can light up a whole room or be so quiet that you hardly know he's there." High praise that sent me to sleep happy.

The last afternoon there Wayne asked me how I was doing. "Made survival plans for the next two years?" He had his own worries and he wanted to talk. He had been accepted in a Master's program at Harvard but was worried about money. He had a proposal.

"You'll probably end up going for some kind of graduate work when you get out in two years. How about if you send me half of your Army pay while you're in? Then I'll be finished and have a job when you get out and I can send you money for your school. We could support one another."

I told him I had to make payments on my various loans, including the loan of two hundred and fifty dollars from Grace that had made it possible for me to squeak through the final semester and graduate. "You can give a payment now and then on the loans and still have enough," he reassured me. "Everything is either free or cheap in the army. I had money in the bank when I got out."

I agreed to send him what I could. As to my own survival plans and how I was doing, I told him that, first of all, I was taking the reading list from my Nineteenth Century Novel course and planned to start with *War and Peace* as soon as I could get to a library that had a copy. I had another idea too.

"You know, like Harry Stack Sullivan figured out that the personality of the particular analyst in the therapy room had to be part of a person's analysis? The observer influences the essential nature and behavior of that which is being observed. I want to observe my own army experience and record it. So I'm going to keep a diary if I can. Maybe it will help me stay sane. And it will be my regular story telling writing practice." It was my reasoned attempt to hold on to my new self, to fight my fear of being immersed once again in the world from which I had struggled to escape. I needed to continue to grow and learn. It was the only hope.

I was an enthusiastic audience for Micheline's garlic laden cuisine in Georgetown. Don loved his new job at the State Department. Together they had made their second floor apartment chic on a limited budget. She had found a part-time sales job in a downtown shop. They were launched as a new young Washington couple.

I had most of each day to myself and concentrated on being a good houseguest, doing grocery shopping each day, keeping the apartment tidy and washing dishes. There was no need to discuss my money situation. They knew. I pretended to sleep late on the sofa each morning until they had finished with the bathroom, had their breakfast together and Don had left for his job. Then I would get up and have coffee with Micheline. She would give me a shopping list and money to pay for it and tell me what I could do to prep the evening meal.

I knew that there was to be one evening in the week when Don had to attend a meeting. By limiting my own spending to one half of a tin of sardines in mustard sauce and two slices of bread per day for my lunch I was able to treat Micheline to an evening out for pizza and wine plus a movie in an air-conditioned theater. Don pretended to be disappointed that he was not able to join us but I knew that he was pleased. I was doing something special for his wife, an extra effort to bond with her.

That week in Georgetown was a vacation for me. After doing my chores, I read, wandered the streets, browsed book stores and pretended that life could go on and on like this forever. It ended too soon.

But Grace was waiting for me, glad to see me, wonderful and wise as always. We drank coffee and ate freshly baked cinnamon rolls at her red-topped kitchen table. We read poetry to one another in the evening. We walked in the woods where she identified the birds that she looked at with joy and wonder each day.

She read the grief and fear in my face as I stood by the staircase after dinner the last evening, ready for bed, knowing I would have only the early morning with her before leaving for my parents and the army.

"They can't really take away your identity, you know," she said. "Nobody can do that. You *are* the person you've become and that's who you are. No matter who they think you are or want you to be, or what sort of uniform you're supposed to wear. No matter what, you are who you are who you are as Gertrude Stein might say."

The brother who had managed to graduate with me from Antioch was at my parents' place, friendly, jocular, ready to take me out for beer in his new car, full of military advice. He was not much changed by his own Antioch experience.

My parents had rented out their house for the summer and retreated farther west to a cheaper, small rental deeper into the woods. It was far from the ocean and I had no way to get to it. My brother and I swam in a nearby pond. Lying in the sun, drying, he said, "Women will go all the way for the uniform." He told me how he had met Norma Jean at a U.S.O. in L.A. when she was an aspiring teen actress, still living with her grandmother, not yet discovered and famous. She had snuck him into her bedroom and he had courteously left a five dollar bill under her pillow before he tiptoed out at dawn. "Get it when and where you can, Buddy," he advised. "Buy them a drink. Be nice to them and treat them like ladies. You'll get plenty."

I woke from my dream at dawn tangled in my blanket. It was the morning that I was to leave. In the dream I had been trying to walk in a marsh like the one beside the pond. My feet had been sinking into the mud and I was having a difficult time keeping my balance. There was dance music. Someone wanted me to dance. It was hot. I was wearing an overcoat and the pockets were stuffed with books. I couldn't do it. I was going to fall. My feet were sinking. I was falling. Before breakfast I wrote the dream in my diary. I wondered what other dreams would fill the pages during the next two years.

Both of my parents dressed up in their best and drove me to the Greyhound Station six miles away in Asbury Park early in the morning. My mother drove, as always. My father puffed on his pipe sitting beside her in the front seat. Standing back away from the door of the bus, wearing her hat trimmed with artificial flowers and a short veil, carrying her purse, she leaned forward and kissed me as she had when she left me at kindergarten and when they took me to the train station the day I left for college. She wore her uneasy smile. My father puffed his pipe and shook my hand, a slight smile that may have been patriotic pride deepening the lines at the corners of his eyes. Never in uniform himself, he had sent four of his five children off to wars. In the chartered bus I got a window seat and waved to them.

As the door of the bus closed and we began to move, there they stood; side by side, not touching, looking up at my window, uneasy in this public place, unsure as always. It was an exact repeat of the Belmar train station scene five years earlier. The stranger who was their son, the one who had become even more a stranger, was leaving again now, off to his military service in a war. Side by side they stood as the bus pulled away. They waved, this American Gothic couple now in 1953, another son gone, another war, this time in a place called Korea, some place far away where people had slanted eyes.

It was a quiet ride to the Processing Center at Fort Monmouth, New Jersey. There were only a few feeble attempts at camaraderie, jokes and bravado. We all knew that any assumed masks might be stripped away when we got there anyway. Humiliation was anticipated.

The drill sergeant who collected us when the bus door opened inside the gate did not disappoint. He looked angry. "Okay, you sorry shits, get this clear. You are now the property of the United States Government and for three days here your ass is mine – totally. You understand? No whining and no pissing, you sorry fucks. Form three lines and stand up straight. Your Mama's not here now. We're marching to the barracks. You'll drop your shit there and then we get uniforms and stuff. Haircuts tomorrow."

After lunch in the mess hall we spent the hot afternoon getting cursory physical examinations, shots and then taking paper and pencil tests. We spent the evening and night scrubbing the floor of the barracks on hands and knees, never quite to the Sergeant's satisfaction.

"You call this clean?" he would shout, kicking over a bucket of soapy water. "Start again." We were allowed to go to bed at midnight finally only to have the bright overhead lights snap on at 2 AM with the sound of his baton banging against the metal bunk frames. "Okay," he screamed. "Drop your cocks and grab your socks, get your sorry asses out of the sack and get busy on these floors and get them *clean* this time or you'll have your sorry asses on twenty-four hour K.P."

Three days of sleep deprivation, exhaustion, insults and exams. By the end of the three days we had learned how to wear our uniforms, how to march and how to take any form of insult without any hint of a reaction to it. Lists were published and posted. People were assigned orders for the next two months at various Basic Training destinations in the east and mid-west.

Of the hundreds being shipped out that day a few dozen of us were detained, continued in the breaking routines of this special Hell designed to last three days. We lucky few had scored high in the tests, we were told, and in combination with enough education and professional experience in our records, we had qualified for a new *S & P* program, a corps of *Scientific and Professional Personnel*. We were told that our orders had to be cut by the Adjutant General's Office in Washington on an individual basis. We could not be sent out on quotas or in groups. One or two left the base within the first week. My own orders took a full month to appear, another month of sadistic *processing*.

But finally, with relief, I was off to Fort Dix for Basic. Not many miles away, still in New Jersey but I was glad. The eight weeks there could be no worse than the insanity and exhaustion of the month of rituals designed to break individuals and make them into units.

A good example had been the dawn reveille after a twenty-four hour shift of back-breaking work in the mess hall during which, given a ten-minute break, we would lie down on the cement floor and immediately fall asleep. "You six men who just came off twenty-four hour K.P. fall out separate over here," the sergeant barked at reveille. We assumed, of course, that we would be allowed to sleep finally. "Okay, you six men, you get another twenty-four hour shift *more*. Move your asses. Report to the mess hall. Other men, at-ease!"

On the bus ride to Fort Dix I realized that the drill sergeants had known no more about this new program than we designated S & P's did. But we were seen as privileged ones, almost like officers, a new elite corps soon to be their superiors, possibly, but their *inferiors* for the time being while there in the Reception Center, targets for their own years of resentment in America's enduring social class caste system.

I did not like the combat boots and other equipment or having to carry the heavy M-16 rifle everywhere, *my piece* as we were required to call it. The games designed to break us hardly fazed me. The previous month had done as much breaking as was going to get done. There was a record-setting heat wave that sent some recruits to the hospital and actually killed a few during their training. Green fatigue jackets marching out in front of me in early morning sunshine soon grew dark green from wet perspiration and then changed to powdered white from dried body salts as we marched in the late afternoon. We were issued salt tablets to put in our cartridge belts but restricted in water intake from our canteens.

There is method in the madness of Basic Training, of course, but it is madness all the same. Individuals in military training are expendable, just as those who survive will be if they later are sent into battle, pieces on a general's chessboard. Individuals who show physical or emotional weakness are worked harder, no mercy. They grow strong or they break. The broken are discarded, shipped off to hospital repair, psychiatric wards, stockades and less than honorable discharges that will interfere with jobs, education, and personal relationships for many years. They are *collateral damage*, innocents bent, wounded, killed or forever broken by their society's war rituals.

There was a Jewish boy in another platoon in our company who got pressured every morning when we fell out for reveille. Some of it was thinly veiled anti-Semitism, some homophobic, some simply sadistic. He was ridiculed for his glasses, the way he stood at attention, they way he marched and walked and the pitch of his voice. It went on every morning and probably for the entire day as his platoon went through its training.

Just before sunrise one beautiful morning at the start of our fourth week, his drill sergeant started on him for some imagined infraction, maybe he had forgotten to button one of the buttons on his fly. He simply sat down on the dirt and cried that morning, dropping his rifle, giving up. He cried as the sergeant ordered him to stand. Five full minutes of humiliation were heaped on him as an example before he was dragged off by two M.P.s, headed for the stockade or the hospital and a probable court martial. "And let that show the rest of you wet pussies. We know which ones you are and your ass gonna' get fried."

Basic training offered a distilled view of the army. It is a container of small and huge cruelty, a rigidly enforced required code of behavior replacing any genuine morality. But then its business is to murder, maim and destroy in the false name of honor, gaining power for the current political and religious chiefs in their unending tribal wars.

I was surprised to find myself gaining muscle and weight rapidly, surprised to find biceps, triceps and a muscular chest. I had trouble with the rope climbs but I did them somehow.

I tried not to laugh and cry at the stupidity of the choreographed bayonet practice. We were told to scream and growl "Killers!" in response when the sergeant barked out "What are you?" Each was then to lunge forward, bayonet pointed at the back of the man three paces in front. The choreography was not very complicated: turn right, turn left, turn all the way around. But not all killers are dancers, not all dancers are killers; many simply cannot dance, look menacing and scream "killers" all at the same time. Some lacked the requisite talent for any of it.

I was reprimanded in front of the entire platoon when laughter took me one day. The comic stimulus was an amiable klutz from New York. Irving was overweight, sweating off his baby fat day by day. He was the imagined enemy in front of me who, when I turned forcefully to my right, as instructed, had managed a three-quarter pirouette in his combat outfit and now lunged directly toward me, dark plastic-framed glasses askew on his pudgy face, sliding down his nose, helmet nearly covering his eyes, shouting "killers" on cue but managing to put a question mark into his scream, possibly as a result of finding himself facing a lot of oncoming traffic. It was a theatrical moment of golden absurdity worth the presumed peer humiliation of the scolding and the extra latrine cleaning duty for forty-eight hours.

I found two buddies, Fred Gemm, Jr., who referred to himself as 'Mrs. Gemm's little boy who does not play well or follow orders' and John G. Gebhard III from Princeton. The sergeant called Fred 'Yo, *Lover boy*'. Since John and I were approximately the same size, both wore glasses and often stood side by side, he called either of us "You, *Glasses*, no not you *Slim*."

Fred Gemm was married and lived nearby. He found a hole in the fence the first week and often went home to sleep for some of the hours of the night, leaving his bunk rumpled, having his wife drive to the hole in the fence after lights-out and wait for him there. Amazingly he was never officially recognized as A.W.O.L., confounding the suspicious sergeant twice by saying simply, "No, Sarge, I was here, honest. Maybe I got up to take a dump."

Since rifles were stacked leaning against one another in threes in the field, forming a stable tripod, Fred, John and I sometimes managed to step backward, melting into the woods when everyone was told to step forward and line up for exercises such as learning to crawl under barbed wire or sit on the ground and listen to a teenaged corporal deliver a canned lecture on how rifles worked or why it was important to brush your teeth and to wipe yourself after defecation. "Hygiene is required, men, otherwise you can spread disease and wipe out your unit."

I was not good at throwing hand grenades. I knew it. I knew it would cause me trouble. In practicing field attacks I had to scheme to make sure that I was not the person at either end of the line because these two carried the extra grenades, throwing far ahead as we advanced, killing hidden enemies.

But, alas, on the final practice day of battle attack the lines were re-formed at the last minute and I was a grenade thrower. I tried. As we ran up the hill I got one off okay, then a second and a third, but I sensed that the fourth was going to be a disaster. It seemed to hit the last blade of grass at the top of the hill, hesitate, then leisurely begin its roll back down towards us as we advanced. It met us with perfect timing, releasing its plume of black smoke, simulating its deadly explosion.

The sergeant screamed out his order to stop our advance on the enemy hill. He was at my side, his mouth close to my ear as he screamed, "You, you fucking asshole! You just wiped out your entire God-damned platoon!"

Since they were all dead they got to retire to a shady grove of trees as a ghost audience while I lay on my stomach in the hot sun, or stood, or crouched, or ran and threw grenade after grenade for the next half hour. The sergeant was disgusted. "You throw like a fuckin' girl. You're a hopeless sorry, mother-fucker."

But full failure was never allowed. We all got medals as sharpshooters, because the rules stated that unless you were a sharpshooter you could not be sent into battle. All it took was some behind the scenes target readjustment now and then.

I did get into legitimate trouble on the rifle range. Nervous Irving was terrified. He confessed to me that, unseen by the sergeant, he had dropped his rifle in the sand. Now, he feared there might be sand inside it and that it would misfire. Since the sergeant was way down at the other end of the firing line, I helpfully crawled forward a bit and peered into the barrel of Irving's rifle. It looked clean.

Then I heard the distraught scream of the sergeant, "Are you fucking insane? You get your fuckin' head blown off that way. And that nut's got his finger on the fuckin' trigger!" He had a point. Especially since it was Irving. I got punished. I deserved it.

The final few days were filled with graduation exercises of nearly real battle conditions, war games. John, Fred and I created a subversive scheme to excuse ourselves from the chaos of the worst of it, the dreaded "full scale night combat with shit coming at you from every direction."

"Hey, it's night," Fred said. "Who can see?" We had to recruit a fourth person since we were to dig two-man foxholes. We refined our plan as we lay in the woods watching the afternoon rehearsal of foxhole digging.

That night Fred and I were one team. John and the fourth subversive were another. We dug our foxholes in the dark, lined the bottom of each with a poncho, got in and put our rifles down, then covered ourselves with the other poncho, snug and ready to ride out the night battle.

We did not know that there would be so many colorful and bright explosions around us once the action began. Our nest was discovered when a bright orange, loud explosion happened only three or four feet away. Then someone threw a tear gas canister into our hole. Next we were choking, tearing and scrambling to get our gas masks in place. Several large firecrackers were thrown directly at us.

I learned then how it happens in a real battle. My rational mind deserted me and the ancient animal brain took over. I was being attacked. I picked up my rifle and began firing its fake bullets in all directions. I wanted it all to stop. I used what I had, not thinking of what sort of harm I might do. I just wanted it all to stop and I had become, for that insane moment, an insane killer.

There it was, too clear, never to be forgotten. They had won. I had seen it, the tragic flaw that our species has dragged forward through countless thousands of years, a mixture of ready fear and greed that makes us too willing and sometimes eager to kill other creatures of any kind, including other people. Dressed up in flags of *patriotism* or codes of *honor* the primitive killer in us waits for supposed justification to strike. We have been unable to use our honed intelligence, compassion and education to subdue the seed of our social cancer. Real men fight and kill, women too.

Finally, Basic was finished. I turned in my rifle, bayonet, cartridge belt, helmet and all of the other battle gear. They were alien, evil. My association with them disgusted me. My platoon and my entire company got orders to ship out immediately, though the *Police Action* war in Korea had been halted with a cease-fire agreement. I stayed.

I was to report directly to the Major who was the Commanding Officer of the Battalion. My S&P orders had not arrived from the Adjutant General's Office. There was a complication also. It seemed that My Basic Training Company was being phased out. Its barracks were to be closed and mothballed. But I could not be actually sent elsewhere until my orders came.

Cooler weather had arrived in New Jersey. Winter was coming. I was to be allowed to keep my bed, footlocker and wall locker and would have to be responsible for keeping the furnace going. On paper I remained in the Ninth Infantry Division, but was transferred from the Thirty-fourth Battalion to the Sixty-first Tank Battalion. I celebrated this non-event by authorizing myself to move into the cadre room of the empty barracks.

I offered my typing and filing skills at the new Battalion Headquarters. Not needed. I was assigned to a corporal who would oversee me and the mothballing of the three empty barracks.

He was nineteen years old, had red hair and a bad case of acne, came from a coal mining town in Pennsylvania and was clearly uncomfortable having to take charge of this twenty-three year old college graduate who read books and had some kind of fancy special orders coming from Washington.

He was suspicious of me. Could I really be dumb enough to let the coal fire die out three times? Also, I seemed to disappear in the confusion of moving the bunks, mattresses and lockers to storage. It happened more than once, sometimes for hours, once for an entire weekend. I had learned well from Fred.

For no particular reason, many of the mattresses had been put into the cadre room in one of the other empty barracks. I made a nest there where I could recline on a stack of a dozen mattresses with a higher wall of mattresses blocking the windows and another between me and the door. He looked for me there only once. I froze when I heard his footsteps and my name called. I stopped breathing when he opened the door. But, convinced that the room held only the mattresses he could see, he closed the door and left and I returned to my reading of *Precious Bane.*

I went through the proper channels, beginning with the corporal, to ask for a weekend pass. It did not make it to the Major's desk before he left for his own weekend off post. The next try, I jumped channels. I went to the Major's secretary but it was denied because it had not gone through the corporal. The third time I got on a bus on Saturday and returned on Sunday evening, asking no one. I was A.W.O.L., but only if I got caught. I knew the M.P.s boarded only every third bus returning on Sunday evenings, checking pass and leave papers. They did not board my bus.

When I left that Saturday at noon I was beyond caring about what sort of show of stupidity and manipulation I might have to employ if I was caught or even what punishment might be heaped on me. I had been out of contact with the surrounding world for more than four months, a prisoner restricted to an army base.

The young corporal looked angry and scared when I reported for duty Monday morning. "Where the hell were you, Man? I looked everywhere. Your bed was empty and you let the goddamned fire go out *again.*"

"I was at the library and the service club," I said. "Fell asleep in the library and got locked in, too. Got drunk at the Service Club and puked my brains out and got lost wandering around the post. Got in real late but got up early with a hangover and went wandering and then to the P.X. for coffee and a donut. Didn't want to go to the Mess Hall or I'd puke again."

He looked like he was thinking. "Yeah. Whatever. You're goddamn supposed to report to me so's I know whereabouts you are. You're in big trouble. You're spending today straightening out the coal pile in front of Battalion Headquarters. You make it shine, boy, and don't tell nobody I couldn't find you all weekend. Goddamn smartass college bastards!" He sulked.

I had taken the bus to Philadelphia, then the suburban train to Grace's for fresh-baked cinnamon rolls, coffee and talk at the red-topped table in her kitchen. We read poetry, talked, visited friends, talked more and slept.

Sitting by the fire just before bedtime she said, "That's something that you had to do I guess, leaving there without permission. I hope it doesn't cause you trouble. But you had to do what you had to do."

On our morning walk in the woods she stooped and touched the moist, dark, resilient earth. "You know it takes three hundred years to make one inch of this top soil. And people are a part of it, our skin and bones."

I decided I would write one letter each day to Wayne, describing my bizarre army life. It would be part of my diary. I asked him to save them for me. He said he would.

I tried for a job at the Post Library. I had discovered that it had a music room with classical music records. There was also a typewriter anyone could use and daily newspapers. And there were books, of course. I started Faulkner's *As I Lay Dying*. The director thought it might be possible to get me assigned there since I was temporarily surplus and read books. The sergeant in charge of the Battalion Supply told me that he also thought he might be able to get me assigned there. He knew the Major's assistant.

On the day that I was to start in Supply, word came down that the eight temporarily surplus men left in the Sixty-first Tank Battalion were to be transferred immediately to the Thirty-fourth Battalion, assigned daily to work details as needed. That meant being available for any messy job no one wanted. The reassignment also, of course, meant that I had lost the indoor job at Supply.

But the C.O. decided that our squad could have weekend passes every week. That was worth something. The passes were good from noon on Saturday to Sunday evening. I could make bus trips or hitchhike to New York and Philadelphia. I also decided to ask for a dental check-up and to get new partial plates made if possible. The appointments would take me out of squad duty many days.

In another service club I found an available typewriter I could use for my letter writing project. The Information and Education Office had German language learning records that I could make use of several evenings each week. I tried writing poetry, too. I made a pest of myself at Battalion Headquarters asking if there had been any news of my orders from the Washington A.G.'s Office.

November. I had been at Fort Dix three months. There was a flu epidemic. The weather was rotten. Rain and cold everyday, mud and puddles everywhere. I faked a dental appointment one morning and walked to the P.X. in another section of the post to get warm. I treated myself to two donuts, hot coffee and the New York Times. That afternoon I was told that my orders had arrived. I could begin clearing the post the next day. I was to report to Camp Atterbury in Indiana the next week.

My second day of making appointments to get all of the necessary paper clearances the weather changed. The sun came out. I was glad to see it. I also was worried. I realized that I did not feel well and that I probably had a fever. I had not yet gotten my medical clearance. The following day it was worse. I was hot and dizzy. I slipped off the curb crossing a street and fell into the gutter.

I thought that if I could get a shot of an antibiotic it might take care of whatever was bothering me. I approached a medical corpsman after sick call was over and explained my situation. I told him that I finally had gotten my orders and was desperate to get out of Fort Dix. I begged him to give me a shot.

He was kind and clever. He said he would make a deal. "If your temperature is under a hundred I'll give you a shot. If it's over a hundred you go to the hospital. We've got a really bad flu epidemic here." The thermometer read one hundred and two.

The hospital stay was a fiasco. My fever mounted. My temperature went to a hundred and four. A kind Gray Lady volunteer asked if she could do anything. I asked for a toothbrush. I would have to buy one in the hospital P.X. she told me. But I could not get out of bed or stand and certainly could not get at my money or walk to the P.X. The next day she whispered that she had broken the rules and bought me a toothbrush with her own money. In the blur of my fever all I could do was clutch the toothbrush and cry my gratitude.

The fourth day there I managed to grab the sleeve of a white coat sweeping through the ward and croak out the words "no medicine". The doctor looked at me, checked the chart on the foot of my bed, looked at me again for some seconds and called a nurse.

There had been a chart mix-up. The soldier in the bed opposite had been sitting up, cheerfully playing cards while being treated as me. Quickly there was an I.V. pole, a needle and fluids were started. I had been getting no treatment, too weak to stand, unable to speak clearly, drifting in and out of consciousness, making my way along a path to death in an impersonal army hospital ward with rows of beds, soldiers with serial numbers, some getting well, some not.

After the hospital stay I was back at square one. The A.G.'s Office in Washington was notified that I was again available for orders. More work details, hiding out and resting in the mattress storage room when possible, letter writing, language records and books. Finally, just before Christmas my reissued orders arrived. I cleared the post and took a bus to visit both Wayne and Bobbie in New York on a three-day pass. From there I would board a train to Indiana.

Two months earlier Wayne had met a very nice woman, Nan, who was a cultured, well-educated heiress a dozen years older than he. Taking the train from Harvard most Fridays, they spent the weekends in the tasteful apartment she kept on Manhattan's expensive mid-town East Side. He thought it might lead to marriage. He wanted me to meet her. Wayne met me at the Port Authority Bus Terminal. "I don't think I told you, did I? Bobbie and Elsie are sharing an apartment a few blocks from here on Eighth Avenue."

Elsie was the thirty-year-old sexually liberated divorcee I had met three years earlier while working at Chestnut Lodge on a job assignment from Antioch. She had taken me into her convertible to visit her book and music filled Silver Spring apartment. She had also taken me into her bed regularly and increased my sexual competence. There had been only a few letters between us since then.

But now she had quit her job at the Lodge, moved to Manhattan, met Bobbie and shared an apartment with her. "They're in the same building with Charles Weidman, the modern dance guru," Wayne said. "He has an apartment and studio right above them. I met him there, a fascinating guy with tons of divine stories about Martha Graham,

Doris Humphrey and, of course, Isadora Duncan. They said you can stay at their place. No problem." It looked complicated to me.

Within the first twelve hours in New York I had drinks with Elsie, Bobbie and Charles Weidman followed by dinner with Wayne and Nan in her apartment, a long after-dinner walk with Wayne from Nan's to Elsie's and Bobbie's apartment and a plunge into deep sleep on the living room couch they had made up for me with extra bedding. They shared the bedroom. It looked like it was going to be a sexually frustrating weekend.

Until the last night it was. I was like a character in a comic bedroom farce, quick moments of seductive intimacy with both Elsie and Bobbie when the other was out of the room. Wayne was resourceful, as always, however. We had several long talks during which I told him truthfully that I really liked Nan a lot and could easily imagine them married. I also told him that the weekend was proving to me that while Elsie probably was more fun sexually, I had deeper feelings for Bobbie and could imagine myself married to her. He suggested that I propose.

Filled with enthusiasm for his mission he asked Nan to arrange "a night away" one block further east in the apartment of a friend of hers who had gone to an island in the Caribbean. Bobbie and I could stay in Nan's apartment my last night in town. He and Bobbie could see me off at Pennsylvania Station in my uniform the next morning. I would have an opportunity to propose.

Nan's apartment was filled with the perfume of fresh cut flowers. There were candles ready for lighting, a tray of bottles and glasses on a table near the fireplace and some romantic classical music albums stacked near the stereo. The cupids had been busy. It was a wonderful night but I did not propose. I wanted to be more certain.

But during the long train ride the next day I made up my mind. I wrote a draft of a letter to Bobbie, a proposal. I also wrote a long letter to Elsie, apologizing for the rude skipping out the last night and explaining my decision to marry Bobbie. I was going to grow up.

I learned when I got there that Camp Atterbury was closing down. There was confusion about exactly where I was to report. Finally, since my papers indicated that though I was a Scientific and Professional specialist I was still a medical corpsman, it was decided that I should report to the hospital. I was restricted to the base for the weekend until my assignment could be sorted out on Monday and told that I was assigned to guard duty for Sunday evening.

The large hospital was being totally shut down and mothballed. It was a big job that would take many months. The Commanding Officer needed more bodies to do the job than he could get in a requisition quota, but he had discovered a loophole. Since it was a hospital he could request additional Scientific and Professional personnel with medical corps specialties without having them counted in his quota of laborers.

There were many young soldiers with Master's degrees or better carrying the stacks of bedpans and wheeling the beds and surgical equipment down the long corridors of highly polished and freshly buffed floors. It was a good place to meet interesting people, exchange interesting ideas and engage in interesting conversations in the mess hall. It was an upside down world in which the drafted privates were better educated than the few officers who were our presumed masters, an ongoing joke that was an endless source of laughs as we privates tested the limits of the structure.

Assigned to a detail moving coat racks that first week along with a former graduate student of music history, I learned a lot about Wagner. He even sang parts of Tristan for me. But trouble came, as it often did if we were found enjoying ourselves. In our afternoon boredom each of us put a coat rack over a shoulder rifle-style. We smartly marched a long hallway calling cadence, taking turns with the lines.

> *I don't know but I've been told*
> *McCarthy's war is more than cold*
> *He sees Commies everywhere*
> *Unless you kiss his fat red rear*
>
> *Sound off,*
> *One, two,*
> *Sound off,*
> *Three, four,*
> *One, two, three, four,*
> *One, two,*
> *Three, four.*

As we rounded a corner we were confronted by the puzzled, displeased red face of a Major. "What in God's name do you men think you are doing?"

Feeling good humored and sassy, my mouth out of control, I quickly answered, "Saving the world from Communism, Sir?"

Wrong answer. His response was "How would you like a Court Martial, Soldier? You don't speak to an officer that way. I want your name and number. Where are you assigned and what are you supposed to be doing? God damned smart mouth college kids. You need some time in the stockade, all of you."

We stood at attention until he had finished his ranting and dismissed us, then looked meek and duly subdued until he was well out of sight and we took turns imitating him. It was one of the best stories in the mess hall that night.

No letters came for a week. No response came from Bobbie. Elsie's letter arrived first, a full blast telling me that I was "an unfeeling bastard." I felt guilty about rejecting her so the knife found its mark. I had been reading Antoine de Saint-Exupery's *Wind Sand and Stars*. I went to the library and got what they had by and about Walt Whitman. I was alone and needed a friend.

Bobbie's letter came the third week. She was sorry but she could not marry me. She did not know why. She did love me and respected me but she could not marry me, at least not now.

I saw every distracting movie that came to the post, got more poetry from the library and wrote to Wayne every day. I wrote to Bobbie too and said that I would be patient and that it seemed a good ingredient to add to a relationship that might one day grow into marriage.

February, my eighth month in the army, was a big month for me. I had settled in and learned my way around. I was able to get assigned as assistant to a sergeant who ran the supply room responsible for sorting and shipping things to the warehouse. There was a typewriter. I was the only person who knew how to type. I got permission to use it after hours. My letter writing went into high gear.

Weekend passes were now routine. Often I was able to get permission to leave early or return late, sometimes using a day or two of leave time. There was a central bulletin board where notices of rides wanted or offered for the price of sharing gas money were posted. When that failed, staying in uniform for hitching worked well.

Friends started writing to me often now in response to the blizzard of mail flying out from my typewriter. Wayne sent me books on loan that were not available in the library. I was enjoying Margaret Mead and the poetry of e. e. cummings. Bobbie seldom responded to my letters, excusing herself by saying that she was not a letter writer like me.

But David and I resumed our correspondence. David, the handsome Jewish young man from New York with whom I had read poetry on his bed at Chestnut Lodge and with whom there had been the forbidden intimacy of touch as we sat on Janet's sofa listening to Max Bruch's Violin Concerto. He was now in Chicago on an Antioch job, his final college year. He would be there through March and hoped that I would come and see him.

The first weekend in February I was able to get a round trip ride that would give me most of Saturday there, leaving late afternoon on Sunday to return. He was as funny, bright and handsome as I remembered. His girlfriend, Sue, was in Chicago on a job too but was working late so we would not see her until late breakfast on Sunday. David had a small one-room apartment in a rundown part of the city. We went out to an inexpensive Italian restaurant for a spaghetti and Chianti meal. The restaurant was not full so we were not hurried. We seemed to have an endless amount of talking to do. He was tired of college and glad to be near the end, unsure of whether he would be drafted, go to graduate school or "maybe become a hobo and ride the rails." He listened to my army tales and we laughed a lot as we finished the bottle of Chianti.

We took a walk and bought a small bottle of scotch for a nightcap. The nightcap took another hour of talk, laughs, trading poetry snips, recollections of experiences at the Lodge as we emptied the bottle of Scotch. We were both tired and needed to go to sleep.

David stripped in the cold air and plunged into his double bed, pulling the covers up to his chin. I stripped down to underwear and socks, flopped down on the worn studio couch with the pillow and thin blanket he had put there before we went to dinner, then got up and got my overcoat and put that on too. I was happy if chilly. David and I were friends. He was a wonderful friend. I was lucky.

Then his voice in the cold dark air, "You can bring your pillow and come on over here if you want to, it's warmer." I did. It was warmer.

I lay there quiet, aware of his warming nearness. "You're cold," he said, putting an arm across my chest as he turned on his side and cuddled close to me. I dared to touch his arm affectionately, turning my face toward him to speak. His face was there, close. We kissed quietly, then more forcefully as we let hands, arms and legs find one another in mounting passion. There was not much sleep.

The door buzzer woke us. It was Sue. We scrambled into our underwear. He buzzed her into the building, opened the door a crack to tell her we had overslept and would be ready in a minute. She waited in the hall for the few minutes it took to pull on cloths, splash water in our faces and run a wet comb through misbehaving hair.

Sue laughed when we apologized and David told her, "We got attacked by a Commie bottle of Scotch we got at the People's Proletariat Cheap Booze Store and oye, we need aspirin."

We had breakfast in a student hangout where both Sue and David saw a few friends. We talked about her job, David's job, my army experiences and the sorry state of U. S. politics. It did not have the easy flow of David's and my talk the evening before. She kissed him before she went to the ladies' room at the end of the meal.

Seizing the moment alone with him, I said, "David, about last night…"

"Man, I've got a headache. We need to find some aspirin."

My stomach tightened. He had looked away from me. He was not going to talk about it. "Here comes Sue," he said. "Let's get out of here and get some air."

"First time in Chicago?" Sue asked. "We have to show you some sights before you leave."

When it was time for me to leave, Sue kissed me and David shook my hand. "Don't let them send you to Korea," he said. "Tell them it's Paris or the deal's off."

On the long drive back to camp I could smell him on my skin. There had been no time for a shower. I was full of emotion, hiding it as best I could from the other three in the car. I was short on sleep and did mention both that and the hangover which were, of course, honorable topics. The others assumed there was a girl but the frustration, confusion, longing, surprise, hope and fear had to be kept out of view. I wanted to talk about it with David. And I wanted to touch him and feel his touch again.

A new kind of love had opened in me. I wrote to David the next evening, tearing up the first two attempts. I told him that I thought that what had happened had brought us closer in our friendship, that we should not be ashamed of it but, of course, that I understood we would have to guard against it happening in the future.

It was my attempt to integrate what I had learned in psychotherapy, my own true feelings, all that I had ingested from reading psychoanalytic theories and what I thought he might be feeling and thinking. I told him that I hoped to come and visit again soon and that he was my excellent friend and I loved him. I told myself that I loved him and it was more true than I yet was ready to admit to myself. I told myself that it was a type of ideal deep love one male might have for another, something honorable.

He did not answer. Three days passed, then five, ten, two weeks. I had stomach cramps and headaches. I got dizzy walking. I vomited in the mess hall one evening and came very close to fainting. I went to sick call and was told I must have a bug that was going around.

After two weeks of waiting I poured it all out, the sex part slightly censored, in a letter to Wayne. I noticed that the long daily letters that I sent to him also looked like love letters sent from one man to another. In a long and painful analysis I had to admit that with Wayne it actually was that ideal of one male friend being unafraid to admit and speak his love to his intimate friend, regardless of gender. But it was different with David. It was all that I felt in my friendship with Wayne and more, much more. I lay in bed at night calling up the now heartbreaking memories of David kissing me, David's naked body next to mine, the tenderness and strength in his touch, his physical responsiveness, the smell of him and the sound of his voice.

At the same time it spurred thoughts of marriage to Bobbie. David seemed to be choosing to disappear. It hurt in every way and that seemed proof that it was a wrong path. I had to get back onto a healthy, respectable path. There was shame. In all I sent half a dozen letters to him, each shorter with more time between them, pleading finally for any word just to let me know that he was alive and well. Silence.

I visited the few friends still on campus at Antioch. I visited Wayne's parents and watched the Army-McCarthy drama on television there. I went to movies on the post. I endured the army reminders that I was only a soldier at the mercy of any higher-ranking person, sober or drunk, manipulative, competitive or just plain stupid. And I wrote my long letters to Wayne, integrating ideas from reading and musings on philosophical questions. I was marking time, waiting.

I read The Man With the Golden Arm, Chicago slums, depressing, no one wins and that led to a decision to concentrate on the question of whether or not to try to go to graduate school and, if so, where and how to pay for it. Do something worthwhile. Try. I would make my life respectable.

A renegade plan also found its way in to my daydreams. What if I just said to hell with it all and went to Europe when I got out of the army, hitchhiked around there for a year and tried to learn to be a real writer. Maybe Wayne would be able to repay the money I was lending him and maybe he would go too. Maybe I would live there forever and be a real writer like Somerset Maugham.

Someone half a dozen beds from where I slept mentioned that he was driving into Indianapolis on the weekend to go to the Symphony. I asked if I could get a ride with him. Deal. It was a Beethoven and Brahms evening. I got a cheap military admission and a great seat. Sitting alone in the darkened hall my eyes moistened. Finally a few tears found their way down my face. I was able to get lost in the music. I became the music. All that I wanted to do was to continue to live in such music.

At the end of that evening I sensed that, somehow, I really had become the person I had once hoped that I might be someday. I had found my way to books and music. I liked me. I was happy. I had found a home in myself. I was me.

On Monday my orders came. I was to leave in ten days to report to the U. S. Army Hospital in Camp Crowder, Missouri, eight miles short of the southwest corner of the state, right in the middle of nowhere. Several guys at Atterbury had come from that post. They said that there was absolutely nothing there except the hospital, a large Disciplinary

Barracks and a small Headquarters Company. It was a prison in more ways than one. I could expect guard duty, physical training once a week, a road march once a week, no promotions and no jobs with any amount of respect attached to them. "You'll be following prisoners around with a rifle in your hand," one of a group recently arrived from there told me. "It's a ghost town. No decent movies and no radio station. Most guys are there about two months before they're reassigned but a few get dumped there permanently."

I was in deep despair for a day and then decided to grow up, do what I could about it, make the best of a bad situation and find ways to use the time well. I would write to my two Senators and complain that, ironically, my Scientific and Professional classification seemed to be getting in the way of my being used well. I would also ask permission to write to Fifth Army Headquarters asking that the same complaint be forwarded to the A.G.'s Office in Washington. I requested four days of leave time so that I could have a small vacation en route in St. Louis, staying at the Y, maybe catching a symphony performance or two.

Chapter 11

The Army

I t was raining in St. Louis, a very dreary day when I awoke there on Friday morning. I impulsively decided to check out of the Y.M.C.A. and catch the next train south, saving my leave days for better weather. Reporting in to the new base on the weekend would give me time to look around.

As usual, no one knew what to do with me when I reported in, so, based on my specialty number, I was assigned to the hospital. Half of the hospital had been closed down. A great surprise, however, was that we lowly privates, corporals and sergeants in the hospital were housed in surplus Bachelor Officers Quarters, which meant we each had a small private room with a door that could be closed. I was told it was considered a very posh assignment compared with being assigned to the Disciplinary Barracks at the other end of the post. I wanted to stay. But my fate would not be known until I was processed officially on Monday.

The hospital had been a large one, a labyrinth of buildings connected by interior corridors. Everyone I met seemed friendly, a bunch of intelligent, educated draftees, most doing some sort of reasonably interesting work in the hospital.

As I walked the ramps and hallways with two others housed in the same quarters, heading for Sunday lunch in the Mess Hall, we passed an office marked *Professional Services*. "Yo, Lou, how short are you?" one of my guides called in to the young soldier working at a desk facing the door.

"Three more days, Man, and I'm on the train to the Bronx." Lou joined us for lunch. I learned that he enjoyed working in his office and that his boss had been too busy to look for a replacement and had left it to him to check available personnel on Monday. Why was he working on Sunday? Because he had fallen behind and did not want to leave the place in a mess. He liked his boss. The other enlisted man in the office was a lazy corporal due out in two weeks who had been going to sick call and generally goofing off.

I told him I had just arrived the day before, knew touch-typing and filing, had a college degree and hospital experience as well as office experience. I offered to spend the afternoon helping him to catch up. Nothing better to do. Deal.

"Jeez," he said, watching me at the typewriter. He was from the slower hunt and peck school. "Jeez" again for my quick grasp of some of the forms, rules and procedures. The tasks were many and varied but most were simple.

The office seemed to be a sort of public relations place that coordinated the medical staff and ran interference for them with those above and below them in the Army, as well as keeping good relations with civilians and generally overseeing treatment to make sure that patients got a fair deal in their hospitalization whether they were soldiers, nurses, prisoners or civilians.

Then there was the job Lou hated most, constantly looking up army regulations and keeping them up to date as they changed so as to keep the medical staff and the forms that they filed out of trouble. The job he found routine and most annoying was the coordination and certification of medical records as departing soldiers did their final medical clearance before discharge.

The audition worked. Three days later I processed Lou's final medical papers. I was in charge of the office for the afternoon that day and was designated to be fully in charge starting the following week when the corporal left.

"You'll need to get more help, of course," said my new boss. "I'll leave that up to you."

I liked him. He was a Lt. Colonel who occupied the office directly behind where I sat at my own desk. He was in his late forties, graying at the temples, and had been activated from the Reserves, not Regular Army. He had been a small town general practitioner, on active duty only four months longer than I. The standing and saluting when he and the other officer draftee doctors came and went was dispensed with the first day. They called me by either my first or last name but I stuck to using their rank and last name when addressing them. I knew it did not matter to them and sometimes did drop it when the door to the corridor was closed and I was in the office alone with one of them.

They were nice guys and competent, all of them, mostly young and fresh out of residency when called up. Like me, they were counting the months until they would be released. I worked hard and my stock quickly soared. With each new army directive they would pop into the office and say, "Hey, what am I supposed to do about this?" "Not worry about it," I would answer. "I'll take care of it; just sign the paper when I put it in your box." They loved it. I was happy. I had a real job.

I got Wayne to mail me a few large museum and airline posters as well as a few cheap Degas prints to use as my *pin-up girls*. I also bought paper curtains and two cheap glass vases and set about decorating both my room and office. Spring had hit and there were wildflowers in the nearby deserted fields so I kept fresh cut flowers in my room and in the office. Apparently no one had ever done that before. I got teased at first but it soon turned to admiration.

At the beginning of the third week I asked the surgeon if I might observe surgery sometime. He said, "Sure. We're got a couple this afternoon if you've got time. Just get permission from the O.R. nurse, she runs the place. She'll show you how to get into scrubs. Oh, and stand back from the table first time and sit down or leave if you feel dizzy. No fainting onto the table. That's a mess."

She okayed it and I made time, my new assistant covering the office. The surgery suite was just across the hall. Halfway through the second operation however, I got called out. The sergeant who worked in the Hospital Commander's Office was sick and I was to fill in there until he was well.

It was a very different atmosphere, definitely a stand and salute place. The Commander was a Regular Army doctor. He occupied the largest office. His Administrative Assistant, also Regular Army, was a spit and polish Lt. Colonel who affected a General MacArthur look with dark aviator sunglasses. He barked commands as he searched the hospital for infractions of army regulations and lapses in proper military discipline. He occupied the smaller of the two inner offices. It was he who capriciously ordered bizarre sudden emergency drills and call-ups of enlisted men to "clip that shoddy looking grass around the insignia by the front entrance on your hands and knees, using god-damned sharp scissors so it looks sharp the way it should."

I worked in my precious Professional Services Office in the evenings and snuck some of the work from there into the Commander's Office during the day because there was too little work there. I did not want to look idle and did not want to lose my regular job.

Near the end of the first week of this double duty, the hospital psychiatrist took me aside at lunchtime. "How about if I spring you from there for a few hours this afternoon?" He was not a real psychiatrist but fresh out of medical school he had been drafted and sent to Fort Sam Houston for the eight weeks of training that made him an army psychiatrist. I had told him about the mental hospital jobs I had held during my Antioch years and about the concentrated experiences and training in group dynamics during my five years at Antioch.

"Starting today you could sit in as kind of a co-therapist with me one afternoon a week and I'm thinking maybe we could start a therapy group. Maybe you could also administer some psychological tests."

I was more than enthusiastic. He talked to the Sergeant Major who ran the Commander's outer office who simply shrugged and said, "Yeah, why not? We're not busy."

It was great. I was being well used at last. We interviewed nine men, six of them prisoners with little or no insight or understanding as to what part they had played in ending up where they were. They talked to me more easily than to an officer doctor.

Arriving back at the Commander's Office the Sergeant Major looked pale. The Commander wanted to see me right away in his office. He wanted to know where I had been and what in the hell I thought gave me the right to bail out of the most important office in the hospital on a whim. There was more, and he did not want to hear any explanations. His vanity was wounded. He needed me to stand in front of his desk at full attention, staring straight ahead while he sat in his leather swivel chair behind the desk and berated me for a full fifteen minutes.

Fortunately the man I was replacing returned to work the following day and I returned to my sympathetic doctors, all of whom had missed me. The message from them was clear. "We need you. Keep your head down. You cover for us and we'll cover for you."

I settled in. No real friends but I had cheap movies on the post, a library that produced *Second Tree from the Corner* and *One Man's Meat*, both by E. B. White, who became my invisible but valuable companion. I also got permission to read anything that was in the hospital's medical library. I had seen psychiatric books and journals there.

By the end of April it was hot but there was a very large swimming pool within walking distance on the post. Also there were weekend barbeques and mixer dances at the Service Club to which local girls were invited provided that they wore shoes in the Club. I met an elementary school teacher who had qualified for the position because she had one year of Junior College. She did not seem to have any enthusiasm, intellectual curiosity, knowledge of current events or interest in reading but she liked to dance and said she hoped to find the right man and marry soon. This was the Ozarks, it was 1954 and her clock was ticking.

Back on the east coast Wayne had gotten himself into a soap opera involving several women. He was thinking about accepting an offer to lead a Quaker international workcamp in Germany for the summer and had two job offers for teaching in the Fall, one on Long Island and the other back in the Philadelphia area, possibly as Grace's replacement. He asked if I would continue to send some money each month. Things were tight.

I asked his parents if they would mind going into my storage in their attic and sending me some civilian summer clothes. Gracious, friendly and eager to help, as always, a box from them arrived one week after I wrote.

At the beginning of May, my eleventh month in uniform, I was asked, commanded really, to be on a panel about the H Bomb at that month's Information and Education Training for the hospital's Enlisted Personnel. The Commander of the hospital, plus the *little MacArthur* Lt. Colonel, a staff medical doctor and a nurse also would speak. The prospect made me anxious but as I said in a letter to Wayne, "What the hell, they asked for it. They want psychology but even if I start out with Freud's libido theory in a military twist I'm going to end up in the ethics involved in throwing around joy-pops that go three times higher than anticipated, burn Japanese fisherman, wipe out cities full of civilians who don't read the newspapers any more than Americans do, and manage to bring reserved Britains out of their reserve yelling *stop.*"

The Commander stayed only long enough to bless the noble efforts of the panel. There were about a hundred and fifty men in the audience, most tired and sleepy, none there by choice. I was determined to keep them awake during my twelve minutes and it worked.

In the days that followed I was surprised to receive many congratulations and thanks for giving real food for thought for a change. Most surprisingly, *little MacArthur* went out of his way to offer thanks and congratulations several times. And even more surprisingly, the Information Office suggested I do it again at Post Officers' Call. I wanted to say "how about a promotion to a first stripe at last" but I held my tongue and agreed. Weird. There was no one on the base with a lower rank than me except those prisoners who had been stripped of all rank.

Wayne tried to persuade me to take some leave and show up in New York in June. But since I had been sending him part of my paycheck each month and had a payment on my educational loan due I had to tell him it was out of the question. I was broke but secure in knowing that, however much I hated the army, I did not have to worry about meals, shelter or clothing. I even had a job I enjoyed. I went to the library and found Nietzsche and studied his writing. I also found *The Naked and the Dead*. The reading kept my interest but did not cheer me.

A lively and satisfying correspondence with Don Brown and Micheline had developed also. The State Department was about to send them to Iran for two years. Don was going to be making much more money and they were thinking of buying a house in Washington when they returned. Wayne wrote that he definitely was going to Germany for the summer. Everyone was going somewhere interesting. Their lives were moving on. I felt stranded.

More books from the library, *The Execution of Private Slovak* and John Gunther's *Death Be Not Proud*. A man at the other end of my barracks was shipping out to an overseas post and selling his belongings. I bought his old portable phonograph for fifteen dollars, joined a classical music club that gave three L.P. records free and only required me to buy four more within a year.

The weather was getting very hot. I spent free time by the swimming pool. I decided that I had to do something worthwhile. I would take the life plunge I needed to take. I would apply to a few graduate schools. Nothing ventured, nothing gained. If I was not able to get in, so be it. If I got in but washed out because of inability or too little money I at least would have gotten a bit more education and it might help me to get a better job.

I sent to the University of Kansas for the first application. I had been told by former classmates that the clinical psychology program there had a very good reputation. When the application was complete I got a weekend pass plus two days' leave and hand delivered it. Maybe being in uniform made a difference. I had worn it to help with hitchhiking and military fares on the train. The Chairman of the Psychology Department and a lead professor in the graduate Clinical Program agreed to look over my application on the spot and give me interviews. In the end they told me that while it was too early and they could not say so officially I could consider myself accepted for September one year hence, two months after my discharge.

Mid-May it was announced that there would be a Company Barbeque and Beer Bust to celebrate Memorial Day on the next Saturday afternoon. It was not an exciting prospect but it would be outdoors and the beer would be free. As I wandered past one small group, none of whom I knew, a tall, handsome young blond said, "No, really, this Senator McCarthy is a fascist maniac."

"Fuck McCarthy," I said.

"Friend!" he said, reaching out a hand to me.

An hour later he and I plus two others of like mind had joined together, gathered up some cans of beer and headed unsteadily back toward our barracks, settling down on the top of a flight of outdoor steps to stare in wonder at a six-foot long black snake which had made it up a different flight of outdoor steps and lay draped across the landing in front of the door catching the last of the sun.

One of the other two, a farm boy, announced that he didn't like black snakes any more than he liked black people and he was "gonna go get that sucka' by the tail and bang his head against the wall till he be dead."

Steve, my new blond pal, told him to let it be. "He means you no harm." The quite drunk third guy, Rully, agreed. But the farm boy went for the snake anyway.

Having thus disqualified himself from our liberal club, we other three decided to retire to my room without him for a final beer as well as a final political analysis of the world. Rully fell asleep on my bed. Steve and I sat on the floor and talked and talked. Eventually we half carried Rully back to their barracks, two over from mine. Rully's room was two down the hall from Steve's so Steve and I returned to his room for another hour of talk about his life and mine before calling it quits for the night.

We were friends. From then on we ate together whenever possible. We always had more to tell one another about our day or something we had read. Only twenty years old, he had been drafted two days after he finished Junior College. He came from a small town in Oklahoma and, like me, he somehow knew that all of the prejudice and bigotry he had grown up with was wrong. He had thought, felt and read his way free of it. Naturally he was considered an oddball in his hometown but the local girls chased him anyway because he was big and very good looking. He wanted to meet a girl with brains who looked at the world the ways he did.

Constant companions through the first weeks of June, we spent our free time at the swimming pool. We signed up to swim two full lengths of the large pool and were each awarded an *Expert Swimmer's Certificate* from the Red Cross. It was something to do.

The local girls were allowed to come to the pool on weekends and they invariably congregated around Steve. Rully was his hanger-on, never far away, a lost soul who always drank too much. Steve felt sorry for Rully, but it was Steve and I who talked and laughed at each other's jokes. We understood one another.

Steve had a car. To celebrate his birthday on the last Saturday in June, we decided to drive twenty miles to Joplin for drinks and a good meal. We had cocktails, wine with dinner and a drink after dinner. Rully came along and had a few extra beers. We tried to take a walk after dinner but Rully was too drunk. I asked Steve if he felt clear-headed enough to drive. He said he was. I confessed to feeling a little sleepy and he said, "I'm okay, doze off if you want to."

I sat in the middle of the front seat with Rully on my right, snoring, Steve and I laughing at it. Steve smiled at me. "Thanks, friend. This was a good birthday, maybe the best."

Somewhere along the way I did doze off. As I was waking I was aware of Rully's head on my right shoulder and Steve's movement to my left. My hand had been resting lightly on his leg and he was moving closer, thereby maneuvering my hand into very intimate contact. Suddenly I was awake and alert. I looked at him and he looked at me. "Hi," he said.

We put Rully in his room and quietly went to my barracks and into my room. The room next to mine on one side was empty and the man in the room on the other side was away on leave, but we were quiet. Sound carried easily in the barracks as we both knew and what we were doing was extremely dangerous.

No words but we could see one another in the light coming through my window. Temperatures in the area had been running unusually high. Even with the window fully open it was hot in the room. I closed the door carefully and we undressed, looking at one another silently, then quietly we moved onto the bed.

An hour later I went to the bathroom and checked to be certain no one was up and about. Steve then made his way out quietly, heading off to his own room in his own barracks.

At lunch the next day, Rully said, "Boy, was I drunk last night!" It broke whatever tension there might have been. Both Steve and I laughed heartily. "What?" asked Rully. "You guys must have put me to bed. Did I do anything weird? Never mind, don't tell me." More laughter.

Fourth of July was a three-day weekend. We took Rully and the farm boy along with us on a trip to Roaring River State Park in the Ozarks and rented a cabin. We bought beer and Chianti. I cooked with lots of garlic. We worked on the farm boy's prejudices with some small amount of success. He could see what we were saying but... The water was too muddy for swimming that day but we had the good Ozarks scenery.

At the end of the drive back we all had a beer together. Steve and I decided to take a walk. The other two declined. We touched as we walked, seemingly by accident at first, then more, at last returning and entering my room again silently.

There was a rumor that there was to be a large shipment of men out in the middle of July. Too many surplus at Crowder. I hoped I would not be on the list and doubted that I would be. The letters to my Senators in March had caused a small stir on the Senate Armed Services Committee one of my Senators had informed me. After paperwork going from one office to another for some weeks I was informed of the regulation I already knew. If any S. & P. rated personnel believed they were being underutilized they had the right, after ninety days in an assignment, to file a complaint stating their objections to their assignment. I now could start the paperwork merry-go-round again if I so chose.

My birthday fell on the second Saturday in July. I was given a surprise party in the Mess Hall at lunch, a first I was told by the cook who had baked the large cake and put the twenty-four candles on it. Several of the doctors stopped by for cake and ice cream and to wish me well.

Steve wanted to take me to dinner in Joplin, just the two of us. It felt like there was something unsaid between us and I debated with myself about bringing it up. "You having a good time?" he asked during dinner, his own blue eyes dancing with enjoyment as they looked into mine. "I am," he said. It was the right question and declaration at the right time. Simple.

Yes, I was having a good time. I loved being with him. His grammar was not always correct but he was good, sweet, intelligent and direct. Alone in the car on the drive back to the base we held hands when the driving permitted. He looked at me with a happy smile and said, "You're my friend."

As if by agreement we headed to my room. A couple of other people were up and about so we sat on my bed with the light on and played some of my classical music, the Brahams' Academic Festival Overture and then the Beethoven Violin Concerto.

Once the others turned in I closed my door and turned out the light. Once again we were lucky, the room on either side being vacant for the weekend. But we had to be quiet. This time I realized how easy that was for us. We were not riding any great wave of lust or passion. We were friends, doing this for and with one another because we really liked one another. I told myself that I knew it was wrong, backsliding rather than preparing myself for the marriage and family I wanted. Yet it seemed right. I knew I would have to talk it out with him when we had the opportunity.

Two days later, Monday, he was told that he would be shipping out in three days. He was to be assigned to a field hospital unit in another part of the state. I thanked whatever gods may be that this Korean Police Action seemed to have ended in a stalemate, a diplomatically brokered long-term cease-fire. I also instructed myself to be cheerful about his departure since we could do nothing about it except to reassure one another that we would write.

The last night we took a last chance on my bed though there was snoring coming through the walls on both sides. Later, in the early morning hours, we went outside and sat on some steps far from anyone's windows. I told him I needed to put some things into words. I explained that I knew that what we had been doing on my bed together was not really healthy but that we should not let it bother us too much. It was just something that happened and it did no harm to anyone else in the world. He let me talk and listened quietly.

Pulling me into nearby shadows before we parted, he held my hand to his face, looked into my eyes, smiled and said, "Friends."

Squeezing my hand before letting it go, he left swiftly and quietly. Gone.

I was grief stricken in the days that followed. It was real grief. There were a dozen times each day that I thought of something I wanted to tell him when I saw him at lunch or in the evening. Three of the doctors asked me if I was coming down with something and I said it was just the heat. The temperatures had been running between 105° and 115° in the daytime, getting down towards 90° at night. It was necessary to keep the hospital thermometers in refrigerators.

I got busy. I made friends with Anna. She worked for Special Services, director of the post Service Club. She had noticed Steve and me together there. "Your buddy shipped out, huh? That's tough to lose a good buddy." Her eyes held mine.

She was a graduate of Julliard, somewhere in her late thirties I guessed, tailored, slim, short hair, sweet smile and witty. I thought she might be a lesbian or ambivalent. The Club was empty most nights during the early and late hours. She would sit at the grand piano and play Chopin nocturnes or rip into Rachmaninoff.

"You should learn to play," she said. I confessed that I had always wanted to learn but did not even know how to read music. "I'll teach you," she said, "but you have to practice scales. Practice, practice." I said I would like to try and I did. But then she received directives saying more people had to be brought in or the Club would be closed and both she and her rolly-poly cheerful assistant would be transferred to another post.

Anna had a car so we went to town for dinner and a movie a few times. She lived in the Women's Officer's Quarters with the nurses. She and I drank beer in the Day Room there some evenings after the Club closed. It was strictly off-limits for me as an enlisted man but after the first time the Major who was the Head Nurse and the highest ranking woman on the post wandered into the room in her bathrobe to get a beer and only flashed me a cheerful smile and said, "Hi, how are you?" it felt safe. Anna and I lowered the lights, snuggled, kissed and made out a bit sometimes. All out sex seemed a real possibility but I suspected that neither of us was sure we wanted to go there.

We hatched some good event ideas to increase attendance at the Club. Anna hired me for the unfilled N.C.O. slot of paid helper in the Club on evenings and weekends. Our Talent Show Night brought people in and showcased some surprises, including a meek and mild young private who filled the enormous Club with sound when he opened his mouth and sang a Puccini aria. Who knew he had operatic training and was headed for the Met?

The regular weekend dance once a month with a live five-piece band and girls from nearby Neosho (wearing shoes) was very successful. And then came Anna's great idea for Tuesday and Thursday evenings. "You cut quite a rug. Why don't you teach these lugs how to dance so they can stop sitting on their thumbs while the music's playing or tramping all over the girls' pretty shoes?"

Very successful. The boys even chipped in a little something each lesson to give me a tip. I got very good at being able to switch back and forth, doing the girl's part with one of the guys to demonstrate the steps in slow and fast motion. The tango was funny but the best was the Charleston lesson which happened to fall on the evening of a day when most of the Disciplinary Barracks guards had endured Field Training and were wearing their fatigues and heavy combat boots.

I wrote long letters to Wayne, confessing and trying to sort out my feelings and behavior with Steve. I almost got it right, catching glimpses of the truth as I wrote. I realized that I had been blaming this *wrong* behavior on not getting married and getting on the *right* track. I caught the insight that I had been mistaking repression for progress. These erotic feelings with some men were a real part of who I was and I needed to learn to accept my true whole self. But it was a difficult insight. Maybe psychoanalysis would do it for me some day, I thought. Maybe I could accept my whole self and live in peace in a wonderful marriage with a wonderful wife and family and be respected in my work by my peers. And maybe, somehow, the *other* would go away.

Looking at my letters to Wayne I saw again how much they looked like love letters written from one man to another. Well, they were. But it was a very different love than the passionate love awakened by David and also different from the simple love with Steve. It was love but there was no sensual desire in it. Strange.

I read *The Man Who Died* by D. H. Lawrence for the second time. It comforted me somehow in my missing Steve. I loved the sensual words and images in a story of a man who learned that he could find joy in being alone. Steve and I wrote, not too often. Almost healed, I thought, as I noticed his bad grammar, but at times I missed him deeply. My friend. I began to understand that I would never ever forget him, maybe not in my whole life. Friend.

Bobbie surfaced again, sending me a long soul-searching letter saying that she wondered where she was going. Wondering, I thought, like me. Good luck to both of us. But our moment seemed to have passed.

Still sending some money to Wayne, trying to pay off my loans, wanting to go East to see my friends in early autumn and knowing I could not afford it, I began to worry, wondering if Wayne really would come through with the money to me when and if I got to graduate school. He always needed money for one thing or another. I knew he was a spender and not a saver. And what about graduate school? I had been told already that I could go to Kansas but I wanted to be in the East nearer to my friends.

Then Dr. Pressley saw me filling out an application to Boston University. "Why don't you go to Medical School? You're the kind of talent we're looking for at Emory." He was due out the same month as I and had a teaching position waiting for him there. "It's an excellent school and I'm sure we could get you a full scholarship."

"But I don't think I'm suited for it. The human body is fascinating but what really gets my interest is the human mind. You know, why are people the way they are? Why aren't we nicer to one another, easier on ourselves and happier?"

"Well, why not psychiatry, the body and the mind?"

"Maybe. I don't know. It seems like taking the long way around. I saw Dr. Van put that guy's hand back together after the accident last week. Fantastic and really dedicated art but all that time learning about the hand might be spent learning something more about the mind."

"Think about it. You could be in Med School one year from today."

Then a letter from my mother. My oldest sister "had to quit her job because of her nerves," so my father quit his job as a janitor in the nearby army camp, they were selling the little tract house they had been buying with no money down and the help of my sister's G.I. Bill and were moving to California at long last. They wanted me to get a leave and come East and help with the driving to the West Coast. They would have money from the sale of the house and could pay my way to New Jersey.

Driving them to California was not a very attractive prospect but I did have the leave time accumulated, could see my friends in New York and have a first-hand look at New York University and Boston University where I had made applications for graduate school.

My parents were innocents when it came to selling their house. I made my leave and travel arrangements twice and cancelled them twice. They had sold the house they told me, definitely, then no, not quite. They would have the money next Wednesday. No, they wouldn't. Not September but early October for sure. Yes, the money was definitely coming next Monday.

I was able to get a military fare on a night flight on the first of October. I did see Bobbie and Wayne and others, I did visit N.Y.U. but my parents were not ready to leave because the money had not come yet. Wayne's very generous sometimes-girlfriend, Nan, the heiress, lent her apartment to Bobbie and me again for my last night in New York and I was able to get a military fare on another night flight returning to Missouri.

The good news I discovered when I walked into my office the first morning back was that a promotion to Private First Class had come through at last, sixteen months into my two years. It meant a little more money. Anna increased the number of paid hours for me in the evenings at the Service Club. The work had expanded in the Professional Services Office. My Lt. Colonel boss noticed my struggle and suggested that I take on a second assistant. He was prepared to authorize and demand it.

A letter from my mother arrived. They had gotten the money, were packing up belongings and getting ready to leave. They would see me when they got to Neosho, the little town nearby. Maybe I could get more leave time and drive them from Missouri to Los Angeles.

It was not clear when they would arrive but they showed up on a Friday, at the start of the first weekend in November, staying in a tourist cabin in Neosho. They wanted to stay a few days and rest. They seemed disoriented but happy. By Sunday they had decided to push on the next morning and that they could manage the drive without me. It would help them to keep expenses down. They would write to me when they arrived in Long Beach where my mother's sister, Edna, had settled with her husband and children.

I was lonely without Steve so I made myself too busy, cramming reading into every gap that was not filled by my work or some other activity that I considered worthwhile and constructive like listening to German tapes or practicing piano scales. I read about a new graduate clinical psychology training program at Adelphi on Long Island. It was not yet accredited by the A.P.A. and that made it a risk but it offered twenty hours per week of field training to supplement and enhance the academic classroom hours. My years at Antioch had taught me the value to be found in field work. I sent in an application.

I had made one weekend trip to Kansas City to rendezvous with Sandy, a buddy from the Camp Atterbury time and Henry, a friend of his. The three of us were at different posts but it was easy to get rides to Kansas City so we decided to try to do it once a month. All three of us were interested in the Symphony, the Art Museum and any other cultural events we could find. Sharing one hotel room Saturday night would keep the cost down. I discovered Evelyn Waugh and some good laughs when Sandy recommended *Vile Bodies*. I recommended *The Well of Loneliness* to him but he found it boring. He was a liberal in politics but some facets of social justice eluded him.

As Christmas neared I volunteered to cover for the guys in two other offices who wanted to go home for the holidays and also in the Service Club so that Anna and her assistant could get some time away. I was counting the weeks until spring. I had made a good life for myself. I was satisfied, at least as satisfied as I could be in the army.

One week before Christmas I received notice that my personnel records had been reviewed in a random spot check at Fifth Army Headquarters. I would have to be moved because I had a Scientific and Professional rating and I was being underutilized in my present job. I was nearing the end of a year and a half in the army, six months remaining. I could only hope that the usual military inefficiency would now leave me where I was in the life I had carved out for myself, lonely but okay.

I got a letter from Bobbie saying that life in New York was dull and that she had been seeing a lot of Peter, a mutual friend of ours from Antioch days. In fact, she was going to drive to Mexico with him to stay in a house his parents had rented. If she wanted to shove me away this was a very good start, I thought.

The hospital emptied as people headed out for the holidays. From Christmas Day through New Years' Day there were no more than six of us taking meals in the Mess Hall. On New Years' Day I sat in my room, read and drank Scotch, missing my friends and wondering whether I had chosen to stay in order to save money or in order to prove that I was strong and different from other people.

But I made friends with Joe while the others were away. He was a loner from Appalachia. He asked me to go bowling with him and told me I had a natural hook. He was sweet, unaffected, uneducated and bright. We adopted one another. My mission was to convince him that he should use G. I. Benefits to go to college when he got out. His mission was to turn me into an athlete who exercised every day.

During January things got exciting. There was a rumor that since there was no shooting in Korea the army was instituting an early release program for draftees as a way to save money, maybe shaving as much as a month off the two years. I had to get serious about graduate school plans and find a way to support myself during the summer. I had to get ready. I had been having tonsillitis off and on for several months. I would not be able to afford medical treatment once I was discharged so I asked our E.N.T. doctor if he would take my tonsils out. He would and he did. Since I knew everyone in the hospital and had done favors for many of them I got V.I.P treatment, plenty of drugs, four days in a private room and six days convalescent leave.

My friend, Judy, from Antioch had done one year of psychology graduate school at Boston University, got married to Abe in the summer and was now living in Chicago where he was finishing Medical School and she was taking psychology courses. They invited me to stay with them during my convalescent leave and I accepted.

Judy and I had dated some in Antioch. I liked her a lot. She had heard of Adelphi also and was giving thought to transferring there the next year when Abe finished Medical School. We talked and talked and talked. I went to a couple of her classes with her.

Adelphi seemed more attractive than the other schools. My dilemma was that I had been accepted at Kansas and Judy had word from a friend that I was to be accepted at Boston. At both Boston and Kansas I could have a good paying V.A. Assistantship starting the second year and could have room and board as a dorm counselor the first year. Those jobs plus G. I. Benefits would allow me to pay my way. Since Adelphi was not yet accredited there were no V.A. Assistantships and money would be as big a headache as it had been for five years at Antioch.

Abe and I were not comfortable with one another. I noticed that he seemed to go out of his way to disagree with me about any topic. Judy and I were hoping we could be in school together. We had been writing letters to one another faithfully since Antioch. We were a good pair. We helped one another and had fun together. She mentioned almost casually the final day of my stay that she easily could have married me. I was surprised but not entirely. Maybe Bobbie had been a wrong choice. Clearly Judy would have been easier. But she was married to Abe now.

Joe was waiting impatiently for me when I returned. "Let's go bowling or how about out for a run?" He looked at me in the shower and said "We've got to get you back on those push-ups and crunches. Your muscles are disappearing."

The two of us acted as a magnet for others and a group of friends began to form, all college graduates except Joe. We were gentle but persistent with him, insisting that he start getting applications in to colleges. The rumors about early release had turned to fact. Discharge dates had not yet been posted but word had it that most of us would leave about six weeks early. That would put Joe out at the end of April.

He was scared, afraid he would not be able to make it in college, afraid he would be cutting himself off from his family and unsure of who or what he might become. He drifted into my room often to sit on the edge of my bed and talk. There was more than a little physical touching between us. Others noticed it sometimes even though there was less of it when others were around. Jokes were made that eased the tension. There was no doubt in my mind that Joe and I shared an attraction, more conscious for me than it was for him. We handled it as simple *liking*, innocent affection.

I took two weeks leave in April and went to New York. It involved a grueling two nights and one full day each way on the train, but the military fare on trains was cheap. While there Wayne and I tried to make plans for the summer.

There were too many possibilities. I put in an application for a Quaker international student work camp in Europe but I would need a full scholarship and Wayne was not sure he wanted to do a work camp two summers in a row. Nan might not be using her apartment in New York City for the summer. There was a chance of a summer job in Philadelphia. There was also a very slight chance that we might be able to use someone's cabin on an island in Maine.

My parents wanted me to spend the summer with them in California, helping to fix up the house with rental units that they and my sister had bought in Long Beach using my sister's World War II G.I. Bill again. If I had to go to school *again*, my mother said, I should do it right there in California. "If you had done what I said and gone to the Asbury Park Business College you would be done a long time ago and not have to go to college all over again," she added.

My Lt. Colonel boss got out early and unexpectedly while I was away. He very happily went home to his wife, kids and small town Midwest general practice. The Captain who replaced him was an Internist and a devout Catholic. We had endless discussions about atheism, agnosticism and faith.

We circled the questions of belief and faith. He wanted me to surrender my disbelief that was based on history's record of massive crimes against humanity committed in the names of the world's religions. I wanted him to have faith in the individual's ability to develop a personal code of morality and ethics that would do no harm.

We liked one another. He just wanted to help me to see the light. He agreed with the Emory University doctor who wanted to see me go to Medical School. I did not join a church but I did begin to consider a remote possibility that if I could earn a Ph.D. in psychology I might follow that miracle by going on to Medical School after that if it was all paid for with scholarships.

Fearing that the office would fall apart with both the Lt. Colonel and me leaving, the administration assigned another corporal to the office and a civilian employee for me to train as my replacement. They also assigned a regular army non-doctor Captain as the official administrator. It was crowded and the administrator Captain was worse than useless, conducting office inspections and silly drills to fill his time.

In my off-duty time I was reading *The Mature Mind* and *Memoirs of Hadrian* and enjoying both, carrying them to and from the office. The administrator Captain viewed me and my books with suspicion. The spring weather was beautiful so I often snuck out and went to the pool. I had gotten several of my doctors more interested in reading also as well as a dental technician who was seeing to it that every possible amount of dental work was done for me before I faced years of not being able to afford a dental visit.

Ron, one of the group of pals that had formed around Joe and me bought a brand new car that he intended to drive home to Delaware when he got out sometime in June. He invited three of us to use up remaining leave time, share the expenses and drive to Los Angeles by way of the Grand Canyon and then back from San Francisco by way of Salt Lake City and Denver. It was a perfect plan for me, allowing me to visit my family for a few days while the other three drove the coast to San Francisco, catching a commuter flight from Long Beach to San Francisco to rejoin them there.

The trip was successful. I soothed my parents' hurt feelings and managed to make school seem more sensible since I was to become a *doctor*. The price of this was to hear all of my mother's psychosomatic aches and pains, past and present.

My being away had given everyone in the office an opportunity to adjust to one another and claim their shares of the territory. I was needed only as a consultant and for moral and religion discussions with the Captain internist.

The other Captain wanted me to account for the time I was spending at the swimming pool. I made up far-fetched explanations that he did not quite believe but he was afraid that if he pushed me too far the intricately constructed house of cards in which he tried to have some importance might come crashing down around him.

May came and those of us getting out early in June rather than July were given our assigned release dates. I was due out June 4 but I asked to be released on the 14th instead so that I could catch a ride to Delaware with Ron in his new car. It would be cheap, easy and luxurious. He was eager to have the driving help.

A letter came from Judy. Abe had finished Medical School and his parents were sending them to Europe for the summer as a reward. But the bad news was that he had accepted an offer of a residency in Boston so she would not be able to go to Adelphi. Was I still thinking about Boston?

Down to the final three weeks and counting. A new guy, Potter, shipped into our unit from his Basic Training. It was only two days after seeing Joe off with the hope that he really would go to the local Junior College as he promised us. I was missing him.

Potter walked into that empty place in my heart. He was so good looking that, except for needing to shave twice a day and having masculine muscles, he might have been mistaken for a pretty girl. He moved gracefully. He had been an all-star competitive gymnast.

He liked my room and he liked me. He asked if he could go to the mess hall with me for his first meal. He wanted to know if he could buy my curtains, pictures and phonograph when I left. He also told me that he gave great backrubs. Everyone on the team had learned to give rubdowns. He showed up in my room late most evenings in his bright and tight white jockey shorts wanting to trade backrubs.

It happened so fast that it worried me. He took my breath away. He was not only beautiful to look at and to touch but he was smart, sweet, unaffected and wanting to learn more about books and music. I kept as much distance as I could. It was clear that we had a lot going on between us. No one came into my room when he was there.

I was aware that if I gave in to my feelings I could be in very big trouble. It was almost time for me to leave the Army. If we were caught it would mean the Stockade for months and a Dishonorable Discharge. There was a homosexual purge going on just then on the post. It happened periodically. This time it was officers and men not in the hospital but at the Disciplinary Barracks. I had seen the evidence on their Discharge papers when they were getting their medical clearance to leave the post.

Wayne wrote saying that he had landed a non-paying job for the summer. He had a place for us to live. We would be the summer caretakers for a fifteen room, beautifully restored, old Colonial house on a hilltop, with acres of gardens with both flowers and vegetables. It belonged to a couple who wrote gardening books and would be away all summer. It was outside of Philadelphia. He also had a tutoring job and I could get unemployment pay in Pennsylvania while watering the gardens and getting ready for graduate school.

N.Y.U. turned me down but Adelphi accepted me, offering me a job as a research assistant to a new young professor with a federal grant. It would pay almost as much as a V.A. Assistantship. I decided to turn down Boston and Kansas and take a chance on Adelphi. Everything was falling into place. It was happening. I sold the phonograph to Potter for almost nothing and gave him the curtains and posters. I went out of my way to avoid him the final few nights.

In an act of defiance and vengeance on my last day in the office I actually altered the forms of two men receiving Dishonorable Discharges for homosexual activity, changing checkmarks, replacing forms, and dropping the unchangeable, most damaging papers behind the filing cabinets in the regular Army Captain's office.

One of the two men, a former Second Lieutenant, looked at his papers when I handed them to him. "This doesn't look right," he said. "It's a medical discharge."

I shrugged my shoulders. "A lot of dumb clerks in the army," I answered. "Somebody must have made a mistake and you got lucky." The look that passed between us made me want to stand and embrace him, hold him and wish him luck. I wished that I had been able to do the same for more of these trapped men. I almost understood that this good man was not one of *them*, the supposed unhealthy inferiors. I almost understood that he was my true brother, a decent and respectable man.

As Ron and I loaded our things into his car, Potter ran out of the barracks. He shook Ron's hand first, then mine. Then he hugged me. There were tears in his eyes. Ron turned away and got into the car, pretending he had not seen the tears. "Take care," Potter said. He stood by the side of the road waving until we were out of sight. I could see him in the mirror. I had a pain in my stomach. I was deserting him.

"Hey Man, this is our day!" Ron said. "What's wrong? Missing the army already? We're free!"

"Guess it doesn't feel like I'm really free of it yet," I answered. "I wonder if I'll ever let go of these years and forget them or if the army will ever let go of me. I chose the longer term in the Inactive Reserves rather than the two years in the Active Reserves but if somebody starts shooting again, back we go."

Passing the sign that read "Leaving Missouri", Ron said, "We're on our way, Man, back to civilization and back to our own lives. What's eating you? Missing the army chow or the bullshit boy scout stuff?"

"Definitely not," I answered. "But we're not home yet and I don't know where home is, just the next stop. We're not where we were and we're not where we're going yet. I'm not who I was two years ago and I'm not who I'm going to be. Neither here nor there, inside or out."

"Always the philosopher," Ron laughed. "I know who I am again and I know what they used us for. My Master's in chemistry got me a lab tech job in this rinky-dink hospital for two years. *Mendacity!* That's the big word in that new play in New York, *Cat on a Hot Tin Roof*, by the guy who wrote *Streetcar Named Desire*. *Mendacity* – all lies. My Dad has a buddy in the Pentagon. We spent two years being part of a secret weapon, Man. That fancy S&P rating labeled us part of a living sperm bank. That's why we couldn't be stationed near cities. If the A bombs started leveling cities, they wanted us out in the Boondocks ready to start the repopulation of America. How's that for mendacity, Stud? You know what they say about being drafted and the army. Wouldn't have missed it for a million dollars and wouldn't do it again for two."

I shut my eyes and saw Potter standing by the side of the dusty road, waving as we left him there alone. Mendacity. We definitely lived in a world of lies.

Chapter 12

Graduate School

The house on the hill was a lovingly restored Colonial. It had antique glass windows, hand hewn polished plank floors, many rooms and Dutch doors that opened out onto acres of gardens that yielded vegetables for the kitchen and cut flowers for the vases in each room. All that was required of us was to tend the compost heap, water gardens and lawns each morning and evening when there was no rain and do some weeding each day. There was house cleaning, cooking and laundry also, of course. Wayne had acquired a friend's old convertible at a very friendly price to be paid off in convenient installments. He needed it to commute the thirty miles to Philadelphia and the suburbs for tutoring jobs.

As a newly released veteran I qualified for unemployment benefits for the summer. I was twenty-four years old. For the first time in more than ten years I did not have to worry about having a regular job. It was strange. I had time to myself as well as peace and quiet. I decided to spend mornings writing poetry, fiction and essays. Some portion of each afternoon would be devoted to studying German in preparation for the graduate school language requirement.

The summer was half gone before I was able to rid myself of the uneasy feeling that came with the freedom and the sense that I was trespassing in someone else's home and life. What if they returned unexpectedly and found me there cooking their vegetables in their kitchen and sleeping in one of their beds? I was like an unemployed vagrant who had broken in while they were away. They knew Wayne through mutual acquaintances but who was I? I was Wayne's friend but what else? I was not a soldier any longer, not a student, and not yet a real writer. My identity fit no standard form.

We invited our friends to flee hot New York City on the weekends and visit us at our country estate. Bobbie came, friendly, funny and unavailable. Anne, the daughter of landed gentry in Vermont and a good friend from Antioch who also had worked at Chestnut Lodge, had settled into a brownstone apartment on West Sixty-ninth Street with a woman friend from prep school days. When she came to visit us she mentioned that she had seen David in the city. She had his telephone number.

David. There had been no word from him since that wrenching parting in cold Chicago after our night in his bed. Wayne wanted to call him and invite him out for a weekend. "End the mystery," he said blithely. "What's the big deal?"

His own affair with Nan had ended but Wayne invited her for the same weekend with David. "It will all be very awkward or not awkward at all," he said. "It should be interesting, maybe amusing. We have enough bedrooms, but maybe Nan and David will have a fling. Who knows?"

I hoped that David would talk to me and tell me why he had not answered my worried pleading letters from Indiana. Wayne was right, one way or another the mystery would be resolved. I would see to it.

But the choreography of the weekend seemed to get in the way. Nan and David arrived together, having arranged to meet in New York and take the same train. They both looked good. Nan seemed radiant, happy in this sudden newfound friendship with David. He was tan and fit, witty and handsome as always. He had discovered a new favorite poet. It was hot and he spent most of the weekend wearing only short shorts. Invariably, if he and I were in the same room either Nan or Wayne would appear. Real talk seemed impossible.

Sunday afternoon I made up an excuse to go to his room when I knew he was there. He was sprawled on the bed, naked, dark hair damp and slicked back, fresh from a shower. I showed him the book that I was reading, my excuse for coming to the room. We talked about it. His pose on the bed could be interpreted as inviting. I did not touch him. He did not reach to touch me. We touched the book together, my hand on one half of it, his on the other, arms close enough that I could feel the hairs on his. We talked about the book and opportunity for resolution faded.

As we were getting into the car to take them to the train station Wayne asked David where he was living. "My brother's gone on a month long safari of some kind to Mexico and asked me to use his apartment in the wrong part of Harlem so that he won't find somebody else living in it when he gets back. Visit anytime. I'll be there a few more weeks, and then I'm heading west for grad school finally."

"Go," Wayne said when I confessed that David and I had not had our talk. "You have to go to New York anyway. Stay with David."

I did have to go to New York. The grant money had come through for the young research professor at Adelphi. The assistantship was probably mine but I had to go for an official face-to-face interview plus paperwork. I made the Adelphi arrangements and then called David and asked if I could stay at his place for the night after my day on Long Island.

"Sure. Just be prepared. You don't know my brother but I can tell you it ain't the Waldorf. He likes to live with the *real* people."

The interviews at Adelphi went well. Gordon Derner, the head of the Clinical Program was the practical dreamer who had created it. It was more clinical than most. All doctoral programs in psychology in 1955 still were weighed down with time-honored academic customs and requirements. Clinical psychology was the fledgling newcomer with two faces. It was designed to produce practitioners dedicated to increasing clinical skills in the art of healing emotional wounds and woes but also was required to have a social science *research* orientation

Gordon sat in his small office wearing a western string tie rather than a necktie. His cowboy boots, a self-conscious touch of non-conformity, were propped against the desk. He boasted often that this maverick clinical program required both course learning and real field experience with such topics as anatomy, physiology, neurology and clinical medicine. He was the oldest member of the professorial staff, "the *only* faculty member over forty," he boasted, though he was not very far over that age line himself.

He introduced me to Gerald Lesser, the good-looking faculty newcomer who was bringing in real research as well as the grant money and prestige that came with it. Like Gordon, Gerry was more comfortable on a first name basis. He and I had lunch together and spent several hours talking about his research on parent-child relationships and education.

He had a clean-cut Ivy League look, blond, dark-rimmed glasses, trim and was very articulate. He was Jewish and married to a young woman who was not. In those days of overt and covert segregation that particular fact made me like him more. He was also a political liberal.

I got the job as his primary research assistant, twenty hours per week. I confessed that I was worried about money. I had not realized that the university rule forbade doctoral candidates from taking any job that required more than twenty hours per week. I had the Korean G.I. Bill but it was far less generous than the one granted after the Second World War. It was limited to a monthly check that would not quite cover school fees and books, much less any living expenses.

"Maybe we can find other ways," Gerry said. "There are other research projects. Grad students are hired to score tests sometimes. After you pass the Qualifying Exam next year we might be able to get an evening course for you to teach. And then there's baby-sitting. Several of us have kids." I could work forty or fifty hours at low paying part-time jobs but could not take a better paying forty hours a week job. The rules and wisdom of Academia.

I found David's brother's apartment in Harlem early that evening. It was definitely in a less desirable part of the city, complete with mail boxes broken open in the entry hall and a man reeking of alcohol and urine asleep on the dirty second floor landing.

It was hot and the apartment had only two small windows. One was in a kitchen stacked with dishes, newspapers, pans and mousetraps, the other in a bedroom just large enough to hold a double bed and a broken bureau. We went out for pizza and beer.

The place was cheap, bright and loud, not right for the conversation I still hoped to have. I asked how his girlfriend, Sue, was. She was visiting her parents for the summer. Graduate schools were putting more than a thousand miles between them and her parents were relieved. "Guess they don't think a nice Jewish boy from Brooklyn would fit in at their country club."

I made a try on our walk back to the apartment. "David, I'd like to say something about that night in Chicago."

"Don't worry about it," he said quickly. "Too much scotch and vino. It was very cold out."

I wanted to say, "That's it? Just like that? That's all? Why didn't you answer my letters? I love you David." I said nothing. The topic had been dismissed.

We stripped and got onto the bed, kicking off the top sheet. It was too hot for clothing or a sheet. Sleep would be a problem. I lay in the darkness listening to police sirens and a variety of loud street sounds. David had turned onto his side, his back to me. We lay like that, quiet for a long time until one of his feet moved and touched my leg. I thought he must be asleep. But then his leg reached back farther, crossing over mine as I lay on my back. He was awake. I touched his back gently and he turned toward me.

It was another sleepless night, the dam of reserve and denial broken again. We drifted into sleep sometime before the first light of day appeared in the window. We were awakened mid-morning by a crash in the kitchen. A hungry rat was exploring.

"Gotta get going," David said. "I'm supposed to go visit cousins in Queens. I'm due there for lunch."

I asked if he might visit us in the country again before the summer ended. "Maybe," he said. His eyes avoided mine. I could see that the real answer was "no".

I wrote about it. I talked to Wayne about it. Wayne said, "Why make such a big deal of it? The boy's obviously confused." Neither of us paid attention to my own sexual confusion or his.

But David did show up again for our work house-party the last weekend before the owners returned. Most of our friends from the city came. Nan had a car and brought David, Anne, Joanie and Anne's roommate, Ava. Bobbie and several others came by train. Everyone helped with the weeding, harvesting, cleaning and cooking. From their interaction I saw that a summer friendship or more had blossomed between Nan and David. It was mutual. Wayne seemed a bit put out even though he and Nan were officially finished as lovers. "He really is some kind of a confused person," Wayne said about David. "It's annoying."

There were two people in each bedroom. I shared Wayne's room and put David in the room I had been using, with Bobbie in the second bed in that room. "Might as well make myself totally crazy," I told Wayne.

Bobbie was funny and as distant as she had been on the first visit of the summer. She seemed vague, unhappy with her job but no plans to change it or go to graduate school, just drifting.

The only moment of real tension happened while several of us were picking tomatoes. David and I had been working on the same row of plants from opposite directions and on opposite sides. Then there we were picking from the same plant. He was wearing his shorts, barefoot, squatting down to pluck a tomato that was heavy and ripe, touching the earth. His hand on it, he looked up at me. Arrested in the moment, eyes on one another's eyes, I thought I saw tears. His lips parted, about to speak.

"Hey you guys, where am I supposed to dump these things when my basket gets full?" Bobbie called to us from the next row, laughing.

"In the kitchen," David called back to her. The moment evaporated. Eyes disengaged, his unspoken words retreated to their birth place.

We had a big dinner at sunset; hamburgers, many vegetables and several jugs of wine. Joanie told us that her husband, Jim, was being shipped to Panama for his last year in the Army and wanted her to join him there, living off-post. She was having trouble deciding. The letter had come Friday. Her plan had been to continue taking graduate courses in social work, live with her parents on Long Island and work part-time in a hospital.

The wine helped us all to convince her that a year in Panama in a new culture with her new husband, helping him to get out of barracks life, was much more sane than going back home again, living with her parents for another year and missing a paid adventure. Before she left at the end of the weekend I asked her if she would check the local paper on Long Island and ask around to see if she could find a cheap studio apartment somewhere near Garden City and the school. I needed to be near public transportation and thought that with luck I could afford fifty dollars a month.

She called on Tuesday, four days before we were to surrender the house to its owners, to say that she had found "an adorable little apartment in East Meadow on a quiet street." It was two blocks from a bus line that would take me to Hempstead where I could catch a Long Island Railroad commuter train to Garden City. The station there was within walking distance of the school. The only problem was that the rent was sixty-five dollars a month.

I went to New York on Wednesday to look at the apartment and search for cheaper possibilities closer to Adelphi. The only less expensive places I could find were rented rooms, a few with limited cooking possibilities.

The apartment was really small and not conveniently located. It was on a suburban residential street, a cute dormered addition that had been built on top of a one-car garage. The door opened onto a narrow staircase that led up to a small kitchen with a window, stove, sink and an enamel-topped table with two chairs. Under the staircase was an area for storage and a small bathroom with a stall shower. From the kitchen upstairs one stepped into a small living room where there was a table, upholstered chair, a standing lamp and a day bed with a few scattered pillows. There were two small windows facing the street and one facing the house next door. The bedroom, on the other side of the kitchen wall, was just large enough for its double bed but there was a small side window and a rear window. A tiny closet in the living room over the staircase had a bar for hanging clothes and a few shelves. Every inch had been well planned. From my experience of brief residences while on Antioch jobs I could see the possibilities with some paint, a textured oil cloth cover for the kitchen table, plants, another lamp and a fabric remnant and tacks to cover the old chair.

I wanted to make it home. The English landlady was truly sorry but her husband would not permit her to come down on the rent price even though I was a graduate student who might stay as long as four or five years. She did offer, however, to change linens and clean once a week. She wanted to rent it to me and I wanted to live there. I would have to find the money somehow. We agreed. I would move in on the first day of September.

We surrendered the house on the hill the last Saturday in August. The owners arrived early in the afternoon and invited us to stay for dinner. They were appreciative of our good caretaking of their home and its gardens. There were a few items in the kitchen that were not in their accustomed places and the compost pile needed adjustment they thought, but all in all, they were glad we had enjoyed their home. We expressed gratitude for having it as our temporary home.

The dinner was careful if not formal or fun. There were no candles lit and iced tea was served rather than wine. It was strange to see them using what seemed to be our dishes with such familiarity.

We entertained them with the story of the flood that had happened halfway through the summer. A Finnish friend of Wayne's from his international work camp in Germany the previous summer had been visiting. We thought it would be interesting for him to visit Wayne's parents' in Ohio and see a different part of America. He was enthusiastic in his quiet way.

First we took him to the beach, leaving early in the morning. After lunch, we put clams in a basket in the trunk of the convertible as a treat for Wayne's parents. But it started to rain. By the time we had been on the road for an hour it was raining really hard.

At the entrance to the New Jersey Turnpike we were turned away due to flash floods. Our trip was cancelled. We drove slowly through large pools of water as we neared the house. Daylight was gone but we could see lights in other houses at the bottom of the hill. We gave no thought to the small concrete bridge that crossed above a tiny creek. It had never been more than a musical trickle of water over rocks and moss. But as we approached it we drove into water that splashed up onto the windshield. The creek had become a raging river fed by water coursing down the hill along the road and elsewhere.

The car was stalled. We could not open its doors because of the water pressure around us nor could we put the top down. We climbed out the windows into waist deep water, each of us putting a suitcase on our head, bare feet feeling our way carefully in case the bridge had washed out. The Finnish boy was laughing, delighted, assuming this sort of entertainment happened every summer. He was having his great American adventure. We debated about whether to climb the hill through the woods where there would be trees to hold. But it offered the danger of unsteady footing in the strong current. Deciding finally that the road would be safer even though the downhill current was powerful we made our way from thigh to knee high water.

Once safely in the house we discovered that the electricity had gone out but the house was dry. We lit candles, and let ourselves realize that we had been in real danger. Still in towels after drying ourselves, our Finnish guest opened his suitcase and, with beaming smile, revealed the prized gift he secretly had been taking to Wayne's parents. It was a bottle of Finnish vodka. "We must drink it. For medical reasons," he said. A joke.

We assured the owners again that there had been no damage to the property and referred to the vodka consumption as "a sip."

Wayne told how the local garage had towed the car the next day, calling him later to say "No great damage done once it gets all dried. Them clams in the trunk is real happy."

They declined our offer to wash dishes and tidy up in the kitchen. They wanted to retire early. So off we went to see Grace in Rose Valley. She poured a glass of sherry for each of us. "Tell me about your summer," she said.

There was a separate registration line for graduate students at Adelphi. A very attractive woman with long dark hair and bright red lipstick got in line just in front of me.

"Are you registering for the clinical psych program?" I asked.

"No, I'm starting the two year social work program," she said.

A definite dating possibility I thought. We were enjoying a mild mutual flirtation. I told her that I had been stuck in the Army for two years in out of the way locations and it felt great to be in New York again. She was from San Francisco and was looking forward to getting to know New York. Her name was Dottie.

As we neared the registration table a man a few years older approached. She seemed to know him. "Nick, this is Don. He's here for the psych program, too."

They were married. Before we three left the registration area we were friends. They had an apartment in Queens and a car. I was invited for dinner. "A pitcher of Manhattans first and then Dottie's tamale pie," Nick said. "We'll introduce you to California food and you can give us an orientation to New York City." Nick had a Master's degree already and would be a year ahead of me in the program.

The incoming first-year class of ten included Allen—whom I recognized from Antioch though I had not known him there. He had a physical limitation that had saved him from the army.

We were a diverse group, though mostly male, mostly New Yorkers and mostly single. We drew together for protection in what we assumed would be a challenging and competitive environment. We knew that doctoral programs in clinical psychology weeded people out along the way. Supposedly, it was possible to finish in four years but we knew that most of us would need more years to do the final dissertation research and it was certain that at least a few of us would not make it to the finish line.

Our first class on Monday was Statistics, taught by a fastidious, meticulous man who appeared cold and effeminate. I was surprised when he made reference to his wife in an example of a basic statistical concept. Looking around the conference table I guessed that this was going to be a least favorite course for all of us. It was boring and seemed to have nothing to do with the dramatic work of curing madness.

The psychological testing course was taught by Gordon Derner himself, filling in for Jack, a young professor who was recovering from hepatitis and would be along in a few weeks. We started off with the Wechsler Intelligence Scale and the Rorschach inkblot test. He had our full attention. This was the stuff we were there for, clinical tools.

Gerry, my faculty advisor and boss on the research project, filled me in on the research that we would be doing. We were funded for three years but the amount of funding for the later years was to be decided each year as we sent reports on progress. Two other students had been hired for fewer hours but I was the half-time assistant. And, he asked, would I be interested in coming to dinner on Friday to meet his wife and possibly baby-sit for them on Saturday evening? Definitely.

I had hoped that one or two of the other students might live near me and offer carpool opportunities but that was not the case. It rained that week, reminding me that snow would be coming in the winter. The bus and train drained time. That was going to be a problem.

Fortunately, Gerry lived in Hempstead so the bus was all that I needed that first Friday and Saturday. He said that he would drive me back to East Meadow when they returned on Saturday. I liked his wife, Stella, and their little girl, Julie. So I had the beginnings of a second job that permitted me to study while earning money. Gerry said he would spread the word on my baby-sitting availability to other faculty members.

My first field placement was working with a young school psychologist, Harry, who had finished his doctorate just two years earlier. He lived only a few miles from me and generously offered to pick me up and drop me off on the days I was in the schools.

Money was, as always, tight. Wayne was not yet making enough, he said, to send me any money to repay what I had sent to him while I was in the Army. But I knew how to economize on food. School was going well. I liked my snug, neat apartment. I was happy.

A problem surfaced the third week, oddly sent to me by rumor, a leak from a faculty meeting confirmed by Gerry. I had been using what I could of my left-over Army clothes, usually dressing neatly in conservative sport shirt, dress khaki pants and army dress shoes, sometimes adding a sweater or my one sport jacket. It was considered inappropriate professional attire by some faculty members. I would have to find a way to buy a cheap, conservative suit. I had two white shirts and two neckties that would do.

Gerry did stir up more baby-sitting work for me, taking Stella out more often than usual I think. Gordon and his wife, Margaret, hired me also. And although Joanie had left Long Island to join Jim in Panama, her wonderful mother hired me to do some yard work and baby sit Joanie's young brother. As always, she urged me to help myself to the always well-stocked refrigerator. I soon had enough money saved to buy a cheap, dark brown suit.

Most weeks, if I had no baby-sitting job, I joined Nick and Dottie for Friday dinner at their apartment or they came to my place where I made a meat loaf, green beans and mashed potatoes. The pitcher of

Manhattans became our ritual, permitting us to unload the week's events, talking freely, trading gossip and aspirations, and to laugh.

In October I was approached by Allen, the former Antioch student, who said his father had sent him enough money to get a better used car and wondered if I might be interested in buying the one his father wanted him to junk. It was an old Morris Minor with dimly illuminated mechanical turn signals that flipped out from the sides near the windshield. "Sort of a classic," he said, "but it stalls and doesn't go very fast."

I persuaded Wayne to come up with a hundred dollars. Allen had been truthful. The car did stall, often, usually while driving on an expressway or thruway where it generated anger from other drivers since it could not be urged to go faster than thirty miles per hour at its very best. I used side roads when possible.

In early November I saw an ad in the local newspaper and signed up with a bonded baby-sitting agency. I also found a used car dealer who took the dying Morris Minor and gave me a twelve-year-old Dodge sedan for the promise of twenty-four monthly payments at maximum interest. The good news was that I was a big hit with the wealthy customers of the agency who made reservations in advance and tipped well for the bonded young veteran who was a graduate student in clinical psychology and was able to somehow quiet and charm their otherwise unruly children by making up stories for them until he got them to bed and turned quietly to his studies. The bad news was that I had to become expert at changing patched tires on my car at two, three or four o'clock in the morning. I was making ends meet but definitely could not afford new tires.

Jack was a very glamorous addition to the faculty when he appeared and took over the psychological testing course. He was stylish, quick and interested in us students as individuals. He lived in a penthouse apartment in Manhattan's East Side, gave cocktail parties and socialized with people whose names appeared in newspapers. "New York's most eligible bachelor," Gordon called him. At his first class meeting with us he said he was fascinated with the way I phrased my thoughts. He had my attention.

In individual supervision sessions going over reports I had written after administering and interpreting batteries of psychological tests he would listen carefully to my use of recently mastered psychological jargon and then ask me to put the draft of the report aside. "Now just tell me what you think is going on with this patient, informally, in your own words."

That I could do. I was enthralled by the amount of coded information revealed in a person's responses to the tests. Jack listened to me. "That's great. That's much clearer. Say it plainly your own way, your own words. That tells the story."

Our class of ten remained friendly. We did not gossip about one another but did pass along rumors about tests, grades and faculty foibles. One at a time, I invited a few for dinner, but, except for Nick and Dottie, there did not seem to be much interest in real friendship.

I contacted Antioch friends in New York and Boston. Bobbie did not seem very interested but Anne did. She, in turn, introduced me to her own New York friends, some from Prep School days and some from jobs in New York.

One girl, Lila, was particularly interesting to me. She was fun, lively, active, had a good sense of humor and a love of theater and books. She was a year younger than me and was already an editor in a publishing house. That really impressed me. We dated. She worked in Manhattan but lived at home on Long Island, not far from East Meadow, with her sister and mother. I could not afford to take her to the theater as often as she liked to go but I took her to movies and once managed discount tickets to a Saturday matinee preview of *Bells Are Ringing* with Judy Holliday.

Someone had told me about a cheap but good French restaurant near Ninth Avenue in the Fifties. We went there later. Both of us loved Broadway shows and this one had been really good. The treasure of *our* romantic little restaurant near the theater district made it perfect. Lila was endlessly flirtatious and seemed sexually inclined. We came close several times but I suspected it was the traditional campaign in those days that would require me to have more definite future prospects and offer a ring.

Anne invited seven of us to a skiing weekend at her parents' place in northern New England. Lila and I went as did Allen whom Anne also had known at Antioch. My roommate for the weekend was Johnny, tall, athletic and very attractive to me. I had been spared the burden of attraction to any other males since the night I had spent in Harlem with David. Fortunately there was no indication that Johnny was attracted to me but he was friendly.

There was also a very sweet, soft-spoken June Allyson type girl whose name actually was June. Anne had invited two other friends, a radiology resident in a New York hospital and his wife, a nurse. I had met them once at a party at Anne's and liked them. His on-call schedule changed at the last minute, however, and they had to cancel.

Only two of us, Allen and I, did not know how to ski. Anne gave us quick lessons on how to herringbone uphill and snowplow downhill and said the rest was just a matter of dancing and falling down. She had been skiing since she was two years old. The group decided to spend Sunday morning at a nearby ski resort. We could rent skis and boots there, Anne said.

I had brought along my army combat boots and asked if she had any old skis I could borrow. "Just those antique ones on the wall," she said. "They have leather straps and they lace up around your boots." I thought they would do since I really could not afford rentals.

Anne advised Allen and me to warm up on the rope tow's small runs a few times before trying the J-bar lift that the others took right away. Allen took longer to begin to feel comfortable but then, I was the dancer.

Just before noon we assembled at the J-bar lift, deciding to go up and have lunch at the little restaurant at the top before skiing down. On the way up, I noticed that the left track people's skis had made in the snow came dangerously close to the edge of the small concrete bridges along the way but there was plenty of snowy space to the right. I reasoned that by moving the tracks to the right it would be safer for all of the skiers using the lift in the afternoon.

Edging the tracks to the right proved tougher than I had thought it would be so I decided to start a new right track altogether; then I could put my left ski in the old right track. While doing that I lost my balance. Falling, I grabbed at the J-bar, hooking it with my right arm. I was being dragged uphill on my back, my fatigue jacket sturdy against the snow and ice though. I was facing the skiers on the J-bars coming along behind me. It was not glamorous but it was better than hiking up the mountain. A man on the next J-bar repeatedly called "Are you okay?"

"Yes," I yelled back each time. "I'm fine."

This went on until I saw his face register horror. "Oh, my God," he yelled. "You're going to hit your head on the concrete! Get off! Roll to the side!"

I did. I let go and rolled quickly to the side, my army training of some use at last. The man rode by pointing down at the concrete bridge his skis were now crossing. "You missed this!"

I lay in the snow looking. It was the same as all the other bridges we had crossed. I had been aware of them and in no danger since I had been keeping my head up. Now, however, I faced the task of unlacing the antique skis, putting them over my shoulders and hiking up uneven terrain to get to the top where my friends would be waiting.

Thirty-five minutes later, fatigued, I got to the top of the lift and trudged to the restaurant. They had just finished lunch and were ready to ski down. "Maybe you should get some lunch and catch your breath," Anne said.

"No, I'll go down with you and get a bite to eat when we get back to your parents' place, before we leave." I would be able to save the food money.

Anne stayed with me for the first minutes of the run. "You're a natural," she said. "You look like a pro." Then she zoomed off on her faster skis. I was content to swoop from left to right and back, descending more slowly, enjoying the scenery.

But disaster struck. On a sharp bend in the run the tip of my right ski somehow caught in the snow bank on the left side of the run. I twisted in the air, landing face down, the ski still caught in the snow, my right leg twisted.

Seconds later June arrived. I was chewing snow, loudly swearing in pain. "Are you alright?" she asked in her sweet, soft voice. "No!" I answered. "Get the goddamned fucking ski off." My language must have shocked her, but she and the next person along managed to unlace the leather straps and free my leg.

I sat in the snow for a couple of minutes, then tried standing and then tied the ski on again and tried to ski, all the while assuring a small group of people now assembled that I was fine. I fell. I could stand but I could not ski.

Handsome, athletic Johnny was there. "You're going down with the ski patrol," he said, taking charge of the situation. "You stay here with him," he told June. "I'll get the ski patrol," and he was off, fast.

I wondered what the sled ride down between the legs of the two ski patrolmen was going to cost and whom I would ask for a loan. The good news at the bottom was that there was no charge. But they wanted me to go to a hospital for an x-ray. I declined, fearing the cost. I had to promise to get an x-ray when we got back to the city. It would be a five-hour drive. I took aspirin.

We guessed we would get there sometime around ten in the evening. Anne called her friend, the radiology resident, who said it would be no problem. He expected to be in the hospital all night.

Anne drove with June beside her. Lila chose to ride in the other car for the return to the city. I stretched out in the back seat, my leg elevated on a pillow, my head in Johnny's lap. He was as tender and concerned as any mother. I was in pain. I also felt hurt. Lila had abandoned me in a time of need. But I was grateful and comforted that Johnny was there holding me.

The x-ray was free. "No broken bones but, frankly, you'd be better off if you had broken a bone," our resident friend said. "You'll need crutches for at least six weeks but you'll be aware of the damage for months, maybe years." He refused payment and borrowed a new pair of crutches from hospital supply. "Just get them back to me when you don't need them anymore. And you definitely should see a doctor as this heals. Keep weight off of it and keep it elevated when you can."

Fortunately the car I had gotten had automatic transmission. I learned to drive with my left foot working both the accelerator and the brake. I also learned to go up and down the steps to the bathroom in my apartment sitting, one step at a time. I took aspirin.

I did not see a doctor but I did invite the resident and his wife out to dinner at the little French restaurant near the theater district. Lila was no longer available for dates. She was seeing Johnny. Anne thought she had marriage in mind. The resident and his wife insisted that I come to their place for dinner instead. I could bring the crutches. They wanted me to meet a nurse friend.

Her name was Marie and she was suffering with one of her allergies which produced both sneezes and a rash. However, she was quite attractive and, from the dinner table conversation, it seemed that she was intelligent, a reader and an extremely competent nurse. I drove her home that evening and we soon began dating.

She was often sick and the ailments usually got in the way of any seriously amorous activity. I opened the medicine cabinet in her bathroom one June evening and found it crammed full of prescription medicines with her name on them. My diagnosis was hypochondria and probably drug addiction.

Our final date was on my twenty-sixth birthday, in July. I took her out for a candle-lit dinner, hoping once more that the evening would end in our first sexual tryst. When we got back to her apartment she vomited three times. I tucked her in and left.

On the long subway ride back into Manhattan where I could change to a train that would take me to the end of the line in Queens and to my parked car, I noticed a sailor sitting opposite me. We made eye contact, serious eye contact. I was attracted, more attracted than I was to Marie. We both got off the train at Columbus Circle. He looked back over his shoulder. I followed.

He stopped. We spoke. His name was Ron. "Mine's Don."

"Ron and Don," he smiled. "We rhyme." His friendly wide smile caused dimples in his strong face.

Why was I working so hard to resist? Why would it be wrong? He was in the Coast Guard, stationed on Staten Island, he told me. I was a graduate student, taking a train to the end of the line in Queens where I would get into my old car hoping to not have a flat tire and drive to my garage apartment in the middle of Nassau County.

We were miles and lifetimes apart with an instant bond. When we separated I admitted to myself that I had more feelings of affection and longing for this young unknown man my own age than I had had for any girl I had met on a first or a tenth date. Whatever this homosexuality problem was I was strongly afflicted. I would have to cure myself somehow if I wanted to get to a decent, respectable life.

Chapter 13

Europe

I worked at every job I could find that summer and made some headway paying off old Antioch debts. Wayne was able to send a payment on the money he owed me. I visited Wayne and Grace for a couple of restful weekends and went to the Jersey shore with Wayne one weekend to visit a headmaster friend of his as well as his wife and a strange friend of the wife who slept the entire weekend, emerging from their room in her nightgown only for visits to the bathroom or the refrigerator, not seeming to notice us. "She's very tired," the headmaster's wife said.

The second year of graduate school began. Gerry was able to raise my pay on the research assistantship and I continued baby-sitting for the agency and various faculty members. I was earning money more than forty hours each week but abiding by the dean's rule of not holding any one job for more than twenty hours per week.

The big challenge of the year would be passing the Qualifying Exam. Failing it would mean leaving the program. I knew that I did not have enough time to study for it properly. My solution was to use several libraries to collect as many of the books that were on the suggested reading list as possible, stock up on groceries and cancel everything except required classes for the four days before the exam.

I stacked the books in my living room next to the chair. Except for classes, quick meals, seven hours of sleep each night and going to the bathroom, every minute of those four days was spent systematically reading the first sentence of each paragraph of each book, whether or not it was of any interest or made any sense. I did well on the exam and Gerry helped me to get an extra job teaching an evening course in educational psychology for people working on a teaching credential. I stayed two chapters ahead in the textbook and read three other textbooks on educational psychology.

Jack invited several of us to a cocktail party in his penthouse apartment. It was elegant. I felt intimidated by all of the important names. "Don't be nervous," Jack said. "Have a drink and interview people. Everyone loves to tell their story." He was right. It worked.

He invited me to a second and then a third cocktail party. I was learning. He also passed along opera tickets twice that someone had given to him and he could not use. Once it was Tebaldi and once Callas. I loved it. It also gave me conversation filler at the cocktail parties.

The third cocktail party was in honor of Anne Morrow Lindbergh. I was near the door, the party well underway when the buzzer sounded. I opened the door and welcomed a small woman, telling her that Jack was out on the terrace. "I'm a bit shy at these parties," I said, getting ready to do a cocktail party interview as I helped her out of her coat.

"Me too," she said. "I'm late because I was having my hair done. I was not the pretty one in my family and I guess it's always made me self-conscious." I introduced myself and told her that Jack was a professor at my graduate school. "I'm Anne Lindbergh," she said. "I guess I really should find him and meet people." We drifted back to one another repeatedly during the party. We were safety nets for one another, easy, like old friends.

Toward spring word was forwarded to me through Wayne that the American Friends Service Committee might have an expense-paid opening for me in one of their European International Student Work Camps. I sent back word that if there was an opening I was available. They sent an application form.

It did not make sense financially. I knew that I should stay in New York and take any and all jobs as I had done in the summer between the first and second years. But I hoped I might finish all my course work by the end of the third year and, if so, I would be starting a full year of internship and working on my dissertation research then and not have another chance to go to Europe for years.

I was accepted. There was to be a German co-leader. He had experience but was quite young and not as responsible as they might wish. The camp would have students from around the world and two official languages, German and English. It was in a refugee camp in Southern Austria, not far from Italy. Its dual purpose was the opportunity for students from different cultures to learn about one another and to help dig foundations for refugee cottages to be built by the Austrian and local governments. I would travel on a small student ship across the Atlantic and have three weeks of free travel time before meeting my co-leader on-site and introducing myself to the town's mayor. Yes!

I took on every job that I could find. I had more than two hundred dollars put aside for spending money by the end of the school year. Wayne agreed to send me some money but he was not sure how much. Then I got a telegram asking me to telephone the A.F.S.C. office. There was a problem.

My German co-leader had fallen and broken a leg. Would I be willing to be the sole leader? A few of the students coming, one from Sweden, one from Denmark and one from Austria would speak both English and German and could help with language problems. But it might be a good idea for me to brush up on any German that I knew.

I bought a small dictionary and a phrase book. On our nine-day crossing on the tiny *Johan von Olden Barnevelt* I studied phrases, checked double meanings in the dictionary and spoke to myself in German when I was alone. Two Americans, Paul and Lenore, were on the same ship and would be in my work camp. Lenore was slim, nervous and full of anxious questions. Paul had a blond crew cut and robins' egg blue eyes. He played Rugby in college and had a great smile. He planned to climb the Matterhorn before going to the camp.

Seeing real English Bobbies on the dock in London and hearing the longshoremen's cockney accent was exhilarating. I actually was having a foreign adventure. Paul tried to give me a quick course in useful French phrases since we were to dock in Le Havre the next day and we were to be billeted in a dormitory at the Université in Paris the first night.

At breakfast in the cafeteria after that first night on French soil, I thought through my phrases and ordered a simple breakfast of fruit, croissant and coffee with warm milk, all in French. A charming young woman behind the counter with a devilish sparkle in her eyes asked in heavily accented English, "Oh, no, Monsieur. You would like watercress with your coffee? I think perhaps you like a pastry better." Lesson learned: Ask first if you might speak English and, if not, try the other language. It would be easier on all concerned.

I fell in love with the France, Italy and Austria of 1957. Picture books came to life. I stepped into stories I had read and movies I had seen. But attractive and seemingly available young men seemed to appear everywhere. My secret problem loomed.

I checked a number of hotels in Paris and found a servants' attic room in one on Rue Jacob. It was five flights up the stairs with a shared bathroom at the end of the hall, but I could have it if I wished for five American dollars for each of two nights. It had two small dormer windows that opened out, looking down on the cobblestone street. The faded, wine red velvet on the wall around the bed corner matched a worn cover on the bed.

Caught in a sudden thunderstorm the second evening I met Luke who I thought was French when a dozen of us dashed for cover under a blue awning. He was more free and forward than I. He wanted to see my charming hotel room. He was sweet and funny with a sad story. His very wealthy American family paid him to stay in Europe while they devised acceptable cover stories for their social circles to hide his sexual preference.

In the morning when I ran to the corner store to get bread, wine, water and cheese, as he had advised, for the bus I was taking to Lyon, I looked back up at the dormer windows. He was leaning out of one, naked, hair disheveled, smiling and waving. We had shared a night of tenderness, tales and touch, intimate strangers. I did not feel guilty. I suspected that I would never forget him.

Then there was the surprising flirtation initiated by the young man wearing a very thin bikini on the beach near the train station in Cannes. There were no inexpensive rooms to be found and he lived with his family. But he walked me to the train station to see me on my way, barefoot with a white towel draped around his neck accenting a tanned chest, he kissed me before I boarded the train.

When a bus dropped me in Rome I let a guide take me to his sister's pensione and rented a room including three meals, all for five dollars. "But no visitors," she commanded. Her dinner was delicious. After dinner I walked directly to the Coliseum without a map. The moon was nearly full and I cautiously went inside the ruin. There were men in the shadows identifiable at first only by the glow of cigarettes.

A beautiful boy of nineteen who communicated his age by counting off raised fingers in Italian kissed me on my neck, took my hand and led me to a nook hidden behind shrubs across the road and expressed his passion as we rested against the famous historic wall that I had seen in pictures. He wanted to join me for the night in my pensione room but I communicated that it was forbidden by the mistress. Corners of his mouth turned down, he asked, "Divertimenti, no?"

"Si, si," I quickly assured him. Then, whether to save face or as per plan, he extended a palm and asked for lira. I showed him that I had less than the equivalent of a dollar in my pocket. I gave it to him. He shook my hand, kissed me on the cheek, whispered *"arrivederci"* and smiled over his shoulder as he ambled away.

In the magic city of Florence I spent several hours in the presence of Michelangelo's David, stepping outside only for an intermission slice of pizza and a glass of wine. I permitted myself to be picked up and seduced by a passionate young man in the shadows by the river that evening. Somehow he also managed to pick my pocket of the two dollars worth of lire I had put there for beer.

I was not winning my battle against my homosexual desires, but I was in Europe. For the time being it did not matter, I told myself.

In Spittal, Austria, we were housed in a boarding school that was unused in the summers, a fifteen-minute walk from the refugee camp where our work was to be done. The mayor's younger brother spoke English. He showed me around the village and walked me to the work site where I met the man in charge of the refugee camp and the man in charge of construction. Our job would be to dig as directed so that the concrete foundations could be poured. The work would begin early each morning and finish late in the afternoon with mid-morning and mid-afternoon breaks plus a lunch break long enough to return to the school for a meal.

"It would be a suggestion that someone stay behind each morning to market maybe and cook the lunch," the mayor's brother advised. "If your people are arriving tomorrow, the next day for work might not be so beautiful since we expect maybe a tempest with rains."

I wrote, edited and memorized a little welcoming speech to be given in English and German at the end of our first dinner together. We fifteen young men and women were from Japan, Turkey, Lebanon, the United States, Great Britain, Denmark, Sweden, Germany, the Netherlands and Austria.

I delivered my small welcoming speech in German first. It was greeted at the end with silence and startled looks. The English version went better. After laughter an Austrian explained that in the German version of my little joke, saying that since we had labored so hard this first day (when all we had done was prepare a communal meal) we should now be entitled to relax together and play, had translated instead into something indicating that we now had permission to relax, let go and play with ourselves.

The work was tough, picks and shovels digging into hard earth filled with rocks of all sizes. Wheelbarrows were filled with stones to be thrown into piles for later use in the building. A very hot sun shone almost every day.

We were free to explore on weekends. People went off in groups of three or four, usually to Vienna, Salzburg or Venice. Or, since we were in the foothills of the Alps, we joined the locals in their weekend pastime of walking the steep mountain paths. They actually dressed up in traditional native costumes on weekends, looking like extras from *The Sound of Music*, the women in their laced bodice dirndls and the men in leather shorts, Tyrolean hats and walking sticks.

Paul and I usually opted for the same weekend adventure, alone together or with others. We slept in our underwear in the same bed in Venice and Verona to save money. I was attracted to him but I was determined that nothing untoward would happen between us. I was, after all, the leader of the work camp. Paul was one of five of the work camp participants who looked like models or movie stars, turning heads wherever they went, especially our slim-hipped young man from Turkey with dark curls, hairy chest and muscles, and our shapely young woman from Denmark with her boyish short blond hair, pale blue eyes and tiny waist. Both had very long eyelashes, very white teeth and dazzling smiles.

I made one important executive decision at the beginning of our weeks together in the camp. Seeing that the projected budget allowed almost the same amounts of money for food and for medical expenses, I told everyone that I was combining the two with the hope that if we ate well we would stay healthy. It was a good choice. Ours was the only camp that ended the summer with no accidents, no sickness and no medical expense.

The wonderful, hoped-for affectionate international bonds formed. Adnon, from Lebanon, introduced us males to the sweet custom of washing one another's backs in communal shower room. Yuri, from Japan, patiently taught us all to sing a traditional folk song in Japanese. We took turns cooking, introducing culinary twists from each culture and inventing our own special *international stew* served at the beginning of each evening meal. It had to contain all leftovers from the day before with something added new that day. Sometimes peculiar, sometimes fabulous, the pot never emptied.

When the small student ship sailed from Rotterdam I was sad, missing my new friends, aware that I would never see most of them again. But I was happy to see Paul. He and I were assigned to the same small six-bunk cabin with one porthole window at the water line through which the six of us would see the Northern Lights the night Paul woke us a few hours after we had gone to sleep. He and I stood close to one another, very close.

Wayne and Bobbie were at the dock to welcome me back home to New York. Bobbie seemed unusually welcoming with her kiss and I noticed that her shirt front dress was unbuttoned enough to show more cleavage than usual. She now had her own studio apartment in Manhattan she told me. We slept there that night.

I had stuffed a few inexpensive gifts into my suitcase. I knew that Gerry's wife, Stella, liked unusual modern ceramics so I had carried a vase with a polka-dot pattern from Austria for her. She was appreciative. "And did you bring back a beautiful European girl for yourself?" she teased.

Nick and Dottie were in their final year. She would have her Masters' in Social Work and Nick was due to take his Oral Defense of his dissertation after the Christmas vacation. They would return to San Francisco in January.

Through a psychoanalyst Nick had met in one of his field placements, he had gotten a job the previous year taking a college-aged schizophrenic, Chad, on outings twice each week. Chad's wealthy parents had opted to keep him at home rather than place him in a mental hospital so that he could see their psychoanalyst several times each week.

Nick was paid well for these outings and he recommended me as his replacement, phasing me in sometime in November with each of us taking Chad out one evening each week. He warned me that it would be an adventure but I reassured him, telling him about similar escorting experiences I had had while at Chestnut Lodge.

Chad spoke a Pidgin English similar to the Lone Ranger's Tonto. He was unpredictable, indecisive and seemed to take secret pleasure in creating embarrassing situations. Changing his mind a half dozen times about what he wanted on his hot dog on one occasion, the exasperated vendor said, "Hey, Mack, quit givin' me a fuckin' hard-on." Chad, silent a moment, looked into the man's eyes and said, "You like Chad this much?"

As usual, at a Friday evening get-together with Nick and Dottie, tamale pie and a pitcher of Manhattans, I said, "So what do we really want to do in our lives when we're grown up." We were quiet for a minute or two.

"I want to be President of the American Psychological Association," Nick said finally. "I want to get settled in our own home and have babies," Dottie said. "I want to write a book and do something that makes some kind of social difference," I said, "make life better for people."

"It's time for you to find the right girl," Dottie said. The gods were listening to all three of us.

It was beginning to look like Bobbie might be the right girl. We had started to date regularly. We spoke on the telephone almost every day between Manhattan and East Meadow. By mid-October I was sleeping at her place one or two nights a week. It seemed clear where we were heading. We had been friends for nine years. We seemed to have the same values. We had the same college friends. Sex was good and a love was developing.

Two fundamental differences between us were being ignored, however. The first was our assumptions about work and careers, the second was our sexual preferences. My future professional course seemed set and attainable but Bobbie was drifting occupationally. She was working for a public relations firm but did not really like her job. As to sexual preference I only knew that I had to take control of myself and overcome my distracting sexual attraction to some males. It seemed logical that unless I was happily married I would not ever be able to do that.

I was doing well in my classes and field placements. I selected a dissertation topic related to Gerry's research on persuasibility in young children and how it develops, and wrote and submitted a proposal. It seemed reasonable to assume that I would complete my course work and go on to an internship. I had a good chance of getting a V.A. internship which would bring in more than I was earning at present. With my Research Assistantship, baby sitting and evenings with Chad I was meeting financial expenses.

Bobbie was waiting for me to ask. I knew it. I could feel it. On a rainy Saturday night when neither of us was sleeping I decided to overcome whatever inhibition it was that was keeping me from asking. I rolled over and faced her in the darkness. "How long are we going to wait to get married," I asked.

Her parents asked only that we be married by a rabbi. We talked to several who were not willing. We would be a *mixed marriage*, still a taboo in 1957. On a Thanksgiving visit to her parents they introduced us to a young rabbi whom friends had said was very liberal.

He asked if I was willing to take classes and convert to Judaism. I said that I would feel perfectly comfortable doing that. He said that there would have to be a *briss*. Blushing a lot since both Bobbie's mother and father were present, I said that I was already circumcised. "Just symbolic," he said, "a Minion, a circle of Jewish men, and a ceremonial drop of blood."

After he left, her mother said, "Never mind. Enough already. You've tried hard enough. Find somebody you like to perform the ceremony. We'll do it out of town."

There was a family precedent. Bobbie's mother's brother was considered the big success in the family. The senior partner in his own law firm, and a member of the town's exclusive non-Jewish country club, he had fallen for a non-Jewish legal secretary. They had married quietly.

We found Algernon Black, the head of the Ethical Culture Society in New York. He interviewed us. We liked him very much. The date was set for January, between semesters. We wanted a small wedding, just ten or twelve people.

We were going to get married. *Bobbie* suddenly seemed like a child's nickname. I tried calling her Barbara. It took.

She found a one bedroom apartment for us on West Sixty-Eighth Street between Central Park West and Columbus that would be available the first of January. It would cost the same amount that the two of us, combined, were paying at the time. I gave notice to my landlady in East Meadow. We also telephoned friends to let them know. Announcements would be sent after the wedding. We went to a small shop in Greenwich Village and picked out rings. We were happy.

When I told Jack he said, "If you don't have to get married, why not wait a while?" It seemed a strange reaction.

Paul was in his senior year of college, still on the rugby team, anticipating the law school years that would lead him into his father's prestigious firm. When I told him by telephone that I was getting married, he said that he had been wanting to come to New York and spend a weekend with me. "How about next weekend?"

He arrived on Saturday afternoon. "I had to skip practice but the team will survive." We met in the city and I took him to meet Barbara. She was meeting her mother and a friend later. They would help her shop for a wedding dress before a shower of sorts with a few others that evening. Her mother also wanted to take me shopping the following weekend to a suit wholesaler friend of a friend. "My present," she said.

"You doing the whole white veil, bridesmaids and promise to obey thing?" Paul asked.

"No, just a really nice cocktail dress that I can use later," she answered.

Paul and I went out to East Meadow, had dinner in a little Italian restaurant and talked about our friends from the summer, our travels together and our futures. The neon lights in the window were playing color tricks on his blond crew cut; the glow of the candle was warming his dimpled smile. "Quite a change from the summer. All of a sudden the future gets set," he said. "It's like another world."

Back at my small apartment we showered and I offered him the choice of the day bed in the living room or sharing the larger bed in the bedroom. He opted for the latter, stripped down to white jockey shorts and hopped into it. "Like old times," he said smiling. I could feel his warmth when I too stripped down to underwear and climbed in beside him.

"Remember that fancy bed in Verona with those fluffy covers?" he asked. I did. "Nice memory," he said. It began to rain. "It's cozy in here," he said.

I woke some hours later to find us snuggled together spoon fashion, his back to me. I wanted to say "I love you, Paul," to say it aloud to his angelic sleeping form, dimly visible in the ambient light. But it might wake him. My old problem, I thought. He looked so beautiful and felt so good there close to me. He smelled fresh and manly.

Craziness. In another month I would marry. It was time to put these thoughts and feelings aside.

At the first light of dawn I woke again. We had turned in the bed. My back was to him and he was snuggled close, his chest against my back, his left arm across me, his hand near my heart. He was snoring softly, safe in sleep. I did not dare to move.

Chapter 14

Marriage

It was an afternoon wedding at the Plaza Hotel, in the Vanderbilt Suite with views of both Fifth Avenue and Central Park South. Barbara's father, Barney, was footing the bill. He and Barbara's mother, Grace, had driven to the city with Grace's important lawyer brother and his non-Jewish wife. They brought along a case of champagne. The hotel would be catering the cake and hors d'oeuvres. There were to be just ten of us, the other four people were friends, one of whom was Wayne. I had not invited anyone from my family.

Barney had given us a wedding gift of five hundred dollars to cover a week's vacation in San Juan, Puerto Rico, plus a dinner downstairs at the Venetian Room before taking a taxi to the airport. It all seemed very luxurious to me, part of a new chapter of life beginning.

It had been a busy couple of weeks since our move into the apartment on West Sixty-Eighth Street the first week in January. The same doctor friend who had come to my rescue after my skiing accident offered to help me again when I missed the deadline for having my blood work done so that a marriage license could be issued. Believing me to be free of venereal disease, he drew the blood, sent it in and signed the form certifying that I was clean.

The morning of the wedding Barbara went to the Plaza to meet her parents for brunch. I had to drive out to Long Island to turn in one last paper and grades for the evening course I had been teaching. I also had to pack for our honeymoon.

An hour before the ceremony I was packing and dressing, watching the time. Half an hour later I closed the suitcase and checked my necktie in the mirror. Maybe not handsome, but I looked good. I took the gold ring out of my pocket and slipped it onto my finger. Very soon I would be a twenty-seven year old married man wearing this ring.

I thought of the movies and stories in which the bride or groom gets cold feet at the last minute. Could that happen? A second of panic gripped me but I pushed it aside. Go downstairs, hail a cab, go to the Plaza, get married. Another beginning. Go. As the other Grace in Rose Valley said in the telegram she had sent, "Let joy be unconfined – the best is yet to be."

Barbara looked beautiful in a champagne colored chiffon cocktail dress. Algernon Black asked the ten of us to stand in a circle in the living room of the suite. He said that, aside from the power vested in him by the State of New York, he could not marry us. Only we could marry one another. He talked about the values we shared, the home we would create together, the good that we could bring to the world and sincerely blessed us as we embarked on this unknowable journey that would be shaped by our joining together in a partnership of equals, individuals strengthened by honesty, trust and willingness to explore.

We fumbled a bit getting the rings onto one another's fingers which made Barbara burst into giggles. We cut the cake together and fed it to one another as cameras clicked. The ten of us drank far less than half of the case of champagne. It was a wonderful wedding.

The two of us, sporting our wedding rings, went downstairs to the Venetian Room for dinner. Ella Logan was performing, singing *Look to the Rainbow* and several of her other songs from *Finian's Rainbow*. Dinner was delicious. Everything was glamorous.

After dinner we went back upstairs, changed into less dressy clothes, said goodbye to our wedding suite in which we had used only the living room and headed to the airport for our eight-hour flight to San Juan. We knew we would be tired when we arrived in the morning. We had a room reserved in a motel on the beach that a travel agent had told us was not far from the famous Caribé Hilton Hotel and was one-third the price.

I was not feeling at all well when we landed but thought it must be a hangover. Aspirin and a nap did not fix it, however. By late afternoon I realized that I had a fever. By two o'clock in the morning I was shivering in the warm tropical night and asking for more blankets. Barbara was frightened. The fever eased the next day but I was weak, not a good start to a honeymoon.

In 1957 San Juan was not yet a popular vacation destination. Tourists were advised to keep a low profile walking the streets of Old San Juan. But Barbara's mother had picked out a trousseau of bold, brightly colored cruise wear for her daughter and Barbara wore it. I suggested we try to speak quietly in public but Barbara was giddy in her new life. In the restaurant dining room of our motel Barbara fainted and had to be laid across several chairs. "The heat and the alcohol," the manager sagely suggested. "It happens."

Most bothersome to me was a new behavior that appeared suddenly now that Barbara was my wife. She would take my arm when we walked and leaned heavily against me. On the narrow walkways in San Juan the leaning forced me off the sidewalk and into the street repeatedly. Calling her attention to it seemed to have no effect.

When we arrived back in New York my doctor friend called. There was a problem. He was more than a good sport about it but my blood test, on which he had signed off, had registered positive in the V.D. screening. His guess was that I had been coming down with the flu before I left. I had to go to the New York City Health Department and be thoroughly tested for V.D. there. I apologized to him profusely and sincerely. My punishment was the half-day spent at the City Health Department's downtown clinic where I was presumed guilty unless proven innocent. I came up clean. The flu diagnosis had been correct.

I loved our Manhattan home. The tall and extremely shapely young woman in the apartment directly under us was a puzzle though. I mentioned to Barbara that when I passed her on the stairs there seemed to be a lot of squeezing by and she gave me a weird impression of wearing too much make-up, though when I looked she actually seemed to be wearing no make-up at all. Twice in the early weeks, preoccupied with other things, I went to her door rather than ours and wondered why my key did not work in the lock. Both times she opened the door to see who was there while holding only a towel around her shapely naked body. And then there were her singing lessons. We mentioned her to friends, laughing about the odd neighbors to be found in Manhattan.

A classmate passed her at the front door when arriving for dinner one evening. He bounded up the stairs breathlessly and solved the mystery. "Hey, guys, I just bumped into Julie Newmar on the front steps. She must be on her way to the theater. She's the babe who's the star of Li'l Abner. Man, I wish she was my neighbor." I told him about the naked with towel encounters. "And you didn't ask to borrow a cup of sugar or a stick of butter? Man, you're killing me. Oh, right, you're married. Loyal husband. Good for you."

Driving to school the next day it occurred to me that my reaction might have been different, had it been her co-star or James Dean at the door with a towel. But then my attractions to men were always more charged, simply because I was psychologically conflicted about them, I reasoned. I loved Barbara. Our sex was good. I was having a great life and it was getting better. Time to put the problematic thinking out of my mind and remember the advice I had gotten in therapy. I was going to concentrate on making a good, decent, respectable life.

I was trying for a V.A. internship in Brooklyn with a later transfer to the famous V.A. Hospital in Menlo Park, California where the avant-garde research in group therapy, family therapy and psychedelic drugs was happening. But we could be content with either staying in New York or going to California we decided. Barbara still disliked her job but we had friends in to our new home for dinner often and life was good. We were creating our new life together.

We had some early disputes about money. I was continuing my job as a research assistant, teaching an evening course at the college and escorting the young schizophrenic on outings. I had done a budget for us but it was tight and did not work well for Barbara. When she had left home for college her father had given her a checkbook with instructions to use it as needed but to let him know when she wrote a check, just telling him how much and what it was for. It had given the desired sense of security to her parents and to her and she had not abused it.

Naturally, her solution to our first money argument was that she would write a check. It had started when I saw the refrigerator suddenly stocked with expensive meats. She explained that she had opened a charge account in the "really nice butcher shop around the corner on Columbus Avenue." How much had she charged there that week? She was not sure. I telephoned them. The amount was the same amount of money that I earned from all of my jobs in that week.

She surprised me again a couple of months later while we were driving back to the city after a fun weekend visiting a wealthy graduate student friend's *cottage* in Southampton. Barbara said that she wanted to have a baby. I was stunned. I had anticipated that we would start a family sometime after I was finished with graduate school and had a job but that was years away.

"We can't afford it now," I said.

"My parents would help," she said. "They want grandchildren and I'm twenty-eight years old already."

I persuaded her to put the question on hold for a few months. Six weeks later we discovered that she had an ovarian cyst that would require surgery. Her parents insisted that the surgery be done in Philadelphia by the *best* expert. They would pay. She would have a private room and private nurses, recuperating at home with them after the hospital.

I stayed for two days, sleeping in a chair in her hospital room the first night and then returned to New York. I could not afford to stay away from my jobs. She was away two weeks. I commuted three times and we talked on the telephone each day. The doctor reassured us that she would be able to have children.

My dissertation topic was approved and I began collecting data. My internship at the Brooklyn V.A. was also approved to start in June. After our first few arguments Barbara and I got along extremely well. We both had healthy sexual appetites and were completely available to one another.

My one perpetual source of dissatisfaction and irritation was what seemed to be her willful determination to sabotage my best efforts to keep the apartment neat. Clothing was dropped on the floor and dishes were left in the sink. I learned to pick up her clothes and keep the kitchen neat. Otherwise we were winning the prize for happy newlyweds. We were friends, we enjoyed one another and our friends envied our marriage.

Once a month we took a bus from the Port Authority Terminal to visit her parents for the weekend. I liked them and wanted to build a stronger family relationship with them, to be a real member of the family.

Barney had a life story that was not terribly different from my own, the son of immigrant parents from Russia who had failed in the New Jersey farming community to which they were sent. His father left the family when Barney was a youngster, but Barney had worked his way up and out, doing his law studies in night school. He was positive and optimistic, passing along jokes, quotes and snippets of wisdom from his reading but he had a difficult time developing a genuinely close relationship with anyone but his wife. He and I shared a martini ritual together before dinner always and he took prideful pleasure in taking us out to popular restaurants for dinner each weekend that we visited, always introducing me as his son-in-law, the psychologist.

Grace was smart, funny and overweight. Her passion was playing bridge. She was a master. She warmed to me more quickly than Barney, sometimes confiding her concerns and asking my opinion or advice. I planted a small flower garden for her as the weather warmed. It was an unspoken but understood and appreciated offering.

Grace managed Barney and the household which included supervising Nellie, the maid who commuted from the other side of town where all of the Black people lived. Nellie was not young and it was an offense to Barbara's and my liberal values to see her shuffling around the house most days in her bedroom slippers, vacuuming, dusting, cooking and doing laundry in the basement. I developed an appreciation for the ways in which she took care of herself though, occasionally putting her employers in their place. We had what I imagined to be a silent but shared respect for one another. She missed very little of what went on around her and knew that I was not long out from the wrong side of the tracks.

Grace had a button on the floor under the dining room table with which she could call or signal Nellie in the kitchen. Nellie kept the door to the kitchen open, however, and was no farther than seven feet from Grace's chair usually. She almost always ignored the buzzer, feigning poor hearing, and waited until Grace called her.

At one of the first dinner parties with the four of us plus Grace's lawyer brother and his wife, Eleanor, Grace pushed the floor button to no avail as usual. When it was time for dessert she had to call Nellie to clear the dishes. She said we had both ice cream and watermelon for dessert. She asked preferences while Nellie was in the room clearing the dishes. I asked for the ice cream. When Nellie brought the desserts she put a plate of watermelon in front of me.

"Nellie, Dr. Clark asked for ice cream," Grace said.

"Yeah, but we got to get rid of this leftover watermelon," Nellie said, putting her back to Grace and offering me a theatrical wink. "Anyways it's better for you." We all laughed. Score one for Nellie.

It was difficult for me to believe but in June, at the age of twenty-seven, I was done with all academic requirements except the dissertation and was starting a full time one year internship at the Brooklyn V.A. Hospital earning five thousand dollars a year plus medical and retirement benefits. With the exception of my time in the army it was the first time in my life that I had not had to worry about the cost of a sick day or a visit to a doctor.

I could not have asked for a better office than the one assigned to me the first day. It was small but its window looked directly out on the Hudson River and the Verrazano Bridge. As I stepped into my office in my new suit, tie, shined shoes and briefcase I saw the Ile de France moving under the bridge, heading for home.

The first case assigned to me that day was a young former sergeant who had been liberated from a German concentration camp at the age of sixteen before entering the United States Army. He was having nightmares and other assorted symptoms and his V.A. doctor wondered if he was a hypochondriac or was malingering. Hearing his story in our first few hours together, I wondered at how well he was doing. He had been a pretty boy slave to his German captors.

The diagnosis of Post Traumatic Stress Syndrome was not yet in the manual but the psychological test battery I administered showed a man damaged and haunted by his awful war and camp experiences, now drowning in guilt about his survival behavior and being the only person in his family to survive. He was humiliated by all that he had done as a young teenager to stay alive. I recommended psychotherapy and volunteered to take him on as a client but he was discharged from the hospital and referred to the downtown outpatient clinic.

As an intern I was stuck doing psychological evaluations. It was good experience but I wanted a more varied experience. I persevered in my application for transfer to the Palo Alto V.A. Hospital in Menlo Park, California. In August I was told that the transfer had been approved. I was to report there the second week in September.

Because we were in a rent controlled building the landlord was happy to have us leave before having been there a full year, since it meant an early rent increase for him. I was allowed travel time plus vacation days so we would have almost three weeks to make the cross-country trip. We could store things in Barbara's parents' basement for the year, just taking clothes and a few other things. I bought a heavy canvas tent second hand. We could camp out in state parks and save money as we went. Somehow it would all fit in our new little Nash Metropolitan convertible.

Our one worry was telling Barbara's parents. To our surprise they were totally understanding. "We'll miss you but we'll talk on the telephone," Grace said. "Listen, you have to do whatever is good for your career," Barney said. We were excited.

Barbara's driver's license, earned in high school, had lapsed while she was in college. She took the test again twice on our final two weekend visits to her parents and failed both times. I would have to do all of the driving until we got to Alabama where we would stay for a few days visiting Barney's youngest brother and his wife. She could take the test there. It was a small town and her uncle was a well-known and respected physician there. It would not be a problem, he assured us.

Our cross-country drive was scenic and mostly fun. Leaving from her parents' home early in the morning, we planned to do a long drive the first two days, staying in motels at night, arriving in Alabama the third day and then camping out in state and national parks after our stay there.

Mid-afternoon, driving along a scenic stretch on a mountain road in Virginia the first day, I noticed a police car behind us. I had not been speeding so there was no cause for alarm but twenty miles later, as we entered a small town I slowed to well below the posted speed limit and the police car slowed also, staying behind us. Finally, I pulled over to the curb across the street from a coffee shop. The police car stopped. I suggested we put the convertible top up, go across the street for coffee and a snack and then drive on until near dark, looking for a motel and restaurant along the way.

As we got out of the car, one of the policemen who had been following us approached and asked to see my driver's license. I asked if there was a problem and he told us that he needed us to wait where we were while he checked something. Returning from his car radio a few minutes later he said he would have to ask us to stay.

"What's the problem?" I asked again.

His hand now resting on his gun, he said, "Seems there was a hold-up of a gas station and you folks match the description. The fella' who works there's the only witness so they're gonna' drive him on over here to see. Shouldn't be more than a half hour or so, maybe an hour."

Ever efficient I said, "We're headed for North Carolina and were going to drive until dark but maybe we could have dinner across the street in the coffee shop while we're waiting. Are we under arrest?"

"Not exactly," he answered. "Just don't want you to go nowheres. Reckon you could eat."

We ordered hot sandwiches, salad and coffee. I laughed. "Here we are, first day away from civilization and already we're Bonnie and Clyde." But when the witness arrived an hour and a half later I got scared.

He was a twelve year old kid who looked younger and whose "uncle was mad as hell" that he had "let some smart-ass New York people steal all the money" while he was minding the gas station. "He wants somebody in jail, right quick, today," the policeman who brought him said. "He's mayor of the town, you know."

The kid was under pressure. His forehead was wet with nervous perspiration. "I don't know," he said, looking at us. I had sudden visions of us spending time in a small town southern Virginia jail because of a frightened twelve year old who, at that moment, had the power to put us there.

He looked at our car across the street. "I think the car was bigger maybe," he said. Bit by bit the picture emerged. It had been an old full-sized convertible, black and white rather than red and cream, and there had been two men he was pretty sure. But it definitely was a convertible and definitely had New York license plates.

After a bit more discussion and a "sorry we had to delay you folks," we were permitted to go on our way, though the police car followed for another few miles. "Darkness be damned," I said. I was ready to drive until we crossed the state line and found a motel in North Carolina. I did not want to be at the mercy of a nervous twelve year old who might change his mind about details.

We enjoyed our visit in Alabama. Barbara's uncle and aunt were halfway between her parents' age and ours. They were political liberals and she was not Jewish. They were helping to build a new South. We became friends.

But the new driver's license was not to be. The town had one traffic light and Barbara drove through the quiet intersection while the light was red. Her uncle and aunt laughed, saying that it reminded them of an *I Love* Lucy show and commiserated with me for having to do all of the driving to California. I was rested and refreshed though after three nights as their guest, given full run of their lake front house seven miles outside of the town. We put the top down an hour after dawn and headed off in the direction of New Orleans.

The old camping stove did not work well and Barbara was not enthusiastic about cooking in the wild so we ate most meals at inexpensive restaurants but we made good use of the tent, air mattresses and sleeping bags. It took effort setting it all up in the late afternoons as well as taking the tent down and folding it up again in the mornings, especially since dew usually made the heavy canvas heavier.

Our only misadventure camping happened in a state park outside of Amarillo, Texas. It was in a canyon and I asked jokingly at the gate, "What happens down there when it rains?"

"We thank the good Lord for a miracle," the ranger said, laughing. "It just don't rain here."

We were awakened during the night by thunder and lightning. I reached out in the darkness for the flashlight and found my hand in water. We were being flooded. Fortunately the top on the car was up but our clothes were wet and the tent had gained considerable weight.

It took two days to get everything thoroughly dry. By then we had made it to Santa Fe and Taos and were looking forward to the Grand Canyon. After two days there we headed off in the direction of Los Angeles where we would make a duty visit to my parents and oldest sister so that they could meet my new wife and she could meet them.

We bought the suggested water bottles that people strapped to the fronts of their cars when driving across the desert to protect radiators from overheating but gave little thought to ourselves. The desert scenery was beautiful and we kept the top down until late morning when Barbara began to feel sick.

Remembering the heat stroke problems during army basic training I thought I knew what was happening. We put the top up and drank water. Finding salt was another matter but we did finally get to a small town with a pharmacy. It was air conditioned and had a soda fountain. The pharmacist concurred in the diagnosis and they did have salt tablets. We checked into a motel in Twenty-Nine Palms, swam in their pool, slept and rested for a day before going on to Los Angeles.

My parents and oldest sister had recently moved into a new subdivision house near Long beach, thanks to Alice's steady job at Douglas Aircraft and her G.I. Bill housing rights. It had three bedrooms, two baths, air conditioning and a back yard big enough for a garden. It was, by far, the nicest of the many houses in which they had lived.

It was the end of the first week in September and it was hot. The air conditioning in the house was on high, windows and sliding glass doors wide open. We tried, tactfully, to explain that the air conditioning would work better if doors and windows were closed but they would have none of it.

My parents seemed to like Barbara but it was difficult to know for sure. I presumed they were grappling with the reality that they had a real live Jewish person sleeping in their house for the first time ever. They were studying her. My sister clearly liked her, marveling aloud at her free and easy ways, her laughter and her ability to say what she thought. Barbara was amazed that this was the family in which I had grown up.

I had not thought to mention that conversations were rare events. Growing up it had been the radio that filled the void once we could afford to own one and pay the electricity bill. It was snapped on first thing each morning and turned off last thing each night. There was an occasional soap opera or Sunday evening comedy that was listened to but most of the time it was just sound filling dead air. Declarations of displeasure, on-going quarrels and the sound of the vacuum cleaner punctuated and overrode the radio sometimes but most of the time it made its sounds alone, a welcome, talkative but ignored guest. It had been replaced in California now by a television set, turned on full volume in the morning, off at bedtime, no possibility of real conversation.

And I had not thought to mention the meals either. It was expected that people would appear at more or less the same time for breakfast and assemble it for themselves, choosing from coffee, tea or cocoa plus shredded wheat, corn flakes or some other boxed cereal and maybe a buttered slice of toasted white bread. My mother had cocoa, her first chocolate of the day. My father had coffee sweetened with condensed milk and sugar, poured from the cup into a saucer and slurped from there.

Dinner was something that happened on Sunday and special holidays, early in the afternoon. Lunch was done on your own. The evening meal was called *supper*, and it varied. I could see Barbara's eyes widen when she went into the kitchen insisting on helping with the cooking and again later when she sat across from me at the table. We had sliced tomatoes sprinkled with sugar, corn on the cob, heated beans from the can, potatoes that had been boiled a very long time, plus mashed potatoes, fried potatoes and ketchup. There was also a pitcher of Kool-Aid, a loaf of Wonder Bread and butter.

She gamely tried to make conversation by telling and showing the trick we had learned in Alabama, putting butter on a slice of bread and sliding it along the cob of corn. My father, whose corn had to be cut off the cob, smiled at her with his three yellowed teeth, enjoying her spunky unorthodox approach to corn eating. In deference to company he was not wearing his hat and had put on a short-sleeved shirt over his undershirt.

"Crackers," my mother said. "Southern crackers do all kinds of funny things. We seen plenty of them. That's no way to butter corn." The attempt at conversation lost momentum. End of discussion.

"Three kinds of potatoes and no main dish?" Barbara asked me later.

"It could have been leftover chicken, meat loaf and cold cuts plus boiled potatoes," I answered. "It all depends on mood and what's around but you can usually count on the boiled potatoes"

They took us for an outing to their favorite place, Knott's Berry Farm, and bought us some preserves to take with us to San Francisco. The visit was, as always, tedious and difficult for me – the strain of straddling two worlds with no common ground and no possible basis for conversation other than, "Remember the time when…"

We said goodbye to Alice early in the morning when she left for work. "I wish you was living down here with us," she said. "It's too far away off there in San Francisco."

After breakfast I packed the car, eager to leave. My father came out to the driveway to watch. He showed me how he had very neatly packed boxes and tools in their garage, a trait we had in common.

My mother appeared in the driveway holding a nest of four colored Pyrex bowls with floral designs. They had been collected, one by one, as rewards for shopping at the new nearby supermarket. "We didn't send you nothing for your wedding," she said, handing them to me.

"They're wonderful," Barbara said. "We'll need them in San Francisco. We didn't bring any dishes." My mother smiled a bit. My father, hands deep in his pockets looked proud. They were pleased. But the timid goodbye kisses and handshakes were, as always, stiff and awkward. What to say? "We'll write," I called out as we drove away.

We telephoned Nick and Dot along the way. When we arrived at their home late in the afternoon they were waiting with a pitcher of Manhattans in the refrigerator. "To be poured as soon as you've unpacked the car, taken showers and gotten settled in the guest room," Dot said.

Chapter 15

Internship

Their house was new. They had moved in earlier in the summer. Its two most unusual features were a large bedrock boulder, mostly in the garage but peeking into the entryway also, and a stunning view from their living room and kitchen, peering down San Francisco's Market Street all the way to the Bay and the hills of Oakland on the other side of the water.

I had a full week before the first day of my internship and we needed to find an apartment in that time if possible. They had maps and want ads ready and promised us a Saturday ride around the city to get us oriented. Dot had gotten a job as a social worker and Nick was just about to start at Kaiser as their first and only clinical psychologist. "That will make me the Chief Psychologist," he said with a laugh.

The apartment hunting proved difficult and took more than three weeks, during which time Nick and Dot were steadfastly supportive and encouraging, repeatedly telling us to take our time and that they were in no hurry to get us out of the guest room. An ad in a weekday afternoon paper was almost missed. Barbara and I were discouraged by experience with similar ads but decided to check it when Nick said, "It's nearby, the next hill over on the other side of Market Street, above the Castro Theater on the way up toward Twin Peaks. You can see it from here."

Barbara was less enthusiastic than I by what greeted us in the late afternoon light. The house was an old Victorian in need of paint, two flights of steps up to the front door and another long flight up once inside the door to the flat. There were six flats altogether on three floors. The one for rent was on the top floor facing east, about the same view that Dot and Nick had. The windows on the side looked south, the kitchen sun porch and rear windows looked west. And it had space to spare. "If you count the sun porch, pantry, laundry room, bathroom and the two parlors it has twelve rooms!" I marveled. Impossible by New York standards.

Barbara saw the multiple layers of wallpaper that had come loose and leaned out from the walls, cobwebs in the corners of the high ceilings, left over broken furniture, ceiling fixtures with dead light bulbs, stained window shades, a gas stove in the dining room that was the only source of heat, a crack in the top pane of the bathroom window and no shower in the large old bathtub that stood on its aged clawed feet.

The landlady was a recently retired social worker who said she had decided that real estate investment was easier. "The rent is ninety-five dollars a month and I can let you have the garage for five dollars more if you want. I just bought a railroad carload of surplus Navy paint and you're welcome to as much of that as you want. You could change it from gray by using paint tints, I guess. Some of this furniture could be fixed up, you could get one of those shower attachments and they left that old refrigerator which works. There were a whole bunch of students living here and I don't want so many people next time. It'll rent this weekend so don't take too long to make up your mind."

Barbara was reluctant but I was enthusiastic. I loved the place. It was a grand old lady fallen into disrepair waiting to be tended, loved and brought back. My enthusiasm won.

We repaired and used the Victorian dining room table and chairs, putting new plywood seats on them, covering those with thin foam rubber and a gold and white brocade fabric that Barbara found in a remnants store. Then I painted the whole set in several layers of white enamel. The room had open wainscoting so I painted the framing in the same white enamel and the remainder of the walls in a muted gold achieved by adding bright yellow pigment to battleship gray. That was after steaming off the many layers of wallpaper. The floor got painted in dark red enamel and we hung false family portraits in important looking frames bought at give-away prices in junk shops. It was an elegant room when finished, especially in candlelight.

The kitchen had a table and two chairs that needed only paint. We bought a bureau for the bedroom and one for a guest room plus a spare bed, a rocking chair and a matching heavy sleigh-front set of loveseat and chair plus two carpet remnants, all for less than seventy-five dollars in attic leftovers stores on McAllister Street.

I painted a sturdy wood desk in black and red enamel. We bought a few cheap small folding tables found in the open crates in the new Cost Plus warehouse outlet. All I had to do was steam all of that wallpaper with a rented steamer, then paint every wall and floor in the apartment. Barbara's mother offered to buy us a new box spring and mattress set plus a blanket and sheets from Macy's. Barbara bleached the old, thin see-through curtains and trimmed them with red rickrack from the Five and Ten. She also had the great idea of gluing colorful fabric remnants to the insides of the stained paper window shades in the bedrooms. In less than two months we had a beautiful apartment with outstanding views.

The Palo Alto Veteran's Administration Hospital was not in Palo Alto. It was just off the freeway in Menlo Park, the next town. It was a pleasant forty-five minute drive from our apartment. After signing in at the Chief Psychologist's office I was given the name of my supervisor and told to report to his office after the morning orientation assembly for incoming psychology interns and psychiatry residents. There were twenty-four incoming psychology interns I was told, twenty from the clinical programs at Stanford and U.C. Berkeley and four of us transferred from out-of-state V.A. hospitals.

Seated at the assembly, I was surrounded by interns from Stanford, all wearing suits and neckties, as was I. They were wondering where Grant was. "I heard he took off for Mexico on his motorcycle last week," one of them said.

Five minutes after the welcoming officially began the missing Grant arrived in a black leather motorcycle jacket and squeezed into an empty seat directly in front of me. Dark blond hair, broad shoulders and muscular, I noted, as he shed his leather jacket. I also noticed that the collar of his white shirt was worn and frayed. Two psychology interns were to be assigned to each ward. A few minutes after I reported to the office of my supervisor, Grant reported in also. He was to be the other intern.

Dr. Light was shorter than both Grant and I, not fat but definitely more round than angular. He was relaxed, wore a suit and tie but was informal and had a genuine smile. He took the world around him in stride. "Call me Bernie," he said. He wanted to get to know us and let us get to know him.

"Why did you come all the way across the country to intern in this hospital?" he asked me, smiling. Grant too seemed eager to hear my answer. In his shirtsleeves I could see that he was indeed very muscular. He was handsome also, an unusual angular face with high cheekbones, dimples and arresting pale blue eyes.

"Tell us the truth," Bernie prodded.

"First of all I wanted a V.A. internship because it pays enough to live on. I've always wanted to try living in California, particularly San Francisco. The word back East is that this is the best V.A. training hospital in the country. And last but not least it seems to be the only one that offers training in group therapy and I have a big interest in that, starting with a lot of group experience at Antioch College where I got my undergraduate degree. You can help more people at lower cost with group therapy and it offers some things that are missing in individual therapy."

"So you want to save many souls," Bernie said with a smile. "Well, that's good. We've got many souls to save here." He was not being sarcastic. He had heard me.

Grant's answer was less revealing. He was at Stanford. This was nearby and had a good reputation. He was hoping to find a dissertation topic.

Next came an introduction to our ward. It was in a separate building across the lawns with puddles of sun shifting as the tree leaves overhead moved in the breeze. The charge nurse was a large, welcoming, authoritative woman in white uniform and cap. Her nickname was *The Duchess*. Wally was the seldom seen, easy-going ward psychiatrist who was nearing retirement. The Duchess ran the ward. That was clear. She was looking us over. I could see that if I did not get on her approved list the year would be wasted or worse. Many of the patients seemed to have learned a similar lesson.

I gave her my full attention then and throughout my stay there. Whenever I disagreed I did so in a questioning tone, someone trying to understand and learn. I never contradicted her openly or questioned her authority and often thanked her for helping me to learn. She rewarded me by granting all my requests. I asked for particular patients to be assigned to me for individual therapy and she approved. I told her that I wanted to try putting together a group for group therapy and she approved. In fact, she said, she also wanted to learn to do group therapy. She told me she would sit-in on the group sessions whenever she had time.

I hesitated but told her that since she was such an important person in their lives and *the* authority it might be a problem. It would be therapeutic for them to talk about their feelings about everything as much as possible and that would no doubt include feelings about the hospital, the ward, each other and also her, I was certain.

"Oh, that's fine," she said. "I've heard it all before once or twice. I can take it. I can also straighten them out. You set up the time you want to use the day room and tell me which of them you want in your group. I'll see to it that others are kept out and I'll sit in when I can."

The best I could do was to set the hours for days and times when I knew she would be most likely to be busy and unable to attend. She was not a mean or evil person. She truly wanted to help. But she also wanted her ward run her way. Bernie, watching my interactions with her said, "You have a way with you, Doctor. I think you're going to save many, many souls before you're done."

One of Grant's friends, another intern named Vic, had a friend named Ken Kesey who was an aspiring writer, working on a novel. Vic helped him get a job as a ward aide, sometimes working on our ward, sometimes other wards. Like any good writer he was a keen observer whose composite characters had many of the characteristics of available vivid models, altered as needed to fit the story. We did have a Native American on our ward, though he was not a *chief* and not the only Native American veteran in the hospital. One of my individual therapy patients was a charismatic alcoholic who tangled with the Duchess too often for his own good. The inspiration for people who would appear in Kesey's *One Flew Over the Cuckoo's Nest* could be seen when I later read the book.

And there was Grant. At the end of the first day at the hospital I told Barbara about everyone I had met and that I thought several of the interns would become friends. I talked about my fellow ward intern Grant, particularly. "He's twenty-five years old, rides a motorcycle, doesn't seem to own a suit and I noticed his collar is frayed. I think he's probably in a bad way for money and we should make it a point to invite him for dinner often."

We did. He accepted. Our friendship grew effortlessly as it did with several of the other interns. But it was different with Grant. He fascinated me. He had a great affection for Mexico and spoke Spanish. He was a reader, liked to travel and was dedicated to gym workouts and weight lifting. He was different. He also seemed to avoid conversation about family background in the same way that I did.

The fourth time he came for dinner was on a weekday evening. We had invited him to stay overnight in the guest room so that he could ride into the city and back to the hospital the next morning with me. Barbara had not yet found a job but was becoming an excellent cook. Grant insisted on stopping to buy a bottle of wine on the way home. Food and conversation were rich and satisfying. Grant promised to bring his new girlfriend next time. He was becoming family.

I tiptoed into the guest room early the next morning to wake him after I had showered. It was early, the first light of day was filling the window, erasing the room's shadows. As I neared the bed and saw his face, peaceful in sleep I stopped before speaking. I saw long lashes on closed eyes, the parted full lips of his relaxed mouth almost smiling. He was beautiful. There was a surge of feelings I had not known were there. I wanted to touch him. I touched one bare shoulder quickly and said, "Time to get up, sleepy head. Bathroom's all yours."

"Thanks," he said, sitting up in the bed yawning and stretching, revealing a naked torso shaped by his dedication to the gym. I left the room quickly.

He was not present a few weeks later when two other intern friends, Al and Fred, joined me at my desk for lunch from our brown paper bags. In conversation one of them, Al, who was his classmate said, "Well, of course, if I had Grant's money, my worries would be over."

I got Al aside later and asked about his remark. "I thought Grant was poor," I said.

He laughed. "You don't know who his parents are?" He told me that Grant came from a famous family. The last name immediately clicked into place. Both parents were famous, both wealthy. I was surprised but it explained a lot, including the brand new large convertible that he had parked in front of our house when he brought his glamorous new girlfriend to dinner. I had assumed that the car was hers.

I told him later about my mistaken impression. We talked about our very different, yet in some ways similar, growing up experiences in the weeks that followed, both of us isolated though for different reasons. He was as shocked to learn about my years in poverty as I had been to learn about his in luxury. The differences and similarities seemed to bring us closer together, like brothers, lovers or twins in a fable, separated by fate, prince and pauper, now reunited.

After that moment of awakened feelings in the guest room I was aware of my attraction to him but told myself that it would have to remain my secret, hidden along with all other such longings, mine alone to know, not to be spoken to anyone ever. And maybe it would go away.

Nick and Dot tried several times to engage Barbara in serious discussion about her career interests. They had no better luck than I when I had tried during our drive across the country. She wanted to have a baby and she liked art, painting in particular, but she could not think of any work that really interested her.

I had not really noticed her lack of focus or interest as clearly before. I had known that she did not like her job in a public relations firm in Manhattan but assumed that she was putting up with it because it offered a paycheck and, thus, a chance to study art and the time to decide her future occupational course. All of our friends at Antioch, regardless of gender, had looked forward to finding productive and socially responsible careers in the future. Barbara had seemed indecisive but that, in and of itself, was not unusual. What now did begin to seem unusual was that five years after Antioch there still was no sign of a focused or occupational interest forming.

She did find a low paying office assistant's job downtown finally. It was a cause for celebration. Her payday was on Fridays so we developed a Friday ritual. I would park downtown when I drove into the city after work and meet her at her office. Many of the better downtown bars had plentiful, hot hors d'oeuvres at cocktail time and they were free. We would order a drink, eat modestly but without cost, then go see a double feature either downtown or back at the Castro Theater near home.

As Christmas neared we shopped carefully and secretively for one another. We bought a small tree and decorated it with homemade ornaments. My best gift for her was a moss green soft wool sweater I found on a sale table at Macy's. We had found other small, inexpensive gifts for one another, all of them appreciated, none returned. It was a happy time for both of us.

San Francisco prided itself on its history of tolerance and acceptance of differences. The swell of social change seeded by veterans returning from the Second World War had gained a momentum in the two decades since and that was seen easily in this small city of many neighborhood cultures. Ours was a working class neighborhood in transition.

Three young homosexual men had moved into the apartment under ours just two weeks after we moved in and, though they made us uneasy at first, we quickly became friends, helping one another move furniture up the many steps, mixing paints, or sharing food and laughs. Fortunately I was attracted to only one of them and he was the most shy and least often present.

The most outgoing of the three, Harris, told us immediately that he was otherwise known as Big Hilda, "Not only tall but big in all parts, if you know what I mean." They were regulars at the city's popular gay watering hole, The Black Cat. "Y'all should come with us sometime," Big Hilda said repeatedly. "You'd be a real hit, Mister Doctor Hubby, but we'd protect you. We want to keep you for ourselves."

On Halloween evening we were having dinner in our dining room with Nick and Dot when the three of them plus three of their friends came noisily up the back stairs that connected the two kitchen sun porches. They were all in elaborate drag, gowns, wigs, heels and lots of make-up. "We wanted y'all to be the first privileged straight folks to see this bevy of beauty," Big Hilda announced as they paraded around the dining room. We four applauded appreciatively. "And just for tonight I am revealing myself as a theater celebrity whose *nom de plumage* is Back Row Betty."

At Christmas they had gifts for us. Barbara had baked a pie for them. For Barbara they had a small box of fancy cosmetics, for me a miniature trophy inscribed *World's Most Patient Husband*. At the time I was not aware of its possible multiple meanings.

It was an excellent year of learning for me at the hospital. Bernie greeted me each morning with a smile and his standard "Did you save any souls yesterday?" He was always available for support and supervision but never pushed or acted superior. And he backed me up the few times I needed it.

One of those times was when I did a diagnostic evaluation on a young psychotic veteran and discovered that he had been mercilessly hounded throughout his time in Korea and later because he had fallen in love with a young Korean man. "I got called a lot of names and got beat up lots of times." I asked to have him assigned to me for psychotherapy and Bernie arranged it.

Though homosexuality officially was considered diagnostic, symptomatic evidence of mental illness at the time, I did not include it in his diagnosis. I told Bernie that I thought instead, he needed strong support for his homosexual feelings to help repair some of the damage done to him. He began to improve.

Our downstairs neighbors mentioned a new homosexual support organization in the city called *The Mattachine Society*. I mentioned it to the patient. He was interested. I requested a pass for him so that he could attend one of its meetings. He went. It helped. It was a needed boost to his self-esteem and self-respect.

The psychiatrist on his ward found out about it though and demanded that I present this patient's case, including diagnostic psychological test results and progress notes, at the hospital's monthly full staff meeting. He was angry. He wanted to know why the patient had been permitted to consort with avowed homosexuals. I could see that he was suspicious of me but held his suspicions in check since I was a married man with a wedding ring.

With Bernie's support I stood my ground for the presentation, nervous and scared but refusing to consider the patient's homosexual feelings to be pathological. The battle was won, the war was lost. Pass privileges were cancelled by the ward psychiatrist and the patient had another full psychotic episode. Bernie assured me that I had done the right thing. "This man will always know that you were on his side and went to bat for him. That counts, really. It will help."

Spring came early, fruit trees blossoming in February. On weekends I packed the tent and our camping gear into the little convertible and we explored the wonderful variety of the California countryside. We toured the wine country as far north as Mendocino, went south along the coast to Monterey, Carmel and Big Sur and inland to Yosemite and Squaw Valley. I would put up our tent in the campground, we would explore the area, then before dinner Barbara would change into a dress, heels and dangling earrings. We would put the top down and drive off to a nearby not-too-expensive restaurant. "Elegant camping," we called it. "Campy camping," the boys downstairs called it.

The return drive each Sunday was timed so that we could stop for a sunset sandwich in Sausalito or a pizza in North Beach listening to *Fledger at the Opera* on the car radio. I was in love with California, in love with life and in love with our marriage.

Barbara created a painting studio in one of our spare rooms and made a large sketch painting of Joanie and Jim's first child, their son, at eleven months of age. It was a less than subtle hint. She wanted to get pregnant. "I could use the smaller room across the hall as a studio and this could be the nursery," she said. We stopped using birth control. Maybe we could stay in San Francisco and raise our child in this beautiful city.

Bernie began reminding me that the internship year would be ending in June. "Will your dissertation be done? When will you actually have the Ph.D.? Any interest in a staff job here? We'll probably have funds to hire one or two interns. We need you."

I had collected all of the data for my dissertation before leaving New York and had been doing the statistical analysis some evenings in the hospital's calculator room. The rules at the time required the Ph.D.

candidate to process data manually using calculators that then were machines too heavy and bulky to be considered portable. There was a huge computer at Stanford University that could be rented expensively by the quarter hour. It could have done all of my needed statistics in less than half an hour but that was against academic rules.

In March, Wayne wrote to say that he was marrying. His bride-to-be was wholesome, bright, competent Jeane. I was glad for him. The wedding was set for April and he wanted me to be his Best Man. Barbara and I agreed that we had to find a way to make the trip to Philadelphia. But there was no way that we could afford to fly there in April and then make another trip to New York in June to defend my thesis at the required final Oral Examination.

I wrote to Gerry as the head of my dissertation committee and to Gordon as head of the Clinical Program and told them there was a family emergency that required me to be in Philadelphia near the end of April, assuring them that I could have the data analysis done and the dissertation written by then and pleading to take the Oral Exam while there because I could not afford two trips East. They agreed.

We then spent two weekends and several evenings in the hospital's calculator room. The calculations were not difficult but they were tedious and took time. Barbara helped. That done, I set to work writing the dissertation, sending drafts to committee members for comments. *Firmness of Parental Control as an Antecedent in the Development of Persuasibility in Young Children* was the less than literary title. I was more than ready to be done with it.

A part of the final agonizing academic ritual required a clean, no carbon, copy of the thesis for each faculty member at the examination. The morning after we flew into Philadelphia, we rented several typewriters and set up shop on the dining room table at Barbara's parents'. Barbara, her mother, her aunt Eleanor, who had once been a legal stenographer, and I took turns churning out pages.

On the day of the exam we got up very early to catch a train to New York. I had pains in my stomach that had started during the night. I had to make repeated quick trips to the bathroom. I was sick. It felt like food poisoning. I could not eat. Barbara and her mother both thought I should call the school and cancel or postpone. I put a handful of pills into my suit pocket and announced that I was going to go if I had to go in an ambulance. I was too close to the finish line. The examination was scheduled for the afternoon.

It was ritualistic, each faculty examiner showing his or her academic prowess by asking complicated questions designed to impress other faculty members. I endured respectfully. To the statistician's very long-winded, complex and foolish question near the end I chose to simply answer, "I do not know the answer to that question." He seemed pleased.

Waiting in the hall outside while they discussed my performance I was keenly aware of my aching, empty stomach. Finally, the door opened. Gordon emerged, shook my hand and said, "Congratulations, Doctor." The stomach pains disappeared and I was very, very hungry suddenly. Barbara and I went out to a nearby restaurant to celebrate. I ate an appetizer and two main dishes plus dessert. I also managed to down a martini and some wine.

Wayne's wedding to Jeane was Quaker oriented, simple, intimate and very sweet, only six of us plus music and beautiful flowers. We had drinks, cake, took pictures and they went off on their honeymoon. We flew back to San Francisco.

Bernie was very pleased. The Duchess had a surprise for me. Though I would not be officially entitled to be called *Doctor* until the full year of internship ended in June she had a sign made with the new title, ready and waiting until she heard the verdict, then up it went immediately on the door of my ward office. She also made sure that everyone, including the ward psychiatrist, addressed me at least once as *Doctor*.

Bernie persisted. "Looks like we may be having only one hire. Think about it. It's a good job. It's kind of a dead end professionally, but there are souls to be saved and you're good. You'd float to the top." I decided that I should wait and go to the American Psychological Association's convention meetings and see what jobs were available for new clinical Ph.D.s. "Why don't we see if we can get you a six month post-doc at the V.A. Clinic in the city?" Bernie said. He arranged it.

Our final day on the ward Grant said, "Hey, call Barbara and tell her we're having a farewell guy's night out. That kid I told you about, Joanie Baez, is singing at the coffee house. We can go out later and get some drinks. Stay overnight at my place."

"I'm tempted, but I think I'd better not. How about you and Jo come into the city tomorrow night for dinner?" Jo was his newest girlfriend.

We saw a lot of Grant and his girlfriends. Jo was stylish, a Hollywood aspirant. High maintenance, she often lost a contact lens and had everyone on hands and knees looking for it. We liked Marge better. He began pursuing her seriously the month before we left. "She's kind of a socialist, though," Grant said. "I think she doesn't approve of money."

The downtown clinic was a dull disappointment after the exciting year of learning and making friends at the hospital. It was an easy commute, taking the trolley down Market to Fourth Street. Sometimes Barbara and I met at lunch for a walk. Most of the patients came in to the clinic to have prescriptions refilled. Few were interested in therapy. We did have a very bright, dynamic consultant and I managed to get an hour with her each week. I learned what I could from her.

At the convention there were two jobs that interested me. One was working on the Blackfoot Indian reservation. The other was a federally funded clinical research into the rehabilitation possibilities for long-term chronic patients at the Philadelphia State Hospital. That job would put us back near New York, old friends and Barbara's family. I was offered both jobs. Barbara and I talked it over and I chose Philadelphia. I was to start the first Monday in January, 1960.

That brought up the question of a driver's license for Barbara again. We practiced on deserted country roads outside of the city. We practiced on flat roads in the city. We attempted a few of the less steep hills in the city. Amazingly, she took the driving test in hilly San Francisco and passed.

"His last name was Clark," she told me. "Maybe he thinks we're related. I think he was afraid he'd be assigned to me another time if he didn't pass me. He seemed relieved to get out of the car."

"Go to Mexico," Grant said. "Why not? It can be on the way East, a side trip down to Mexico. You'll love it." He planted the seed. Barbara and I started reading about Mexico. I arranged to use accumulated sick leave and vacation time and take advantage of the Thanksgiving holiday, leaving for Philadelphia late in November we drove down the West Coast Highway to Mexico City.

The last time that Grant and Marge came to the apartment on Ord Street he startled me when I found him alone in the front parlor, lights off, looking out at the view. Marge and Barbara were in the kitchen. "It gets dark so early in November," he said. "Great view. I'm gonna' miss this place." He pulled me close and held me tight in muscular, weight-lifter's arms. "I'm gonna miss you too, Man."

"Yeah, me too," I answered, wrapping my arms around him. Faces close, I could feel the stubble on his cheek, his thighs against mine, warmth as our bodies pressed together.

"Hey, let's meet in New York," he said. "Or you come on back out here and visit."

"It's a deal," I said.

"Deal." He loosened the embrace, our hands brushed against each other, fumbling in the dark to find one another to shake. Eyes met and held. "*Mano a mano,*" he said.

Barbara and Marge called from the kitchen. "Hey, guys, come on, everything's ready. Get it while it's warm."

Chapter 16

Psychologist and Professor

We sold or gave away all of the furniture bargains. I felt sad closing the door of our flat on Ord Street but our little convertible was packed full and the road south was waiting. We arrived in the Los Angeles area late in the afternoon, in time to sit down to an evening meal with my parents and sister.

Except for the Thanksgiving turkey, our two days there were a repeat of the earlier visit, including a trip to Knott's Berry Farm. There were questions about why I was going all the way back to Philadelphia to be a doctor and why in the world we wanted to drive all the way down to Mexico City. They were a bit more relaxed with Barbara and she with them. As my father said while he was helping me to repack the car, "The novelty's wore off. She seems okay."

Early Friday morning we put the top down, waved goodbye and headed for Tucson, Arizona where we would spend the night before crossing into Mexico at Nogales. Barbara felt comfortable driving for an hour at a time on U.S. highways but feared Mexico would be another story.

It was. The first day we somehow got off the road while following detour signs and found ourselves driving along a dry riverbed. I used limited Spanish to ask the two children who were playing there and startled to see us, where we could find the road. Speechless, they pointed to the embankment. The road ran parallel to the riverbed. Its lowest point seemed to be less than a quarter of a mile ahead. I hoped for the best and aimed for it. We made it. The children cheered and we breathed easier, vowing to pay more attention to future detour signs. We made it to Guaymas on the west coast at the end of that first day just as darkness approached and found an available room in a small resort shaded by palm trees on a clean, raked beach.

After fresh papaya and pineapple at breakfast I managed a quick swim in Golfo de California before we headed out onto the West Coast Highway toward Mazatlan. Barbara took short turns driving between towns and we stayed on the road. I felt happy. I had developed a taste for Mexican food, music and art during our time in San Francisco. Now we were in Mexico, the sun was shining and it was warm even though it was November. I knew enough to stay overnight only in places where the car was secure, to drink only Coca Cola or beer and to avoid ice cubes.

I had not been warned to be careful about what I ate, however, and not to eat snacks offered by street vendors. We spent two nights in Mazatlan and two in Guadalajara. By the time I drove into Mexico City for our five day stay there my stomach was complaining, a result of the street vendors' snacks probably. By the second day in Mexico City I could not leave the hotel room's bed and bathroom. It felt like I had swallowed razor blades. I developed a fever. Barbara was worried. The hotel doctor was consulted. He recommended fluids and rest. "It will pass."

It did. But it left me weak and without appetite. We had planned to splurge on a few *authentic* restaurants in Mexico City. Instead I was cautiously appreciative of soft-boiled eggs and toast. We cancelled our tentative plan to drive south from Mexico City and extended our stay at the hotel by two days. The final days I was able to do some sightseeing and the final evening we did eat in the most expensive of the recommended restaurants where Barbara dined amid the fountains and violins as I cautiously combed the menu for a few bland items.

We drove north on the inland highway toward Laredo, no unnecessary stops, crossing the border late in the afternoon of the second day. My stomach had not yet stopped complaining and I was happy to find a big American motel and restaurant with safe drinking water on the outskirts of San Antonio. We stayed there two nights, swam in the pool and happily dined from an unimaginative menu. We stopped in New Orleans and in Alabama again where Barbara was congratulated by her uncle and aunt on the California drivers' license she had obtained in the famously hilly city of San Francisco. We were driving into winter. It was snowing as we approached Philadelphia.

Barbara's parents were happy to see us. Nellie had prepared a meal of comfort food. "Heard your stomach wasn't doin' too good," she said with a smile. "Home style cookin's what you need. Some good macaroni and cheese here, creamed peas. This'll fix you up."

Two days later the streets had been cleared of snow. Christmas was three days away. Barbara and I drove into Philadelphia to do some modest Christmas shopping. We had lunch and then drove out to the edge of the city to see the hospital where I would be working. We wanted to see what housing possibilities were like in the neighborhood.

The Philadelphia State Hospital was huge. It was a hidden town with seven thousand patients and hundreds of employees. Locals still referred to it as Byberry, the name of the city's old Insane Asylum. Housing nearby did not look promising.

I got lost driving the small rural roads around the circumference of the grounds and came upon a *For Rent* sign. There were two Tudor style houses next to a farm, the larger house was clearly occupied, a car in its driveway and smoke curling into the pale winter sky from its chimney. The smaller cottage nearby, shielded from the house by trees, overlooked the farm and appeared to be empty. It was a long shot but we wrote down the telephone number.

I was not yet out of debt from college and graduate school and even on a salary that was two thousand dollars a year more than my internship pay had been it seemed likely that we would need to find an apartment, perhaps on the other side of the Delaware River in

New Jersey. The ninety-five dollars for the apartment plus five dollars for the garage that we had been paying in San Francisco had been a financial strain. One hundred a month was our agreed limit now.

But we telephoned. Indeed, it was the cottage that was for rent, "available right now" the welcoming voice of the woman said. "Two dormered bedrooms, one quite large, living room with fireplace, an eat-in kitchen, laundry room and flagstone patio." But the rent was one hundred and twenty-five dollars.

We looked elsewhere. January was approaching fast and I was to start work three days after New Year's Day. The hospital was a thirty-five minute drive from Barbara's parents, the same to the center of Philadelphia. Everything seemed to be either run-down and dangerous or too expensive.

"Let's go look at that place you saw near the hospital," Grace said. "I want to take Barbara shopping in the city anyway. Maybe they'll like you and lower the rent. Try bargaining."

We loved the cottage. The landlady loved us. But the price was firm, she said. We lingered. "We can't do it," I said finally to Barbara. "We'll have to find an apartment in the city somewhere. My pay isn't enough yet." Grace shocked me as I closed the door behind us. "Well, Barbara *could* get a job and work, you know," she said.

I was stunned. I guess I had expected that Grace would want me to take care of her daughter in all of the ways that Barney took care of her with total, unquestioning financial support. She, though, was a person who had opened a store with a friend during the war when ladies worked. She had enjoyed it. But when the war ended, she had returned to her proper role as the wife of a lawyer, entertaining at home or at the Country Club and "playing bridge with the girls." I glimpsed her own frustration in being the country club wife and mother rather than having her own independent part in life.

There was a glimpse of something else too but it lasted only a moment. I was on a path to respectability, imitating others as I thought they were, but I was not moving forward as myself. That momentary glimpse scared me. Barbara and I were on different paths. I was becoming someone respectable but it was not me, at least not all of me.

I had given in to Barbara's wish for a baby and assumed that we would model our lives after her parents until our child or children were old enough for Barbara to begin work in her field of choice, whatever that might be. Barbara was not eager to go job hunting. She wanted to be a housewife and mother. Another two days of looking at apartments too far away or too dilapidated and I gave up. I telephoned the landlady and tried again but she held firm on the price. "But we could include heat and water," she said.

I would have to find additional income. "Maybe I can start a part-time private practice in Philadelphia," I told Barbara. My accumulated hours and experience, including the Army years, had grandfathered me in to the new certification licensing law in California just before we left. Pennsylvania did not yet have a licensing law.

We moved into our cottage four days before my first day at the hospital with the furniture we had stored in Barbara's parents' basement, plus some pieces of furniture Grace had been "just looking for an excuse to replace." She also bought us a small wrought-iron, glass-topped outdoor table and four chairs that we could use in the kitchen or on the flagstone patio in summer. Wayne and Jeane, who lived in a rural area on the far other side of Philadelphia, also lent two tables and two lamps that they were not using. We had our first meal in front of our fireplace as snow was falling at the end of New Year's Day.

The first few days of the hospital were devoted to meeting the staff of our Clinical Research Program and key staff members in the hospital. The hospital's seven thousand patient population was tended by just a handful of psychiatrists, a few social workers, one psychologist and a large number of nurses, nursing assistants and ward attendants. Most of the labor in the kitchens, dining halls, laundry and maintenance departments was supplied by patients who had been there for many years.

Our small, federally funded rehabilitation program study was staffed by a dozen psychologists, psychiatrists and social workers. I had a private office and my own secretary. We ate in a serene cottage dining room with starched white tablecloths, waited on by patients who had been serving doctors for a long time.

I liked my boss, J.G., immediately. He was an unusual mix of tough, tender, smart and compassionate. He could be personally open and warm or closed and cold, depending on the circumstance and the person with whom he was talking. He had been a very young Marine in dress uniform serving as a guard at the U. S. Embassy in Tokyo on December 7, 1941 and, therefore, had spent all of the war years in various prison-of-war labor camps. He told me about some of his experiences but I knew that I would never learn them all. I could never know what he knew of the deep potential people have to harm one another, to torture, hate, love and sometimes heal.

My job was to go into the general hospital population, to read patients' charts and interview those patients who had been named as possible candidates for our program. The males transferred to our unit were then my administrative responsibility. I received nursing reports on them, interviewed and counseled them, wrote progress notes and, finally, recommendations. I coordinated efforts with the assigned social worker and sat on a monthly interdisciplinary review board making final release decisions.

Our patients had been hospitalized for as long as fifteen to thirty years. The clinical research question was whether they could be released and live on their own in society again. The answer seemed painfully clear to me after the first few months.

Most of those selected could be *rehabilitated* to survive outside of the hospital setting. Relatives usually wanted little or nothing to do with them but they could manage in a rooming house or half-way house, getting by on welfare. Few returned to the hospital but, while harmless, they were lonely social isolates, separated from *normal* people by odd mannerisms.

Separated by miles from the friends and associates who had accepted them, fed them, washed their linens and said hello to them every day in the unusual town known as the State Hospital, they became lonely. For many, perhaps most of the patients, this giant hospital was a snake pit offering little hope, yet for these untroublesome old-timers it had become home.

I liked my co-workers and hated the hospital. When I went into the locked wards there were people tugging at my sleeve, begging for someone in authority to listen for just one minute. My work seemed futile. Except for the very few people I might help, I was useless.

It was the wrong job. It would look good on a resume if I stayed at least a year but it would eat away at my humanity in a serious way if I stayed too long. Workers there protected themselves by becoming insensitive. After six months on the job I decided to look for another job with a start date sometime after I had put in a full year. I missed San Francisco and our friends there. I missed Grant the most. Maybe we could go back to California or to New York, depending on what Barbara wanted. New York would be closer to her family.

We enjoyed watching the changing seasons from our cottage. We saw Wayne and Jeane often. They came to dinner and we visited them, driving around the central city nearly an hour to get to one another. Joanie and Jim, Anne and our other New York friends came and we made trips to New York to visit them. We visited Barbara's parents every week usually.

On my lunch hour one sunny winter day we sat at our glass-topped table in the kitchen, looking at a pair of peacocks perched on the bare branches of the cherry tree outside the window. We were being thrilled by John F. Kennedy's inauguration words: "Ask not what your country can do for you..." coming from the radio.

Joanie gave birth to their second child, a girl. We had not been using any form of birth control for more than a year and Barbara was not pregnant. We decided that our next move would be to New York. If she was not pregnant by then, we would consult specialists and also seriously consider adoption. I began to investigate school psychologist job possibilities on Long Island. I had enjoyed the work as a graduate student, was good at it and felt like it made a difference. It would give me more free time in summers to indulge my urge to write fiction and I could still have a small private practice. In the meantime I sublet an office in downtown Philadelphia two evenings a week and started with my first private patients.

Perhaps I should have seen the problem with Wayne coming but I did not. We were best friends and confidants. I was aware that we drank too much when we went to their house for dinner and I also was dimly aware that he and I had unfinished business related to such things as money and sexual secrets but I was unaware there was hidden envy. It seemed clear to me that Wayne knew more about most things than I did. It was true that I had a Ph.D. and that he often teasingly called me *doctor* but his Masters' Degree was from *Harvard* and he was in demand as a private school teacher and administrator.

We sat in their large garden late one summer Saturday, drinking gin and tonics, telling tales from work and trading stories about mutual friends. There seemed to be an increasing edge to Wayne's remarks, a tension in the air. But we made it through the dinner with wine. I was telling about our planned move to New York and made a throw away remark for a laugh. "Everyone says the Village is out but there's an apartment there somewhere and we should have it."

Suddenly, Wayne attacked. "You always think you can do whatever you want. You're so God damned superior and I, for one, am sick of it." I sat, mouth open, shocked as Jeane and Barbara frantically tried to soothe, distract and put out the fire. "You're just a superficial nobody," he ranted.

It was time to leave. I felt confused and overwhelmed. My friend had become an enemy. As we headed for the car I handed the keys to Barbara and asked her to drive. I felt the tears coming and I had a sudden, piercing, incapacitating headache. I did not understand what had just happened or why it had happened. It was crazy. My world had turned upside down.

I tried writing to him, telling him that I did not understand what I had done to provide the attack. He did not answer. It hurt. We had communicated about everything always. It did not occur to me that he was too humiliated by his outburst to respond. Pressure had been building behind a dam I had not known was there. Since I was not sexually attracted to him it also did not occur to me that we had been in love. Time passed and I constructed defenses to put distance between awareness and the hurt.

The next time I saw Wayne in person, many years later, he said it was all quite simple. "Envy. I'd been envious of you since college days. You were the one who was funny and bright, who could dance, who could be really serious and sincere. And then you went and got a Ph.D. and had your pick of jobs and places to live." I was dumbfounded. I always had seen him as the one who had read more books, knew all of the famous names and charmed important people.

Our friendship never recovered. The trust and intimacy had been irrevocably destroyed, real repair impossible.

Barbara and I contacted everyone in New York that we knew, telling them we would be moving there again, possibly to Long Island. In May, Gerry, my mentor from Adelphi contacted me. He had moved up the academic ladder to Hunter College in Manhattan and suggested that I join him there. He had taken Federal grant money with him and was a full professor.

I told him that I already had one definite offer for a job as school psychologist on Long Island with decent pay and summers free. I also confessed my need to do something that I could see clearly helped people. Children in school offered a great possibility, I thought, remembering my own years of misery as a school child.

Gerry was persuasive, as always. He persuaded me that working in the Psychological Clinic run by the Education Department at Hunter, participating in research and teaching teachers could do more good for children. I applied and was officially offered the job. I was to begin the last week of August.

Barbara and I started an earnest search for a decent apartment in Manhattan, spending most weekends in New York, usually staying with Joan, Jim and their two children in Brooklyn, continually asking everyone we knew to ask everyone they knew for any clue to a rent controlled, two bedroom apartment, preferably in Greenwich Village. I was excited again.

We met a young woman on the street in Manhattan who had worked with Barbara at her last job there in the public relations firm. Becky was beautiful. She had married while we were in California and now lived in the Village, she said, just west of Fifth Avenue. She invited us to a cocktail party the following weekend. She said it would be a great opportunity to pester people about apartment possibilities.

Her new husband, George, was as Hollywood handsome as Becky was beautiful, tanned and dressed in expensive, elegant, casual clothing. They seemed a perfectly matched pair. They introduced us to the other guests, a diverse group, mixed and balanced for intellect, accomplishment and looks--a stimulating Greenwich Village cocktail party in the summer of 1961. My questions about apartments seemed to fall on deaf ears but the party was fun.

As Barbara and I were getting ready to leave I mentioned that I had met a woman I liked a lot and hoped we might invite her to dinner once we were settled in the city. Her name was Barbara, also, a teacher who was married and the mother of two young children. "She's lively, beautiful, and has an amazingly broad range of interests, including psychology, literature, music and art."

Barbara said she had met a man she liked a lot too. "Maybe we could invite them together." Frank, she said, was a painter and historian who taught high school. We agreed to get their telephone numbers before leaving. We all had a good laugh when we learned that they were married to one another and had been having the same conversation about the two of us. As we were leaving I asked Becky's husband, George, to please keep us in mind if he heard of anyone planning to move out of an apartment anywhere in the Village. "Please," I said, "we want to live near here. We've got to find a place soon."

"Hey, wait a minute," he said. "My father and stepmother have a brownstone on Charles Street near Seventh Avenue. That's not far from here. I think the woman who lives on the top floor is moving out, or already has. He says the place is a mess and he's pretty discouraged about fixing it up."

We called his father and went to see the apartment the next day. It was empty, a third floor walk-up, the full top floor, two bedrooms facing the street, a funky ancient bathroom with a pull chain toilet, an impossibly small kitchen that measured five feet by five feet, wall to wall, a living room with a fireplace wall of partially exposed old red brick and a fireplace that did not work. There were decaying parts of a deck visible outside the windows at the rear and spaces between the living room floorboards large enough to see into the apartment below. It was, as promised, a real mess.

"The rent controlled price is ridiculous," his father said. "She was here when we got the building, lived here twenty-two years. It doesn't really pay or make it worthwhile to rent it, let alone even think of the cost of fixing it up. I'd have to get rid of that rotten deck and put in a whole new kitchen."

I loved the place. Barbara was worried. I had caught the hint from George's father. "Maybe we could figure out a way to make it work," I

said to him. "We fixed up an apartment in bad shape in San Francisco."
He was interested. He smiled. He liked us.

"Well, you're friends of the family," he said, "maybe we can do
something. If you could *unofficially* pay maybe two hundred and
seventy-five a month. Unofficially, you understand. I could have
someone get rid of that deck debris, I suppose. I don't know about the
kitchen though. I'd have to put in a new stove and refrigerator, maybe
get second hand ones." He said he would talk to Florence, his wife.

I told him we would have a very hard time coming up with two
hundred and seventy five but could promise to work with him on
fixing the place up. He was thinking. The apartment was going to be
ours. I knew it. We continued negotiations through the next week by
telephone from Philadelphia.

"Florence has been after me to get her a bigger refrigerator so I
might put our old one in there and a cousin of hers has a small stove
that he said he could let me have for twenty bucks," he said in the
second call. "I like your pegboard walls idea for hanging things in the
kitchen. If you pay for materials I could have my handy-man put in
shelves in the kitchen. He could nail up the pegboard and fill in the
floorboards too while he's taking out the deck parts. In fact, if you
want a new deck, he says the supports are good still. I could pay part
of the cost of a new deck I suppose. It would run about four or five
hundred he guesses. You'd have to paint everything though, including
the deck."

Barbara's father said he could lend us six hundred dollars. The
unofficial rent was set at two hundred and thirty dollars finally. We
sold our car and did split the cost of a new deck. I fully exposed the
red brick fireplace wall, put down a black and white checkerboard
floor of vinyl tiles in the small entry way and the bathroom, glued
burgundy-dyed burlap to uneven walls in both areas and finished the
cheap and newly very efficient little kitchen.

We painted the old tub and pipes in the bathroom as well as
bedroom walls and floors. Barbara found a small, slightly dented,
brass chandelier that had been badly wired for electricity. We took out
the wiring, polished it up, put candles in it and hung it over our small
expandable dining table between the windows that opened out onto
our deck and looked toward Sheridan Square beyond.

After we moved in I began work on a floor to ceiling bookcase that I carefully wedged between the irregular wall at the end of the fireplace and the irregular wall of the bedroom. The smaller bedroom was made into a combination guest room, painting studio and study, ready to be easily converted to a nursery.

We were both thirty-one years old. It was time. We made doctors' appointments to be checked for fertility problems. Barbara had a slight infection that was cleared quickly with an antibiotic and after I made an embarrassing visit to a doctor's closet with a plastic cup and a girlie magazine handed to me by the nurse, we received reports pronouncing us fit and fertile.

As a new hire I had to sign papers in the college first. "A loyalty oath?" I asked, surprised. "I thought those things died a well deserved death when that fascist demagogue McCarthy fell." The payroll clerk was not impressed. The law was still on the books. In my world it had been the people who refused to sign the oaths who were the heroes, those who signed became pawns in his game.

"If it's not signed we can't put you on the payroll."

Walking from the college along the south side of Sixty-ninth Street, I looked across the street at the quote from Emerson carved high into the stone façade of the college. "Yeah, *truth*," I said aloud, still smarting from the requirement.

Hunter's Educational Clinic was in an old brick building at Sixty-Ninth Street and Lexington Avenue, diagonally across the street from the college. Its rooms were large and smelled of fresh paint applied during the summer. The windows were large, drafty, metal barred and caked with grime around their aged edges.

I was not the only new hire. June, the woman who was the Director, was new also. Though not young, her life had taken a turn. In addition to her new job, she was newly married and had a new doctorate. She had brought in an old friend and colleague from work in the schools. Mary had not quite finished her own doctorate but had a Master's degree in educational psychology and many years of experience in various school districts.

There was a new young social worker, Ellie; a young woman psychology graduate student, Sarah, working on her doctoral thesis study; and another newly minted psychologist, Clarence, who presented the only ethnic face of color to be seen. The senior social worker, Mrs. Edwards, had been there for years and let everyone know it.

June had an affinity for meetings and forms. Each of us had a full one hour supervision meeting with her each week. There was also one whole morning and one two hour afternoon staff meeting each week. We all filled out forms which were typed by the very efficient and all-knowing secretary, Ruth, before being passed on to June for review. It seemed to me that our most important mission was to provide paperwork that would convince the administrators of the Education Department that we were a busy lot of professionals deserving consideration for promotions.

Our main job, I was told, was to use the large one-way mirrored room to administer psychological tests to children, then interpret the tests and explain the whole process to college students who came in classes to observe and listen. We were to show them how an up-to-date educational psychiatric team made use of the psychologist, psychiatrist, social worker and teacher. June's orientation was decidedly psychoanalytic, also in keeping with the style of the day.

Style counted. We all dressed well. June and the senior social worker were the most stylish, often complimenting one another on a hat or other article of clothing picked up at Henri Bendel, Saks or Peck & Peck. Stylish private schools were a favorite topic of discussion for them.

The psychologists on the staff were assigned to administer and interpret the individual intelligence tests and interview the four year olds whose parents were hoping to get them enrolled in the Hunter Elementary School. The school was stylish but not private, a free public school for intellectually gifted children. It was a laboratory school for Hunter's Education Department. Admission was fiercely competitive.

To be considered for admission a child had to score in the top one percent on an individually administered standard intelligence test. Admission offered parents the best parental bragging rights in the city. Though they could not buy their way in, many did spend large amounts of time and money having their poor children coached for the testing. Part of our job was to factor out any extra help and pressure given to the child.

At the end of the first week on the job I told Gerry honestly that I did not think I was going to feel constructively challenged there. He promised the problem could be fixed. "This current policy of bringing in new Ph.D.s at the Instructor level is as insulting as requiring us to sign loyalty oaths before we can be put on the payroll. But we're going to get this department on its feet. Let's get you involved in my new research, get some night and summer course teaching for you so you can make a bit more money, and if you want more clinical contact with kids, why not make yourself known at the Hunter Elementary School? They just got a new young guy as principal and he's pretty sharp."

Done. I was off and running. By the second semester I had volunteered to be the school psychologist for the Elementary school, was to be a co-author of a monograph that would be coming out of a research project Gerry had involved me in and I was teaching two evenings a week. It was the beginning of a delicate dance with June who was suspicious of my engaging in activities under the Department's control that were not under her control. "You're young and eager," she observed with an anxious smile.

I also had to go through the ordeal of taking the new psychology licensing examination in New York. Though I had been grandfathered in California there was no reciprocity between the two states and the new examination was a haphazard mess of multiple choice questions contributed by senior psychologists engaged in all sorts of work in New York. I had to guess at answers to questions about work in advertising agencies, prisons and drug companies in the morning, but the afternoon essay questions permitted *clinical* as one of the choices in answering posed questions and designing a research project. I passed.

In the second semester, June brought in a highly respected psychoanalyst as a consultant. Asya had started life in Russia, before emigrating to Europe as a very young woman. She had then moved on to New York as war clouds gathered. She knew or had met all of the stars of her day in psychoanalysis, was a keen observer and had ideas of her own.

She told the clinic staff that she would like to set up a demonstration of group therapy with young children. She was a leading expert in the use of group psychotherapy but using it with six year olds was definitely different. She said that she would offer private consultation weekly with "whoever is brave enough to volunteer to do such group play in the mirror room with first graders from your Hunter Elementary School."

No one volunteered. "Come on people," she said. "Nobody bites you. We're watching behind the mirrors one hour each week to learn, the whole staff, then all talk about what we see one hour following. Then I meet later in the week at my home apartment office with the therapist one hour. Nobody?"

I raised my hand. "Good man," she said. "We select children and start in two weeks."

The first play session was awful. I sat on a stool, being a good, reflective and non-directive therapist as these very bright six year olds poured finger paints, water and sand on the floor of the observation room, tried using blocks to skate or ski, and screamed and laughed as they made me wish I had not been stupid enough to volunteer.

"Very, very different," Asya said when it was over. "You're a very patient man and brave." Later in the week, at her apartment office, uptown on Park Avenue, she said, "First of all, my darling, children *move*, and they need everything should move. You don't move, so they need to get you moving." We both knew, and years later admitted to one another, that from that first week we had been aware that we were going to be very good friends. We trusted one another. I was ready to learn from her. She was ready to guide.

Barbara had found occasional work as a proofreader at a printing plant where a woman whom she had known in earlier years in New York now worked. It was dull work, lasting a few days at a time but it helped us financially. The pregnancy was not happening. She looked into attending open art classes.

In January of 1962 her doctor recommended we plot ovulation and fertility by keeping daily temperature records and plan intercourse accordingly. Sex became, at least in part, a scheduled job to be done to produce a baby.

In March she became pregnant. We were excited and joyful. We celebrated with dinner at our favorite neighborhood restaurant, *Fedora's*, around the corner on Fourth Street. Barbara did not want to tell anyone until June, after the third moth. The miscarriage happened near the end of May. We told her parents and we told Joan and Jim. It was a private grief that took us by surprise. We had not really realized how many dreams and hopes we had invested in our unseen child.

We had been seeing Joan and Jim and their two children fairly often. They lived across the Williamsburg Bridge in Brooklyn, where rents were cheaper. Taxis sometimes refused to go there so we learned to get into the cab and check the driver's name and number first before telling our destination. When they could get a sitter for the children, they joined us in the Village for a welcome change of scene. We saw other old friends too and we got to know Barbara and Frank, whom we had met at the cocktail party the day we learned of the apartment. We were developing a close friendship with them.

Summer came. Barbara painted and worked some days. I taught summer school for extra pay. We went to neighborhood movies. I repainted the deck blue and white. We had an old-fashioned red and white striped awning installed over it, the kind that had to be hand cranked open. It kept the deck relatively free of soot and made it cozy for candle lit summer evening dinners.

Grant and Marge came from California. They had married a few months after we left San Francisco. They were staying in a fancy midtown hotel with Grant's father but escaped for an evening and came for dinner at our place. Barbara and Marge squeezed into the tiny kitchen. Grant and I sat on the deck drinking gin and tonics. Dinner was delayed.

The combination of the drinks and street noise caused a misunderstanding. I thought Grant was confessing an attraction to me. I reciprocated. The confusion was brief and embarrassing. We laughed. Then he put his hand on my arm and said, "Actually, it probably is true. We're married men but, after all, the Greeks did that sort of thing, no? I mean maybe we can."

After dinner he and I announced that we wanted to go to Julius' for beer. We had never seen it. "I hear a lot of strange types go there.

A tourist attraction, part of my education I've missed," he said. Marge said she didn't mind if he went but she was tired and would take a cab back to the hotel. Barbara said she also was tired and wanted to go to sleep.

Men drink beer, sometimes a lot of it. We did. It facilitates confessions of caring, affection, even love. It permits intimate talk and gentle touching. *Greek* became our code word. In the months that followed we used the word in notes and letters, signaling that we remembered our new bond. "Who knows, maybe someday we'll go crazy and run away to Greece," he said as we left Julius' that night.

I confessed to myself and drunkenly hinted to him that I was in love with him and had been for a long time but kept it a secret even from myself. He was exotic, a renegade motorcyclist, a muscular handsome rich guy who could afford to be different. And he had feelings for me too it seemed.

I now owned a love, a love of my own that had come into being and had been spoken out loud to another man, to *the* man, a respectable man. Maybe it was possible, after all, to wholly love another man and have it be part of a respectable life. Grant was with me in my thoughts and fantasies at work and at home every day. He appeared in my dreams.

Chapter 17

Love and Death

Shortly after their visit Barbara realized that she was pregnant again. We planned to be careful. We told no one. We ate healthy foods, took walks, got plenty of sleep. But early in September there was another miscarriage. The tiny fetus was saved as per the doctor's instructions for laboratory examination, checking for abnormalities.

"We can't do this," I said to Barbara. "We can't just go from pregnancy to pregnancy. Our lives have to have a broader focus." I urged and prodded her to be sensible and plan an occupational future. "Kids grow up. Even if we have a child or two, you'll need a profession or occupation." We agreed, finally, that teaching would be good. It could lead her in a number of possible other career directions. The prestigious Bank Street College of Education was only a few blocks away. She could earn a Master's degree in two years or less, even with a pregnancy and birth. She enrolled.

I signed up for a course in creative writing at the New School, also only a few blocks away. During the half dozen years of writing clinical reports, school papers and my final thesis I had lost the writing voice

that had been with me since childhood. It had flowered in the army
years and then disappeared. I needed to prime the pump.

Both of our school projects worked. Barbara liked the faculty
and students at Bank Street. After the first few assignments and very
helpful commentaries from the teacher, Hayes Jacobs, my writing
began to flow again. I got up at dawn and sat bundled in pajamas, robe
and blanket in the living room writing each morning until Barbara got
up.

I did not realize how distant or distracted I was becoming. In
addition to my writing and my private thoughts of Grant, I had been
spending more time at the Hunter Elementary School. The principal
and I got along well and the secretary, Julie, and I got along extremely
well. She was smart, funny and capable, definitely the queen behind
the throne keeping the school on course. I did not realize how often I
talked about Julie at home.

On Thanksgiving weekend Barbara confronted me in a tearful
session. "You're always talking about Julie. Are you having an affair?
Are you in love with her? You're not really here anymore. Do you
want a divorce? Tell me!"

It took my breath away. I knew it was Grant. I had thought my
secret was safe, but she had read me, mistakenly thinking it was
Julie. I was the deer caught in the headlights, the kid caught with a
hand in the cookie jar. And did this have something to do with the
miscarriages? That jagged thought cut through the tangle of feelings
and other thoughts. Divorce was inconceivable, wasn't it? We were
married for life. Marriage was an integral, essential part of the new
life I had been developing. Wasn't it?

"No, Julie is just a friend," I said truthfully. "I like her. I'm not
in love with Julie. I don't want a divorce. I'm sorry if it seems like
my mind is elsewhere. Maybe it's the writing. I'll slow it down. We'll
take a vacation, maybe Puerto Rico for a few days during Christmas
vacation."

But did I want a divorce? I wondered. Did she have the wrong
person but the right question? I was confused and scared.

We did go to Puerto Rico, this time away from San Juan, up into
the mountains to Barranquitas and then over to the little village at

Parguerra where we swam at night making neon phosphorescent trails in the water.

A few weeks after the vacation Barbara told me that she was pregnant again. I privately vowed to put thoughts of Grant out of my mind and to refrain from mentioning Julie. I pampered Barbara in every way I could. I cooked. We went to the theater and to movies. We saw friends. I shopped for elegant maternity clothes in little Village shops.

Then David telephoned. He had heard that we were living in the Village. Anne had given him our number. Would it be possible to get together for a drink or dinner? We invited him for dinner.

He was seven years older than when I had last seen him at the end of that summer before graduate school. I had carried that picture of him in my mind, naked except for his shorts, the green of the vines and the ripe red of the tomato, his tanned arm and hand reaching toward me, our eyes locked on one another in a moment of stillness. He was quieter now, more settled, more solid, less angular. He wore maturity well, still handsome, still sexy, still funny, but different. He was in graduate school in California, visiting New York briefly for his brother's wedding.

He and I took a walk after dinner. Did I dare to speak of it; the night in Chicago, the unanswered letters, the night in Harlem? I took a deep breath and said "I owe you an apology, I think."

He touched my arm and turned me to face him. "No, don't. I liked it, a lot. It's okay, really okay. I wanted it, maybe more than you. I'm glad you're married now. I don't think I ever will be." He took both of my hands, close, facing me. "It was good to see you both. Good luck." I stood where he left me, not knowing what I felt or what I thought. I walked home slowly. Had I done this to him? Had I tainted his life? Had I been the person who started him down an unhappy path?

Barbara grew large. At the end of the fourth month her doctor told her it was either twins or an abnormal fetus. A few weeks more and twins were confirmed. "They're happy and doing well," the doctor said.

Barbara was glad to be having a full pregnancy at last but was physically uncomfortable and irritable. Stairs were a problem. I took over all tasks possible. The doctor became concerned. "It should be alright if you can make it to the seventh month," he said. "That would be early June."

We waited anxiously. The school year ended. We checked off the days on the calendar. We talked with Barbara and Frank and with Joan and Jim often. Joan had given birth to their third child, a second girl.

Allen, the man who had gone to Antioch and then through Adelphi in my class, had gotten married and moved into the Village near us, an apartment on Tenth Street, just three blocks away. They were going to Europe for the summer and he offered to rent his old red VW Bug, kept in a garage just across Seventh Avenue. "You pay the monthly twenty-five bucks for the garage plus fifteen and it's yours until we get back in September. You can get out of the city when it's hot." It seemed like a good idea with babies coming.

We drove over the Williamsburg Bridge to have dinner with Joan and Jim the night we calculated to be the end of the sixth month. We took wine. It was a celebration. "We can stop holding our breath," Barbara said. "We've made it into the seventh month."

We got home late and there was a parking place on the street so I did not bother to put the car in the garage. At dawn Barbara woke me. "I think I'm going into labor." We put in an emergency call to the doctor's answering service and got dressed. The doctor called and told us to meet him as quickly as possible at the Emergency Room of the hospital which was across town on the East Side and way uptown on Fifth Avenue in the Nineties. I was grateful that I did not have to retrieve the car from the garage. Every minute counted.

We had taken Lamaze classes together and I knew what to do if birth happened in the car before we got to the hospital. But that would apply only if there were no complications. Barbara was saying "Hurry. It's happening."

I was prepared to speed and go through red lights. I sped across town on Fourteenth Street, to Fifth Avenue and pointed the car uptown, my foot down on the accelerator, hand on the horn, hyper alert at intersections especially when the light was red. As we sped through a red light at the intersection at Forty-Second Street, other drivers honking and cursing I wondered why a police car had not found us. We needed one to escort us.

No police car, just Barbara groaning and cursing and saying "Hurry." They were waiting with a gurney at the entrance to the Emergency Room. I parked the car in a no-parking zone, ran to the door and took the elevator to the Waiting Room as instructed. I did not know what to do. I asked a nurse. I was told that she was in the Delivery Room. Time was suspended.

I had no idea of how long I had been waiting when her doctor appeared looking serious. "Identical twin boys," he said, "but we couldn't save them. I'm sorry. We had a heart beat when she got here but they're gone."

"Is she alright? How is she?"

"She's okay. She's resting. You can see her soon. You okay?"

"Yeah. I guess so."

"Why don't you sit down for a couple of minutes? We're going to need you to view them and sign some papers."

I was not okay. I was in some other world. Able to speak and hear but in some other place, where space and time had joined and thickened. He left the room, returning with papers and a pen, showing me where I needed to sign. I saw *Baby A Clark* and *Baby B Clark* had been filled in on lines in the papers. I signed, or the me who was holding a pen signed.

The doctor led me down the hall to a small room. A table had been covered with a fresh white towel. On the towel two perfect little boy babies had been placed, eyes closed as if in sleep, mouths open as if gasping for air. I have no idea how long I stood there looking at them, loving them, stunned by their perfection and horrified by their stillness. Those moments are engraved in me. I will never forget them.

A hand on my arm steered me back to the Waiting Room. "You'll be able to see your wife in a little while," the voice said. There was a phone booth in the room. I wondered how it would be to break the glass. I dialed Joan's and Jim's number but when they answered I could not get any words out, just awful hoarse animal crying sounds. They guessed. "Which hospital?" But they guessed that too. "We're coming" Joan said. I stayed in the phone booth a while, holding a dead receiver, crying.

I was sitting on a chair when the nurse came and said that I could see Barbara. The tears stopped. Done. She needed me. But, no, when I reached her bed she did not need me. "I'm okay," she said, "just tired. Go home and get some rest." They had given her a sedative.

"But Joan and Jim are coming."

"Why did you call them?" She seemed amazed. She had turned the page, moved on, the ordeal done.

I was grateful to them for coming. They sat with me. Joan called Barbara's parents who arrived in the afternoon. I walked on Fifth Avenue with Barney, looking across the avenue at the play of sunlight on new green leaves in the park. "That's why I always say not to count your chickens until they're hatched," he said. I was horrified by his words but knew he must be trying to comfort me or himself. Like Barbara maybe, he had turned the page and moved on, the ordeal finished.

He took a bus home that evening but Grace stayed. I wanted to make up our bedroom for her but she insisted on sleeping on the sofa bed in the living room. "She's alright," Grace said. "They said we could pick her up tomorrow at about eleven. She'll be alright. These things happen."

The still air seemed too thick to breathe. Sounds were muted and distorted. Food had no meaning or use. I did not want a drink. We ate scrambled eggs and toast. I stared at the ceiling in the bedroom unable to sleep, but sleep did take me finally.

The next few days moved from morning to night as if being pulled by the determined hands of the clock. I bought groceries and cooked. Barbara rested.

Then, waking up one morning, I said "We have to get out of here. We have the car. Let's go somewhere out of the city. Let's go to the ocean. Let's follow the shore south. Let's go visit your uncle and aunt in Alabama." Yes. Run away. The ocean, my old friend.

We did run away, New Jersey to Delaware, the Outer Banks of North Carolina, all the way to Alabama and back. It was a good trip. It was what was needed. We got back in time for work and our classes, ready for autumn in New York. The twins were gone, lifeless bodies gone with the papers I had signed. But the twins would be there in the shadows of my mind always and death was not done with us.

Barbara began to worry about her final project and paper and considered quitting. I told her I would help her. "Look, you're so close to a Master's. You could be done by the end of this year. Start the new year with a graduate degree."

I had hope of being promoted to Assistant Professor. The research I had been working on with Gerry had to do with looking at intelligence in inner city children from differing cultural groups without using the standard tests that worked best only in the suburbs. We were beginning to think out the first monograph to be published.

"There's an international conference in London at the end of August, almost a year away. You could present a little preliminary paper there. It would look good on your résumé," Gerry said.

In November, Julie told me that one of the teachers in Hunter Elementary would be taking a leave the next semester and wondered if my wife would be finished at Bank Street by then. I asked the school principal about the job and he suggested Barbara come in for an interview.

She was there for the interview on November twenty-second, the day that the clinic secretary, Ruth, dared to knock on June's door to interrupt the meeting she and I were having. "President Kennedy's been shot in Dallas and is being rushed to a hospital." The entire staff was gathered around Ruth's desk, listening to her small radio, hoping. Ruth was holding her rosary, praying and burst into tears as we heard: "It's confirmed. President Kennedy is dead. Vice President Lyndon Johnson is to be sworn in."

Disbelief and tears. Barbara hurried in from across the street. There would be no more school or clinic that day or for several days thereafter. We took a taxi home. The driver too was stunned, his radio on as if it might bring an announcement that it had all been a hideous mistake. Dazed people on sidewalks were weeping openly. Hope had been killed.

We had an old small second-hand television set that we seldom turned on but we clicked it on when we got to the apartment and kept it on in the bedroom as the ghastly drama continued for hours and then days. Sad music replaced commercials. When I went out for groceries in the morning the Village streets were deserted. I had a sort of hallucination, imagining my son, one of the twins perhaps, running toward me, fair-haired and freckled, smiling. The funeral on television was for all of us.

Two weeks later the telephone rang as I was getting ready to leave for work. It was my mother. "I think you better come," she said. "It's my heart. The doctor says I have to go to the hospital."

I could not trust her report. She always had one medical complaint or another. I called the clinic to tell them I would be late. I tracked down her doctor at the Orange County Hospital. "Well, it could be very serious," he said. "I'm admitting her. The heart is fibrillating." I was able to get hold of my sister and told her we were coming. We had to borrow money from Barney. Barbara and I were able to get on a late flight that would get into Los Angeles at five in the morning.

We rented a car there and drove directly to the Orange County Hospital. She was in Intensive Care and had lost consciousness. I sat with her during the ten minute periods allowed throughout the day. I asked her to squeeze my hand if she could hear me. She squeezed my hand. I told her that I loved her and was sorry that her life had been so hard.

I thought I saw symptoms of a stroke in the one-sided way her face moved and reported it to the nurse. My brother arrived from Sacramento that evening. My other sister, Hazel, and her husband arrived the third day. Hazel had broken her leg and it was in a cast so she arrived in a wheel chair, sensibly dressed in black. The stroke was confirmed.

My mother did not regain consciousness. She died the third day. No one knew what to do. My brother and I went to a funeral home and picked out a relatively inexpensive casket and some recommended simple casket clothing. Everyone promised to chip in for their share of the cost. He and I made funeral arrangements.

I bought three adjoining cemetery plots that were for sale in a peaceful park like cemetery since my eldest sister, Alice, wanted to be buried near her parents. I took my father out shopping and bought him a very dark blue suit, a shirt and a necktie. "I can save it to be laid out in," he said. Barbara cooked meals that pleased everyone except my brother-in-law who wanted "more grease on the potatoes, not that gravy stuff." We were an unlikely collection of people.

The funeral was impersonal and grim. The open casket showed the woman who had disapproved of women wearing make-up, now smiling, rouged, coated with lipstick and sporting rhinestone hairpins in curled gray hair that had experienced its first blue rinse. I had shed no tears in the hospital and I shed none during the generic funeral.

We were put into first-class on the return flight. I drank too much red wine and finally burst into tears that I could not stop. "She never had a chance," I said. Nor did the twins. Nor did the only president I ever believed might help. Barbara had to lead me to a cab at the airport as tears continued. I slept for fifteen hours.

Barbara got the job, filling in as a teacher at Hunter Elementary. "She can sub after this semester if she wants to," Julie said. "And, who knows, maybe someone else will leave."

The unexpected phone call in the second week of January was from my sister, Alice. My father had been arrested. "He was hanging around where they was building new houses and a couple of little girls was playing there. He got one of them to pull her panties down and she told her mother."

I had to make use of the pay phone booth outside the clinic to talk to the psychiatrist who examined him, later to the social worker and the judge. Jail had been the first option, a group home the second. Finally it was agreed that he could stay with my sister after several months in a group home, if they moved to another town, closer to other relatives who could help to keep an eye on him. That meant Long Beach. We agreed on a diagnosis of "early stage dementia".

Barbara and I got through the semester. I helped her to finish an outline for her final thesis but she put off writing it. In March she had another miscarriage. Her full time income for the semester had helped us to get out of debt and for once we had some dollars in the bank. "I think we need to get out of here again," I said. "I think we need to run away and relax for the whole summer. Let's go to Europe. Let's use birth control for the summer and forget about babies."

"Greece maybe," she said. "It's supposed to be cheap there."

She was congratulated on her teaching at Hunter Elementary. "Keep us in mind," the principal told her. She and Julie had become friends. "You're family," Julie said, sweet and warm as always.

"Your promotion's coming through," Ruth told me at the start of the last week. "But only the secretaries know. June doesn't know yet."

Allen, our neighbor on Tenth Street, knew about deals. "You should get a new car while you're in Europe." He produced an ad that showed how to get a loan to buy a VW at the factory in Germany and thereby save on the cost of the car and on the transportation to and from Europe. "You can dock in France, take a train down to Sicily, a boat from Greece to Italy, train to Germany and then drive to England and have the car shipped back *used* from there. You can always sell it for more here, especially if you get a convertible."

Greece was cheap, as was Sicily where we spent the first two weeks. For the whole summer we lived cheap and worry free. The biggest decision was which island to ferry to next or how long to float in the clear, warm water of the Adriatic. The closest we came to elegance was during one of our stops in Athens to get cleaned up, eat an American breakfast and use the marble bathrooms and the lobby of the Hilton. An older woman, a local travel agent in Athens, Maria, had become our friend. We met her for coffee.

"I want to take you to a special little taverna in the Plaka for dinner, but late," she said, "everybody's a little drunk then and singing." She looked down at Barbara's sandaled feet. "You're Jewish," she said. "Jewish women always have such pretty feet." We laughed. "No, I'm serious. I *love* Jewish feet."

"Thanks," Barbara said.

"Anyway, right now though I have to go see clients in the nice hotel right across the square there. Why don't you come too? They're Jewish, I think. Ashkenazy. Isn't that Jewish? That's his name. He plays the piano. They'll love you."

"I think he's the one Barbara and Frank were telling us about," I said to Barbara. "The guy who won the Tchaikovsky contest a couple of years ago." We told her that we did not want to intrude.

Maria left us there, reluctantly, after we promised to meet her at ten o'clock for dinner. Later, in the dark Plaka we stepped carefully on the loose, ancient stones. "It's the damned Nazis and Communists," Maria said. "They make disaster and loose stones and I don't care who hears me say it. To hell with Communists and Nazis." She stopped suddenly and in a stage whisper said, "Look at that beautiful young couple. You can see them in that window over there. They're making love. Isn't that beautiful?"

I discreetly said that maybe we should give them their privacy. "Nonsense," Maria announced in her warm, somewhat hoarse voice. "Don't be a Communist. This is 1964. Beautiful young people have beautiful young bodies for making beautiful love and, of course, they leave the light on so everyone can enjoy seeing." Maria was a fresh and fierce life force, not to be restrained by silly ideas of propriety, political or otherwise.

We took the Yugoslav boat overnight from Piraeus to Venice on the way home. I sat on the deck drinking fifteen-cent glasses of plum brandy, tearful. I did not want to go home. But we had to get to Germany and pick up our car. It was a shiny black convertible bug with a white top. We watched it roll off the assembly line.

We took the ferry from Calais and stayed in London only the two nights needed for me to speak my paper. London was expensive. I was terribly nervous giving the paper. The formal academic setting did not fit our relaxed summer. But the drive through the English countryside and Wales was enjoyable. I went through every Agatha Christie book I could find.

Our ship slid past the Statue of Liberty very early in the morning. We stood on deck drinking coffee, having emerged from our tiny, dark inside cabin to witness the arrival. Our usual life there was waiting for us. I had to be on campus to help with registration two days after we docked but Barbara's parents were eager to see her so she took the bus and went to visit for the weekend. Our car would not arrive for another month or two.

"It was a good visit," she said when she got back. "I told them all our stories. It's as close to Sicily and Greece as they'll get. I think they enjoyed it vicariously."

That Friday evening her distraught father telephoned. They had been at a big Bar Mitzvah party at the Jewish Country Club. "The kids were doing that new dance they call the Twist and she wanted to learn." Grace had dropped on the dance floor, a cerebral hemorrhage. "She didn't even say goodbye. She was only fifty-nine," her father sobbed. We went immediately.

Though I was not a flesh and blood member of the family my grief was sincere. I had grown to love Grace. At the time I did not associate her death with all of the death that had come in the months before but that must have been part of the grief I felt.

To watch Barney's deep, inarticulate mourning was awful. I wanted to help and knew that nothing that I could say or do would help. Barbara stayed and I returned the following weekend. We invited him to come and visit us but that did not start to happen until a few months later.

In early November, Barbara realized that she was pregnant again. She was working a few days each month at the proofreading job and was visiting her father for a few days at a time. Joan and Jim were feeling cramped with the three children in their two-bedroom Brooklyn apartment and were yearning to live in Manhattan. Their parents had said they might be able to help with loans for a down payment and they wondered if we would be interested in sharing a brownstone in the Village, two floors for each family. Barney said he might be able to lend us some money.

We began hunting but the price was always too high. The best bargain was one near our apartment but the seventy-eight thousand dollars price tag, or thirty-nine thousand each was beyond our reach.

We went to visit Barney for Thanksgiving. Barbara and her mother's best friend prepared the dinner with help from Nellie. Grace was missed. It was her sense of humor that had made family dinners there fun.

Climbing the stairs to our apartment ahead of Barbara on our return home, I saw that our apartment door was open. Foolishly, I dropped the suitcases and rushed inside. Fortunately no one was there but the apartment was a mess. Kitchen drawers, bureau drawers and file drawers had been partly emptied. The old television, jewelry, including the antique ring I had bought Barbara at the hockshop near the clinic in San Francisco, and our new music system were gone. There was an open bottle of prune juice and a large kitchen knife on the hall table. The front door was off its hinges.

We called the police and an hour later two large uniformed policemen appeared. I pointed out the knife and the juice bottle and said that they must contain fingerprints. They jotted notes as we told our story about coming home and discovering the burglary.

"What I want to tell you," one of them said, "is that if anything like this ever happens again do not go running into the apartment. That is very stupid. That is why the knife was there. Sometimes there's a gun. The juice bottle is there because this crime was done by junkies looking for stuff to hock so's they could get drugs. They like sweet things to drink."

"What about the prints on the bottle?" I persisted.

"Mister," he said in a kindly tone, "you both got your health, thank God. We'd never find them but your stuff might show up in a hock shop somewheres in Queens, Brooklyn or the Bronx."

In addition to the two dead bolt locks that had been on the door, we had a cumbersome *police lock* installed. It was a metal rod bolted awkwardly to the hall floor that locked into place leaning against the front door from the inside. The city was becoming less safe and we were thinking about raising a family. Having seen the equipment Joan and Jim required we also began to wonder about moving a baby carriage or stroller between the street and our top floor apartment.

At the clinic there was a lot of talk about an impending split of the Park Avenue and Bronx campuses of Hunter. The clinic in the Bronx had been neglected, supposedly staffed by the Park Avenue staff with only one person assigned there half-time. I let it be known that I was a candidate for what would soon be the Assistant Director of the Educational Clinic, a person who would be at the clinic on the Bronx campus probably three or four days a week, preparing for the separation.

I was eligible for tenure and fairly sure that I would get it by the end of the academic year but I knew that I would never make it up the next rung of the promotional ladder to Associate Professor while June was my boss since she had just gotten there herself. I also realized that as Assistant Director I would be in line to possibly become Director of the clinic on the Bronx campus when the total separation of the two campuses happened.

We were watching the calendar yet were less worried about this pregnancy. The doctor reassured us. June reluctantly let me have the several days per week Assistant Director position in the Bronx because, of the few people interested, I was the most qualified and the best connected within the large Education Department. I also was part of the best research that was happening, had given a paper at an international meeting in London, was the only Clinic person connected to the Hunter Elementary School, had excellent student evaluations for my teaching and was an Assistant Professor. I would soon have tenure; I knew how to write and would go far beyond her in the publishing that was so valued in the academic world. We had a child coming and needed to get our world ready.

In January, during the break between semesters I suggested that we look at housing north of the Bronx. Barbara and Frank had moved from their Yonkers apartment and rented a charming gate house on Arturo Toscanini's estate in Riverdale. The rentals were not promising, most being dull, ordinary and expensive. But we continued looking in February on weekends. We were talking about it with Barney during a visit to us in the Village one weekend, wondering what to do.

"This city is no place for kids," Barney said. "Look for something to buy outside the city. Bricks are as good a place to put money as anywhere." I told him that I had us on a budget that allowed us to get by on my regular pay, putting my pay for evening teaching and summer teaching aside but it wasn't enough. "I can lend you part of the down payment," he offered. "What's money for?"

Our search went into high gear but the interesting places were too expensive. Our limit was twenty thousand dollars. We did find one house that we liked a lot in Westchester County but it was twenty-four thousand. It was at the end of a rural suburban road with woods on one side and a steep slope of woods behind the large yard that, in winter, showed the Hudson River and sunsets in the distance. It had a cathedral ceiling over an all wood paneled kitchen, dining room and living room combination plus three bedrooms, a bathroom, a finished but unheated attic suite with its own bathroom and a finished basement with a third bathroom, plus a garage. We looked at it several times and finally told Barney the problem. "What kind of mortgage can you get?" he asked.

"Five per cent fixed, thirty years," I answered.

"Get it," he said. "Try to bargain for twenty-two, but a few thousand on a thirty year loan is nothing." We got it for twenty-two and a half. Barbara was entering her seventh month of pregnancy when we moved in April into our own house in Ardsley. The surrounding dogwood trees were in flower but we still could see the Hudson and the sunsets.

There had been so much loss in the past few years. But a new life was on its way, a baby. We were going to be a family in our sheltering nest. We were making our real home. It seemed like there was a chance that the next chapter in life might be a truly good one.

Chapter 18

Suburban Parent

We settled into our new home quickly and easily. The baby's room was next to ours. Freshly painted, it had starched white café curtains, a chaise for nursing and the same bassinet Barbara had slept in during the early months of her life. I gave its wicker a fresh coat of white enamel and Barbara trimmed it with the same white fabric she had used to make the café curtains. We hung a colorful mobile over it to offer the baby visual stimulation and entertainment.

The due date was late in May. I was now the Administrator, soon to be named Director, of the Educational Clinic on the Bronx campus. The commute by car was an easy fifteen minutes. My secretary, Evelyn, knew my whereabouts at all times. Barbara's hospital suitcase was packed. We practiced Lamaze breathing together. We were ready.

Though Gerry Lesser was at Harvard, he and I had continued a long distance collaboration on a book of readings about school learning for more than two years. My copies of the book arrived. I disliked the mottled gray and black cover the publisher had chosen but swelled with private pride, holding and looking at my first published book. Gerry and I also had a prestigious monograph in process and I had started to outline another book of readings that I would do alone. Other than articles, this was to be my first published work. Colleagues were generous with their congratulations.

Asya Kadis and I had started work on a book two years earlier in 1963. We had met for breakfast weekly since then in the sunny breakfast room of her uptown Park Avenue apartment, me bringing along a reel-to-reel tape recorder. We had achieved a decent outline though it changed a bit each time we met. She had a writing block. She said the roots of the block were in childhood when a teacher in Petrograd refused to believe that a young schoolgirl could have possibly produced the mature paper that she had written on the Tartar influence on Russia.

We had become good friends. She was a rich source of wisdom and compassionate acceptance, the product of life experiences in very different cultures. We seldom disagreed but liked to let our differing vantage points play and shape our writing. She loved babies, children and families and knew the struggle that Barbara and I had been through. She waited now in joyous anticipation of the impending birth of our first child.

The grass around the house had turned a vivid green. I mowed it and planted colorful flowers around the front and side of the house. By the end of the first week of June, Barbara was more than ready. Her doctor assured us that all was well.

By the second week of June, classes were finished, grades had been turned in and the clinic was down to a small summer staff. Summer school classes had not yet begun. I stayed close to home, away only for quick necessary errands and an hour each day to take care of business at the clinic.

Early in the morning on June fourteenth Barbara thought something might be happening. By afternoon she was sure. We called the doctor, had a light afternoon meal, drove into Manhattan and checked in at the new New York University Hospital on First Avenue.

The nurse and resident who examined Barbara confirmed that she was in labor. They admitted her, prepped her and put her in a room with a great view of the East River. We had been warned in our classes that it was called *labor* for good reason. It was hard work but Barbara was strong during the first hours, doing the special breathing with me at the bedside, coaching, urging and doing the breathing with her.

Her doctor was waiting for the resident to call him in for the delivery but dilation was happening very slowly. We went through the entire night. Barbara was exhausted. She developed back pain and I rubbed my knuckles bloody on the sheets giving her the back massage I had been taught. We were worried. In the early morning her doctor appeared and he looked concerned. He put her on an I.V. drip to increase the speed of dilation and in an hour we were sent to the delivery room.

It happened. A new baby girl appeared. Her appearance had been slowed they reasoned because the umbilical cord was wrapped around her neck. A foreign-born pediatric resident murmured heavily accented words of concern and hurriedly took the baby away for tests.

I telephoned the pediatrician we had hired, a gentle, skilled German woman with a tattooed number on her arm. An hour later she arrived, did a full examination, double checked the tests and told us that the baby was perfectly healthy. "Not to worry," she said. "She's a lovely baby with that beautiful reddish blond hair. Just put a ribbon in that hair and love her."

Barbara and our new daughter, Victoria, were to stay in the hospital three days, standard procedure in 1965. In keeping with what Barbara's mother, Grace, would have wanted, we had hired a baby nurse. Lucille was ready and waiting for the call.

I picked her up at the train station the morning of the day I was to collect Barbara and Vicki at the hospital. She was a stout, tall African-American with light freckled skin, her dark ironed hair in a net, white uniform dress, white shoes and a small black suitcase. She was not young and moved slowly but I soon saw that she was constantly in motion and accomplished a lot. She came well recommended by friends as a baby nurse. Her additional claim to fame was that she once had been Tallulah Bankhead's personal backstage maid. She had stories to tell and enjoyed telling them in a deadpan style, the droll delivery followed by an involuntary chortle.

"What names did y'all name her? Victoria and then what?"

I explained that her middle name, Grace, was to honor both Barbara's mother and my mentor, Grace Rotzel, who had been the director of the School in Rose Valley when I assisted in the kindergarten there as an Antioch student.

Lucille took over the entire household, including the preparation of meals for us. She knew what she was doing and softly reprimanded me when I said that the starched white uniform was not necessary. "This is what I wear when I'm on professional duty," she said, "same as a doctor or any other nurse."

She was pleased with the upstairs dormered room and bath that would give her privacy. "But I'll be sleeping in the baby's room," she said. And she did, disappearing upstairs only for quick naps while Barbara was nursing.

During the six weeks that Lucille was with us I made sure that I was there on duty all day and night when she took her one day off each week. I discovered that I needed to hold the baby. I needed to study her and let her study me. I loved the new soft feel of her skin and the sweet smell of her. If she woke with distress during the night, I rushed to the bassinet, picked her up and carried her to the rocking chair in the living room where she could settle comfortably against my chest as I rocked slowly, looking out the window at trees moving in the night, both of us snug and happy.

Though I was teaching summer classes I spent very little time on campus after Lucille's six weeks of duty was finished. We had hired a cleaning woman, Mrs. Kashee, who lived nearby and had five children of her own, the youngest now in high school. She loved babies and volunteered to babysit anytime. We arranged to have her come one evening each week so that we could have an evening out. Life was good.

The intrusive cloud hovering over our sunny summer days in 1965 was the unavoidable news out of Vietnam. A major war was taking shape. Male students at the college were facing the draft when they finished school. Friends and neighbors were involved, taking sides. We were firmly anti-war and I joined the protests.

My sense of self, who I was and who I wanted to become was expanding. In college I had wanted to become a respectable citizen voting for positive social change. It had shifted when we married as I tried to make myself into a thoughtful, caring, sensitive and generous husband. Now I wanted to be all of that plus the best father anyone could imagine and that included setting a good example as a respected professional and a person who worked hard, spent time with his child, pushed hard for social change and spoke out for human rights.

I was on the right track, I thought. I was popular with students, respected by colleagues and admired by our friends. I was an assistant professor with tenure. I had job security, health insurance, a good pay scale and an admirable retirement package waiting. I was co-author of an important monograph to be published in a few months and, with more publications, I was sure to be promoted to associate professor soon. I was young, healthy and promised myself that I would work ever harder to achieve my goals.

I was like an émigré from a troubled land. I had worked hard to make my escape from the world I had known in Belmar. I knew that. But I also knew that I was one of the very lucky ones who had made it to this better, safer place in the world. I did not question whether it fit me exactly, that would come later. For now, I knew only that I needed to work hard, consolidate gains, fit in and try to make sure I could stay.

The two campus system of Hunter College was splitting, with the Bronx campus soon to be the Herbert H. Lehman College of the City University of New York. As Director of the Educational Clinic there I intended to set to work changing our way of helping to educate future teachers for New York City's schools.

Rather than entertaining the students who would become schoolteachers by having them watch a psychologist administer psychological tests to children through a one-way vision mirrored wall and then having the interpreted results explained to them, or have social workers explain their possible role in schools, I wanted to start a demonstration program that would be entirely new.

Each student would be assigned an inner-city child as a *buddy*. The college student was to visit the child's classes, neighborhood and home, getting a feel for the real world in which these children lived. Then our students would meet at the clinic in small groups facilitated by a staff psychologist or social worker and share their experiences, reactions, and personal feelings about the child, the classrooms, the teachers and the child's home environment. The aim would be to lower the failure rate of first-year teachers and to capture the interest and enthusiasm of the most talented aspirants early.

By January, 1966, I had persuaded the department and a sufficient number of school principals. We started. There were tears shed, shock shared and friendships formed. There was new life in the clinic. The plan was working.

The entire world was changing. Reading newspapers, I noticed gains being made by *admitted homosexuals*. By April, 1966 when we celebrated Vicki's ten month birthday, the Society for Individual Rights in San Francisco had opened the first Gay Community Center in the U.S. and an activist named Dick Leitech and others had organized a *sip-in* at Julius' in Greenwich Village to protest the New York state law forbidding the serving of alcoholic beverages to gay men and lesbians in bars. The newspaper headlines also announced U.S. troops with helicopters and armored vehicles north of Saigon, killing 100 Vietcong.

In my own private, protected world, I received a contract from Free Press to publish my book of readings to be titled, *The Psychology of Education*. The big news, however, was that Barbara had finished breastfeeding and had become pregnant again. Our second child was due in October.

Barbara told me that when she was a child, her mother and aunt would take their children to Atlantic City for the hot summers. Their husbands would join them on weekends. I knew that I could not afford to do that yet but we could begin to approximate it. In addition to my full time job I taught two evening classes and also taught during summer sessions for extra income.

I thought it would be good for Barbara to get a restful vacation during the second pregnancy so in the break before summer classes we rented a small house for two weeks in Harvey Cedars on Long Beach Island in New Jersey. Barbara was entering her sixth month of pregnancy and she was tense.

We hired an athletic and enthusiastic local teenager who seemed mature, responsible and able. She was quite willing to take care of the baby as needed and to do some cooking and cleaning in exchange for minimum wage plus the two weeks of room and board at the shore.

Unfortunately, while being athletic she broke her leg one week before we were to leave. She assured us that, though in a cast, she would be able to perform all duties, if a bit more carefully and slowly. She came along. Hobbled, she was no match for a frisky one year old. It did not work. I drove her home near the end of the first week and took over her duties.

By mid-July Barbara was entering the seventh month of the pregnancy and having a difficult time taking care both of Vicki and the house, even with my help. I suggested that we go a bit deeper in debt to have the garage made into a maid's live-in quarters and hire foreign help as some of our neighbors and friends had done. We could keep someone for a year or two by which time we should be able to manage two children and the household ourselves.

The agency had dossiers on many eager applicants. Maria was in San Salvador and spoke English. She was the eldest of fifteen children and had helped care for all of her siblings. A bonus was that her best friend was on her way to a household just thirty miles north of us and they could get together on their days off.

We picked Maria up at the International Terminal at Kennedy after she and her friend cleared customs. We exchanged telephone numbers with the other employer. The first surprise was that while her friend had a working knowledge of English words Maria did not. I bought two Spanish-English dictionaries, one for her and one for us.

She liked her large, new, freshly painted room and bath, but she was homesick. She spoke with her friend by telephone, long conversations. She cried. She did not want to leave her room because she missed home so much her friend explained.

At the end of the first week, on her friend's day off, I drove the thirty miles, picked her up and brought her to visit our crying maid. Barbara and I made a dinner for them. At one point we passed one another carrying dishes to and from the table where they happily dined, chatted in Spanish and laughed. I caught Barbara's eye and said, "I think we're doing something wrong. It isn't supposed to be this way."

The next day she was in her room crying again. I telephoned her friend. "She misses home too much." The friend was doing fine. I

telephoned the agency. We would have to pay an additional fee as
well as her return airfare. "Sometimes it just doesn't work out," the
woman in the Scarsdale agency said cheerfully.

By now Barbara was in her eighth month. It was a hot end of
August. She was uncomfortable. Mrs. Kashee came several times
a week to help. We heard about another agency where one could
interview applicants in person. I telephoned. They had three people
coming in that day and I could interview all three. Barbara was not
feeling well and could not go.

Two of the three young African-American women from the South
were so laconic that an interview consisted of their mute presence,
sitting as the employment counselor told of their wonderful skills and
willingness to work hard. Maybe, or maybe they were homesick.

Ethel, the third, seemed to have some life, at least, and did seem
interested in the job. She was slim, nineteen years old and answered
my questions though I needed interpretive help from the counselor
because of the very heavy dialect. Her answer to what her last job
had been sounded like *chomconfil* which, interpreted, turned out to be
"choppin' cotton in the fields".

When I asked which part of the job she thought she might like the
most and which part the least, she chose "holding the baby" or *hlubay*
as best and "doing the dishes" or *'ndsha* as least desirable. Well, she
was honest, able bodied and we could learn to decipher the dialect. I
hired her and brought her and her small suitcase home.

At the agency's suggestion I bought her two full sets of uniform
clothing that afternoon. She fell in love with her quarters and was
willing to come upstairs and help out though she needed more than
a little direction.

She was adjusting to a household with table settings at meals,
a washer, a dryer and an automatic dishwasher. The baby, who was
learning to put words together in meaningful ways, developed an
accent that fell somewhere between Ethel's version of English and the
one used by her parents. Ethel's greeting to Vicki in the morning was a
big smile and "Hah, Bay," and the happy return greeting was "Morn',
Eth."

I was waking each morning at 5 A.M., creeping quietly up the
stairs with a cup of coffee and a muffin to make my daily journal entry

and work on short stories for an hour or two if possible. In the year following the writing course at the New School in Greenwich Village I had churned out half a dozen short stories. Jack Huber, the Adelphi professor who had seen to my social education by inviting me to his penthouse cocktail parties introduced me to a friend who was an agent and, after reading my work, she had taken me on as a client. My agent was enthused about my work as were several of the editors to whom she sent the stories. In September, one of the stories that had not particularly pleased my agent was greeted with great enthusiasm by the editors at *McCalls Magazine*. They wanted it for their November 1966 issue, would pay top rate and hoped to publish another of my stories soon!

The doctor assured us that the pregnancy was proceeding well and there was no cause for worry. Lucille, the baby nurse, had been notified early in the pregnancy and had reserved mid-October and the first half of November for us, maybe more, depending on the time of arrival for another client's baby.

On the morning of October 10, Barbara thought labor was beginning but it subsided. I telephoned Lucille and told her we had Ethel employed but… She said she was available and if labor started to let her know. She would look the situation over and decide if Ethel was up to the job.

Very early the next morning Barbara was sure. I telephoned Lucille and picked her up at the local train station at noon. Her verdict on Ethel was "You can't leave that child in charge of the baby. She can't hardly take care of herself."

We took our time, remembering how long the labor had been the first time. I made a five o'clock reservation for dinner at a nice restaurant a block and a half from the hospital. We left the two white uniformed women and the sixteen-month-old girl in the kitchen and got into the car at four o'clock.

We had a drink, ordered an appetizer, chose our main courses, saying we would think about dessert later. We did not want to be hurried. As we were finishing the appetizer and the waiter was pouring wine Barbara said, "We have to go soon." As the main dishes arrived she said, "We have to go now I think." I had two bites.

"Now," she said. I put more than enough cash on the table and we headed for the door. We made it to the hospital. Less than one hour later our son was born in a fast and easy delivery.

Lucille was called away three weeks later for an early arrival. "You gonna' have to stay on this child," she said, meaning Ethel. "She knows nothing."

I had been referring to our new son, Andrew, as "the little prince" or "Prince Andrew." He was an easy baby, happy, smiling, drooling and laughing. "Ethel asked me yesterday if he sure enough is a real prince," Lucille said, rolling her eyes. "You let me know if you need me to come in on any of my days off."

We managed. I cut my hours on campus to bare minimum. Mrs. Kashee came in whenever more help was needed. Ethel never did get the hang of "which side of the plate that fork go on again?" True to her prophecy she did like to hold the new baby, *the prince*, and had to be encouraged to put him down to do other chores.

We made it to the Christmas and New Year holidays when I could be at home full time to help. We even had a big Christmas tree, wrapped presents and had our friends in for a holiday dinner. My dream had come true. I had a home and a family. We had good friends. I was providing for my family as a good husband and father should. We even had a live-in, uniformed maid of sorts.

But newspapers and TV continued to shower us with grim news. There were close to half a million Americans in and around Vietnam, 6,000 dead and 30,000 wounded. The numbers were reported daily like sports scores. The score for Vietnamese killed and wounded was so huge that I could no more imagine the carnage than I could imagine infinity. What kind of world would our children face?

Early the following semester my own book of selected readings, *The Psychology of Education*, was published. I was talking to textbook publishers about several other possible projects. Wars or no wars I had my work to do and, with luck, it might help promote understanding.

Ethel had become more helpful but required ongoing training and supervision from both Barbara and me. She thought we were peculiar and, from her point of view, no doubt we were. She chuckled for weeks over each newly acquired phrase. When Barbara said, "Ethel, you need to use *elbow grease* when you clean the stove top" she said that was one of the best ones she had heard. She liked to linger nearby, holding Andy, when I sat on the sofa reading to Vicki. Both she and Vicki had questions and both needed to see the pictures.

But Ethel found her way to *bad company* as Lucille pronounced mysteriously when she returned for a few days six months later, after Ethel had disappeared for three days. Two months later Ethel disappeared for good, leaving only her two uniforms and a few pages of a sort of diary describing the effect on her of the special sexual powers of *that man who does it so good that way*.

With Ethel gone the downstairs room and bath were unused. We put thick carpeting on the stairs leading to the finished basement, curtains at the windows and installed a large colorful cardboard playhouse. The washer, dryer and ironing board were down there. It became a large child-proof playroom with a linoleum floor that was easily cleaned, a place where we could do chores and keep an eye on the children.

We turned Ethel's room into a painting studio for Barbara. She could retreat to it when either Mrs. Kashee or I were around to take care of the children.

The spring semester of 1967 ended in very warm weather. I graded exams while sitting in the shade from a tree in our backyard, keeping an eye on Vicki who busied herself with toys on the grass near me. Her second birthday was only days away. I was scheduled to teach classes in the summer as usual but little additional time would be required to keep the clinic going on its reduced summer schedule. By then I had hired a great staff, all very competent, all teaching summer classes and happy to help watch over the clinic.

The news of slaughter in Vietnam continued but there was also other, more positive news that caught my attention. The New Jersey Supreme Court ruled that the state's liquor commission was no longer justified in refusing to permit service for gay men and lesbians in bars, and the New York Supreme Court followed with the same ruling. By contrast, the U. S. Supreme Court ruled that a Canadian man could be deported due to being afflicted with *a psychopathic personality* since he was homosexual.

Gay related news popped up regularly it seemed and I noticed. The New York Civil Service Commission announced a policy permitting city agencies to hire lesbians and gay men. In England sex acts between men twenty-one years of age and older were decriminalized. The American Civil Liberties Union passed a resolution urging decriminalization of consensual sex acts between adults.

Close to home, the new Oscar Wilde Memorial Bookshop was expected to open in November in Greenwich Village. The first gay bookstore in the U.S. was going to be just two blocks from where we had lived on Charles Street. The American Psychiatric Association reported that it was considering a motion to move homosexuality down a step in its list of mental illnesses, from a psychotic level disorder to a *sexual deviation* disorder, but it was still nothing a psychologist like me should be caught having since it would mean losing my license.

When classes resumed in September 1967 the anti-war movement on campus had grown loud and strong. Professors had chosen sides. I was no exception. Faculty meetings became heated with the subtext of national politics never far beneath the surface.

I noticed that we were getting more male students in the teacher-education program. The reason was they had learned that if they took jobs teaching in the most difficult inner city schools they could be exempted from the draft that was feeding the Vietnam War. Many were talented young men who ordinarily would have gone into other fields. I knew that some of them, with help, would discover that they liked the work and were richly rewarded personally by acting as both teacher and role model for disadvantaged children, too many of whom were missing fathers.

I decided to start another demonstration project. We would offer these young men an opportunity to meet for two hours a week in all male groups. The first two groups would be facilitated by me, using new encounter group techniques that encouraged truthful expression of all feelings, including feelings about one another. The groups soon affectionately named themselves the *draft-dodger groups*.

I was only mildly surprised to find that timid admission of feelings of admiration for one another began to surface and were spoken in the second week. Homosexual desire and consequent self-searching came out in the open the fourth week. I was tested, of course, and had to own up to my own feelings of attraction. Having bravely faced down the demon of homosexuality with no harm done, the groups became amazingly strong in their bonding and mutual support. We dared tell any truth. I was learning something.

Barbara, Mrs. Kashee and I kept the household running fairly smoothly. I got a really big tree at Christmas. Joan, Jim and their children helped us to decorate it. Barbara and Frank Alweis came to visit. The Browns were between State Department assignments in Africa and visiting Don's mother in New York so they and their children came too. It was very festive. Everyone helped with the cooking and we had a wonderful holiday banquet.

Chapter 19

Temptations

April, 1968 brought the shock of the assassination of Martin Luther King, Jr. Beyond the grief and despair for the world, my heart went out to Coretta. We had not been close friends and had not had any contact since Antioch but I saw the widow on TV and remembered the spirited young dancer with whom I had shared joyful moments at dances in the school's gym. My shyness overcame my impulse to send a message. I was sure that she was being inundated while mourning and I did not know if she would even remember me – the skinny guy who liked to dance.

Then, two months later, came the attempted assassination of Bobby Kennedy, followed two days later by the announcement of his death. Vicki was going to be three years old in a week and a half, Andy was only a year and a half old. I wished I could explain our grief, shock and worry to them but that was, of course, not possible.

Spring was beginning to show itself in leaf buds on our trees and tiny colorful flowers were emerging from bulbs planted the previous fall. A real estate agent in Harvey Cedars called about a bargain ocean front rental that would be available for the last two and a half weeks of the summer season, including Labor Day weekend. We asked

Barbara's father if he would be interested in sharing the house with us. He took the hint and told us to rent it, saying that he would chip in. He missed the children and would try to get down on weekends. "Ocean front with the kids is worth a million!" he said. I would miss only the first few days because of summer school. Barbara could hire a local babysitter to help.

In May I persuaded the Department to fund a three-day retreat for the clinic staff at a nearby growth center. One of our staff knew Bill Schutz, a psychologist who was becoming famous for his encounter group work at the Esalen Institute in Big Sur, California. He was interested in trying a three day live-in Intensive with a staff and was willing to do it for a very small fee.

In one of the warm-up exercises, he had us doing quick free association and then explanation to assigned partners. I was paired with a very bright and perceptive African-American social worker I had hired the year before. My quick association to *sweet* was *home*. In my elaborated explanation, I said, "I imagine sitting on the sofa in the living room with Andy tucked in close on one side of me and Vicki tucked in close on the other side of me while I read a book to them and Barbara is cooking dinner nearby in the kitchen.

She laughed. "That's you alright. Mister Homebody."

Toward the end of the first morning a competitive struggle between two young male staff members emerged. They wanted my attention and approval. Bill had them sit at my feet, facing one another. To my surprise, tears erupted, coming from deep inside me before I had any inkling of their meaning or source. Looking down at these two caught in their struggle I gasped as I saw, as if superimposed, my dead twin boys, gone before they had ever had any chance of life.

I was wrecked. The group continued productively I was told, as I reentered and emerged periodically from some deep other world of grief and tears for the three days. I had come undone. The last day I feared that the tears would not stop and that I would not be able to resume family and work responsibilities or function in the normal world.

But when Barbara arrived with the children in the rear of the station wagon, the tears cleared as suddenly as they had begun. I was surprised to find myself sliding behind the steering wheel, kissing all three, tired, back in my usual life but somehow better. It was the beginning of my love affair with Esalen and encounter groups.

That summer Vicki turned three and Andy was nearing his second birthday. I taught summer classes and then we drove south to Harvey Cedars for our summer vacation. It really was an ocean front house right on the beach. It had three bedrooms and a bathroom downstairs, a large living room, dining room and kitchen upstairs and huge picture windows facing my beloved New Jersey ocean and beach. We had invited our friends to visit and Barbara's father did come on the weekends. Don and Micheline Brown and their three children were still in the U.S. and able to find a small house nearby to rent for the last week.

I got Vicki and Andy out soon after dawn most mornings so that Barbara could sleep later and get rested. The ritual involved getting juice for them both, then getting them changed, minimally dressed and out of the house as quickly and quietly as possible. I would hoist each of them onto a hip then and, as they clung to an arm and shoulder, walk the beach in the fresh salt air until the bakery opened. A bag of freshly baked, still warm jelly donuts would last us another hour before going home to wash up for the real breakfast with Mommy. We loved it, all of it, one another and the mornings.

Walking with them on the beach while Barbara fixed dinner a few days before Labor Day we passed a good-looking man and his two teenaged children. The three were tanned and fit, laughing together, clearly enjoying one another. I recognized them as the people next door to the Browns. They owned their little beach house, Don had told me, and came for the whole summer every year. That was who I wanted us to become, a family like them.

In September the two Hunter campuses officially separated. We were Lehman College. After classes and the clinic program resumed I made arrangements to be away for one week and flew to California for a week long encounter group and gestalt therapy event at Esalen. I needed to see how it was done at the source and how we might use it in our clinic groups. I returned as a confirmed enthusiast.

Not long after I was approached by a friend of Joan and Jim's who worked for the Carnegie Corporation of New York. He wondered if I thought this new human potential movement, as it was coming to be called, might have application in the field of education. If so, might I be interested in taking a sabbatical to study it and seek funding from Carnegie.

"Absolutely," was my answer. I was past due for a sabbatical and knew that I would have a better chance of its being granted if I asked for only one semester. Sabbaticals paid half salary for a full year or full salary for one semester. The assurance of the time being spent on a legitimate study funded in part by the Carnegie Corporation and requiring a written report at the end would clinch it I thought. It did. My sabbatical leave was granted for the Spring semester, 1969. My normal salary would come from the university and all other expenses would be covered by Carnegie.

I started work on the project immediately, contacting the people I knew or knew about. There were interesting programs developing on the East Coast but most of the innovative work seemed to be centered on the West Coast at Esalen, Carl Rogers' Center for Studies of the Person in La Jolla or scattered groups in Los Angeles, San Diego and San Francisco.

With the help of people at the Center for Studies of the Person I found a two-bedroom house to rent for a month in La Jolla. In late-January Barbara and I, with the two children, boarded a flight to Los Angeles. In an exciting, if unnerving, beginning to the adventure, I looked out the window and saw a small fleet of fire engines and ambulances moving onto the runways as we approached the Los Angeles Airport. The flight attendants looked strained. In a whisper I asked one what the problem was and, after a second of hesitation, she said there was a problem with the hydraulic system.

I put Andy in Barbara's lap and took Vicki in mine and said quietly, "Hold on very tight." We glided in for an extremely soft landing at the farthest end of the runway. I caught the eye of the flight attendant who rolled her eyes and let out a large sigh.

Two days later we were settled in our little cottage amid palm trees and flowers, just two blocks from the ocean. It was winter for the locals but definitely late spring weather for us. Barbara said she did not enjoy being left alone with the children but I had work to do.

I tried to space the overnight trips up and down the coast, making day trips when I could. My aim was to participate in as many new and different experiences as possible. I knew that I could return to California on brief trips in the Spring but I wanted to make good use of the month there, getting to know the innovations at both the Center for Studies of the Person in La Jolla and Esalen in Big Sur especially, talk with Carl Rogers, tag along with Bill Coulson and other CSP staff to look in on work as varied as an encounter group of Catholic nuns in San Francisco. I was also talking to leaders at the Western Behavioral Science Institute in Los Angeles and getting leads on such events as nude swimming pool groups in the Los Angeles area and adult play groups done on a houseboat in Sausalito, north of San Francisco.

Before returning to New York I planned two trips for the spring. For the first, in March, I would participate in a five-day group at Esalen and interview people in Los Angeles and San Diego. On the second, in April, I would stay in the San Francisco area, participating in two weekend group experiences there and interview Michael Murphy, the co-owner of Esalen, and others.

The Esalen five-day encounter group was actually five groups, coordinated by Bill Schutz with each of the groups facilitated in smaller sessions by one of his resident lieutenants. There was plenty of drama, gestalt exercises and exotic physical contact. Sensory awareness and trust exercises were designed by Bernie Gunther. There was also massage and nude late night soaks in the fabled cliffside thermal baths often leading to romance and rivalry.

Ancient woes sealed behind doors of repression flew out into the air in this humanistic carnival. Fresh hurts, unspeakable deeds and mummified desires emerged. The pain of a woman's missing breast, a man's years immersed in incest tangles, a child's illness and death. And then, unexpected, the twins appeared again, present, haunting me, sending me into a torrent of hot tears for the loss of that love that nearly was, for all that might have been. They were a murdered part of my self. I understood that this loss was something wedged in me like a broken knife blade I could not get out. I would carry it as a part of me always.

The *Esalen massage* was achieving its own notoriety and acclaim. I signed up to return for a week in May for the Massage & Meditation workshop. My report would be missing something if I did not experience it. Somehow this was integral to the entire human potential movement. Humans touching one another truthfully, figuratively or actual skin to skin, was at the core.

I had learned that the best way to interview the leaders of this new, disorganized and vibrant culture of the human potential movement was to ground the conversation with plenty of self-disclosure, thereby encouraging them to do likewise. Michael Murphy was young, handsome, charming, sexy and, therefore, charismatic. He was also very bright, energetic and dedicated. As the owner and director of the Esalen Institute, he was the person who was making much of this phenomenon happen. He was interested in the all-male groups that I had been doing in New York and invited me to schedule one at Esalen. I was thrilled to be asked, but said I thought I ought to wait until after my study was finished and the report had been completed.

One of the weekend groups in April was being facilitated by Al Haimson, an old pal from internship days. I stayed with him and his family in Menlo Park. His encounter group weekends were part of an ongoing group therapy and encounter group community, wider in extended boundaries yet more therapeutic in focus than the Esalen groups in which I had participated. Participants had a history with one another and a possible future together.

Near the end of April I saw that Barbara was having a hard time. She looked tired. I asked Mrs. Kashee if she would consider moving in for a weekend so that Barbara and I could get away. She was delighted.

It was a chilly and inexpensive time at the Jersey shore so we went to Harvey Cedars and got a motel room. During the lazy weekend we saw a small ramshackle house that was for sale, just three houses in from the oceanfront. We called the realtor for fun. "The owners want $15,000 dollars but will probably take less. You know it's on pilings, one of the few old places that made it through that really bad hurricane a few years back."

We called Barney. "It's a great place for kids to be in the summer," I said. If we fixed it up we could rent it out for half of the summer and cover costs, I thought. "We can get it for $13,500," I reported to Barney, "$2,750 down but we will need some money put aside to paint it." Yes, he could lend us a down payment. He gave his approval.

In May, I was at Esalen once again for the Massage & Meditation Workshop. It was excellent. For five days, when not sleeping or eating, we were meditating, massaging, being massaged or soaking in the tubs. It amounted to wordless psychotherapy as we listened to ourselves and listened to others by touching them or being touched by them in compassionate silence. Inner change happened naturally without verbal insight.

On the airplane, flying back from San Francisco to New York, I put down the book I had meant to read and looked out the windows at the sky still blue and the clouds still white as we raced toward the approaching darkness. I was remembering the individuals who had touched me with such caring. I remembered the erotic moments touching several of them, one young male athlete especially. I was carrying all of that home with me. I would try to communicate most of it to Barbara, though maybe not the feelings stirred by the young athlete.

Then I remembered a movie we had seen soon after moving into the apartment in Greenwich Village. *Victim* starred Dirk Bogarde as a successful young London lawyer named Farr who was both married and gay. The woman who played his wife looked and dressed like Barbara except for the blonde hair. I remembered her angry words in confronting him about his infidelity with a loving, good looking laborer, her awful fear as she learned that he was caught up in a blackmail scheme and her noble words at the end of the film when he decided to come out and confront the real crimes rather than hide and try to ride out the storm.

I also remembered the ghastly scene that led to her discovery of his infidelity when she and her brother innocently closed the garage door after putting the car in it. One of the blackmailers had painted *Farr is Queer* in huge crude letters on the door. The scene had struck terror into me at the time and I had totally forgotten the film during the six years since.

By the time I got home I knew what I had to do. I needed to communicate as much as I could about my hidden inner self. I had gotten a new large heavy wood desk that I could use also as a massage table. After I gave Barbara a massage I sat with her in the bathroom while she soaked in very warm water.

I told her about all of the experiences of the week and about me. The twins were on my mind as I spoke though I did not make any direct reference to them. I said that I knew that she already knew and maybe did not want to know that I was sexually attracted to some men. I tried to describe the deep longing for full loving, including sex, with some of these men. I could not, and did not want to, kill that part of me. I wanted it to live. *I* wanted to live fully. If I was going to be the best father I could be, I needed to show our children, by example, that it is best to tell the truth, to live truthfully and be your full self even when it is uncomfortable or displeases some other people.

I did not want to leave our marriage I reassured her, but I did need to let people know that I was homosexually inclined, gay, and that it was an important part of my identity. It was a part of me that needed to be given life. I could see that my full disclosure was making her very uncomfortable. "I guess we'll have to see how it goes," she said. Clearly she needed time to sort all of this.

I did and did not see the contradictions. The various parts of me did not fit together easily. Yet, it seemed to me, since they were all very real parts of me it had to be possible to integrate them somehow. I was striving for integrity. I was a happily married man in a heterosexual, community approved marriage and I was a gay man also since I longed for sex and love with other men. Somehow it all had to fit together. It was the first of many related conversations that we would have over the following years.

I would not be teaching that summer of 1969 since I was on sabbatical until late August. Instead I would be researching groups in the New York area, reading and writing the report to the Carnegie Corporation. That meant that we could spend most of the summer at Harvey Cedars.

Before leaving New York I had to do some catch-up work at the clinic even though I was officially away. I also made a lunch date with Gerry Lesser who was in town from Harvard and another lunch date with the contact man from Wadsworth Publishing, a handsome New Yorker soon to be transplanted to the company's new offices in the San Francisco Bay area. In lunch conversations he had been suggesting for more than a year that I do one or more textbooks for them.

Gerry sensed my restlessness and we talked about it. "You're well positioned for a change right now," he said. He had been having great success in the academic world. "You're in a small pond," he said. "You should think about Harvard. It's a great place."

Asya and I were coming into the home stretch with our *Humanistic Teaching* book. The Wadsworth man was not particularly enthusiastic about its money-making potential in the textbook market. I told him about another book in the making based on a study being done by me and two social workers on the clinic staff. "It's a textbook for teacher education that will be written as a series of portraits of inner city kids, real ones." I said. The students will read the teacher's referral to the guidance counselor, then the clinic notes, then there's a fictionalized picture of the classroom, the teacher and home life from the point of view of the child."

He was interested but he really wanted me to do a new educational psychology textbook. By the end of our lunch we had a handshake deal for three books. First off the press would be *Those Children*, the book I had described to him that was nearly finished. Next would be the book with Asya and third would be the standard textbook.

"Asya will be relieved," I said to Barbara that evening. "We've had no luck in sniffing out publisher interest and she really wants this book in the world. It represents a lot to her, the end of her writing block. With luck the book should be out less than a year from now, maybe May 1970."

The naming of our beach house was left to the children. They were very cute wrestling with such a weighty decision together. We looked at other signs on other homes. They finally settled on *Mouse House*. I made a rough sign to go over the front door.

The name had come from our reading, of course. *Winnie the Pooh* had been a standard favorite though that summer's favorite books turned out to be a beautiful picture book titled *Seashore Story* by Taro Yashima and *The 14th Dragon*, a group effort with text by James E. Seidelman and Grace Mentonize with dragon drawings by thirteen artists. I had found both books in a little shop in Big Sur.

Barbara was taking morning painting classes elsewhere on the island. On any rainy morning or afternoon the children and I would cuddle together on the screened porch as I read, "On a magical, mystical day like today/Nothing behaves in the usual way...." The dragon book then ended with instructing the child to draw the dragon *you'd like best of all whether tiny, demure, scary or tall, nobody ever has seen the dragon you'll draw – dragon number fourteen!* Then we would scramble for crayons and paper to capture the best dragon of all.

We had the weathered gray asbestos shingles painted dark brown and the woodwork a bright red. We had a simple concrete slab poured in front of the house and topped it with screens and a roof, thereby giving the house a big porch for playing, sitting and dining with friends. The carpenter needed work and said he could put a roof deck on the house "very cheap" so that happened too, along with a half oval wooden walkway running from the front door of the porch, past the outdoor shower and ending at the stairs in the rear that led up to the roof deck.

I painted the inside white and blue, then planted gardens of colorful annual blooms including purple and yellow pansies, bright red petunias and yellow marigolds in the pocket garden areas created by the walkway. From the start it was a wonderful summer punctuated by weekend visits from Barney, and many of our New York friends.

By the end of the summer Barbara had completed several paintings. The one I most admired was a large misty gray gray-green painting, marsh in fog perhaps, that had a mysterious black, gray and orange line wandering across horizontally. It seemed to match the search the children had for the 14th dragon.

I was not reading newspapers so it was not until the July 4th weekend, when Barbara and Frank Alweis came to visit, that I learned about the *gay riots in the Village.* It was bound to happen. Canada had decriminalized private same-sex acts between consenting adults in May. When the New York police sauntered into the Stonewall Bar on Christopher Street expecting another easy conquest, bullying and humiliating patrons, they were surprised to find they had stepped into a strong turning tide. Soon they had locked themselves in, barricading the doors, calling for help because the fags that night had had their fill. They were angry and throwing things, joined by others in the Village, uprooting parking meters, ready for justice. It happened very near our old apartment on Charles Street. I really wished I had been there.

I had a first draft of my report to the Carnegie Corporation done by the end of August. I titled it *Permission to Grow*. It had been difficult to write, like trying to describe and make sense of what you see when you look into a kaleidoscope, full of fascinating colors, shapes and forms, dazzling and changing quickly.

The final Saturday at the beach we hired a babysitter, a mature local woman who became our Harvey Cedars equivalent of Mrs. Kashee. She was a widow who loved children but lived alone there all year around. She said "you have to love the ocean and weather to live here all year." I understood what she meant.

Barbara and I went out to dinner and then to the nearby drive-in theater to see *Midnight Cowboy* starring Jon Voight as the handsome, dumb, would-be hustler and Dustin Hoffman as the crafty but ill-fated human discard sinking in urban blight. From the opening scene of the tanned, muscular and absolutely naked Voight dropping the soap while taking a shower to the final scene of his bewildered loneliness as he cradles the newly dead Ratso Rizzo protectively in his arms to shield him from the gawking of the bus passengers as they arrived in sunny Miami, I was in the film, part of both of them.

I was surprised but not entirely put off by the use of words like *fag, gay,* and *hustler* though they were used disparagingly. Maybe they applied to me, I thought. Like the desperate boy in Times Square who dared to promise twenty-five dollars he did not have in order to touch and possibly make love to the friendly, beautiful, manly hunk in the cowboy costume, I too wanted to touch that erotic warmth. Like the nervous visiting businessman, I too battled desire and need, fearing I might risk the danger he found by pulling such an idol into his world, alone in a hotel room.

But more, I was the naïve small town hick, the phony cowboy, hoping to better myself, testing myself in the mysterious world of my betters, learning love slowly, only to find it far different than I had imagined. And I was Ratso Rizzo, with his hidden needs, daring to dream of crossing final forbidden lines, finding unconditional love at last as the prize, but with death its price.

I drove away with a hole in my being. I could see right through myself. I managed to chat with Barbara about the acting and the symbolism in the film, but there was a hole in me. I was not solid, not complete. There was an empty place. I could feel it. Part of me was missing.

I felt afraid of where the need to fill that empty place would lead me. I had a family at last, the family I wished I had been born into as a child. I did not want to lose my family and my home.

"What's wrong?" Barbara asked.

"I don't know," I answered truthfully. "I guess that movie got to me somehow."

The Humanistic Psychology Association had its yearly meeting at the end of the summer. I needed to go, participate and interview a few people before preparing my final report to the Carnegie Corporation.

One of the available activities was participation in a leaderless encounter group. In one of its meetings an attractive young man, Chris, said that he wanted some help from the group. An assertive woman responded quickly by saying that she knew what his problem was. "Boys," she announced smugly, giving the group a knowing smirk.

He assured her that he was gay and did prefer sex with males but that was not what his problem was about. He wanted help with an upcoming job interview.

I had been sensitized, no doubt, by reading the work of Black authors during that summer and was stunned by the group's pseudo-liberal, condescending and unsolicited acceptance of his homosexuality. All that was needed was to replace *gay* with *Black*. I announced that I too had homosexual feelings and did not like the covert trashing that he was getting from this group of supposedly humanistic liberals.

He and I had a bond. He told me later that he wanted to get more experience facilitating groups. I wanted to get more experience with openly gay men I told him. He knew plenty of gay men and I had lots of experience facilitating groups. We could be a team.

We co-led a weekend group of gay men and it was a mess. Several of the men said they got a lot out of it, but there was more than one who needed far too much attention and would do anything to get it. When he and I did a post-group conference I said I could sum the problem up in two words: *better screening*. "We could have managed one of those guys in that size group but not three."

I knew my feet were on a right path, however. I wanted to work with gay people, men first. If every man in the room was admittedly gay, the group would be off to a running start and I could see some of the places it would need to go.

I designed an encounter group weekend for men that explicitly welcomed exploration of sexual and erotic feelings for other men. It was to be called *The Natural Man* workshop. Like Esalen's weekend groups, it would begin Friday evening and end Sunday afternoon. Men would bring sleeping bags. Food and beverages would be on hand but we would have Saturday dinner out or have take-out delivered. Chris promised to help spread the word among gay friends. I told former students who were gay. The first one was held in a warehouse loft space reached by freight elevator. The space was sometimes used by other experimental human potential groups. It was a success and word spread quickly, assuring a full sign-up for the next group, a month later.

Chapter 20

Coming Out

My classes filled immediately at registration. Students I knew were glad to see me back again, some making whispered pleas to add a friend to one of my classes even though they were officially full. The anti-war feeling was strong. Campus protests against the war and the draft were in progress.

I took Vicki to her first day at nursery school, staying in the back of the room with other parents as the teachers had asked us to do. She did not cling as a few of the others did, nor did she plunge in recklessly either. She watched, observed others and then picked her activities. She was not the ill at ease, timid child I had been but she did seem to have some of my wariness.

In addition to my written report, the people at the Carnegie Corporation wanted me to make a oral presentation to the staff at a lunch there in their Manhattan offices in October. The offices were elegant and the conference room where such presentations were made looked expensive, stiff and formal. "We'll have the lunch catered," I was told.

"How about making the presentation fit the topic?" I asked. "Maybe we could have a brown bag lunch and sit around on big pillows with shoes off instead of chairs and tables. I could introduce some encounter group techniques and everyone could participate."

The compromise was a catered buffet with uniformed servers standing behind a long table covered with a white linen tablecloth and silver serving trays instead of the even more formal sit-down service. My report was received politely but I sensed that my audience was uncomfortable. It was far from the usual recitation of *fact and figures*, tables, graphs and statistical analysis. But not long after that an edited version of the written report was published in five languages, mostly due to the respected name of the Carnegie Corporation I suspect.

I let my naturally curly hair grow longer and began to wear turtleneck sweaters and pendants rather than suits and neckties. The students and younger faculty members liked it. Deans and older faculty members frowned. It was clear that I was on the side that was protesting the endless slaughter and destruction in Vietnam. After my months of immersion in group experiences that ranged from unusual to really bizarre attempts to free people from unnecessary inhibition and repression, I found faculty meetings insufferable.

It seemed clear that I was in the wrong place. I wanted to teach, to help and to heal. I also wanted to learn. I told Barbara that even with the protection of tenure and my current academic rank of associate professor and a probable promotion to full professor in the near future, the prospect of another twenty or twenty-five years in that setting felt like a prison sentence. "Maybe it's time for me to think about a different work life. You too. Are you going to finish your Masters' degree and use it to do something?"

I was pleased with the changed mission of the clinic that I had been able to accomplish but the administrative work was taking too much of my time and was no longer exciting. I decided to resign as clinic director on January 10, 1970, at the end of the Fall semester. There would be time for me to groom a new director. I would ask to be assigned to full time undergraduate and graduate teaching in January.

The October 31, 1969 issue of Time Magazine arrived in the mail a few days before that date. Its cover was unusually colorful, flamboyant in hot pink, green and red, a muted painting of an attractive young man's face, a no-face slim male figure with hands on hips superimposed over the left eye of the portrait and a banner at the top right reading *The Homosexual in America.*

The four full pages of coverage opened with "An exclusive formal ball will mark Halloween in San Francisco this week. In couturier gowns and elaborately confected masquerades, the couples will whisk around the floor until 2 A.M. while judges award prizes for the best costumes and the participants elect an *Empress.*" Seven full pages of text and seven full pages of advertising later, it concluded with "The challenge to American society is simultaneously to devise civilized ways of discouraging the condition and to alleviate the anguish of those who cannot be helped, or do not wish to be."

There were interviews with male homosexuals, lesbians and bisexuals quoted, as well as a lively discussion among presumed academic experts. The word *inverts* was used frequently and there were a number of choice sentences such as "The homosexual subculture, a semi-public world, is, without question, shallow and unstable." Another of the many was "Most experts agree that a child will not become a homosexual unless he undergoes many emotionally disturbing experiences during the course of several years." Actually, even the *experts* they recorded in discussion did not agree to that at all.

I had been reading every article that I could find referenced in the *Psychological Abstracts* having to do with homosexuality. It was clear that the only *research* pointing to pathology was the extremely flawed pseudo-research of such self-appointed experts as psychoanalysts Charles Socarides and Irving Bieber who were earning a very good living from their psychoanalytic party line, expertly insisting that the Emperor's invisible clothing was made of the most amazing fabric. Theirs was a mixture of opinion and sloppy logic, nothing more. And it made me very angry.

I sat down at my typewriter and fired off a letter. The day that the November 14, 1969 issue of Time appeared we got a telephone call from Barbara's father, Barney. He was a loyal subscriber and devoted reader. "Hey, the big lead letter this week is from Don. That's terrific. Of course I don't know anything about what he's talking about, but he's famous!"

Opening our copy I saw an edited version of the longer letter I had sent, my full name and the town we lived in at the bottom lest there be any doubt about people with similar names. The letter began with identifying myself as a clinical psychologist and ended with a plea. "In the name of sane humanity, let us stop our obsessive concern about homosexuality as a condition. Let us stop nervously watching our children until they start dating. Let us encourage expression of all varieties of affection before our denied and twisted desires murder us all in an acceptable war."

I did not say "I am gay" or "I am a homosexual", nor did I imply in any way that I was not. I knew that I would lose my license as a psychologist in both New York and California on the basis of *moral turpitude* by admitting to homosexual behavior. But, for better or worse, one foot was now clearly out of the closet door. I was coming out as a gay man and I was glad. Frightened of the possible consequences, yes, but excited and exhilarated by the taste of truth and freedom also. Barbara and I laughed about her father's words but I could see that she was uneasy.

An off-campus encounter group that some students and their friends had persuaded me to facilitate had continued to meet irregularly for months in an apartment in Greenwich Village. As I emerged from the subway at Sheridan Square for an evening session just before Thanksgiving I saw a new newspaper for sale. Its bold large red-lettered masthead proclaimed itself *GAY*. I walked past but returned to buy a copy.

The two young gay men responsible were Lige Clark and Jack Nichols. I devoured the contents. I wanted to make contact with them. It would be another clear step in coming out in a public way. But my New Year's resolution was to take that step. I telephoned. They were welcoming. They would love to see anything from me and certainly consider it for publication. Perhaps something about the Natural Man workshops I was doing as weekend encounter experiences? Definitely.

Barbara was tired. She had slowed down in her painting after producing a very large canvas of brown trees seen against winter snow that we hung in the living room above the sofa. Now she seldom went down to her studio.

Though Mrs. Kashee was available to help, tending to a three year old and a four year old seemed to exhaust her. During the winter break before the new January, 1970 semester, we hired Mrs. Kashee's teenaged daughter to babysit some evenings with the assurance that she would call her mother if need be. They lived only five minutes away.

We went out to dinner and a movie one evening and to the theater in Manhattan another evening. The outings did not help. Barbara seemed depressed. It worried me. Early on a Friday morning I asked her if she had any idea what might make her feel better. She looked out the large picture window at the darkened, cloudy sky from which freezing rain had begun to fall onto the snow already on the ground. "Some sunshine might help if you could arrange that," she said.

I went upstairs to my desk and called Mrs. Kashee and asked if she might be available to come and take care of the children for the weekend. She was delighted at the prospect. I thought about Miami but the travel agent said flights were full. "What about Puerto Rico?" I asked. There were two seats on a flight out at three o'clock that afternoon if we could make it. And there were two seats returning on Sunday afternoon. There was a room available at El Convento in Old San Juan. We got to the airport with five minutes to spare. And it worked. Her depression lifted.

The change of scenery, if worrisomely expensive, was good for me too. I decided that I needed to try a professional life outside of the limitations of the college. I was going to try to start a private practice devoted to helping gay people, their families and their friends. Within two weeks I had found a therapy office in the Columbus Circle area of Manhattan that I could sublet for one afternoon and evening each week. Two weeks after that I had my first two clients.

I told Barbara that I thought it might be fun to have an open house on a Sunday each month for favorite students and their friends. "I could cook up a batch of spaghetti, make a big salad, heat some baguettes and let them bring other things if they want to."

She agreed. "It would be fun. Let's try it."

I knew that the daily care of the children was becoming a chore. "We might even get a few child care volunteers out of the deal," I said.

It was a great success. The children reveled in the attention. There were guitar players and other musicians as well as photographers. We sang Joan Baez songs and Simon and Garfunkel songs. I feigned ignorance and did not notice those who smoked marijuana. More than one of them said, "I want to live here. Do I have to go back to the Bronx?"

My first article for *GAY* was published. Whispered word of it traveled through the faculty. I was asked about it by a brave activist assistant professor during lunch in the faculty dining room. She was on my side. She winked. The other two faculty members at the table went silent. I admitted it and said that I was thinking about a next piece for them. "It's a damn good thing you have tenure," she said.

It was a cold winter with plenty of snow, rain, winds and slippery ice. Driving to the school one morning on the Expressway I came to an area of slowed traffic in the crowded lanes. Drivers were aware of the ice on the road and were driving with care.

Three or four car lengths ahead I saw a car two lanes to the right begin a slow slide. The net result was an accident involving seven cars. The man just to my right looked at me helplessly as his car slid left and crashed into our station wagon. Everyone involved ended up on the far right shoulder. Drivers' licenses and insurance information was exchanged. The police arrived and an ambulance arrived. Two people had been badly injured. Our car was damaged but I was not hurt beyond a few bruises.

The car could be driven so I went on to the school. My morning class had been dismissed due to my failure to appear. My secretary in the clinic had called home to find me. Barbara had told her that I left at the usual time.

I called Barbara to tell her that I had been in an unavoidable accident that was no one's fault and that the car was damaged but I was not. After reassuring her and again reassuring Evelyn, my secretary, I closed my office door, sat down at my desk and began to shake. I had not realized how frightening it had been. "God damned New York winter," I said aloud. I felt vulnerable. I was miserable.

I had the galley proofs for *Those Children*. While working on the corrections one rainy morning a week later I got a telephone call from Gerry Lesser at Harvard. There was a definite opening there. They were beginning a search to fill the Clinic Director's position left vacant by Richard Alpert's departure, part of the residue of the Timothy Leary LSD exposé there. Would I consider coming for a visit? I said I would talk with Barbara about it.

She was no more interested in moving north to Boston than I was. But she knew that I was restless and did not see a future in my present job. Harvard would be a prestigious step forward if I wanted to remain in the academic world. Gerry called twice more. We decided that I should go for a *visit*, something less than an official invitation or application, in March.

I visited the clinic there with Gerry and then had lunch in the faculty dining room. It was impressive. Handsome, clean-cut, polite young men offered impeccable service with white tablecloths, polished silverware and gleaming glasses. There were a half dozen other faculty members at the table, there to meet me and size me up. After five minutes of polite chatting about the weather there and in New York, Gerry adroitly rolled in a few references to my writing, innovative clinic work and research.

The always polite covert academic combat then began in earnest with references to recent journal articles read flying around and across the table. The point of the exercise seemed to be winning the grudging respect of colleagues because you were more up-to-date and better informed about arcane but respectable research then they were. I hated to disappoint the ever cheerful and optimistic Gerry. He had proven himself repeatedly to be a real friend and devoted booster. But after lunch I said, "I don't belong here, Gerry. I am outclassed." He protested. I insisted. There were a couple of follow up phone calls but it was done.

I would not go to Harvard but the visit there had helped me to see that I was definitely ready to leave my present safe, secure nest and venture out of the academic world. Maybe the answer was to develop a full-time private practice in Manhattan focusing as much as possible on the needs of gay people and their loved ones.

I telephoned Jack Nichols to talk about doing another article for GAY. We agreed to meet for lunch and get better acquainted. The New York police had raided a gay bar in March and arrested 167 persons. A young man from Argentina, fearing deportation, had leaped from a second story police station window and impaled himself on a wrought iron fence.

A few days before our conversation, gay activists had disrupted a special session of the American Psychiatric Association. They were protesting a paper on the use of genital electroshock aversion therapy to treat homosexuality. Bella Abzug, running for Congress, was going to ask for support from gay and lesbian activists. Things were moving fast, change was happening.

Barbara and I had our evening out at the movies with Joan and Jim. We went to see the newly released *Boys in the Band*. It was not a flattering picture of gay men certainly, yet it stirred me. "These are my people," I thought. "What am I doing in the suburbs?"

I needed to try something like a year's leave of absence. If I applied for one before the end of the semester I would know by September if it had been granted and I could have the entire 1971 year to try full-time private practice with the safety-net of the leave, returning in January 1972 if I failed.

We decided to take two weeks at Mouse House in June, before the start of summer classes, then rent it out for the weeks of summer most in demand and return to it after classes ended in August, staying through Labor Day weekend. Before we left I applied for the leave for 1971.

Also before we left I got bad news from Wadsworth. The publishers had decided not to take the book Asya and I had written. I was very angry. "It was part of our three book deal," I said. I felt protective of Asya who happily believed they would publish it soon. *Those Children* had arrived as a handsome book.

"We still want the textbook," my earnest, handsome friend said into the telephone in California. "We have a signed contract for it."

"We have a contract for *Humanistic Teaching* too," I answered. "I am going to put the phone down on the desk," I said, "so that you can hear me tearing up the contract for the textbook. The deal was three books." I tore up the contract and hung up the phone.

During the summer it occurred to me that if the leave was granted and I had all of 1971 to make a new start I need not be restricted to New York. We could go back to the San Francisco Bay area. We had been happy there. We had friends there who could help. Our children might have a good life growing up in California. Certainly, the weather would be better.

I brought the idea up with Barbara. I knew that she too had enjoyed our stay in San Francisco. She was cautious but finally said her only real concern was her father. Later she said, "I guess it's no worse then it would have been moving to Boston. He probably wouldn't have gone there to visit us either and he didn't seem upset at the idea of you going to Harvard."

He was wonderful about it. He would have liked it if we lived in the same town so that he could see the children often, he said, but we should do whatever was good for our future. He even said that if we went to California he would fly out for a visit. I reassured him that if we went we would come back to Mouse House the next year for summer vacation.

Returning to the city and the school after Labor Day I began to catch up on the news. The religions had begun to weigh in on gay rights during the summer with the Lutherans stating their opposition to the discrimination and oppression of gay people, the Unitarians not only demanding an end to the discrimination but officially recognizing its own gay, lesbian and bisexual clergy and the Roman Catholic Church stating its sour official view of homosexuality as a *moral aberration.*

The New York City police had been busy too. Since 1970 was an election year, they had done their traditional August *clean-up,* inspecting gay bars and arresting 300 gay men and lesbians for *loitering.* Just before Labor Day a peaceful demonstration protesting police harassment had evolved into an evening of rioting in the Village.

A week after classes started I was told that my request for a leave had been approved. My faculty ally, the young activist said, "Are you kidding? The deans are probably dancing or in a prayer meeting right now, hoping God will see to it that you don't come back. You're a very hot potato around here."

I told favorite students and the clinic staff. I was surprised at how much affection there was for me and how genuinely sorry many people, mostly students, were to hear that I would be away for a whole year and possibly gone for good. "We still going to have one Sunday a month at your house?" a small delegation asked me. "Absolutely," I answered.

Once Barney had given his reluctant blessing, the next difficulty was breaking the news to our close friends. We had many friends but were closest to Joan and Jim with whom we had been friends since college days and to Barbara and Frank with whom we had grown ever fonder since meeting them at the cocktail party in Greenwich Village the day we found our apartment on Charles Street through mutual friends. They had bought a large house in Yonkers earlier in the year and we had helped them with the taking down of old wallpaper, scraping and painting. Promises and intentions aside, we all knew that even if they made a trip to California and we invited them to visit during our summer vacation at Mouse House, the everyday intimacy would be lost.

I telephoned the real estate agent who had sold us our house in Ardsley and asked what price we might expect to get for it as well as advice about renting it out furnished for a year. After he visited and saw the improvements we had made he guessed that we could expect to sell it for half again as much as we had paid for it. "I don't think renting is a good option though, really. People rent in the city but they buy in Westchester County mostly."

I telephoned Al Haimson in Menlo Park, California. He and his wife, Jean, would begin to ask around about home prices and rentals. They had two children also and were familiar with the quality of schools in their area. Al said that he would be glad to introduce me to everyone he knew who might be a source of referrals, would sublet his office to me one day a week plus a few other stray hours when he was occupied elsewhere. He also suggested I might think about teaching a course or two in the evenings at the local community college. "It's a beautiful campus and they'd be lucky to get you."

I also spoke with Bill Coulson in La Jolla and told him I thought we were heading back to California but to the San Francisco area where I had done my internship. He asked how my writing and publishing was going. I told him about the soured deal with Wadsworth. He reminded me that he and Carl Rogers were editing a series of books called *Studies of the Person* for Merrill and asked if I would send them the manuscript.

It was time to take Andy, now almost four years old to nursery school and Vicki, now five years old to kindergarten. They started the same day so Barbara took our daughter to school and I took our son. He had none of the reserve his sister had shown a year earlier, letting go of my hand immediately and heading for the climbing apparatus with a look of clear delight.

I suggested to Barbara that since both children were now occupied for half of the day and Mrs. Kashee was available if one of them had a sick day, it would be a good opportunity to return to the Bank Street School and finish up her Master's degree before we left. Or she might want to get a job or start on some other occupational preparation. We had most of four months left in New York.

She was not interested. "I have to think about packing and moving," she said. It was true that we had less than a full four months but finishing her Master's work was really only a formality. No. She was not interested.

We decided that it made sense to sell our house and buy one in California. We would have enough money from the sale to make a down payment on a new place and have a cushion of money to help us get through the first year. We were making a definite move. If the venture failed, the cost would be the moving expenses. I could return if need be and resume my tenured position on the faculty. We could buy a home in New York again.

The *for sale* sign went out on the front lawn and we decided on a one week trip for Barbara in October to visit the Haimsons and look around at home sales. We wanted to live in Los Altos, Menlo Park or Palo Alto. The prices were best in Los Altos. Al's practice was in Menlo Park but Palo Alto was the next town south and Los Altos was just south of it. All were suburbs of San Francisco.

Mrs. Kashee and I took care of the children while Barbara was away. She and I spoke on the telephone each evening. There were houses we could afford, she found, some better than others. She had seen two in the Los Altos area that seemed like good bets. The real estate agent there suggested that one or both of us return in November and make a definite bid on a house with the closing to take place the day after New Year's Day. We had a time line. The pressure was on to get our present house sold. The local market was slow and prices were down slightly.

At the end of the first week of November Barney called us. He was exhilarated. I had made it into Time again in the November 9, 1970 issue. This time I was being quoted frequently in an article about the developing human potential movement. "He's the expert!" Barney said. And this time it had nothing to do with that other topic that he had said he knew nothing about.

We went to California for three days during the Thanksgiving holiday. The two houses Barbara had seen were for sale still. The one she liked best had been sold but the financing had not gone through. I agreed that it was the better of the two. It was charming but the rooms were small and the ceilings low. It had a beautiful large garden full of flowers in bloom. It was in sunny Los Altos and the schools were good.

The agent mentioned a new listing that had come on the market just after Barbara's October visit. "The place is a real bargain if you can afford a larger than usual down payment." It was indeed a bargain. It had more rooms and higher ceilings, a large garage and guest quarters and a long sweeping driveway up from the street. It was on a hill looking out toward the distant Bay and the hills to the east beyond. It was in Los Altos Hills where the zoning required a minimum of three acres.

Neither Barbara nor I really liked the house. It seemed cold, formal, boring and built to be impressive rather than welcoming. But it was empty, the price had been lowered and it was a bargain. The owners needed to sell quickly. It would require a larger down payment and that was worrisome but I knew that we would make a profit when we were ready to sell it and move on. We made a low offer, hoping that if the offer was rejected the smaller house would be available still. Two days after our return to New York the offer was accepted.

Bill Coulson telephoned after our return. He and Carl Rogers liked Asya's and my book and would like to publish it as part of their series. That made me happy. I told Bill more about Asya and why it was so important to her. She had been ill in recent months and I was worried that time was limited if she was actually going to see the book finished.

I also told Bill about my coming out process. He was a devout Catholic with a large family, a follower of the church, but he wanted to understand. "Bill, it's about loving. Men love men sometimes and women love women. I am one of those men. Some church leaders and some other people are stubborn in their determination to remain ignorant and not see the loving. They do a lot of damage. I guess you could call that evil. I want to be who I am and do what I can do to help make things right."

"You always said that you're not religious," he said, "but you can't say you're not spiritual."

A friend of a student told us at our monthly Sunday open house that he too had decided to move to San Francisco. Two of the students wanted to go along with him for a vacation while classes were out and he wondered if we might want him to drive our car there. We decided to move out the week of the last day of classes, and, if possible, go to visit Barney and then fly from Philadelphia to San Francisco. Barney was delighted.

Our real estate broker was not much help but I knew that two of the parties who had seen our home were very interested but could not meet our price. I got in touch with both parties directly, explained that we were moving in December and told them that whichever of them offered the better price would get it for the price offered.

It worked. We had a sale but it was lower than we had hoped. That plus the larger than expected down payment in California, the cost of the movers and the airplane tickets for the four of us cut deeply into the cushion I had hoped that we would have for the year. But both children would be in school and it was possible that Barbara might find a job.

We arrived on the day before New Year's Day and checked into a motel in Los Altos. There was sunshine and there were flowers. Our car arrived the next day. After paying the motel bill and the movers, I calculated that there would be one hundred dollars in our pockets and five hundred dollars in the bank. I would have to get moving fast. It was freedom, hampered by money concerns, but freedom nonetheless. I hoped that we could make good use of it.

Chapter 21

Gay Activist

I got to work immediately, writing, meeting colleagues of Al's who might send me referrals and introducing myself to the handful of visible gay activists in San Francisco.

The book Asya and I had written was going into galley proofs. Judy, the book's editor in Ohio, and I had many long telephone conversations. We became friends. I told her that Asya was very ill and I feared that she might not live to see the finished book. Judy sent a set of galley proofs to her, though I was the only author who would be involved in the final edit.

I had completed a requested chapter for one book while still in New York and had begun work on another to be published in 1972. They were about male encounter groups. They would not yield any income beyond a small token honorarium for each. But just before leaving New York I was contacted by the editor of Mothers' Manual inviting me to write a column for each issue on a topic of interest to young parents. It would bring in a check every two months. Together, the three assignments reflected the contradictions in my life but, in a peculiar way, that seemed right.

Another early project was an article for *The Humanist*. I titled it *The Happy Man is Sometimes Gay* and in it I cited the small amount of relevant psychological research on homosexuality that had made it into print and challenged sexual conformity and our society's damaging attraction to artificial sexual categorization and labels. My own sexual identity could be seen. It was another step in my public emergence from the closet.

I managed to get three referrals the first month. They were difficult patients, poorly motivated but in need of help. I understood these were referrals that the established therapists were happy to pass on to a willing newcomer.

Talking with colleagues I explained that, though happily married I considered myself gay and really wanted to work with gay clients. Several said that they thought it was a mistake. More than once it was pointed out that I could lose my license since homosexual acts, consensual or not, were illegal still in California. "Why not be more discreet about it?" was the repeated question.

I knew that I wanted to meet Phyllis Lyon and Del Martin, the lesbians who had founded *The Daughters of Bilitis*. I also wanted to meet the members of the Gay Men's Collective in Berkeley. I had read about them in New York and heard of them during my time in California while researching the human potential movement. I knew that the men in the collective were using encounter group and sensory awareness techniques in their weekly gay men's rap group evenings.

It was easy to find Phyllis. Reverend Cecil Williams had provided office space at Glide Memorial Church for the Council on Religion and the Homosexual and that was where Phyllis worked. She was wary but interested when I told her that though I was a heterosexually married man and a licensed clinical psychologist, I was also openly gay and wanted to work with gay men and women as well as with their families and friends.

The slash of bright red lipstick was still for a moment and then, "You said you wanted to make contact with the Gay Men's Collective in Berkeley?" She gave me a contact name, Gary Titus, and his telephone number. "Gary's also a member of a task force working to get the local Mental Hygiene Association to word some kind of a resolution that says homosexuality is not a mental illness. It's slow work but it has to be done."

I telephoned Gary Titus and he suggested that we meet in San Francisco the next day just before the Mental Hygiene Association Task Force meeting. "You could stay for the meeting and see if you'd be interested in being on the task force."

I liked Gary immediately. He was tall, broad shouldered, handsome, warm, welcoming and bright. He was one of several people at the meeting who were calmly effective at cutting through illogical bureaucratic nonsense and fear while not grandstanding or pushing others faster than they could go.

Another was Sally Gearhart, a lesbian dressed in a dark blue business suit, stockings and heels. She spoke clear English that wasted no words but was softened by hints of a Texas accent. She also seemed to have a thorough quotable knowledge of the bible.

It was indeed slow going, educating people who feared learning. But the work was happening and there would be a resolution formulated that would influence mental health professionals. I signed on.

Sally and Gary introduced me to Rick Stokes, a prominent San Francisco lawyer who had been sent to a mental hospital earlier in his life because of his homosexual inclinations. Sally, Rick and I became a formidable speaking trio. He knew the law, she knew the bible and I knew the mental health field.

Barbara had gotten the children enrolled in schools. We had boxes unpacked and the pictures hung but the house did not suit us. It was in shadow much of the day and there was no good place on the steep three acres of hillside for a real garden.

But our dog found us and, soon after, our cat. One of the children spotted the dog first, high up on the hill above the house. At first I thought it might be a bear cub lost in suburbia but a look through recently unpacked opera glasses showed him to be a large, unkempt dog with lots of matted fur and a rope around his neck. He was watching us but was afraid, crouching back in shadows when we called to him.

The children put out a bowl of water and a small dish of scraps and waited. It took two days of coaxing before he settled down near the garage, another two before he settled outside the kitchen door and would let us get near. Clearly he had been mistreated but had managed to chew through the thick rope to gain his freedom. He needed our loving and he got it. He, in turn, became our watchdog and defender. The children named him Shaggy, of course. The sleek black cat with big green eyes who adopted us the following month was named Big Eyes.

I found an inexpensive office in a building in San Francisco that had been a large turn of the century whorehouse. The building was in an area that had become fashionable for interior designers' offices. I had two city clients. One had been a student in the Bronx, the other was a friend of one of my fellow interns in Menlo Park.

The Berkeley Gay Men's Collective welcomed me, my experience and my ideas. They were an easygoing group with clear memories of the Bay Area's recent Summer of Love. They were intrigued when I told them that I was happily married and had two children. These men were not doctrinaire defenders of the word *gay*. Each man had a right to identify himself in whatever way he thought best, they believed.

I was very impressed with how well they had adapted various gestalt therapy and sensory awareness exercises into their Friday Night Rap meetings which were open to all gay men in the Bay Area.

I offered to teach a day-long massage workshop for members of the collective. It was a hit. My volunteer demonstration model in the morning was a quiet, blond, bespectacled theology student who quickly shed his clothing and glasses and climbed onto the table while I was talking to someone else. When I turned to the table I thought at first someone new had arrived and had decided to be the demonstration model. He looked like the perfect swimsuit or jockey shorts model except that he was not wearing a swimsuit. His name was Bill Johnson and he was destined, after some struggle, to be ordained sixteen months later in the Spring of 1972 by the United Church of Christ, the first mainstream U.S. denomination to ordain an openly gay man.

I had kept in touch with Brent Wallis, another friend from the Menlo Park internship year. I knew that he was planning to return to the area after finishing studies and training in another state. Al told me that he had seen him during the holidays. "He called last night and I told him you and the family had arrived and that you're getting your practice set up. He wondered if you'd be interested in sharing an office in the city."

Brent and his wife Helen were staying with Brent's father in Los Angeles. Al was planning to visit them on the weekend. Brent had asked him to pass along an invitation to me also.

My sister, Alice, telephoned early in the week to say that my father had been diagnosed with colon cancer and was scheduled for surgery on Friday. Airfare on the commuter airline between San Francisco and Los Angeles was inexpensive. Barbara thought I should go.

I flew to Los Angeles on Thursday and visited with my father in the hospital. He was frightened. "They're gonna' take the knife to me," he said. His hand was trembling when I took it to hold.

"They're good doctors," I said. "They know how to do this. They'll get rid of the problem for you and you'll be asleep while they are doing it." I held his hand and listened. I tried to comfort and give a measure of reassurance without telling any lies or being dishonest. I had become the father and he the child. Those two hours were the closest we had ever been.

I was awakened the next morning at dawn by Brent's stepmother tapping on the guest room door. "There's a telephone call for you. Your sister."

The surgery had been successful. But he was disoriented, agitated and angry when he awoke and discovered the colostomy. "Sometime during the night he pulled out all the tubes and stuff and got out of the bed, they said. He died a couple of hours ago." Would I come and help her to make arrangements?

Brent's father made one of their cars available to me. Brent was good. He stood close to me as I dressed, wanting to help in some way. I was surprised to feel the tears coming. I put my arms around him and sobbed, "I want my Daddy." He knew the story of my life. Both he and I knew that what my inner voice was saying was that I wanted the Daddy I had never had and now, with absolute certainty, would never have. The agonized wail of grief came from my primitive core. For those few minutes I was the hurt and cheated child.

After my return to Los Altos I was asked if I would be part of a panel presentation at the Western States Psychological Association meetings in San Francisco in the spring. The topic was gay identity. I was not the only psychologist who considered himself gay but I was the only one ready to claim gay identity in public in an official meeting of fellow professionals. It was risky but I reasoned that the best defense was a good offense.

Our panel presentation was very well attended. People were curious. When it was my turn to speak I stepped to the microphone and looked out at the faces in the audience. I thought that I saw too many of the bemused smiles one sees on the faces of onlookers at the monkeys' cage in a zoo. Was it self-satisfied condescension? I put aside my prepared words and said, "I am a gay man. As I look at your faces I imagine that I see many, perhaps most of you, being a bit smug and thinking you took care of these childish or adolescent homosexual desires in your fourth or twelfth year of psychoanalysis. Therefore I would like to ask you to put one of your hands in the lap of a person of the same gender seated nearest to you, leave it there for a few minutes and see if it is true that you have no problem with homosexual desires."

To my surprise and delight there was immediate laughter and a standing ovation. During the applause the psychologist who had invited my participation on the panel came close to my ear and said, "You realize there are no laps out there now."

A few more gay clients appeared, one had been referred by a local therapist, the others had heard of me from a friend. They needed reduced fees which I was happy to offer since I had the time. They were students living in communes and activists protesting the war in Vietnam while working for gay rights.

My office in San Francisco was too small for the group work I wanted to do. I hoped that Brent and I could find an office big enough and arrange to share it. He told me that he was not at all put off or intimidated by my openly gay practice.

I went to the Community College that was nearest to Menlo Park to see about the possibility of teaching evening classes there. I presented my credentials and background to the Dean, bolstered by Al's words, "they'd be lucky to get someone like you to teach evening courses."

The Dean listened and then said, "Well, that's very impressive. Your mother must be very proud of you, Doctor, but we don't have any need for new instructors right now." It was a peculiar and insulting dismissal. I wondered if it had to do with my mentioning

my interest in clinical work with gays. The mystery was clarified some
dozen years later when the same closeted Dean came to see me for
psychotherapy.

While doing the research for my Carnegie study I had met John
Levy who was the Executive Director of the Association for Humanistic
Psychology. I liked him. He was a quiet, behind-the-scenes person,
who did not need to take credit for his ideas and his ability to move
them toward fruition. He lived in Tiburon and had an office in San
Francisco.

We renewed our acquaintance, shared ideas and daydreamed
together about where all of the emerging ideas in the human potential
movement might one day take root in the field of psychology. We
agreed that there was a definite need for graduate level education in
clinical psychology that would be a genuine alternative to what was
being offered in accredited programs in established universities. There
was a need for a school that welcomed older students with unique life
experiences who could take hold of the new ideas and make sensible
clinical applications from them. And the school should welcome gay
students and professors. That would be new.

John moved the idea along. He contacted Eleanor Criswell who
taught at Sonoma State and had been making headway in establishing
humanistic psychology studies there. He also talked to Carl Rogers
and members of the A. H. P. Board.

In less than a year he had an agreement to start a skeletal program
called the Humanistic Psychology Institute. He and I were two of the
members of the first Board of Directors. We were clear in our vision of
an educational program that was to be a true alternative to what was
already available elsewhere. It would stand on its own merits and its
cumulative reputation.

But, as other Board members, faculty members and students
appeared, the quest for legitimacy by way of accreditation began.
I tried to make the point that the academic accreditation process
conferred approval only on that which met the *standards* of what
already existed. My plea was lost, however, in the faculty, board and
student needs to be part of an academic establishment that was seen
as legitimate, so I left the board.

Brent found our San Francisco office on Union Street. It was a cottage set back behind the stores fronting the street. It had a living room that would serve as a waiting room and was large enough for group work and a bedroom easily made into an office for private sessions. There also was a bathroom, kitchen and even a dining room. It had a front porch facing a flower garden and there was another garden in back behind the kitchen and bathroom. He and Helen had it furnished quickly and beautifully. I could sublet it two days and evenings a week and use it for weekend groups.

Al and several other therapists were looking for office space in Menlo Park. It was agreed that I could share one office with Ginny, a therapist particularly interested in work with women. By summer it was clear to me that income was a real but temporary problem. I was doing work that I enjoyed with some wonderful gay clients. The children were thriving in the California sunshine. Barbara was meeting people and making friends. It was happening.

We went back to the New Jersey shore in July to vacation for the last time in Mouse House before putting it up for sale. It was the only part of our previous life that I would miss. I decided to write a resignation letter to the university. The safety net would be gone.

Each day I took one long walk on the beach alone and thought about the near future. I was sure that I was doing the right thing. I wanted to start two on-going weekly therapy groups for gay men when we returned to San Francisco, one in Menlo Park and one in the city. I also wanted to do the Natural Man weekend groups for gay men. There was a need for loving and truthful community in which we gay people could safely show ourselves and grow in self-esteem.

The last weekend at the shore we got a babysitter and went to the movies to see *Sunday Bloody Sunday*. Peter Finch played a London physician who reluctantly shared a younger male lover with Glenda Jackson's character. The owned-by-none young man soon leaves them both. I was mesmerized by Peter Finch's monologue, looking straight at the audience at the film's finish, saying that he had walked his own individual path despite what passed for common wisdom and had found his measure of happiness. Willing to admit his shared love was *half a loaf* perhaps, with a soft but defiant look he tells the audience that it was much more than nothing, "It *was* something."

It resonated in me deeply. I knew what he meant. I knew it was truth that I was hearing and I knew I needed to find my own measure of that love that I was missing. I needed love and sex with a man but would have to make sure that it did not disrupt my marriage and family.

The groups for gay men were up and running within two months. I also took Michael Murphy up on his offer and planned a Natural Man weekend for Esalen. It too filled quickly. Maybe soon I would find that man. Meantime there was all of the touching in the groups and sometimes massage that was erotic, especially at places like Esalen.

In September, Vicki went into first grade and Andy into kindergarten. Near the end of his first week of school we got a note from Andy's teacher explaining he had been punished for a discipline problem. His teacher was young and pretty, an insecure first year teacher. I wanted to know what had happened.

When the two kindergartens had been lined up in the morning Andy had recognized a friend from his nursery school in the other line. He had called over excitedly to say hello. "We need to be silent when we are in line and he needs to learn that." I allowed as how it might be better to reward friendliness rather than to punish it and reward silence instead. Then Vicki came home at the end of her third week with a large crayon picture she had produced. In the corner the teacher had placed a large *A-*.

I talked to Al about the progressive private school his boys had attended for several years. He telephoned the director and took me there the next day to introduce me. Their classes were full. I also could not imagine how I would afford the tuition but I asked to have our children considered for the following school year.

The director was more than a little interested in my background. He knew about the School in Rose Valley and had heard of Grace Rotzel. He was happy to learn that she had written a book about the school and her philosophy of education. He was also intrigued to learn that I had gathered experience working as a school psychologist, as a graduate student and later at the Hunter Elementary School. He really wished that they could afford to pay a school psychologist. Perhaps we could work something out.

Barbara had met a number of our neighbors at the schools and elsewhere, and one woman was becoming a good friend for Barbara. We both liked her and her husband. We also were invited to neighborhood parties but did not fit in really. There was heavy drinking and the supposedly titillating possibilities of wife swapping. They were people who worked to make money. I never hid the fact that I considered myself to be gay but I also did not often offer the information. It was confusing to most of them just as it was to the most opinionated, anti-establishment young gay radicals I encountered who were unwilling to share their club with *family types*.

That winter several important new people entered my life. The first, Hal, came as a patient. He was recommended to me by a musicologist friend of his from Berkeley whom I had seen for a few sessions. He considered himself to be gay but was married to a woman. The second, Bill Horstman, telephoned from Berkeley to say that he was gay, had just finished work on his Ph.D. in clinical psychology and would like to work under my supervision as a psychological assistant, gathering the hours of experience needed before taking the licensing examination. The third was Betty Berzon. She lived in the Hollywood Hills and had been told by mutual friends that we should meet. She was closeted still but on her way out. We arranged a meeting while I was in Los Angeles to do a Natural Man Workshop there and we hit it off immediately, inspiring one another in our activism. I enjoyed both her sense of humor and her intellect.

Betty and I became close friends and confidants as well as colleagues for many years. Bill and I also worked together for many years as good friends. We navigated the worst years of the AIDS epidemic together as a seemingly unimaginable number of patients and friends became sick and died. After his therapy Hal and I became good friends. He and his later partner, Mike, became my closest friends until each died in the AIDS epidemic.

We gay professionals were finding our way. Such arrangements as friendships or bartering with clients were frowned upon though not forbidden in those days. It was assumed, unless proven otherwise, that a therapist always would act with the needs of the client as a paramount concern. The gay community, even in San Francisco, was a small one, with personal and professional roles intersecting often. We policed ourselves and talked to one another if it seemed someone was behaving in a way that would reflect badly on us all.

The gay men and women I met professionally and socially who were married and had children were caught in the same strong emotional currents that I was experiencing. We longed to be with imagined or real lovers, to claim our identity fully but we did not want to hurt our wives, husbands and children. The social upheaval of the late 1960s and early 1970s had made divorce commonplace but it still meant pain for all concerned. Most of us did not know where our conflicting emotional tides would carry us.

Many of the friends Barbara and I had in the spring of 1972 were gay. I was very public about my gay identity and also very public about being in a good, loving marriage with wonderful children. Barbara and I talked. We jokingly agreed that what we needed was another husband. Sex outside of marriage was acceptable in our changing world. She said that she was managing and thought that she could continue to manage with the changes as long as I did not become romantically involved with another man. I wondered how that would work since sex was not all that I was missing or had missed.

We agreed that we were not happy with the public schools and wanted to take a closer look at the Peninsula School. We began to visit. It was a place and a community that reflected our values. The director told me that they were interested in trading a partial scholarship for part-time service as their school psychologist. My gay activism would pose no problem. We were glad but not enthusiastic about driving the children back and forth to Los Altos.

One day after visiting the school I saw a new *for sale* sign in front of a house that was directly across the street from the school. A commune of sixteen people was vacating, I learned, going their separate ways. It was more than we could afford but we made an appointment to look.

It was an original Eichler, the architect famous for walls of glass, walls of wood and heated floors that made a cozy nest. It was a large and very private place revealing little of itself to the street but opened to its gardens and trees. We loved it. Four bedrooms and two baths, large living room with a fireplace, large dining room, large garden area with a cute playhouse the commune had built. It also had a two-car garage and a quiet, separate guest room with its own bathroom.

We confessed that it was too expensive but the agent came to look at our place. "There's almost always a way," he said. He calculated that we could get enough from the sale of our house in Los Altos Hills. "We'll get a good enough mortgage so that you can make the switch and have some cash to make repairs on the new house."

We were nervous. What if our place did not sell soon enough? Finally he offered, if necessary, to buy our place himself at a low enough price that he would be sure to re-sell it in a matter of months. It still would give us enough to make the trade, he said. We agreed and made an offer. The offer was accepted and we made another appointment to see the house and look more carefully at whatever might need fixing. The commune was much more casual about our coming after the offer had been accepted.

It was a sunny April afternoon. We arrived, as planned, at six o'clock in the evening. As we stepped into the living room I saw a smiling, handsome young man, quite naked, strolling across the grass on the other side of the screened sliding door. "Oh, hi," he said, at ease as he stepped into the living room. He was wet. "Sorry. I didn't know we had visitors. I just got out of the pool."

"Pool?" I asked.

He pointed to the seven-foot high redwood fence that I had assumed defined the edge of the property. He escorted us to the fence, pushed a panel, and the gate swung open revealing a very large rectangular pool surrounded by night blooming jasmine and loquat trees. Another naked young man was just springing off the diving board. Two women and two children stood in the shallow water at the nearest end. All were comfortably naked and waved a friendly and relaxed hello.

We moved in at the end of that month. The move was made easier because we had kept all of the boxes used in the move from New York. Last to go after the moving truck was loaded was Shaggy. He had looked frightened as men loaded the truck. Large as he was, he was always a source of amusement to others whenever he sat beside me in the front seats of our VW bug. His head was at just about the same height as mine.

He did not understand what was happening and he definitely did not want to leave home. I tried to coax him into the car. No luck. He cowered. I started to pick him up and he rolled over onto his back. I managed to get my arms under his bulk and lift him, belly up, head hanging in resignation or despair.

As I walked the few steps to the car, the children laughed and comforted him. They opened the car door, Shaggy whimpered and sent a stream of urine straight into the air and, of course, onto me. It became the children's favorite tale for months.

The school still did not have space for Andy but they did have a new vacancy in the first grade and the teacher was willing to take Vicki since all of her children would be staying together as a group the following year anyway. Andy was more than willing to trade the Los Altos kindergarten for a swimming pool. The pool brought other children quickly as well as more friends for Barbara and me. It was a very happy move.

I met with the Director and teachers at The Peninsula School. We worked out details. I would be the school psychologist, available fifteen hours a week to observe, confer with staff and parents and attend staff meetings. In exchange there would be the discount in tuition fees for the children. It was a good fit in a good community. We even met a few couples in which the husband was gay-identified or suspected by the wife of being "sort of gay" or, as one wife put it, "almost gay but too scared to say so, I think."

Al Haimson and his colleagues found a perfect house in Menlo Park that could be turned into offices. I borrowed enough money to pay one half of the down payment on one share. Ginny paid the other half since we would be sharing the room between the kitchen and the rear patio. The very large living room served as a waiting room for all of the offices by day but would be mine one evening a week to use for my therapy group for gay men.

I actually was busy. My practice was close to full both in San Francisco and Menlo Park. I had taken on a second and then a third psychological assistant whose clinical work I was supervising. I was writing contributions to gay publications and letters to editors, being very *out* as a gay clinical psychologist. I was also continuing my articles for Mothers' Manual.

Chapter 22

Book Fame

That winter, I invited Martin Hoffman, the psychiatrist who had written *The Gay World* in 1968 and John de Cecco, a prominent San Francisco academic, to lunch in the Union Street cottage to discuss the possibility of setting up a scholarship fund for gay students training to be mental health professionals. They were interested but pessimistic about finding funds and shy about the spotlight it would shine on their own sexual identities. David Goodstein, a closeted and wealthy local philanthropist also was invited but he needed to visit alone and proved to be even more shy about risking coming out and quite ambivalent about donating or asking any of his wealthy, closeted friends to donate.

By then we could afford to hire a babysitter once in a while for an evening out with friends. *Deliverance* was a film that was causing a lot of discussion, so we saw it with another couple. It seemed to me to be a dark meditation on what men could do to one another and for one another, their love and desire for one another having gone dangerously sour in a world that favored male aggression and violence while ladies stayed at home, screened from naked truth. I could see how gay love was a mighty threat to that *normal* societal system. Perhaps if men felt more free to meet in the intimacy of loving sex they would have less need to meet in the intimacy of battle. My opinion seemed interesting, but odd to Barbara and our friends.

Before Christmas the peace talks in Paris between the North Vietnamese and the Nixon Administration fell apart and Nixon ordered a new bombing campaign that lasted twelve days. "Why can't men be encouraged to make love with one another?" I began to ask aloud.

In October several of the men in the Menlo Park group turned up in full drag for the evening meeting closest to Halloween. It had caused much discussion in the following few months, touching off both painful and funny memories of dressing up in Mom's clothes and getting caught.

Someone suggested that we all do drag for one meeting. I thought it was a good idea. A few men refused but we agreed that everyone who could would do it three weeks hence and "you *real* men come in your usual dreary drag," as one person put it.

Neal, a friend from New York who had taken me out to several gay clubs there, had moved to San Francisco and was excited when he heard about it. "Oh, Sweetheart, we have to go shopping. You stay home, Babs," he said to Barbara.

We did. We found a second-hand shop in Menlo Park where society ladies sent their cast off gowns and accessories as charitable donations. There was a dress that fit me, black with many black beads and black sequins individually stitched in place. "You'll look *fabulous* and it must have cost some large dame a fortune." The two ladies running the shop that day were highly amused.

"Now to Macys' and the other places in the Stanford Shopping Center. You need hair, panty hose, shoes and definitely make-up!"

In a large wig department he stopped traffic as he pulled and tugged one blond wig after another onto my head as I sat blushing in front of the mirror. "I guess this one will do, but it needs to be re-styled," he said finally. Then looking at the sales clerk he said, "What about your hair, dear? Is that a wig you're wearing?"

She shook her head "no."

"Pity," he said, rolling his eyes. "Pay the nice lady, we're off to get you some make-up."

The young woman behind the cosmetics counter, having witnessed the wig event, said, "Is this some kind of gag?" as we passed her.

"Don't be silly, dear," he said. "This is serious. It's his first time in drag."

"Far out!" she said, beaming approval.

I had only an hour and a half to dress, get made up and eat dinner on the evening of the big event I had put my new clothes plus some possible accessories Barbara had offered on the bed. The children wandered in and asked what I was doing so I explained. They thought it was really fun so they went outside to tell their friends. Soon I had several of the neighbors' children giggling and watching as I assembled my outfit. I wondered how they would describe it all to their parents.

The big surprise came when I got into the car to drive to the office. First I had to take off the heels since I feared they would interfere with reflexive use of the brake pedal and the accelerator. Then, as I started to back out, I looked in the rear view mirror and gasped as I saw a woman's face, looking at me.

The three men who had come in their usual jeans and work shirts admitted to feeling out of place. Two of the men had gone all out with careful choice of female clothing and makeup. One had spent half the day in a salon having makeup, nails and his own hair styled. A few quickly tried out as caricatures but the acts could not be sustained. It led each of us to search out those strong facets of our real selves usually left in the shadows of the mind, unrecognized and dishonored. We learned more about one another.

The group bond grew stronger. It became a required annual event.

Soon after the Christmas and New Year's holidays I was told by Bill Coulson in San Diego that I would be hearing from the Education Department of the state of South Dakota soon. Each summer the state assembled all of its teachers, up to and including those teaching in the state university. Carl Rogers had been asked to deliver the keynote address that year and could not do it. He had recommended me.

It was a great honor to have been recommended by him. They offered a respectable honorarium which I definitely could use and would, of course, pay all of my expenses. It was a two-day event. The keynote address was to be given to one group in Rapid Falls one day and in Sioux City the other day. They would fly me between the two cities in a private plane.

Though we had met several times I assumed that Carl Rogers had recommended me on the basis of Asya's and my *Humanistic Teaching* book, published in the series that he edited with Bill Coulson. But I wanted to take a more bold step in the keynote address and work gay liberation into it somehow. I did not want to give an hour-long boring speech and maybe I could help gay children. Surely Rogers had seen my *Happy Man is Sometimes Gay* article in the *Humanist*, I thought.

Since I was afraid of public speaking I knew that I would have to craft the address carefully and have it clearly typed out double-spaced. It should have surprise in it to keep the captive audience awake and the words should have a rhythm or cadence when read aloud. I worked hard on it.

The final product was titled *Humanism in Teaching, a Vote for Deviance.* In it I used my own story as a child in poverty with illiterate parents who stumbled into an education and went all the way to a doctorate in a conformity-oriented society that cared little for those it considered non-conforming. As a result, some of the education I earned had done me as much harm as good, devaluing my identity first in poverty and then as a gay male. Teachers could help non-conforming children to feel their worth.

I had their attention. I had been told that there would be a luncheon following the speech. I was to be the guest of honor. When I concluded, the startled audience gave me five seconds of polite applause and then fled. I ate lunch alone.

I went to the men's room to wash up before eating though. I was alone there when a nice looking young man entered and, speaking hurriedly, said, "Thank you so much for that. I just got out of the Marines and came back home here. This is my first year teaching. I'm gay. You've made my year and saved my life. Thanks." With that he left as quickly as he had entered, not wanting to arouse negative suspicion about what he was doing in the men's room with me no doubt.

I was received with simple, polite words in the second city and invited to dinner at the Holiday Inn where I would have a room for the night. After dinner I was taken to the American Legion Hall for a drink. Word of me had traveled quickly by telephone I assumed. The conversation was stilted. The audience the next day was quite alert and quiet.

I was ushered to the airport quickly when I was finished. The best part was the flight between the two cities. It was a small plane, the pilot in the front seat and me in the rear seat. "You want to see Mount Rushmore?" he asked.

Indeed I did and indeed we did see it, up quite close as he flew us to and in front of the massive carved heads. "What do you think?" he asked. I could only muster a "Wow!"

A local gay magazine, *Vector*, asked me if I would be willing to review several sex-education films currently in use and write an article about them. The editor liked the article and asked if I would consider writing a monthly advice column in response to letters. The ethical guideline in place at the time urged psychologists to give advice to individuals only if seeing them face to face for counseling or psychotherapy. I said I could use letters as a jumping off point to offer general observations and professional opinion but not advice to the letter writer. *Dear Don* ran regularly from 1973 to 1975.

Brent's enthusiasm for private practice and, hence, his practice had not grown and he was giving serious thought to stopping it. Our shared cottage office on Union Street had been a great gift from him but it was time to move on.

My first psychological assistant, Bill Horstman, was now ready to start his own practice. We thought about finding an office or buying a building in the Castro, right in the heart of the gay population we wanted to serve and talked about it with several gay therapists who, like most, were closeted within professional circles. One psychiatrist said he would rent from us if we found a good suite of offices. Another said he was interested in being a partner in buying a building but was not sure about having his office there.

After a few months of searching we found a house on Eighteenth Street, two blocks uphill from Castro Street. There was space for three offices and a waiting room on the main floor. A converted basement had two good sized rooms plus a small kitchen and bath that would work for me as office, waiting room and space for the on-going weekly therapy group in the city as well as the weekend groups if I limited groups to twelve participants.

The on-going weekly group in Menlo Park meanwhile had developed into a three-hour group for sixteen gay men. Two of the men in the Menlo Park group were lovers and talented gardeners. Big, handsome, well educated, strapping young men, one blond and one dark, they were dedicated to self improvement and the care of their relationship in turbulent times. Recent hippie college graduate dropouts, they could not afford to pay in money but could pay in gardening service. I decided to give Barbara the big garden she had always wanted as a birthday present. We had the space for it and they were enthusiastic about designing and building a big garden from scratch. It took most of a year but Barbara was very happy with the process, the result and with them. She and they became good friends and it was she who was to become the valued caretaker for them in their terminal illness years later.

A local psychiatrist, Alan, with whom I was developing a good friendship, had a wife, Frieda, who was very interested in art and social causes. She and Barbara met and liked one another. A friend of Barbara's from New York City days had married an actor and moved to the area. He too was gay but closeted.

By now she had a number of friends. Judy, the textbook editor from Ohio, was one. Based in part on our telephone conversations while she was editing *Humanistic Teaching*, she had talked her physician husband into moving to the Bay Area. They lived ten miles away. She brought news that Asya's and my book was being translated into Spanish.

My determination to be totally open and proud of my gay identity worried Barbara. "Why does everything have to be about being gay," she asked in exasperation after I had mentioned it in conversation with the closeted actor. "Why do you have to tell everyone? With you gay is like a religion."

I thought about it. "I guess you're right." I said. "It is. You're Jewish and I'm gay. We don't go to religious services but it's who we are. It's identity."

In January of 1974 Richard Nixon resigned as President of the United States and was replaced by Gerald Ford. Military advisors and

Marines remained in Vietnam though the war was officially over. Of the more than three million Americans who had served in the war, close to fifty-eight thousand were dead, more than a thousand were missing, and one hundred and fifty thousand Americans had been seriously wounded. "If only men could make love together," I said in a speech, "or at least admit that they want to sometimes, we might harm one another less often."

Quality gay oriented books had begun to appear. I was reading Rita Mae Brown's *Rubyfruit Jungle* and Patricia Nell Warren's *Front Runner*. Issues of *The Advocate Magazine* and *Vector* were in the living room. My life was now full of gay men, many of whom were attractive to me. The longing inside of me was building. It made me uneasy.

By then I was having sex with other men discreetly, according to the agreement Barbara and I had fashioned. It was okay as long as she was not confronted with evidence of it. She did not want to have to deal with embarrassing gossip or have it brought into our home life. But I did not have my own special male lover. It was that which I now realized I had been missing all of my life.

My private New Year's resolution for 1974 was to assemble notes, make an outline and begin to write a book for gay people, their families, their friends and the professional service providers with whom they came into contact. I was no longer closeted, I had the right professional credentials and I had the experience. Such a book was needed. I spoke with my literary agent about it. She was not enthusiastic. "I don't know of any publisher who would publish such a book."

But that spring I started. Barbara and I had bought a part time share in a beach house in Pajaro Dunes near Watsonville, south of San Jose, on the coast. I took a school week off and went there alone to write, Monday to Friday, dawn to dark. I was alone with my typewriter, my few notes and the ocean. By noon on Friday when I packed up to go home I had an outline and a very rough draft of the first third of the book.

I sent it to my friend, Betty Berzon, in Los Angeles and showed it to Barbara. Betty encouraged me to go on. Barbara said she thought it might be good. She seemed worried. It was difficult finding time to work on the book but I made a folder of notes.

My friend, Hal, who had finished therapy with me was still married but was out and open with his wife, his two sons and his work colleagues. He had referred a friend, Don, who was also married and had two sons. Don was good looking, athletic, a psychologist and a college professor. We had a lot of life experiences in common.

I had no idea how important our meeting would prove to be a year after his therapy was finished. He telephoned me early in 1975 to see if we might get together for lunch or coffee sometime. I thought he might be a good early reader for my work on the book. Our schedules did not mesh well, however, but in early February I was contacted by Chris, the young gay man who had been attacked by zealous liberals in our leaderless encounter group at the Association for Humanistic Psychology yearly meeting in 1969 and with whom I had done a first try-out weekend gay group.

Chris had become a filmmaker and produced a full-length feature film about gay male love titled *A Very Natural Thing*. He told me that it was opening in San Francisco and invited me to attend. Barbara was not interested so I asked Don if he would like to go since we had not been able to get together for lunch or coffee.

The film was very moving for both of us. We retired to a gay bar some blocks away to talk after the movie. I told him about the book I was writing. There was an odd intensity to our talk, things not being spoken aloud. There was attraction and it seemed to be mutual though neither of us named it. I said that I would mail him a portion of the manuscript.

At its January 24, 1975 meeting, the governing body of the American Psychological Association had voted to support the action taken by the American Psychiatric Association in December 1973 in removing homosexuality per se from the association's official list of mental disorders. It went further, endorsing a policy statement submitted by its Board of Social and Ethical Responsibility urging all psychologists to take the lead in ending discrimination against homosexuals. This was big news. Change was happening. Don and I talked about it.

In May 1975 California became the eleventh state to decriminalize same-sex acts. I could stop looking over my shoulder, wondering if

I would lose my license as a psychologist for admitting that I was gay. In June, the American Medical Association joined the chorus and in July the U. S. Civil Service Commission announced that it would consider applications from gay men and lesbians.

Don and I had managed to find time to see one another many times by then. I had not been mistaken. The attraction was mutual. We talked. We touched. We kissed. We made love. By June we admitted to one another that we were in love and had, in fact, become lovers. We hoped that we could stay in our marriages. Wild as the times were in Berkeley where they lived, Don knew this news would not be welcomed by his wife. I knew that I had to let Barbara know the facts also, even though it was exactly what she had said she did not think she could tolerate.

In those few months I had finished a reasonably good draft of the book. I sent it off to my agent in New York and she began sending it to publishers. She had been right, no one wanted it. I received a scolding letter from a friend of hers who was Editor at Basic Books. She attached a letter from their expert professional reader. Both scolded me for shirking my professional responsibility. Did I not understand that these poor sick people needed help?

My editor friend, Judy, who had moved to California from Ohio meanwhile, had found a job in a small printing company in Millbrae, near the San Francisco Airport. They printed large decorative California posters mostly of the *Have a Nice Day* variety. They had published a few small books also.

Judy read my manuscript and thought it was both good and timely. She pushed her employers but they were reluctant. Finally, to appease her, they agreed that they would publish it in 1976 with a printing of five thousand copies if I would agree to buy back a sufficient number of the unsold copies to guarantee that their cost would be covered. They would let Judy edit the book. It was the best and only offer I had. I wanted to get the book and its message out into the world.

Barbara and I were having problems but we were trying. We talked. We wrote letters to one another, the better to choose our words carefully. We had meetings to talk about the letters. We were both tense. I made efforts to shield the children but they too seemed tense. I dreaded pulling into our driveway at dinnertime and hearing Barbara yelling at the children.

It was not going to work. I knew that something had to give. I had worked too hard at not knowing what I now knew. Sex became a non-verbal battleground, strewn with unasked questions and unspoken desires, mind and body trapped with hidden tests. The ghosts of what was missing jammed the lines of the erotic communication that once had been there between us. The fun was gone. Tenderness was now a memory.

We tried. We both tried. We had evenings out alone together and with friends. We rented a big R.V. and took the children along on a summer camping trip as I drove it up into Oregon and back. The four of us enrolled in family therapy. Barbara and I learned Transcendental Meditation and meditated together. The two of us took an inexpensive charter flight from Oakland to France to visit Barbara and Frank Alweis who were spending a sabbatical year in Provence. When we returned we joined my psychiatrist friend, Alan, and his wife, Frieda, in a Sunday matinee opera subscription.

But the undercurrents were carrying us away from one another. Gay liberation was happening locally, nationally and internationally. The *struggle* had become a *fight* and I was in it every chance I got. In July, nearby Santa Cruz County had become the first U. S. County to make job discrimination against gay men and lesbians illegal. In December, the Washington Star began a series of articles about homosexuality in sports, alluding to football stars. Later in the month Dave Kopay, the former Redskins linebacker came out publicly as gay.

Don and I saw one another whenever we could, sometimes for only an hour in my office in the Castro, a mid-point between our several work places and homes. Our lovemaking seemed magical, transporting me to a luxurious erotic freedom I had not visited since the snowbound night in a rented room with my fellow usher when we were sixteen years old. He was on my mind always and Barbara sensed it. I did not know what to do. I was torn between wanting to be with Don and wanting to keep my family together. He faced the same dilemma.

When school resumed in September Andy's teacher offered to host a parents' evening at his home in the city. Though he had never announced it, the teacher was gay and the school community knew it. He lived in a gay area of the city near the Castro. It was a potluck dinner on a Friday evening. Parents accepted a glass of wine and chatted in the living room or out on the deck as we waited for those having a difficult time finding parking.

As I stepped out onto the deck I saw a car pull into the driveway of the house across the street. Two young men in plaid flannel shirts and jeans got out of the car, each carrying two large brown bags of groceries. When they got to their door, one of them said something to the other. Both laughed and they kissed before unlocking the door and stepping into their home.

There it was. *That* was what I wanted and it was not a frivolous want. It was what I had wanted and needed throughout my life, a real home shared with another man who was the love of my life. Grocery shopping and cooking dinner with the man I admired, respected and slept with, safe always in one another's arms.

It was the good, easy loving, respectable home life that Barbara and I had seemed to create together. But I was gay and wanted what those two men coming home from the grocery store on a Friday evening had together. I *needed* it. I envied Andy's teacher. It was all available to him. I had missed the path because it had not been visible in my earliest adult years when I tried to imagine and work for a decent future life.

It was difficult to pay attention to the discussion that evening. I had a pain in my gut. It hurt. A wound had opened. I could not see a future that would bring resolution to the swirling conflict. I could only take the next careful, most truthful step and hope.

I had begun to make minor corrections on the manuscript of the book, responding to Judy's editorial suggestions. We worked well together as we had on Asya's and my *Humanistic Teaching*. "They don't like your title," she told me. "They think *Loving Someone Gay* is too vague and weird."

"It *is* the title," I said. "It stays."

Watching a television re-run of *Summertime* with Katherine Hepburn one evening in December, we could have been mistaken for a happy family. I had read to the children and put them to bed before the movie began. Barbara was trimming a weaving that she had made on the large loom I had given to her on Valentine's Day. I had seen the movie the first time in the summer before graduate school while wondering if I had made the right choice or if I should have gone to Europe to become a writer.

I saw it differently that December night. I saw her terrible struggle, trying to be good and right, maintaining a façade of satisfaction and cheer, holding back her deep desires when opportunity confronted her. At the start of the film, speaking of Venice supposedly, she says she *has* to like it, "I've waited so long and come such a long way." I knew her desires and I was looking at my own Venice. I too had waited so long and come such a long way. Like her I was trying to fit two very different pictures of myself in two different worlds together and have it make sense. It was impossible. But, unlike her, I could not will myself to return to the closet.

Judy and Barbara had arranged to go into the city and stay overnight in a hotel the day after New Year's. It was a chance to leave family responsibilities behind for a *girl's night out*.

I spent the week between Christmas and New Years' crafting a letter to Barbara. I wanted to choose words very carefully, to be truthful and honor our love while confessing that I needed to leave the marriage that we had built so carefully. I did not want to lose her or the family and pleaded for us to work together to find a new form that would free all of us from the increasingly difficult tangle we were in. I put the letter in her suitcase. Judy was a good friend to both of us and could help her sort her feelings during the day away from me and the children.

She returned at dinnertime the next day. I was in the kitchen. She entered very angry. "I want you out of this house now. Pack up and get out. And explain yourself to the kids before you go." It was a nightmare.

"And don't think you're going to get out of this without taking care of the kids half-time." Did she really know me that little? As I was leaving she said, "You're going to ruin Don's life the same way you ruined mine. You've taken the best years of my life." The words stung. Had we not done this together?

She was in a rage, not her usual self. I knew that. But the words wounded. Neither of us had ever hit below the belt before. Those last minutes struck a blow at the beautiful but delicate structure of our life together, shattering it along its many fault lines.

Before I packed the car I asked the children to come to the kitchen table for a family meeting. Barbara sat opposite me, anger blazing in her eyes but pain now showing also. I reminded them of other children in their school whose parents had separated. I told them that we too were having a hard time and that I would be finding another place to live.

"But it will be another home for you. You'll live here and there both." That would be the change. They would have two homes.

My daughter burst into tears and said that she wanted to come with me. My son asked if he could still go to the overnight at his friend's house that had been planned for that night.

I said that it was a hard time for all of us but that we would get through it and times would get better. I told my son that I would drive him to his friend's house as planned and told my crying daughter that she could come along with us for the ride if she wanted but that I would have to find a place for the three of us before I could take her overnight.

"When?" she asked.

"Very soon," I answered. "I promise."

"You stay here and have dinner," Barbara said to her.

1976 was a tumultuous year. I went from three nights in a motel room to a furnished apartment over a garage, then to a partially furnished two-bedroom house. Always the children were with me half-time, all of the living places were close to the school and the house on Peninsula Way.

Barbara and I managed to be civilized after the first few weeks. We found a no-fault lawyer who officially would represent her but would represent us both in finding our way from separation to divorce, he told us.

I increased my work hours to handle the additional expense. After a few months Barbara got a job in real estate sales. "Is that what you wanted, for me to get a job?" she asked. I did not know how to explain or if it even mattered anymore.

We had entered our marriage with the same basic values but different expectations. She had probably seen me as someone like her father who would treat her as he had treated her mother. I had assumed that she was like the other dedicated young women I had met at Antioch, eager for marriage and family but also eager to have a career, forge individual identity and make a difference in the world. We had both been wrong and neither of us had dreamed that the civil rights struggle we strongly favored would lead to liberation for men and women with suppressed homosexual needs.

Don and his wife had continued to deal with their own problems. Their marriage also seemed destined to end but I certainly did not wish them to have to endure the pain that both Barbara and I now faced every day with the wreckage of the life we had constructed together weighing us down. I did not wish him to have to endure the guilt that was tainting even the most pleasant moments I could find with the children or with him.

But in the spring it happened. His wife asked him to leave. He rented an inexpensive apartment close to his sons' schools. Our schedules did not always match but we could, now and then, have a weekend alone together when the children were with their mothers. It would have to be that way for the foreseeable future.

I concentrated on getting the book manuscript through the editing process. The publication process had delays. As we neared the end of 1976 the publisher decided that the book would be in the warehouse in December but would have an official 1977 publication date, to be released in January.

Christmas would be different. I dreaded it. Barbara took the children to visit her father for Christmas. I decided to take them to Hawaii for the ten days after Christmas and before school started again. It worked. They had good holidays and their parents did something for themselves.

The publisher had hired a good publicist temporarily, an experienced person from New York whose husband's work had brought them to San Francisco. She arranged a book-signing event the first week in January at Paperback Traffic, a new gay-oriented bookstore on Castro Street.

It was a few blocks from my office. I had dinner that evening with Don, Bill Horstman and two other friends. It was an unseasonably warm, balmy evening. As we neared the corner of Castro and

Eighteenth Street I was stunned when I saw a line on the street outside the bookstore!

I spent the next two hours in a state of euphoria, my shyness forgotten. I was no longer the outcast kid on the playground. That was clear. In this world, my world, filled with people like me, I was definitely one of the gang. They liked me. Only the fear of keeping those in line waiting too long stopped me from spending more than a minute chatting with each of them.

Maybe it was going to be a better world for everyone, at last. Maybe my gay brothers and sisters would be not only accepted but appreciated in the world. But less than two weeks later the world heard from a woman best known up to then for doing television commercials to sell frozen Florida orange juice. She was a former beauty queen who said that she was launching a nationwide *crusade* against gay rights in response to Dade County, Florida's new ordinance forbidding discrimination against lesbians and gay men in housing and employment. Overnight Anita Bryant had become someone who stood for something or against something. She called her crusade *The Save Our Children Campaign*, accusing us of corrupting the nation's youth.

The publicist telephoned me. "You did know, didn't you, that the first printing was sold out well before the official publication date? We ordered a larger print run and now we'll need more." Could I free up some time? I was wanted for interviews.

"What kind?"

"Television, radio and newspaper."

"Where?"

"Here… and in a lot of other places. You're a psychologist, you're gay and open about it, you were married *and* a college professor and you have kids. Anita Bryant is making news and they need someone to represent the other side of the issue. You're their dream come true. Get ready."

Chapter 23

Divorce

I t was not anything I had wished for. But it would help to spread the book's message and it could contribute to the struggle for equal civil rights. My appearances on television, radio and in newspaper interviews would put a human face on the word *gay*, for the first time for some people. I realized that The National Gay Task Force never could manage to have as much airtime as I was being offered. It was a responsibility that I did not dare to refuse.

But there was more than a little fear attached to the experience for me, especially that first year. Being more introverted than extraverted, my voice sometimes squeezed down to a hoarse whisper when I had the misfortune to realize that thousands or even millions of people would hear what I was saying. Sometimes I was saved by the genuine warmth and interest of an interviewer. More often not.

There were times when I was saved by a surge of anger as when a morning show pretty-boy host with a very large live studio audience, mostly women, dared to greet me with an assumed look of distaste and ask why in the world I would choose to be an avowed homosexual. I told him I had not taken any vows and had been born the person I was just as he had been born the attractive person that he was.

I then leaned closer to him and went on to say that it was hard for me to believe that he had never been tempted to respond positively to the expressed sexual interest of other men. I saw the beads of sweat popping through the pancake makeup and knew I had adjusted the playing field. Doing live TV shows I quickly came to realize that I would be in another city the next morning while the host would be right in the same spot the next morning, mopping up whatever damage I chose to inflict. I could require respect.

Observing myself, I was amazed to see myself learning the tricks of the trade. An accidental one-liner that worked one day could be tried out again the next day in another appearance and then added to the repertoire if it played well again. I was sometimes flattered, sometimes reviled, and managed to take very little of it personally.

Sometimes, when the interview seemed to be getting too chummy in an unreal way I had to remind the interviewer, the audience and myself that in 1947 I had been a seventeen year old usher in a movie theater and a junior in high school when I saw Gregory Peck in *Gentlemen's Agreement*. My friends were Jewish. I understood the gut message of the movie the first time I saw it.

Nice people are disgusted by ungraceful subtle anti-Semitism and by crude anti-Semitic jokes but they do not speak up. They do not want to spoil a party or upset a business deal just because one person is vulgar for a moment. They let it go. They do not consider themselves to be anti-Semitic. After all, some of their best friends are...

"Anyone who does not challenge a passing remark or joke that panders to homophobic prejudice is no friend of mine," I would say. "I would not trust such a person and neither should you, even if it is yourself that you observe doing such a thing." Then I would smile and say, "Either we're all in the same boat or we're not. Life is full of choices, isn't it? Being gay is not a choice, however. You're gay or you aren't and you're in the boat or you're not."

But threats to my physical safety were scary. Such threats reminded me each time that I had two children at home. One time the TV interviewer and I had done only half of the interview when there was an abrupt cut to a commercial. She put her hand to her ear to better hear the words piped to her from the control room. I saw the look of fear as her face paled.

"Someone called in and the producer thinks it's a credible threat—somebody with a loaded gun on their way here and they have the address right. You have to leave now. We're changing to a piece we were going to do tomorrow."

The receptionist was at the studio door. "There's a taxi waiting." It was the last interview of the day so I had my suitcase with me.

The producer appeared on the run. "This way." She hurried me through hallways to a back door, opened the door of the cab waiting there, handed the driver cash and said, "Take him to the airport now, quickly, absolutely no stops anywhere."

Walking in a light rain from a TV studio to a radio station early in the morning in an Ohio city I heard a screech of brakes close behind me and a blaring horn. I did not turn. Then a voice, "Hey, you, in the raincoat." I might as well see my assailant, I thought. It occurred to me that I might be witnessing my own end. I turned.

"Yeah, you." It was an African-American cab driver, one foot out of his cab, pointing at me. "Wasn't you the guy who was just on the TV?"

"Yes," I answered.

"Right on, Brother," he said smiling and waving. He got back into the cab and sped away. I really wanted to sit down on the wet curb right then and there and cry but I continued my walk. I had the next appointment to keep.

The following day in Cincinnati I sat at the anchor desk in a TV studio watching the monitor as the morning show began. I was between the woman who was the host and the handsome weatherman who seemed to be in his own world, devoted to his appearance and using the monitor as his mirror.

As I watched, a print banner on the screen advised people that the morning's guest was a homosexual and that homosexuality would be mentioned so it might be advisable to have children leave the room. As it moved into the commercial, before the interview began, I covered my lapel microphone so that I would not be heard in the control room and expressed my displeasure at being presented as anything less than a normal person. The host covered her own microphone and told me that it was she who had pushed to have me on the program and would explain later how the compromise of the consumer warning had happened. She turned out to be an excellent, skillful interviewer. The weatherman said nothing during the interview and did not move. Later she told me that a member of her family was gay and she realized how badly my book was needed in her city.

At lunch time that day I went to a restaurant that had been recommended by a radio interviewer. There was a short line. Two women waiting just in front of me were in conversation. "Did you see that homosexual they had on the television this morning?"

"Can you believe it? You'd think they'd keep these people locked up and out of sight."

I thought about tapping one of them on the shoulder and asking if they might like to be my guests for lunch. It would make an amusing story later and might even help to change some prejudice. But I was tired and wanted a quiet lunch before the newspaper interview. I had done enough lonely missionary work for one morning.

Once in a while something funny happened. I did an early morning live TV show with a male host who was genuinely warm and friendly. I was on a tight schedule and he wanted another interview on tape that he could use the following week so it was agreed that we would move immediately from the live interview to the taped one without a break and thereby save time.

"I like this guy," he said on the live show. "I don't know why guys who aren't gay are so scared of guys who are gay. Do you mind if I reach out and touch you?"

"Not at all," I answered. "The feeling is mutual. I like you too."

He put his hand on my upper arm and then on my back.

During the taped segment he reminded viewers that he liked me and had touched me during the previous program. "We cheat ourselves by not making friendly contact with gay people," he said into the camera. Then, slightly off balance, he shifted position and put his hand on my leg as he righted himself. "I guess a gay friend can come in handy when you least expect it," he quipped, laughing.

When the interview finished I reached for my briefcase and shook his hand warmly. One of the cameramen stepped forward into the brightly lit set and said, "You might want to know that his fly is open," as he pointed to me.

The host and I both gasped and I reached down to zip up. "Not to worry," said the cameraman, "expert camera work saved the day—both days." At that the three of us fell into one another's arms laughing.

My basic message in interviews was that we were good people, different in our natural erotic attractions than the so-called *normal* or average citizen, perhaps, but quite capable of civic responsibility and hard work. We were not molesters or recruiters as the Anita Bryants and other bigots charged and were as good at all jobs, including the job of teacher, as anyone. I wanted people to know that we did far more good than harm in the world, were more likely to help than to harm and that we loved as earnestly as anyone. "But we will not volunteer to be victims sacrificed to prejudice," I said often. "We insist on equal civil rights for everyone and that definitely includes us."

My practices in both San Francisco and Menlo Park were full. I insisted on being away on the publicity tours for no more than one week at a time and being home at least two weeks in between. I needed home to restore my sanity after the blur of interviews, hotels and airports, changing to a new location each day. I also worried about the effect of increasing notoriety and my absences on the children.

I hired a half-time secretary. There was no choice. Because of the publicity I was getting a lot of mail forwarded to me from the publisher. Most of it was from people thanking me, some of it was venomous hate mail. I wanted to respond to the favorable mail and I needed help with such simple matters as making and changing appointments. The secretary could also make sure the children could contact me if they needed me. She could always find me in case of an emergency.

Both my daughter and son seemed to be enjoying it all, however. Don and I had worked out schedules with our former wives and usually had the four children at the same time by then but, because of my erratic publicity demands, not always. I took my two out to dinner at least once each week if possible so that we could have our own private family time together.

Sometimes our dinner was interrupted by someone wanting to wish me well, thank me or ask for an autograph. I had become a minor celebrity in San Francisco. But though I did not really like the interruptions, the children seemed to relish them. "You're *somebody*," my son said one evening after our waiter had gone out to the nearby bookstore to get a copy of the book, asked me to autograph it and gave both children free desserts.

"Somebody?" I knew what he meant. "I'm your Dad," I said, "that's what makes me somebody. When I was your age I felt like I was a nobody but that's not true anymore."

"No, he means you're an important *gay* person," my daughter said.

I laughed. "Yeah, I guess that's true right now. I've become *someone gay*."

It was true. I had become someone I had not known I could be. I had a gym membership in the new gay City Athletic Club in the Castro and was looking pretty good if often tired. I was on the Board of Directors of the new public legal defense firm, Gay Rights Advocates. I had finished work on another book to be titled *Living Gay* that would be published early in 1979. I had been a keynote address speaker at the national meeting of the Gay Academic Union in Los Angeles and had been asked to be the keynote address speaker in other cities for various fundraisers.

Yet I could be taken by surprise still. Asked to introduce famous Christopher Isherwood who was to appear in San Francisco for a fundraiser, I was both honored and nervous. He had published *Christopher and His Kind*, a book of memoirs that covered the ten years of his life before emigration to the United States at the age of thirty-five and it was revered as a contribution to American literature and an elegant coming-out gift to gay people. He was twenty-five years my senior, seventy-four years old in 1979, and a very famous person.

I stepped out onto the stage of the large school auditorium and saw that every seat in both the orchestra and balcony was occupied. Some people were standing in the lobby, peering in through open doors. The introducer must also introduce himself before giving some tidbits of interesting background on the star of the evening's event. I intended to simply say, "Hello. I'm Don Clark, a psychologist here in San Francisco" and then praise Mr. Isherwood. I said, "Hello, I'm Don Clark." There was a sudden thunder of applause, stamping feet on the wooden floor and whistles as people began to stand. My jaw dropped. I was stunned.

My partner, Don, seemed to enjoy those moments of fame, basking in the glow that enveloped both of us, yet I believe that the intensity of the affectionate attention focused on me was a major factor causing us problems. It created an artificial imbalance in our relationship. We had moved into a house in the city that had room enough for the four children. We got along very well and had good friends but strains in our relationship had begun to show by the time I introduced Christopher Isherwood that evening.

Don was very good looking and he was pursued by admirers. I knew that he was tempted. I was less tempted by those attracted to my temporary public persona. I wanted to live quietly with him and our children, have meals at home or at the homes of our friends and be peacefully shuttered from the public life I had fallen into. Don wanted to be out and about, flattered by the attention of admirers.

The worst recurrent conflict, which seemed to get worse with time, was about the children. He accused me of putting them first and him second. He was right. We both put our work first, really, but next for me was the welfare of the children. What was left was there for us to delight in, I felt, enjoying our good fortune in having found one another and building a new, good life together that was envied by many.

The annoying demands of his admirers that cut into our home life were a secondary conflict for me. My own admirers were simply part of the gay rights work I was doing for the sake of our community and I kept that separate. It would quiet down eventually just as the children would grow up and leave home eventually. I thought we only needed to be patient and wait until our life could be more about us.

Don and I talked about it but things did not get better. Finally, one evening in 1981 we agreed to leave the children at home and go to a quiet neighborhood bar and restaurant that was currently out of favor and therefore empty and quiet. We agreed to talk until we came to some sort of agreement that would end the troubling disputes.

The talk took only half an hour. Both of us were frank and honest about our feelings, needs and priorities. It suddenly seemed quite clear that his and mine did not fit together and neither of us was willing to change priorities. There it was. Clear. Our time together as a couple had come to an end. It was shocking but true. We would have to explain it to the children and then to friends and others.

We both bore scars from the process of the earlier divorces that had taken two years. We had been wise enough to have a lawyer friend draw up a prenuptial agreement for us. We needed only to follow the steps set forth in that agreement. It took my breath away to see how fast, neat and clean our end was, done in half an hour.

We each had thought that we had found the loves of our lifetime and we had been wrong. Instead we had found the right transitional partnership to bolster us, see us out of our previous marriages and prepare us for what might come next. Certainly each of us knew himself better as a result of our six years together. Now we needed to be careful not to wound one another, to separate with care rather than to rip apart what had been.

It was not easy. It was confusing. We missed the comfort of what had been. We could not pretend to change it suddenly into a friendship. We both were too honest. It had been a flawed love that failed and that hurt a lot. In the following six months we completed our separation. Don was already in another relationship by then and I was facing the world alone again with still more explaining to do to fans and family.

Chapter 24

The Road to Home

At the time we separated there was frightening talk of a mysterious disease attacking gay men. One of my clients had developed the disfiguring skin lesions known as Karposi's Sarcoma. Another was hospitalized with a Cryptosporidium infection. The mystery illness was referred to a *gay cancer* at first, then as *GRID*, for gay related immune deficiency. No one knew the cause but it was thought possibly to be a sexually transmitted disease. It took research time to learn that it was a sexually transmitted retrovirus that had taken root earlier in Africa and found a new home in the American gay male community.

The Federal government of the United States turned its back on the threat of the disease in the ugly, prejudiced belief that it only killed gay men. We were expendable, second class.

We lived in fear of contracting the mysterious disease and facing the pain of symptoms that disfigured and destroyed. There was also real fear of losing jobs, losing health insurance, losing housing, losing independence and being ostracized by society, lepers cast out and condemned. Shamefully, families too often followed the example of trusted government leaders and turned away when the first symptoms appeared.

By the time a test was developed that could determine whether or not a person was infected there was a great debate among gay men about whether or not to be tested since no treatment was yet available and positive test results gave information that was likely to increase worry. Most of my closest friends chose to be tested and of those tested most learned that they were infected.

It seemed to be an endless nightmare as friends and patients spiraled down into sickness and death. But, amazingly, we gay people not only did not turn and run away from one another but instead found ways to help one another, forming volunteer groups for psychological and legal counseling, delivering food, cleaning homes and transporting those in need to doctors' appointments and hospitals. Gay men were barred from donating blood so lesbians organized to do it for us. Most of us agreed that we had never ever been more tired and distressed nor had we ever been more proud to be gay, members of a now quite visible and active gay community.

One of the early cases was Jon Sims, the musician who launched many gay musical groups such as the San Francisco Gay Marching Band and Twirling Corps and the Gay Men's Chorus. I had been an informal adviser to him. When I learned that he had been hospitalized I wanted to go to see him. But I was worried that I might somehow carry this mysterious sickness of as yet unknown origin back into my home, possibly endangering the children.

I opened all windows after I had taken them to school, wore washable clothing and went to the hospital. By chance, the famous drag entertainer and activist known as The Widow Norton arrived there at the same time also dressed in washable male clothing.

Jon was in a small isolation room with large warning signs on the door. We had to put on caps, surgical gowns, masks and gloves before we were allowed to enter. Jon seemed unusually small and terribly alone in that silent, tiny room. Without discussion we lowered the masks and each took off a glove so that we could touch Jon's bare legs, arms and hands. We knew that it was what was needed, skin to skin closeness rather than barriers, affectionate human contact to ease pain and help healing.

Back home I put on cloth gardening gloves before I entered the house, went immediately to the washing machine, stripped and put everything into a hot wash. Next I went into the bathroom and took a long, hot, soapy shower. The children were at their mother's house. I left the windows open until night came. It was the best that I could do. That is how life was.

I counted my blessings. I was not sick. I was not infected. I was busy doing work that I wanted to do and I had excellent friends. There were a few romantic and sexual brief relationships. I counted myself lucky. I was seldom alone but I was lonely. I was also tired, physically and emotionally, and feared that my constant fatigue might lead to illness.

My old friends from New York, Barbara and Frank Alweis, had visited Don and me in San Francisco. They had retired a few years earlier and moved to a small village in the south of France where they rented a house. Frank painted and created weavings. They wanted me to visit. Airfares were cheap. I decided that it would be good medicine for me.

I checked into a small hotel in Paris that they had recommended so that I could get a night's sleep before taking the train south the next day. I wanted to stay awake into the evening if possible so as to get adjusted to local time.

After an early dinner I walked. I was sleepy but it was a beautiful evening. On the Boulevard Sainte Germaine I saw a movie theater that was showing an old American film, *Cover Girl*, in the original English with French subtitles. I remembered it from 1944, the year before I had gotten the theater job as an usher. It was the summer before high school when I was working as a stockboy at the Acme Supermarket. I had gone alone one evening after work on a payday. It was Rita Hayworth, Gene Kelly, Phil Silvers and Eve Arden in a perfect musical. It might keep me awake until bedtime, I thought, as I took French francs from my pocket. I wondered how it would play now forty years later and in another culture.

It was wonderful. It transported me immediately to that summer evening in Belmar, sitting in an aisle seat on the left side of the small, crowded orchestra in the Rivoli Theater, ten or twelve rows from the screen. The faces had seemed so near.

I saw again the close-up of Gene Kelly's face as he sang *Long Ago and Far Away*. It had been intoxicating back then, as if he was singing especially to me. I had since forgotten how mesmerized I had been by his handsome face, the beautiful mouth and the tiny scar just above his lips. I had been excited by his trim male body and his athletic dancing, wishing that I too could dance. I had imagined him guiding me with strong hands the way he guided Rita Hayworth as they danced. She was beautiful too, the perfect glamorous woman, out of reach. He seemed more real.

Sitting alone in the Paris theater, I was myself and I was also the fourteen-year-old boy I had once been. The words washed over me as he sang "I dreamed a dream one day..." I could not have imagined in that crazy summer of 1944 with its huge war carrying all of us on turbulent tides that the dream I was dreaming might ever come true. But it had come true.

It had and then it had ended suddenly and now a new massive, awful tide had us all at its mercy. I sat in the darkness alone again and felt warm tears tracing their path on my face.

Three days later, sitting in the living room while Barbara was out tutoring a local child in English, Frank and I got into a disagreement while talking about the epidemic. He said that he could not believe that the government of the United States really would stand by and knowingly permit a disease holocaust to kill gay men as if it did not matter. Tears came that I tried to stop. Frank immediately said he was sorry. I could not explain. I could not speak.

How could I put into words all of the wounds that had accumulated, the losses, the tears not shed and the dreams destroyed in the horror of what was happening? "You met my friends Hal and Mike," I managed to say finally. "You had dinner in their home. You and Barbara liked them a lot. They're going to die, both of them are going to die and I can't stop it no matter what I do." With that my defenses collapsed entirely and I wept, seeing tears on Frank's face as he moved closer to grasp my hand.

When I returned to San Francisco, I encouraged other therapists to start therapy and support groups for gay men. In my own two on-going weekly groups I saw how tremendously helpful these intimate, truthful communities were in dealing with the fear, sickness, death, grief and mourning that haunted us.

With a friend whose therapist-partner had died of what by then had become known as AIDS, for Acquired Immune Deficiency Syndrome, I started a therapists' volunteer group that we named The Pacific Society. Invited members were psychologists, social workers and psychiatrists. We would take turns hosting the group for dinner once a month for purposes of organization, support and camaraderie. Each member agreed to take on clients who were affected by the AIDS emergency and who could not otherwise afford good care. We would also make use of one another for consultation and refer clients to one another as needed and appropriate.

During our December meeting in 1985 one of the prospective new members being recommended was still a graduate student. Dennis, his friend, said, "He's all done, though, except for the dissertation, I think."

We always wanted to know everything there was to know when one of us recommended someone for membership in our Society. We wanted people we could respect and vouch for and we wanted to feel sure that the person would be generous in helping those in need.

I had told everyone earlier in the meeting that I had agreed to do a second edition of *Loving Someone Gay* and also had started writing a new book to be titled *As We Are* that I hoped would help shed some light on the spiritual as well as the psychological aspects of our gay evolution in this time of trouble. I had added with a laugh that I was still open to introductions for the purpose of romantic dating.

"We have to find a boyfriend for Don," one man said, winking at me. "He's obviously hard to please though if he turned down everyone he met when he was invited by all those gay students to speak both at Colgate and Salt Lake City. Is this new guy you're talking about single by any chance? Maybe a writer also?"

"Like I said, he hasn't finished the dissertation so I don't know that you could call him a writer." Dennis said. "But he's a jock. Does that count? He's used to be the secretary of Front Runners, the gay running club. He's also the President of the Board of Directors of the United Nations Association of San Francisco, works as Program Director at the National Conference of Christians and Jews and is on the President's Advisory Council at his school. And did I mention that he's very good looking and recently single?" That got a laugh.

"What school?" I asked.

"Saybrook Institute. The one that used to be the Humanistic Psychology Institute."

"No wonder he doesn't have time to finish the dissertation," someone said. "Sounds like a busy boy." We all agreed that we should invite him to the January meeting.

He and I gravitated to one another at that meeting. There was an odd feeling of familiarity as if I already knew him. In fact we had met at a party ten years earlier, drawn to one another then too; both recently divorced and in committed relationships with men.

We had talked, indicating our interest with mild flirting. He was a cute curly haired hippie then, with metal-framed granny glasses and shoulder strapped overalls. He had said that he was a carpenter since he was helping a friend renovate his house at the time. I had said that I was a writer since I was doing the final edit of *Loving Someone Gay* at the time. Neither of us had mentioned anything about psychology which helped us to not recognize or clearly remember one another the evening of the Pacific Society meeting.

Dennis told him something about each of us. "And this man," he said, pointing at me, "actually gave an invited address at the recent American Psychological Association meetings in Los Angeles."

"Then you must be *someone*," Michael said with a friendly, sly smile.

"Someone gay," I answered. "Like you."

Memory shapes that which is remembered, recording, but making what is recorded personally useful as one moves into the future. Since the sunny late summer day in 1961 when I first glanced at the words of Ralph Waldo Emerson carved into the stone façade of Hunter College, through all the years, I remembered the play of tree shadows and sunlight on the words. I remembered that it spoke to me of truth in a way that caused me to keep the memory alive.

Fifteen years later, raw and hurting from the end of the marriage that Barbara and I had created, I tried to find guidance in the words as I remembered them. I thought they had read, *the truth will make you free.*

By chance, on another late summer day forty-three years after I first looked at that stone wall, I had the opportunity to see it again. However, the words were not those I thought I remembered. Instead, they read, *we are of different opinions and different hours but we always may be said to be at heart on the side of truth. Ralph Waldo Emerson.*

I had held fast to the word *truth* and used it to shape and examine my choices. My treasured memory had shaped itself into a tool that I needed. But as I stood on the busy New York street reading the words again all those years later I saw that I also had kept the original quote, though less clearly visible, in the back of my mind and had used it too as a guide in my determined efforts to build bridges and work for peace.

The most difficult times in my life have offered me learning. Like the iconic Dorothy on the yellow brick road in the Wizard of Oz, once awakened to the wonder of our inner emotions, we gay people are confronted with adversity as we journey through life. We are forced to discover the fullness of our intelligence, courage, compassion and, finally, the wisdom that will shape our gay identity. Without the wholeness of that gay identity there is no *home.*

We do live in the present only and I now know that the past is best viewed with both acceptance and appreciation. I have learned also that the future is best faced with hope, the earned tool of truthful identity firmly in hand, if one is to maintain a capacity for happiness and ultimately acquire the guiding knowledge that only by helping to make this world better for everyone can one experience real satisfaction.

In the final paragraph of *Christopher and His Kind,* Christopher Isherwood imagined that he and W. H. Auden are each allowed to ask a fortune teller one question as their ship enters the New York harbor in the winter of 1939.

The imaginary fortune teller answers that each of them would "find the person you came here to look for—the ideal companion to whom you can reveal yourself totally and yet be loved for what you are, not for what you pretend to be."

Christopher had to wait a long time, he tells us, though his future husband was already there in the city where Christopher would settle. They would be near for many years without meeting and it would have done little good if they had met since Don Bachardy was only four years old at the time.

When Michael was four years old, living in the suburbs outside of Washington, D.C., I was in the army, miserably alone and lonely. I was in basic training, trying to hold on to the identity that I had formed during my college years, trying to remember that I *was* someone. I had caught sight of the new someone I was becoming while I was a college student working at Chestnut Lodge, only a few miles from Michael's home, quite near the ground on which he was learning to walk.

He was not yet ready to find me then nor was I yet ready to find him. I had more to do before trusting all of my identity, more before I could claim that identity with pride. But on that winter evening in 1986, looking at him, I was ready.

There would be a second edition of *Loving Someone Gay* in 1987, a third in 1997, and a fourth in 2005. Michael and I would lose many of the people we loved but we would grow stronger remembering them.

More than twenty years later we would be sitting in the shade of a macadamia nut tree on a small farm on the island of Hawaii, listening to the birds and enjoying the cooling breeze from the distant ocean as we ate sandwiches packed that morning. We would be dreaming aloud and silently, separately and together, wondering about the help this neglected farm might need and imagining a tiny cottage that could be built and named in honor of a lesbian sister no longer living.

Our paths had come together and stayed together. I knew who I was. We had time.

Acknowledgments

Writing this book has been difficult, sometimes painful and in all ways liberating which, in my experience, seems to describe the path of honesty in search of truth. I am grateful to each and every person mentioned in these pages for helping me, one way or another, to find my footing.

There are many friends, mentioned and not, who are no longer living but who returned to me at times, while I was awake or in my dreams, during this writing adventure. I miss them. I talked to them sometimes and sometimes I could imagine them answering.

I want to thank my friends Bob Carrere, Mark Kelly, David Mattingly, Pamela Owings, Andy Pesce and Ruth Wetherford; my son, Andrew Clark, and my husband, Michael Graves, for their encouragement and insightful comments made while reading earlier versions of this work.

Finally, my thanks go to editor Michael Denneny, typist Norma Fisher and to Toby Johnson for his generous support, useful suggestions and for leading me to Lethe Press.

Don Clark, Ph.D., author, teacher and clinical psychologist, is a Fellow and Lifetime Member of the American Psychological Association. He lives in San Francisco with his husband of 21 years, psychologist Michael Graves. His classic book, *Loving Someone Gay*, now in its fourth edition, has been continuously in print for more than thirty years. More information about him can be found at www.DonClarkPhD.com.

Printed in the United States
99497LV00006B/1-30/A